Children's Literature in Action

Recent Titles in Library and Information Science Text Series

Libraries in the Information Age: An Introduction and Career Exploration, Second Edition
Denise K. Fourie and David R. Dowell

Basic Research Methods for Librarians, Fifth Edition
Lynn Silipigni Connaway and Ronald R. Powell

Public Libraries in the 21st Century
Ann E. Prentice

Introduction to Technical Services, Eighth Edition
G. Edward Evans, Jean Weihs, and Sheila S. Intner

Science and Technology Resources: A Guide for Information Professionals and Researchers
James E. Bobick and G. Lynn Berard

Reference and Information Services: An Introduction, Fourth Edition
Richard E. Bopp and Linda C. Smith, Editors

Collection Management Basics, Sixth Edition
G. Edward Evans and Margaret Zarnosky Saponaro

Library and Information Center Management, Eighth Edition
Barbara B. Moran, Robert D. Stueart, and Claudia J. Morner

Information Resources in the Humanities and Arts, Sixth Edition
Anna H. Perrault and Elizabeth Aversa, with contributing authors Cynthia Miller and Sonia Ramírez Wohlmuth

The Collection Program in Schools: Concepts and Practices, Fifth Edition
Kay Bishop

The School Library Manager, Fifth Edition
Blanche Woolls, Ann C. Weeks, and Sharon Coatney

Young Adult Literature in Action: A Librarian's Guide, Second Edition
Rosemary Chance

CHILDREN'S LITERATURE IN ACTION

A Librarian's Guide

SECOND EDITION

Sylvia M. Vardell

Library and Information Science Text

LIBRARIES UNLIMITED

AN IMPRINT OF ABC-CLIO, LLC
Santa Barbara, California • Denver, Colorado • Oxford, England

Library of Congress Cataloging-in-Publication Data

Vardell, Sylvia M.
  Children's literature in action : a librarian's guide / Sylvia M. Vardell. — Second edition.
        pages cm — (Library and information science text series)
  Includes bibliographical references and index.
  ISBN 978-1-61069-560-2 (hardback) — ISBN 978-1-61069-562-6 (paperback) 1. Children—Books and reading. 2. Children's literature— History and criticism. 3. School libraries—Activity programs. 4. Children's libraries—Activity programs. I. Title.
  Z1037.A1V39 2014
  028.5'5—dc23   2014004200

ISBN: 978-1-61069-560-2
      978-1-61069-562-6 (pbk.)

18 17 16 15 14 1 2 3 4 5

Libraries Unlimited
An Imprint of ABC-CLIO, LLC

ABC-CLIO, LLC
130 Cremona Drive, P.O. Box 1911
Santa Barbara, California 93116-1911

This book is printed on acid-free paper ∞
Manufactured in the United States of America

Contents

Acknowledgments ix
Introduction xi
Theme poem: *This Book* by Joyce Sidman xv

1—An Introduction to Children and Their Literature 1

Becoming Literate 2
Literacy Development 5
Emergent Literacy. 8
Schools and Reading 10
Reading Aloud 11
Sustained Silent Reading (SSR). 12
Readers' Advisory 14
Selecting and Reviewing Children's Books. 15
Awards in Children's Literature 18
Other Major Awards 19
Best Lists 22
What Books? 24
Learning about Authors, Illustrators, and Poets 25
Literature in Action: Launching Literature and
    Literacy Celebrations 31
Ongoing Professional Development 33
Conclusion 34
Professional Resources for Children's Literature 35
Standards in Action: ALSC Competencies 36
Assignments in Action: Getting Started 37

2—Picture Books **39**

   Introduction 39
   Definitions 42
   Types of Picture Books 44
   Major Authors and Illustrators of Picture Books 50
   Children's Picture Book Illustration 55
   Evaluation Criteria 59
   Awards for Picture Books and Illustration 65
   Literature in Action: Sharing Picture Books Aloud 68
   Sharing Picture Books 70
   Conclusion 76
   Professional Resources on the Art of Picture Books 77
   Standards in Action: Common Core State Standards 78
   Assignments in Action: Looking into Picture Books 79

3—Traditional Tales **81**

   Introduction 81
   Definitions 84
   Types of Traditional Tales 87
   Major Retellers of Traditional Tales 92
   Evaluation Criteria 98
   Awards for Traditional Tales 102
   Literature in Action: Featuring Folktale Variants 103
   Sharing Traditional Tales 108
   Conclusion 111
   Professional Resources for Traditional Literature 111
   Standards in Action: AASL Standards for the 21st-Century Learner . . 112
   Assignments in Action: Celebrating Traditional Tales 113

4—Poetry for Children **115**

   Introduction 115
   Definitions 118
   Types of Poetry Books for Children 120
   Major Poets 125
   Evaluation Criteria 132
   Awards for Poetry 136
   Literature in Action: Leading Choral Reading and
      Poetry Performance 138
   Sharing Poetry 140
   Conclusion 145
   Professional Resources in Children's Poetry 146
   Standards in Action: Texas Essential Knowledge and
      Skills (TEKS) for English Language Arts and Reading 146
   Assignments in Action: Exploring Poetry Possibilities 148

5—Contemporary Realistic Fiction **151**

   Introduction 151
   Definitions 154

Types of Contemporary Realistic Fiction 156
Controversy and Contemporary Realism 164
Major Authors of Contemporary Realistic Fiction 166
Evaluation Criteria 171
Awards for Contemporary Realistic Fiction 176
Literature in Action: Guiding Responses. 178
Sharing Contemporary Realistic Fiction 183
Conclusion. 186
Professional Resources in Contemporary Realistic Fiction 186
Standards in Action: NCTE/IRA Standards for the English
    Language Arts 187
Assignments in Action: Checking Out Contemporary
    Realistic Fiction. 189

6—Historical Fiction **191**
Introduction 191
Definitions 193
Types of Historical Fiction. 195
Major Authors of Historical Fiction 201
Evaluation Criteria 207
Awards for Historical Fiction. 211
Literature in Action: Using Community Resources 212
Sharing Historical Fiction 214
Conclusion. 217
Professional Resources for Historical Fiction 217
Standards in Action: National Curriculum Standards
    for Social Studies. 218
Assignments in Action: Digging Deeper into Historical Fiction 219

7—Fantasy. **221**
Introduction 221
Definitions 223
Types of Fantasy. 227
Controversy 231
Major Authors of Fantasy 232
Evaluation Criteria 237
Awards for Fantasy. 240
Literature in Action: Expanding Reading with Audiobooks 242
Sharing Fantasy 244
Conclusion. 248
Professional Resources in Fantasy Literature 249
Standards in Action: YALSA Competencies. 250
Assignments in Action: Delving into Fantasy 251

8—Informational Books **253**
Introduction 253
Definitions 256
Types of Informational Books 258

Major Authors of Informational Books 268
Evaluation Criteria 275
Awards for Informational Books 278
Literature in Action: Introducing Access Features. 281
Sharing Informational Books 283
Conclusion 285
Professional Resources in Nonfiction. 286
Standards in Action: Common Core and Nonfiction 287
Assignments in Action: Investigating Informational Books 288

References 289
Bibliography of Children's Books Cited 305
Copyright Credits 327
Index 331

Acknowledgments

This project is the fulfillment of a professional dream as well as a labor of love; pulling together a lifetime of teaching and a multitude of favorite books and resources to help create this tool for librarians and future librarians. The response to the first edition of this book was so gratifying, and I'm grateful to have the opportunity to update it for even greater relevance and usefulness. Once again, I am indebted to many others for their help and support on this project. Thank you, dear friends:

For the editor who conceived of the project from the very beginning and continues to encourage me, Blanche Woolls

For my colleagues "in action," Sharon Coatney and Rosemary Chance

For being an encouraging and helpful group of early readers and advisors, Leigh Ann Jones, Jane Claes, Kim Kinnaird, June Jacko, and Donna MacKinney

For the generous gift of a wonderful opening poem, Joyce Sidman

For sharing their words, Dean Schneider and Robin Smith, *Horn Book*, Marianne Follis, Mary Ann Scheuer, Marc Aronson, Kiera Parrott, and Cynthia Alaniz

For being such inspiring and magnanimous "authors in action," Pat Mora, Denise Fleming, J. Patrick Lewis, Janet Tashjian, Kirby Larson, Grace Lin, Ashley Bryan, and Seymour Simon, as well as Janet Wong, Kristine O'Connell George, Cynthia Leitich Smith, Laurence Yep, and T. A. Barron

For being such amazing and articulate "librarians in action," Margriet Ruurs, Barbara Kieran, Emily Chasse, Hilary Haygood, Mia Steinkamp, Marlene Horsey, Elizabeth Murphy, Marnie Cushing, Rose Brock, and Xelena Gonzalez

For sample reviews, my *Librarians' Choices* aces, Zulema Bewley, Mary Buckalo, Tammy Korns, and Susi Grissom

For generous permission in sharing book covers, Boyds Mills Press, Clarion, Houghton Mifflin Harcourt, National Geographic, Henry Holt, Little Brown, Pomelo Books, Penguin, Random House, Simon & Schuster, and HarperCollins

For being such kind and generous friends, Janet Wong and Lynn Akin

For being my biggest cheerleaders, my mom, Ingrid Mergeler; my kids, Alex Vardell and Emily Vardell; and especially my husband, Russell Vardell, for Bali and beyond

Thank you, all!
Sylvia

Introduction

The purpose of this book is to provide an activity-oriented survey of children's literature for undergraduate and graduate students seeking licensure and degrees leading to careers working with children in school and public libraries. Most textbooks on children's literature focus on teachers using literature in the classroom. This textbook focuses on librarians and library media specialists. The framework for this text adds a layer of practical application in every chapter for the librarian who shares books with children, plans book-based programs, and collaborates with teachers and families in sharing books and developing literature-based instruction. What does a librarian need to know about how to select and share books in each genre? What are the usual promotion and collaboration activities associated with each genre? This is the driving force of the book, linking literature with active practice in the school and public library. Embedded in a genre approach to literature, it has a unique focus on the librarian or future librarian as the reader.

In my 30 years of university teaching, I have used nearly every major textbook in the area of children's literature. Each has its strengths and weaknesses, but none focuses specifically on the perspective of the librarian. The unique contributions of this textbook are threefold: designed for use by librarians, emphasis on action and library applications, and brevity for an affordable text and more time for reading literature itself.

Each chapter is enriched by brief insets of author comments and interviews, collaborative activities, featured books, special topics and programs, selected awards and celebrations, historical connections, recommended resources, issues for discussion, connections with various standards, and assignment suggestions. The table of contents is organized around these major genre divisions:

Chapter One: An Introduction to Children and Their Literature
Chapter Two: Picture Books
Chapter Three: Traditional Tales
Chapter Four: Poetry for Children
Chapter Five: Contemporary Realistic Fiction
Chapter Six: Historical Fiction
Chapter Seven: Fantasy
Chapter Eight: Informational Books

The "action" components of each chapter include:

- Literature in Action
- Librarians in Action
- Authors in Action
- One Book in Action
- History in Action
- Standards in Action
- Assignments in Action

Backmatter includes professional references and children's books cited throughout the narrative, as well as a comprehensive index of authors, titles, and subjects.

The goal of this approach is to help the new librarian or library media specialist become knowledgeable about the field of children's literature in preparation for guiding young people, ages five through twelve, in their reading. In addition, the book provides practical ideas for generating interest in reading, strategies for connecting with the school curriculum, and guidance for reaching out to families and the wider community through children's literature. It includes:

- The most current, popular, and critically acclaimed books and materials for children
- The selection and evaluation of digital eBooks, apps, and audiobooks
- Short essays by top authors and practitioners in the field
- Practical activities, programming ideas, award information, and teaching strategies
- Both the history of classic books as well as the latest professional and curriculum standards including the Common Core

This new, revised edition features:

New section on "Standards in Action" for every chapter
New information on selecting and evaluating digital books and apps and using social media tools
New section on easy readers and transitional novels
New section on using games and community resources
New author profiles and practitioner contributions
Award updates

Updated links
More than 250 new children's books cited and 75 new sources cited

This book provides the librarian with a practitioner-oriented introduction to literature for children ages five through twelve, with a look at the latest trends, titles, and tools for selecting and evaluating quality books and materials and for planning fun and meaningful programs and activities.

This Book

—Joyce Sidman

Small. Square.
Opens, shuts;
this eye
with cardboard lids.
This tree
of milk-white leaves.
This stack of wings.
This trick window.

This escape route,
travel-pouch,
dream-pillow.

This treasure.
Open it.

1

An Introduction to Children and Their Literature

"Sometimes there was a good reason to break the rules. Even in the library."
From *Library Lion* by Michelle Knudsen (Candlewick, 2006)

Did you like to read when you were a child?
Classics? Comic books? Newbery winners? Nancy Drew?
If you did, what do you think were the factors that contributed to that?
Did your family include avid readers? (Researchers have found that this is the #1 reason that most people become readers.)
Or did you grow up in an environment (in the neighborhood, in school, in a library) where reading was modeled and encouraged? (This can be a major factor in fostering a lifelong love of reading.)

If you were *not* an avid reader as a child, it's not too late to become one. I have found that many adults who missed the reading "bug" in childhood often discover a new love of reading through reading children's books as adults. There's something about immersing oneself in the best books for young people that is interesting, informative, and even inspiring. It connects us with our childhoods, as well as with the children in our circle. Sure, a lovely picture book can take us back to special childhood memories, but it is also a carefully crafted work of art. When we study it we can learn a great deal about writing, illustrating, and bookmaking, about the stories, themes, and characters that are part of the world of childhood. As children's literature expert and critic Betsy Hearne put it, "Childhood is the time and children's books are the place for powerful emotions, powerful language, powerful art. . . . There is no room for cutesy books, dull books, or books that talk down. Children are not inferior. They may be small in stature but not in what they feel, think, listen, and see" (1999, p. 5).

In this chapter, we will consider the variables that contribute to creating literate children. We'll also look at the field of children's literature itself and how libraries, librarians, and library media specialists fit into the bigger picture.

BECOMING LITERATE

Most people agree that one of our major goals in working with children is to help them become literate citizens. When our children grow up and leave our charge, we hope they can read and write and think for themselves. We hope they can use their reading skills to handle the information they'll encounter in the workplace and in their daily lives. And we hope we have also planted a seed that will result in a lifelong pleasure in reading for its own sake. Books we read as children shape us for the rest of our lives. Count yourself lucky if there is a special book you remember fondly from your childhood. Consider how it has shaped your attitudes. Think about how you can provide this same anchor for the children you reach.

As children's literature scholars and teachers Tunnell, Jacobs, Young, and Bryan (2012, p. 1) observe, "Engaged reading, like eating, is one of life's activities that simultaneously yields both pleasure and benefit." Through reading we learn things, but we also experience good feelings and happy memories through books. To take the food metaphor a step further, we also want to expose our children to a healthy "diet" of literature: to easy books, hard books, beautiful books, simple stories, all the genres and types of books; so that all children can discover their favorites and build a lifetime habit of diverse and healthy reading. I would even argue that if children graduate as non-readers or "aliterate" individuals who know how to read, but choose not to, then it's partly our fault. Children who watch television after school every day keep watching television throughout their lives. It's up to us to work with the other adults in children's lives (families, teachers, other caregivers) to create a reading climate. To make reading as much a part of their lives as television, for example. To help children make reading a fun part of their often heavily scheduled lives. We may have to broaden our notion of reading to include all kinds of literature (like graphic novels or joke books) or even all kinds of texts (like eBooks, apps, and websites), but we need to help children learn to value reading in their lives, throughout their lives.

What's the key? It is getting to know the children as individuals and keeping current with our knowledge of their literature, so we can match the child with the just-right book that she or he will find irresistible. It is often said that a child who doesn't like to read has just not found a book that really "grabbed" him or her. That's where we come in. As librarians, we have the privilege of working with children and books all day long (more or less), and we can be the tour guides to the "literate" life. Through our own modeling as we talk about books and through our sensitivity to the special needs of each child reader, we are in a unique place to usher children into the world of books. What a privilege! But what a responsibility, too, because this also means sometimes putting aside our own personal preferences in seeking out the right book for the right reader. Personally, we may not enjoy fantasy novels, but we need to be familiar enough with them that we can recommend the latest adventure to children who *do* enjoy fantasy. Or perhaps we are avid fiction readers, but we also need to know more about nonfiction for the many boys who may prefer it to fiction. We need to be effective booktalkers and reading advisors, while valuing children's freedom of choice, even helping children learn *how* to choose for themselves. And as we consider our diverse classrooms and communities, we also need to be steeped in the best multicultural literature for children, so we can recommend books that reflect a range of experiences for all readers.

In fact, I dream of a world where children grow up reading all kinds of books about all kinds of people. They will grow up thinking and talking about these books with all kinds of kids. They will become grownups who are more tolerant, open, and compassionate because of these experiences. It will be impossible for them to purposely hurt people in other places because the people there are like friends. They will have friends and kindred spirits all around the globe— through their favorite books. I believe you and I can help make that happen. Why bother? Scholar and critic Rudine Sims Bishop (1992, p. 3) reminds us, "Students who do not see any reflections of themselves or who see only distorted or comical ones come to understand that they have little value in society in general and in school in particular. . . . Literature can contribute to the development of self-esteem by holding up to its readers images of themselves." As educator Dierdre Glenn-Paul (1997, 258) stated so eloquently, "I realized that I hadn't chosen books featuring racial and ethnic characters because it was mandated or suggested that I should be 'multicultural' in my selections. I incorporated such books because I fervently believed that my students should see themselves represented in our classroom and within the school. I also hoped that they would see that, even in books that featured characters that they perceived were like them, and lived in settings such as theirs, there was diversity."

Librarians in Action: Libraries around the World

Margriet Ruurs is a children's book author with 30 books to her credit who also works as a presenter and consultant in promoting books, reading, and writing. She is also editor of KIDSWWWRITE, a Web magazine that publishes writing by children: www.kalwriters.com/kidswwwrite. Here she writes about one project that led to her writing the nonfiction picture book *My Librarian Is a Camel* (Boyds Mills Press, 2005) and to ongoing international collaboration developing mobile libraries around the world.

Libraries That Walk and Float
by Margriet Ruurs

Several years ago, I read an article in a newspaper that triggered my curiosity. The article explained how the National Library of Kenya uses camels to bring books to children in remote desert areas of Kenya. It made me realize that I had been taking my local library for granted. I have always lived in cities with easy access to libraries. Weekly, if not more often, I would visit my neighborhood library to check out books. I even worked in a public library conducting children's story times.

But what if you had no access to a public or school library? I wanted to know more. For eight years I used the Internet to search for and contact librarians and others who brings books to people in remote areas of the world. In the process, I learned that libraries are not buildings. They are collections of books that are accessible to readers in one way or another, often thanks to dedicated librarians or volunteers.

In Queensland, Australia, huge trucks full of books are used to reach isolated communities. Solar panels on the truck's roof power computers inside to offer Internet access to patrons. But in countries where budgets or other circumstances do not allow such a fancy mode of transportation, a library can be much more primitive. In Peru, for instance, donkeys are used to pull a wooden cart into mountainous villages to bring books to people. And in Thailand, elephants are used for the transport of books into the jungle.

Mobile library projects are often run by keen volunteers who are aware of the importance of bringing books to people, especially to children. In Papua New Guinea, one mobile library consists of volunteers of Hope International, carrying boxes of books on their shoulders into the jungle. "Along the way, villagers feed us sugarcane to sustain us," says one of the volunteers.

I have had the privilege of visiting Alif Laila, a mobile library project in Lahore, Pakistan. Syeda Basarat Kazim, who runs the project, is proud of the book bus that visits areas of the city where children would not normally have an opportunity to read books. "Reading is not a tradition in Pakistan," she explains. "We try to show children the importance of reading and how it can open a window to the world." One child in Lahore, who visited the book bus for the first time, quickly started copying a poem he read in a book. But then the librarian explained the concept of a library: "This bus full of books will come back next week, and you can keep the book until then and read more books." The idea was a source of wonder for this child and may well have changed his life.

Access to books is important to children in Mongolia as well. Jambyn Dashdondog is a Mongolian writer of children's books. He initiated a project of bringing books to children in the Gobi desert where families live a traditional herders' life. With the use of a camel, a donkey-drawn caravan, and a small bus paid for by donations from Japan, he is fulfilling his dream of bringing children and books together. Dashdondog grins, "We ask these children which is sweeter, candy or books? They always reply 'books'!"

Throughout North America, innovative ways of book transportation are used. Book vans and portable libraries bring books to rural areas, to seniors or homebound parents. Even in the USA, many libraries offer alternatives to library buildings. Mobile library buses (bookmobiles) are quite common in rural areas. Oregon's Crook County is large and rural, with a population of 19,182 spread over 2,979 square miles. To meet the challenge of serving county residents, the Crook County library is starting its first bookmobile. The bookmobile will bring the gift of reading to hundreds of children a month at preschools and daycare facilities who might not otherwise have access to books.

For more details: http://www.margrietruurs.com.

Today's schools and communities have a mix of children from many cultural and linguistic backgrounds. Our goal, however, is not simply to match books and demographics. Black children need to have the opportunity to read African American literature for young people, no doubt. But so do white children. And Asian and Hispanic and all other children. What does your library look like? Do you have books with brown faces on the covers? Children in wheelchairs? It's time to stretch. As Bishop (1992, p. 3) reminds us, "All students need to recognize the diversity that defines this society, learn to respect it, and see it in a positive light." This includes the rich variety of multicultural literature available in the United States, as well as the growing body of wonderful international books from other countries now being published and distributed in the United States.

We need to be advocates for literature and literacy in our schools and communities, working to remind everyone about the value of the simple act of reading and talking about books in a climate of testing pressures, overextended lives, and complicated schedules. We can rely on many of the classics from our own childhood lives, but we also need to go beyond nostalgia to stay current with the future "classics" being published today. We need to be part of the latest children's literature phenomenon, like the popularity of Harry Potter or the appeal of book-based movies, and piggyback on aspects of popular culture that lead children back to books. We are reading activists, lobbying for more time and resources for reading in the lives of our children.

LITERACY DEVELOPMENT

Where do we begin? Where does reading begin? Like so much else in life, we are generally products of our upbringing. If we grow up in a house of music lovers, we tend to appreciate music. If our caregivers enjoy sports, we will too. We know from the foundational work of researchers such as Shirley Brice Heath (1983) and Gordon Wells (1986) that families are the first and foremost influence on developing literacy. We also know that literacy can take many forms from the oral sharing of stories and daily routines to the reading of print matter of various types. What kinds of things do families read?

- Magazines and newspapers
- Books
- The Bible and other religious texts

Parents can be the role models in reading aloud to their children at home. However, siblings, grandparents, cousins, aunts/uncles, friends, other children, and daycare providers can also be leaders of read aloud experiences. In addition, children are exposed to many forms of "everyday" or "environmental" print at home, including the mail, letters, cookbooks, instructions, the dictionary, homework, signs and billboards, comics, diaries, catalogs, the TV guide, the phone book, greeting cards, puzzles, coupon books, and bills. All of these involve reading, too. And where do families get their reading material? From the library, hands down, twice as often as any other source, according to most experts. But also from grocery stores, bookstores, friends and neighbors, book clubs, book fairs, through the mail, at the barber's, at garage sales, at work, at discount and other stores, at church, from school, at the gas station, at the daycare center, and at the hospital.

In a study I conducted with colleagues in an urban setting (Vardell, 2000), we found a variety of literacy-related activities were regularly taking place in family life. Parents, siblings, grandparents, cousins, and aunts/uncles told stories at home. What kind of stories? Children listened to family stories, original stories, bedtime stories, ghost stories, and "once upon a time" stories. Family members and friends sang songs from the radio, as well as religious songs, holiday songs, songs from TV, bedtime songs, songs from tapes and CDs, and family songs. This helps us gain a somewhat broader and more inclusive understanding of literacy, even multiple literacies, among families of all kinds. It can be helpful to see the many literacy activities that are already occurring in family settings. Instead of taking a "deficit" view of family literacy ("why aren't they reading more books?"), we can look to see what kinds of literacy activities are already in place. So often we tend to view the "glass" of urban literacy as "half empty." What kinds of activities promote family literacy? All kinds. And if we begin where the families already are, we can have a greater impact. More reading and writing that is relevant and meaningful to both parents and children is the key.

According to Postlethwaite and Ross (1992), family involvement may be the most critical factor in children's future literacy achievement. However, many parents are not aware of their potential impact or the methods they can utilize to foster their children's literacy development. In fact, often there is a wide gap between the expectations and practices of the school and those of the home regarding the fostering of children's emerging literacy. In order to positively impact children's language acquisition and literacy skills, schools and libraries should examine avenues for collaboration with families and local communities to support and encourage children as they learn to read and read to learn. Linking homes, local communities, and schools in networks of literacy that value and reflect cultural and linguistic diversity has positive, far-reaching outcomes for all concerned. We need to recognize "the need for respectful partnerships that build on the strengths of parents and other family members" (Ordonez-Jasis and Ortiz, 2006, p. 48).

What can we do to make everyone feel welcome in the library, particularly those who are still building their knowledge of English? Librarian Sharon Amastae (2010) offers tips for helping Spanish-speaking children (and families) feel at home in the school library (but these could certainly be adapted for speakers of other languages and can apply to the public library too). They include:

1. Learn a few phrases in Spanish—it will make you more approachable.
2. Purchase Spanish editions of books that are popular at your school, such as Jeff Kinney's *Diario de Greg, un Renacuajo* (*Diary of a Wimpy Kid*).
3. Most young people love magazines, so subscribe to a few in Spanish, like *ESPN Deportes*, often available from your regular vendor.

4. Intershelve your Spanish nonfiction with English nonfiction rather than in 468 so that when Spanish-reading students come to research, they will have resources in their native language.
5. Put up a Spanish Dewey poster (available from ALA Graphics); it will help make sense of the library.
6. Include a general encyclopedia in Spanish in your reference collection, along with an easier elementary-level encyclopedia in English.

More and more libraries are reaching out to families to provide support for promoting literacy development in the home. In a 2013 Pew Report, researchers found that 94 percent of parents said that libraries are important for their children. Book borrowing remains the most important service offered with some 96 percent of parents indicating that borrowing books is important and nine in ten parents agreeing that libraries should "definitely offer free literacy programs" to help young children prepare for school. Whether it's public library programs that provide evening activities for all ages or school libraries connecting daytime and afterschool activities, we have resources that can be instrumental in promoting literacy for children and parents alike. When you plan activities for the year ahead, consider including the whole family in your literacy celebrations (like El día de los niños/El día de los libros) or in your reading programs (like Summer Reading Club or Book It pizza certificates). Create opportunities for intergenerational connection and involvement. Be part of the Decade for Childhood, 2012–2022, a ten-year initiative to consider best policies and practices and support a global conversation about childhood.

Resource Sites for Supporting Family Literacy

These websites offer an excellent starting point for helping parents and families learn more about literacy development.

Colorín Colorado
Serving Families of English Language Learners
http://www.colorincolorado.org/

National Center for Family Literacy
http://www.famlit.org/

Barbara Bush Foundation for Family Literacy
http://www.barbarabushfoundation.com/

Reach Out and Read
Literacy Support from the Doctor's Office
http://www.reachoutandread.org/

Reading Rockets
http://www.readingrockets.org/

Harvard Family Research Project
http://www.hfrp.org/

EMERGENT LITERACY

What do we know about how children develop as literate beings? Experts like Sulzby and Teale (1996) coined the term "emergent literacy" to describe the evolving way that children acquire language skills. It's not as if they are gurgling babies one day and fluent readers the next. Recent brain research has shown that infants are learning from the moment they are born (and some say before they're born); children are listening, learning, and developing language. They are not always able to communicate their thoughts to us, but they are still doing a lot of thinking! Some early childhood experts even advocate using "baby sign language" as an intermediate step in communicating with children before their verbal vocabulary is fully developed.

Public librarians have been particularly active in reaching out to parents and families and their littlest ones, leading regular story times since the 1930s. In fact, the public library sector has long been a source of parent and family support with story times, lapsit programs, toddler activities, and other organized opportunities for promoting children's literature. In recent years, the Public Library Association and the Association for Library Service to Children have collaborated to create the "Every Child Ready to Read @ your library® Project," complete with training opportunities for librarians (see http://everychildready toread.org/). In addition, the current "Born to Read: How to Raise a Reader" project provides brochures and materials to share with families to provide guidance in early literacy development (see http://www.ala.org/alsc/issuesadv/bornto read). They remind us that the essential building blocks of reading skill include three components: developing oral language skills and phonological awareness (or knowing sounds and words), developing print awareness and letter knowledge (or knowing the alphabet and what it represents), and having the motivation to learn and some experience and exposure to books and stories. School librarians can help preschoolers make the adjustment to school easier by making an appearance at story times at the nearest public library, even volunteering when possible, thus becoming a familiar face to the parents and children in the area.

Don Holdaway in *The Foundations of Literacy* (1984, p. 52) claims that children with early literacy experience have developed certain expectations of print and that this serves as a motivational factor. He observes, "They come to print with expectations, not only that they will succeed in unlocking its mysteries, but also that the mysteries are *worth* unlocking." Kathleen Odean (2003) reminds us that parents can promote this development through the old-fashioned practice of reading aloud to their children, but it works best if it isn't approached as an educational exercise. Parents have been known to have children repeat each word after them as a device to teach reading. Such a tedious approach is more likely to squash enthusiasm for books than to promote learning. They should be encouraged to simply enjoy the books together; all the aspects of "reading readiness," such as learning vocabulary and becoming familiar with books, will follow naturally. As Bernice Cullinan (1995, p. 7) observes, "Readers are made in childhood. The models we provide, and the books we select, influence children in lasting ways." The library can help provide support for parents in building this background, can supplement family activities with organized programs, and can provide reference books for parent education on literacy development.

Resources for Parents about Sharing Children's Literature

These are parent-friendly resource books with related websites to recommend to adults who want to help their children become eager readers.

Codell, Esmé Raji. 2003. *How to Get Your Child to Love Reading: For Ravenous and Reluctant Readers Alike*. Chapel Hill, NC: Algonquin. (http://www.planetesme.com/)

Fox, Mem. 2008. *Reading Magic: Why Reading Aloud to Our Children Will Change Their Lives Forever* (Updated and Revised Edition). Boston: Mariner Books. (http://www.memfox.com)

Lipson, Eden Ross. 2000. *The New York Times Parent's Guide to the Best Books for Children* (Third Edition). New York: Three Rivers Press.

Miller, Donalyn. 2009. *The Book Whisperer: Awakening the Inner Reader in Every Child*. San Francisco: Jossey-Bass.

Silvey, Anita. 2005. *100 Best Books for Children: A Parent's Guide to Making the Right Choices for Your Young Reader, Toddler to Preteen*. Boston: Houghton Mifflin.

Silvey, Anita. 2012. *Children's Book-a-Day Almanac*. New York: Roaring Brook Press. (http://www.anitasilvey.com/)

Trelease, Jim. 2013. *The Read-Aloud Handbook* (Seventh Edition). New York: Penguin. (http://www.trelease-on-reading.com)

In this book, however, our focus is on supporting the growing literacy of children ages five to twelve. We need to understand the basics of preschool child development and literacy acquisition in order to build on this foundation appropriately. It is also important to realize that many children do not have the optimal early environment for learning sounds, letters, words, stories, and books—in English or in any language. And learning to read English with a limited knowledge of the spoken language is also challenging for children. Thus, it may fall to us to help older children develop letter and word knowledge and story background if they missed those opportunities earlier. We may need to include board book collections even in school libraries, for example, and adapt our reading aloud practices to be more interactive. It's not their fault that they missed out, and we can try to fill in those gaps, without judgment, whenever possible.

Professional Associations That Specialize in Educating Very Young Children

For more information about the development of very young children, these organizations can be helpful:

National Association for the Education of Young Children (NAEYC)
http://www.naeyc.org/
Association for Childhood Education International (ACEI)
http://www.acei.org/ and their state and local chapters

SCHOOLS AND READING

When children enter school, the emphasis continues to be largely on reading and overall literacy development throughout the primary grades (K–3). Reading instruction focuses on helping children read proficiently "on grade level," a process that may take several years for some children, particularly those children who do not arrive with a rich background of story language and book words. A "basal reader," or anthology of stories, poems, and excerpts makes up the reading diet for instructional purposes in most schools. But the library is essential for supplementing this minimal quantity of reading. Stephen Krashen (2004) reports overwhelming research about the critical role that school and public libraries play in helping children learn to read, as well as to learn English. Children need to be surrounded by a print-rich environment that provides light reading (magazines, comics, etc.) as well as the best in literature. In addition, the library can still be a place where reading occurs for its own sake, not for a grade, a test score, or even a project. A welcoming library is a place for recreational reading and information seeking guided by a sympathetic adult.

In "Letter to a First-Year School Librarian," Justin Ashworth (2006) recommends several tips to the novice, including developing an ongoing working relationship with the school principal or administrator. He emphasizes being assertive, updating the administrator on library successes and happenings, submitting circulation statistics, leading booktalks at faculty meetings, and building a case for library needs and priorities. He suggests we consider offering to be the principal's personal librarian by helping locate needed professional development materials. Ashworth (2006, p. 51) reminds us that "Many administrators aren't aware of how directly involved the librarian is in teaching students, working with staff, and innovating with technology." Show them. Be your school's advocate for campus-wide reading.

The librarian also serves as a kind of consultant and collaborator with the teaching staff of the school(s), offering library resources (books, technology, know-how) to enhance student learning experiences. The American Association of School Librarians identifies the major "Roles & Responsibilities of the School Library Media Specialist," which include serving as teacher, instructional partner, information specialist, and program administrator. Woolls (2004) details the school library media center manager's responsibilities for the facility, the program, the personnel, the budget, and the collection itself. We can organize a class set of books pulled on a designated subject currently under study, or create reading lists on a particular topic for individualized reading. As we plan group activities, we can offer mini-lessons, read alouds, and other opportunities to reinforce the learning that is taking place in the classroom. When we are aware of and involved in the curriculum, we can provide invaluable support—like having two teachers for the price of one. But often this role is the best-kept secret in the school. Sometimes we need to be assertive about what we have to offer, about the pivotal role that the library can play in learning—not just as an occasional book pit stop, but being careful always to reduce classroom teacher work, not increase it. Often the librarian's suggestions are seen as one more obligation, rather than as a way to lighten teachers' loads in the process of offering more and better resources to students. And the collaboration between school and public libraries is also an often underutilized source of student support. Working together, we can help with student homework, science projects, recreational reading, summer reading, transitions between grade levels, and much more.

Take inspiration from one example of a librarian at Lakewood Elementary School in Sunnyvale, California, a state that ranks last in the nation for the number of teaching librarians, particularly in elementary schools. According to the California Department of Education, only one in five California schools has a credentialed librarian on staff (Bartindale, 2007). Librarian Valerie Torres revolutionized the Lakewood school library, putting computers in prominent places, labeling the books and shelves in a more child-friendly way, updating the collection with more current titles, instituting a reading club and chess competitions, and launching a literacy program for Spanish-speaking parents to show them how to build reading routines at home. She worked closely with teachers to identify research material to support what students were learning, finding websites, seeking out video clips and other resources that teachers might not have time to unearth. Now the library is the "heart" of the school, the "academic focal point," and not just a "book depository." An abundance of research supports this idea. In schools with professional library staff, students' achievement is consistently higher. In addition, those intangible variables like "enjoying reading" are also increased in environments like this.

Schools that are especially effective also partner with their local public libraries, helping parents and families utilize literacy resources after school and year round. Applications for public library cards are made available at schools and school library media specialists share their curriculum plans with the children's services personnel at the public library. Additional information about public library programs and resources is also circulated at the school site, particularly regarding the all-important Summer Reading Program. Support for parents and preschoolers is supplemented by the public library, and special events like celebrations for National Children's Book Week in May or El día de los niños/El día de los libros in April are coordinated together. That back-and-forth collaboration between school and public library personnel is the hallmark of a literacy-centered community.

READING ALOUD

One of the fundamental applications of children's literature is the simple act of reading aloud. In *Radical Change: Books for Youth in a Digital Age* (1999), Eliza Dresang reminds us that handheld books still have a place in children's lives, albeit a changing one. In our technological age, there is still great pleasure in sharing a book out loud with a group of children. Here, we provide a model of fluent and enthusiastic reading, build vocabulary and story knowledge, and reinforce the correlation between listening and reading, between spoken and written language. It is also a moment for emotional connection, a time for showing children we care about them by spending time reading to them and enjoying a common book together. In the landmark study *Becoming a Nation of Readers*

(1985), the Commission on Reading found that "The single most important activity for building the knowledge required for eventual success in reading is reading aloud to children. . . . It is a practice that should continue throughout the grades." Children of all ages and language backgrounds benefit from this experience as they can focus on content and story, rather than decoding and word analysis. And we all know that children can understand much more challenging works than they can tackle on their own. Plus, they enjoy the connection and attention from a book-loving adult. According to Jim Trelease, national advocate for reading aloud and author of *The Read-Aloud Handbook* (2013), reading aloud is "the best-kept secret in education today." He also says, "We have concentrated so hard on teaching children how to read, that we have forgotten to teach them to *want* to read. As a result, we have created a nation of schooltime readers, not lifetime readers." Fortunately, many helpful resources are available to guide us in leading engaging read aloud sessions, including the *Books Kids Will Sit Still For* series by Judy Freeman. Even older children enjoy the experience of hearing a book read aloud or reading aloud to each other. There is a social aspect to reading that may be all the more necessary in an online-obsessed age.

SUSTAINED SILENT READING (SSR)

Jim Trelease and other reading experts such as Stephen Krashen also recommend providing time for children to read silently and independently, another key ingredient in becoming a mature, confident reader. Krashen calls this "free voluntary reading," or reading because you want to. In schools, this approach is often called "sustained silent reading," or SSR. Other clever names have been coined such as DEAR time (Drop Everything And Read) and SQUIRT time (Super Quiet UnInterrupted Reading Time).

The idea is that we set aside ten to fifteen minutes (or more) out of each school day (or week), usually during reading or language arts class, and let students read whatever they have chosen, including comics, catalogs, manuals, graphic novels, and magazines. There are no book reports, no assignments, and no grades. And students aren't required to finish their selections if they don't want to; they're free to choose something else to read. During SSR time, library media specialists and teachers (and the entire school staff) also read for pleasure. It's a positive interlude in an otherwise crowded school schedule and often mushrooms into promoting a school-wide emphasis on reading. Consider joining in for national "Drop Everything and Read" Day held on April 12, an initiative designed to encourage families to put aside thirty minutes to enjoy books together in honor of the birthday of Newbery Award–winning author Beverly Cleary. For additional tips, check out *The SSR Handbook* (2000) by Janice Pilgreen.

Storytime Favorites

Marianne Follis is a senior librarian at the Valley Ranch (Irving) Public Library in Texas where she develops and provides story times for ages birth through preschool and their families, instilling a love of books in children and offering tools for parents to continue to grow a lifelong love of books in their homes. She also has a highly attended book club for 'tweens to foster critical skills in discussing books. Programming is her specialty, and she believes that going to the library for fun events helps cement the notion of the "library as a place" vital to her community. Her story times rock, so I asked her for her current list of favorite books for story time sharing. Here are her own annotated recommendations.

1. Bell, Babs. 2004. *The Bridge Is Up.* New York: HarperCollins.
   When the bridge goes up, everyone has to wait. Fun vehicles wait patiently, as do the storytime participants. Simple text and bright illustrations make this a story time favorite.
2. Buss, Deborah. 2001. *Book! Book! Book!* New York: Scholastic.
   When the kids go back to school, the animals on the farm get bored. Going into town, they find the library where the librarian doesn't understand what they want, since she doesn't speak "cow," "pig," and "goat." Thankfully the hen is on hand to save the day, asking for a "book, book, book."
3. Conin, Doreen. 2002. *Giggle Giggle Quack.* New York: Simon & Schuster.
   DUUUUCK! I love Duck. I use this in my "Storytime Behaving Badly" series coupled with the books *No David, Don't Let the Pigeon Drive the Bus,* and *Max Cleans Up.* Here we have some lovable but badly behaving story time characters.
4. Fleming, Denise. 2002. *The First Day of Winter.* New York: Macmillan.
   Done to the tune of "The Twelve Days of Christmas," this fun, sung book builds a snowman while counting its ingredients. I have created a fun "flannel board" to go along with the book and we count as we sing.
5. Fleming, Candace. 2002. *Muncha! Muncha! Muncha!* New York: Simon & Schuster.
   Three clever bunnies and an exasperated farmer make for a fun "tail" of persistence. Onomatopoeic words make this a fun read aloud.
6. Kutner, Merrily. 2009. *Down on the Farm.* New York: Holiday House.
   The repetitive phrase "down on the farm" lends itself to a fun and interactive story time, as do the animal noises. The last refrain is done as a whisper as "Sun goes down . . . shhhhh . . . quiet town . . . down on the farm, down on the farm."
7. Litwin, Eric. 2012. *Pete the Cat and His Four Groovy Buttons.* New York: HarperCollins.
   Author/songwriter Eric Litwin elevates a simple concept book to a fun and interactive story time event. As the laid-back optimist Pete the Cat loses buttons off his favorite shirt, children are invited to explore the concept of numbers through text, symbols, and equations, all of which can be sung to a "rockin'" tune, which you can learn with a little help from YouTube.

8. Rohmann, Eric. 2007. *My Friend Rabbit*. New York: Square Fish.
   I love mismatched friend stories, and this is one of my favorites as the nearly wordless book relies on audience participation in the telling of the tale.
9. Stevens, Janet. 2008. *Help Me Mr. Mutt*. Boston: Houghton Mifflin Harcourt.
   I love this book for the varied voices of the dogs in distress (great for hamming it up) as well as the math components. I use this in my "Dogs vs. Cats" story time along with *Dog's Colorful Day* by Emma Dodd and *There Are Cats in This Book* by Viviane Schwarz.
10. Willems, Mo. 2007. *There Is a Bird on Your Head*. New York: Disney/Hyperion.
    All of the *Elephant and Piggie* books are perfect for readers' theater and just overly dramatic reading, but to me the first is always the best for friendship and fun.

READERS' ADVISORY

Another major activity in children's services focuses on promoting individualized reading through readers' advisory. Recommending books to kids is definitely one of the most fun parts of the job. It's particularly rewarding when a child comes back asking for more. And if not, it can be an interesting challenge to help children find books they like better. Many public libraries, in particular, offer readers' advisory assistance through bookmarks, booklists, and booktalks, as well as via their websites, blogs, and apps. Independent sites such as Kidsreads.com and others offer the opportunity for children to read, respond, rate, and recommend books to each other. Book experts such as Kathleen Odean provide multiple selection guides, such as *Great Books About Things Kids Love: More Than 750 Recommended Books for Children 3 to 14* (2001), among several others, or Walter Mayes's and Valerie Lewis's *Valerie & Walter's Best Books for Children: A Lively, Opinionated Guide* (2004). Reference works such as *A to Zoo: Subject Access to Children's Picture Books* edited by Carolyn Lima and Rebecca Thomas (2010) and *Best Books for Children: Preschool Through Grade 6* edited by Catherine Barr and John T. Gillespie (2010) are invaluable tools for looking up books to recommend by subject, title, and author. Libraries Unlimited even offers a readers' advisory e-newsletter along with *The Reader's Advisor Online* on a subscription basis, helpful for guiding preteen reading. And of course there is no substitute for being well read yourself, keeping up with the latest children's books, so that you can recommend titles and authors with genuine enthusiasm and knowledgeable details. Fortunately, there are also several excellent review and evaluation tools to help us select books worth adding to our collections. Kids are often curious about what the librarian chooses to read and fascinated by what their teachers are reading, including coaches, school staff, math teachers, science folks, and others who are not necessarily viewed as "peddling" reading for a living. Muster these adult resources to create a climate of people of all ages who enjoy talking about books.

The Reader's Bill of Rights

1. The right to not read.
2. The right to skip pages.
3. The right to not finish.
4. The right to reread.
5. The right to read anything.
6. The right to escapism.
7. The right to read anywhere.
8. The right to browse.
9. The right to read out loud.
10. The right not to defend your tastes.

Pennac, Daniel. 1996. *Better Than Life*. Toronto, Ontario, Canada: Coach House Press.

SELECTING AND REVIEWING CHILDREN'S BOOKS

How do we choose which books to read aloud or recommend? How do we know whether a book is "good" or not? Luckily, there are multiple resources to guide us and well-established criteria to rely upon. Standard texts such as K. T. Horning's *From Cover to Cover: Evaluating and Reviewing Children's Books* (2010) are invaluable as a beginning frame of reference. And as we explore each genre here, we'll consider the elements that are particular to each type of book, chapter by chapter. In the meantime, it is also helpful to be familiar with the major review journals in the field of children's literature. There are many emerging online sources of reviews, including databases of comparative reviews via vendors such as Follett's Titlewave, Ingram's iPage, and Mackin. These are helpful for gathering input, but they often abridge or excerpt reviews due to space limitations, so it's important to check primary sources for a complete review picture. For example, I still feel it's important to read my paper copy of the *Horn Book Magazine*, the preeminent journal in the field. Since 1924, the *Horn Book Magazine* (http://www.hbook.com) has been devoted to the critical analysis of children's literature, including articles, book reviews, and the speeches of the Newbery and Caldecott medal recipients. *Horn Book* cosponsors the annual *Boston Globe/Horn Book* awards, prints a yearly "Fanfare" list of best books, and publishes *The Horn Book Guide*, a comprehensive review source published semiannually.

But you should seek out reviews from other sources, too, as you decide which books are just right for your library collection. Indeed, most librarians are required to cite at least two positive reviews from well-regarded sources to justify a book's acquisition. What are other reputable sources?

School Library Journal
http://www.slj.com/
SLJ may be the most comprehensive of the review media since it considers nearly all books published for young people and is available

monthly, with reviews written by a nationwide panel of several hundred librarians. A starred review and/or inclusion on the "Best Books" list in December signifies a particularly noteworthy book.

Booklist
http://www.booklistonline.com
Booklist is the major review publication of the ALA and includes a "Books for Youth" section of reviews of books for older, middle, and young readers. Outstanding books are given starred reviews and an end-of-the-year "Editor's Choice" issue is especially helpful, as are the lists of "Best Books" compiled by various ALA committees. Print subscriptions include issues of *Book Links* magazine as a regular supplement offering columns and articles full of booklists, strategies, and tips.

Bulletin of the Center for Children's Books (BCCB)
http://bccb.lis.illinois.edu/
The Bulletin was founded by children's literature giant Zena Sutherland and is currently published in print and online by The Johns Hopkins University Press for the Graduate School of Library and Information Science, University of Illinois at Urbana-Champaign. Regular staff members review new books on a monthly basis (except August) and issue an annual list of Bulletin Blue Ribbon books.

Kirkus Reviews
http://www.kirkusreviews.com/
Kirkus Reviews, founded in 1933, is published twice monthly and includes reviews written by specialists selected for their knowledge and expertise in a particular field with over 100 freelance reviewers contributing regularly.

Publishers Weekly
http://www.publishersweekly.com/
Although the primary focus of *PW* is on books for adults, there are regular reviews of children's books in various categories such as fiction, picture books, and nonfiction written by permanent staff members. General information about the publishing industry including current bestsellers and publishing statistics is also interesting. Their *PW Children's Bookshelf* is a very popular and helpful digital newsletter.

VOYA (Voice of Youth Advocates)
http://www.voyamagazine.com/
This journal provides reviews for librarians who work with teenagers and preteens and considers everything from fiction and fantasy to graphic novels and audiobooks. In addition, it offers interesting articles on current trends in literature and youth services.

The Cooperative Children's Book Center (CCBC)
http://www.education.wisc.edu/ccbc/
Based at the University of Wisconsin in Madison, the CCBC was established in 1963 as a center for research and study in children's

literature. Currently headed by Kathleen T. (KT) Horning, the center highlights a book of the week, the annual "CCBC Choices" best list, the Charlotte Zolotow award for picture books, and many helpful bibliographies.

Most of these review sources continue to offer print magazines and journals, but they also include electronic access on a subscription basis. Many use their websites to offer additional resources that are updated on a regular basis. And laypeople enjoy reviewing, too. Reviews by librarians, educators, and young people themselves are popping up in all kinds of places, particularly on the Web, on blogs, and in informal publications. This can be a fun and meaningful activity to orchestrate and assist in collection development that more closely aligns with patron needs. It bears repeating that relying on reviews alone is not enough to build a strong collection. We need to know the kids and the community and seek out books that meet their various needs. One colleague, Donna, put it this way: "The bottom line for librarians is that no single source is the best source; you have to learn the sources that work for you and your library and then keep reconsidering your decision."

Best Book Blogs

Blogs are online Web logs that provide an avenue for informal online posting and information sharing, often on a daily basis. These are some of my favorite blogs to check for the latest scoop in children's literature. New blogs and new formats (like Facebook, Twitter, Tumblr, Pinterest, Instagram, etc.) emerge all the time, so keep on the lookout. Or better yet, create your own.

7-Imp: Seven Impossible Things Before Breakfast
    http://www.blaine.org/sevenimpossiblethings/
    Julie Danielson ("Jules") writes primarily about illustration in children's books, particularly in picture books and illustrated novels, with plenty of interviews and behind-the-scenes nuggets.
Blue Rose Girls
    http://bluerosegirls.blogspot.com/
    A group of children's book illustrators began this collective blog with a fresh take on the bookmaking process, publishing business, and the children's literature field.
Chicken Spaghetti
    http://www.chickenspaghetti.typepad.com/chicken_spaghetti
    Susan Thomsen, magazine editor, contributor, theater reviewer, and author, provides reviews, lists, and news. This is a good place to go for information about the latest book awards.
Cynsations
    http://www.cynthialeitichsmith.blogspot.com
    Author Cynthia Leitich Smith offers a range of up-to-the-moment news, interviews, reviews, booklists, and more.

Fuse #8
> http://blogs.slj.com/afuse8production/
> Formerly an independent blogger, Betsy Bird was so successful that her blog is now hosted at *School Library Journal's* blogsite where she covers a range of children's literature topics with her unique sensibility. She is also New York Public Library's Youth Materials Collections Specialist.

Nerdy Book Club
> http://nerdybookclub.wordpress.com
> This group blog, which invites participation on all topics related to literature for young people, is led by a trio of teachers: Donalyn Miller, Colby Sharp, and Cindy Minnich.

ReadRoger
> http://www.hbook.com/category/blogs/read-roger/
> The editor of *Horn Book Magazine* maintains a regular blog with children's literature–related information, opinions, asides, and more.

AWARDS IN CHILDREN'S LITERATURE

Another tool for identifying quality in children's literature is the recognition of awards and prizes. Often it is this element of children's literature that is most familiar, even to the average layperson on the street. Gold seals on book covers have become nearly ubiquitous. They sell well and gain prominent placement. The winners of the two most important awards in children's literature often appear on the *Today Show* television program when the awards are announced. What are these two awards? They are the Newbery medal for the author of a distinguished children's book and the Caldecott medal for an illustrator of a distinguished picture book. Both are awarded by the American Library Association through the Association for Library Service to Children.

The Newbery Award

The John Newbery Medal is probably the most well-known and prestigious award in the field of children's literature. It has been presented annually since 1922 to the author of the most distinguished contribution to children's literature published in the United States in the preceding year. Several honor books are also usually named each year. It nearly guarantees that the award-winning book will be on the shelf of every library in America and establishes reputations of authors, editors, and publishing houses. It was founded by businessman Frederick Melcher and named after an 18th-century British gentleman (John Newbery) who is credited with creating the first publishing market for children in the 1700s. A committee of librarians and other professionals chooses the award-winning book each year, which is usually announced to the public in January. All the award recipients and honor books are also listed in many places, including the ALA website. (By the way, please note that the name "Newbery" has only one "r"!)

The Caldecott Award

The Randolph Caldecott Medal is probably the most well-known and prestigious award in the field of children's book illustration. It has been presented annually since 1938 to the artist of the most distinguished American picture book for children published in the preceding year. Several honor books are also usually named each year. It also nearly guarantees widespread acquisition and establishes reputations. It was founded by Frederick Melcher and named after a 19th-century British illustrator, Randolph Caldecott, who is credited with creating the first lively, humorous, and dynamic illustrations for children's books. A committee of librarians and other professionals chooses the award-winning book each year, which is also announced in January. All the award recipients and honor books are listed in many places, including the ALA website.

And as you look for ways to promote and share the medal books, seek out these resources for help and inspiration: *The Newbery/Printz Companion* by John Gillespie and Corinne Naden (2006) and the latest update of the ALSC book, *Newbery and Caldecott Awards: A Guide to the Medal and Honor Books* published by ALA.

OTHER MAJOR AWARDS

In addition to these two major awards, there are many other recognitions that help us appreciate the very best in children's literature. These consider genre (like nonfiction or poetry) or the author and illustrator's cultural background (like the Coretta Scott King or Pura Belpré awards) or other attributes.

Hans Christian Andersen Award

Since 1956, the International Board on Books for Young People (IBBY) has presented the Hans Christian Andersen award to a living author whose complete works have made a lasting contribution to children's literature. In 1966, they added an award for illustration to a distinguished illustrator for his or her entire body of work. Sometimes called the "Nobel Prize" of children's literature, it is given every two years to one author and one illustrator from around the world. Candidates are nominated by their home countries (a national section of IBBY), and a distinguished international jury of children's literature specialists makes the award decision.

The Sibert Award

In 2001, the American Library Association introduced a new award for informational literature for children called the Robert F. Sibert Informational Book Medal. The award is named in honor of Robert F. Sibert, the longtime president of Bound to Stay Bound Books, Inc. of Jacksonville, Illinois, and is sponsored by the company. ALSC administers the award. The Sibert Information Book Award is intended to honor the author whose work of nonfiction has made a significant contribution to the field of children's literature.

The Coretta Scott King Award

Since 1970, this award has been given annually to African American authors and illustrators for outstanding contributions to literature for children by the American Library Association. Usually one author or novelist and one illustrator are each recognized. The award is intended to encourage the artistic expression of the African American experience by African American authors and illustrators. The award commemorates the life and work of Dr. Martin Luther King Jr. and honors his widow, Coretta Scott King, for her courage and determination in working for peace and world brotherhood.

The Pura Belpré Award

The Pura Belpré Award, established in 1996, is presented to a Latino/Latina writer and illustrator whose work best portrays, affirms, and celebrates the Latino cultural experience in an outstanding work of literature for children and youth. It is cosponsored by the Association for Library Service to Children (ALSC), a division of the American Library Association (ALA) and the National Association to Promote Library Services to the Spanish Speaking (REFORMA), an ALA Affiliate. Books are chosen both for narrative and for illustration.

The NCTE Award for Excellence in Poetry for Children

The National Council of Teachers of English (NCTE) established its Award for Excellence in Poetry for Children in 1977 to honor a living American poet for his or her entire body of work for children. The award is currently given every two years.

The Orbis Pictus Award for Outstanding Nonfiction for Children

In 1990, NCTE established the Orbis Pictus Award for Outstanding Nonfiction for Children for promoting and recognizing excellence in the writing of nonfiction for children. The award commemorates the work of Comenius, the *Orbis Pictus—The World in Pictures* (1657), historically considered the first book actually planned for children. One title for children in grades K–8 is singled out for the award, and several honor books are also recognized.

The Scott O'Dell Award for Historical Fiction

The Scott O'Dell Award is given to the author of a distinguished work of historical fiction written for children or adolescent readers. First presented in 1984, the award was originated and donated by Newbery Award–winning historical author Scott O'Dell himself. The winning book must be published in English in the United States and must be set in the "New World" (North, South, or Central America).

Additional Awards

Additional awards for children's and young adult literature include, but are not limited to:

- Michael L. Printz Award for Young Adult Literature
- Odyssey Audiobook Award
- The Claudia Lewis Award for Poetry
- Lee Bennett Hopkins Poetry Award
- Children's Book Guild and *Washington Post* Award for Nonfiction
- Jane Addams Book Award
- The Edgar Awards for Mystery
- The Cybils awards (Children's and Young Adult Bloggers Literary Awards)
- The National Book Award for Young People's Literature
- National Council for the Social Studies Carter G. Woodson Award
- Tomás Rivera Mexican American Children's Book Award
- The Américas Award for Children's and Young Adult Literature
- Aesop Prize

And many others (watch for announcements of book awards worth noting in other countries, like the Kate Greenaway award in Britain). Keeping up with these and other awards of particular importance to our own local communities can help us build our collections as well as assist with promotional efforts since the public recognizes these prizes more readily. We should not feel bound or limited by these, but they are a helpful barometer of what our colleagues as well as experts with special training deem as the best of the best in literature for young people.

Major Publishers of Children's Literature

Publishers, too, are moving quickly to experiment with various technologies for promoting books, authors, and reading via the Web. Many offer print, audio, and video resources for learning more about children's literature. Most publishing companies, such as Random House (http://www.randomhouse.com/

teachers/) and HarperCollins (http://www.harpercollinschildrens.com/harper
childrens/), even direct their audience to separate layers of information
depending on whether users are children, parents, or educators. Others, such
as Simon & Schuster (http://www.simonsayskids.com), appeal to children at
various age levels. Each offers information, as well as opportunities for interaction via games, contests, free materials, and so on. For adults who work with
children, publisher websites are helpful for keeping up with the latest books,
as well as for mustering creative connections and materials for motivating
young readers to check out those books. Such Web-based resources provide
both commercial and pedagogical value.

BEST LISTS

In addition to awards that single out an individual or a select few titles, there
are many "best" lists published annually that help us highlight books gathered
for particular purposes. Many focus on children's own preferences; others offer
recommended reading or curricular connections. Check in your own state to see
what awards exist for recognizing children's books or consult *Coast to Coast:
Exploring State Book Awards* by Janet Hilbun and Jane Claes (2010). In Texas,
for example, the Texas Library Association sponsors the following:

- The Bluebonnet award (one favorite chosen by children in grades 3–6
  from a list gathered by librarians)
- The 2X2 Reading List (booklist of recommended books for children age
  2 to grade 2)
- The Texas Lone Star Reading List (booklist of recommended books for
  grades 6–8)
- TAYSHAS High School Reading List (booklist of recommended books
  for high school)
- The Maverick List (booklist of recommended graphic novels)

The American Library Association through ALSC sponsors several annual
best lists of children's "notable" books, recordings, videos, and websites. The
Young Adult Library Services Association also orchestrates a variety of "best"
lists including Best Fiction for Young Adults, Quick Picks for Reluctant Young
Adult Readers, Great Graphic Novels for Teens, Popular Paperbacks for Young
Adults, and Teens' Top Ten, Amazing Audiobooks, and Fabulous Films. These
are all announced at the beginning of the year and are a great help for keeping
up with a variety of literature and media. For older children, it can be interesting to do a comparative study, looking at how many different "best" lists their
favorite titles have appeared on.

Various educational organizations also value the role of children's literature in their disciplines. For example, the International Reading Association
(http://www.reading.org) promotes several reading lists including Children's
Choices and Young Adults' Choices based on the voting of children and teens,
Teachers' Choices, and Notable Books for a Global Society. They also sponsor

an award for new authors and poets. The National Council of Teachers of English is responsible for the Notable Books in the Language Arts list, in addition to the Orbis Pictus award and Poetry award already mentioned. Three other discipline-specific "best" lists include:

- Outstanding Science Trade Books for Children (sponsored by the National Science Teachers Association in cooperation with the Children's Book Council)
- Notable Children's Trade Books in the Field of Social Studies (sponsored by the National Council for the Social Studies in cooperation with the Children's Book Council)
- Outstanding International Children's Books (sponsored by the United States Board on Books for Young People)

It's our professional responsibility to seek out the very best literature for children, as well as to balance the unique needs of our particular library and community. Looking for award winners and "best" list choices is helpful, but we also need to consider what other books will appeal to our young readers. Will we also stock #17 in a series that is not prize winning but consistently flies off the shelves? Or movie tie-in books? Or paperbacks? What is your philosophy? I'm a proponent of sharing the best-quality literature with children, offering the most beautiful language, engaging stories, and deeply expressed themes. These are often the works that last, that touch our hearts and minds, that stay with you for a lifetime. But, admit it, we have all read our share of junk. In fact, studies of avid readers have found that they read widely as children, often extensively in series books such as Nancy Drew or Hardy Boys, for example. Indeed, it is this wide reading, this vast volume of reading, that helped us gain our proficiency in reading over the years. I remember when my daughter (always an avid reader) read over 100 of the "Babysitter Club" paperbacks, one after the other. I think it was after reading #134 that she said to me, "You know, Mom, after a while, these are kind of all alike." It only took 134 books! But look how many pages of print she had absorbed in the meantime and how comforting that familiar circle of girl characters had become. Often children who are not fluent readers have simply not had enough practice reading, so reading is still difficult, so they don't want to tackle it, so they don't improve. It can be a vicious circle. These are often the same children who find the Newbery books too challenging. What to do? Fill in the gaps with more "temporary" reading that helps build skill and confidence while continuing to read aloud from the award winners to keep the bar high.

Favorite Websites about Literature for Children

Here are some of my favorite websites in the field of children's literature in addition to those that have been featured earlier in this chapter. Each is a good beginning point for general information on books, authors, and ideas for sharing books with kids.

Professor Kay Vandergrift's Children's Literature Site
   http://comminfo.rutgers.edu/professional-development/childlit/
Carol Otis Hurst's Children's Literature Site
   http://www.carolhurst.com/
Children's Literature Web Guide
   http://people.ucalgary.ca/~dkbrown/
The Center for Children's Books at the University of Illinois at Urbana-Champaign
   http://ccb.lis.illinois.edu/
Children's Book Council
   http://www.CBCBooks.org

WHAT BOOKS?

It's only really been about 100 years since children's books as we know them have been around, often marked by the publication of Beatrix Potter's classic picture book, *The Tale of Peter Rabbit*, in 1902. That little pint-sized book has sold nearly 10 million copies and is the #2 bestselling children's book of all time in the United States, according to statistics from *Publishers Weekly* in 2001 (Roback and Britton, 2001). This gem of a book is the "gold standard" for picture book creation, with the perfect marriage of illustration and text, beautifully conceived and produced, told simply and directly, but with clever phrasing and language. So, what is the #1 bestselling children's book? *The Poky Little Puppy* Golden Book, a nostalgic favorite by Jannette Sebring Lowrey that still sells for only a few dollars. This series of inexpensive Golden Books was launched in 1942 for twenty-five cents apiece, making children's books more widely available than ever before (even outside bookstores). Other books in the series, including *Tootle* and *The Saggy Baggy Elephant*, are also among the bestselling books ever. Several of Richard Scarry's colorful books and many Disney movie tie-ins (e.g., *Lion King*, *Aladdin*) also maintain consistent popularity, whatever you may think of their literary quality. Not surprisingly, fifteen of the top 100 children's books are by Dr. Seuss, including *Green Eggs and Ham*; *The Cat in the Hat*; *One Fish, Two Fish, Red Fish, Blue Fish*; *Hop on Pop*, and others. His legacy to the children's field is enormous, influencing both illustration (with his trademark cartooning) and writing (with his ear-catching nonsense rhymes).

What other books have demonstrated staying power over the years? P. D. Eastman's *Are You My Mother?* and *Go, Dog. Go!* and A. A. Milne's *Winnie-the-Pooh* and *When We Were Very Young* and several of Sandra Boynton's books for very young children such as *The Going to Bed Book* and *Moo Baa La La La*. What variety that represents. Three of Shel Silverstein's poetry collections are in the top 100: *Where the Sidewalk Ends*, *A Light in the Attic*, and *Falling Up*. These helped pave the way for a whole revolution in humorous poetry for children.

Which novels for older readers appear on this same list? You'll probably not be surprised to learn that all of the Harry Potter fantasy novels by J. K. Rowling are there. Since first published in 1998, each one sold better than the last.

Published in 200 territories in 74 languages, the series garnered worldwide sales of more than 450 million copies. And what an impact they have had in encouraging reading on a gigantic scale, as well as the publication of more fantasy, including longer works previously thought too challenging for children. At the other end of the spectrum, the gentle fantasy *Charlotte's Web* by E. B. White published in 1952 also holds its place on the bestseller list. In between, various editions of the Nancy Drew and Hardy Boys mystery series still maintain a loyal fan base.

This quick bird's eye view reflects the variety of children's books popular in the marketplace. It reminds us that there is quite an appetite for the familiar touchstones of the past, as well as room for something new and different, like a fat fantasy novel or a wacky book of poetry. The following chapters will focus on each major genre of children's literature in greater depth. We'll look at the major titles, authors, and trends in each genre and consider how to take good books into action, sharing them with children in all kinds of meaningful ways.

History in Action: Anthologies of Children's Literature

Although our focus in this text is on studying individual titles of children's books, it is also worth knowing about some of the notable anthologies that gather examples and excerpts of some of the most noteworthy children's literature across genres and generations. In particular, these big fat anthologies gather historical gems that are no longer widely available on library shelves, such as original works by John Newbery and Randolph Caldecott. Plus, they offer scholarly commentary that helps us understand the significance of these selections in a historical, social, and cultural context. For anyone interested in the "big picture" of the body of children's literature, they are valuable reference tools. Here are some of these most notable anthologies:

Children's Literature: An Anthology, 1801–1902 edited by Peter Hunt (Oxford: Blackwell, 2000)

Crosscurrents of Children's Literature: An Anthology of Texts and Criticism by J. D. Stahl, Tina L. Hanlon, and Elizabeth Lennox Keyser (Oxford: Oxford University Press, 2006)

The Norton Anthology of Children's Literature edited by Jack Zipes, Lissa Paul, Lynne Vallone, Peter Hunt, and Gillian Avery (New York: W. W. Norton, 2005)

The Riverside Anthology of Children's Literature (Sixth Edition) collected by Judith Saltman (Boston: Houghton Mifflin, 1985)

The Scott, Foresman Anthology of Children's Literature edited by Zena Sutherland (New York: Scott, Foresman, 1983)

LEARNING ABOUT AUTHORS, ILLUSTRATORS, AND POETS

It's the authors, illustrators, and poets who create the literature we love, so learning more about them, their lives, and their creative processes can be a fascinating aspect of the study of children's literature. We can rely on the traditional "Something about the Author" reference tool or "Google" them on the Web or look for them on YouTube. Subscription-based electronic databases such as Contemporary Literary Criticism, Contemporary Authors, or the Dictionary of Literary Biography offer additional support. The Society of Children's Book Writers and Illustrators (http://www.scbwi.org/) provides resources for aspiring authors and artists, as well as information and links relevant to the field of children's literature in general. TeachingBooks.net, a subscription-based multimedia website, specializes in hosting mini-movies that feature authors reading aloud or talking about their work. There's even an online tip sheet of authors and illustrators pronouncing their names for you. The Children's Book Council website (http://www.cbcbooks.org) provides guidelines for author and illustrator visits and publisher contacts. A wonderful Canadian website, Just One More Book (http://www.justonemorebook.com/), offers podcasts of interviews with authors and illustrators, as well as book reviews and other audio commentary.

Inviting an author to speak at a school or library program can be the "icing on the cake" for eager readers who have prepared by reading the author's (or illustrator's or poet's) books. This can be a literacy event, creating lifelong memories while reinforcing reading, writing, and language development. Nowadays, some authors even do "virtual" visits via the Internet (using Skype or FaceTime) that can also be enjoyable and effective. For one example, consult Cynthia Leitich Smith's website for tips on booking a "cyber speaker" (http://www.cynthialeitichsmith.com). Another option to consider includes "Special Appearance Videos," a series of videos and DVDs featuring a variety of individual authors and illustrators produced by Spoken Arts.

Many, many authors, illustrators, and poets now host their own private websites (usually labeled with their name in the URL), and they offer a variety of information geared to readers of various ages. Some, like poet Kristine O'Connell George (http://www.kristinegeorge.com/), have even received awards, such as her site's recognition as "An American Library Association Great Website for Kids." Others are experimenting with blogs (such as Leitich Smith's "Cynsations"), podcasts, videos, and digital trailers available on sites like YouTube. More innovations are on the horizon. Child readers are certainly attuned to searching for information on the Web and expect to see their favorite author and illustrator "celebrities" online. For information about authors, about becoming an author, and for communicating with authors, the Internet has made it possible to connect with creators of children's books in a way that was only possible for a select few in the past.

Author Study Resources

For professional resources to assist with in-depth study of children's book creators, these titles can provide valuable assistance:

Buzzeo, Toni, and Jane Kurtz. 1999. *Terrific Connections with Authors, Illustrators, and Storytellers: Real Space and Virtual Links.* Englewood, CO: Libraries Unlimited.

Follos, Alison M. G. 2006. *Reviving Reading: School Library Programming, Author Visits and Books That Rock!* Englewood, CO: Libraries Unlimited.

James, Helen Foster. 2002. *Author Day Adventures: Bringing Literacy to Life with an Author Visit.* Lanham, MD: Scarecrow.

Jenkins, Carol Brennan. 1999. *The Allure of Authors: Author Studies in the Elementary Classroom.* Portsmouth, NH: Heinemann.

Jenkins, Carol Brennan, and Deborah White. 2007. *Nonfiction Author Studies in the Elementary Classroom.* Portsmouth, NH: Heinemann.

McElmeel, Sharron L. 2001. *ABCs of an Author/Illustrator Visit* (Second Edition). Columbus, OH: Linworth.

McElmeel, Sharron L., and Deborah L. McElmeel. 2005. *Authors in the Kitchen: Recipes, Stories, and More.* Englewood, CO: Libraries Unlimited.

McElmeel, Sharron L., and Deborah L. McElmeel. 2006. *Authors in the Pantry: Recipes, Stories, and More.* Englewood, CO: Libraries Unlimited.

Rockman, Connie. Ed. 2008. *Tenth Book of Junior Authors and Illustrators.* New York: H. W. Wilson.

Silvey, Anita. 2002. *The Essential Guide to Children's Books and Their Creators.* Boston: Mariner Books.

Vardell, Sylvia M. 2007. *Poetry People: A Practical Guide to Children's Poets.* Englewood, CO: Libraries Unlimited.

There are also books available by and about children's book authors that can support the close study of individual writers. For example, the Libraries Unlimited *Author and YOU* series features the life and work of several authors such as Jane Kurtz, Mary Casanova, Bob Barner, Jacqueline Briggs Martin, Alma Flor Ada, Jim Aylesworth, Toni Buzzeo, and Gerald McDermott. The Richard C. Owen "Meet the Author" series includes photo-illustrated autobiographical picture books for children on more than 35 different authors, illustrators, and poets.

The more you immerse yourself in reading children's literature, the more names you will come to know—and love. We all have our favorite writers and artists and look for their next works with great anticipation. Let's create that same appreciation and enthusiasm in children, recognizing that their choices may be very individualistic and surprising. Thank goodness there's an abundance of talent to choose from, with new names emerging all the time. Don't rely only on your own old favorites or on fiction writers exclusively. Be open to poets, nonfiction writers, authors of color, and more. Look for creative ways to promote new and popular authors, such as:

- Collecting the author's works and making them prominent and available
- Creating a bulletin board, poster, or display featuring the author (include a photo, a printout of their website home page, a few "fun facts" about their lives)
- Reading the author's works aloud
- Looking up biographical information about the author and sharing with children
- Seeking out autobiographies, video/audio interviews, and author websites to share

- Setting up an online chat or even a guest appearance by the author, being sure to prepare the children beforehand with extensive reading
- Involving children in choosing authors to study and in developing rotating featured author centers
- Featuring children's authors, illustrators, and poets in your booktalks, displays, and activities

Creating time and space for featured authors helps introduce their work and encourages children to read more. In addition, it can be inspiring for young would-be writers to see that there are successful adults who have made writing their careers.

Authors in Action: Pat Mora

Pat Mora has written in a variety of genres including poetry for children and adults, nonfiction, and children's picture books, including *Tomás and the Library Lady* (Knopf, 1997), *Confetti: Poems for Children* (Lee & Low Books, 1996/1999), *Dizzy in Your Eyes: Poems About Love* (Knopf, 2010), and *Zing! Seven Creativity Practices for Educators and Students* (Corwin, 2010), among others. Many of her works are written in two languages (English interwoven with Spanish words and phrases) and in bilingual editions, which is especially inviting for Spanish-speaking children and also instructional for children not fluent in Spanish. Her work has garnered many awards and recognitions, including a Kellogg National Fellowship, a National Endowment for the Arts Fellowship, the Cooperative Children's Book Center Choices Award, inclusion on the Américas Award Commended List, an International Reading Association Notable Books for Global Society distinction, and the Tomás Rivera Mexican American Children's Book Award, among others. Mora has worked as an administrator, lecturer, and activist, and gives poetry readings, workshops, and presentations around the world. She is also a literacy advocate and a powerhouse in promoting El día de los niños/El día de los libros (Children's Day/Book Day) held on April 30, a national day to celebrate children and literacy.

Zapped by "Día"
by Pat Mora

Imagine a delightful March day in Tucson, 1996. It's almost noon, and at the University of Arizona's public radio station, I've finished an interview about poetry. The radio host asks if I'll read a few of my children's books in Spanish for El día del niño. El día del niño? As a Latina writer, I'd quickly discovered the book world's reluctance to include diverse voices in what we call our national children's literature. I'd also become more aware of underserved children and families.

"I'm from the border, from El Paso, Texas," I say, "and I've never heard of the Day of the Child. When is it? What happens?"

I learn that annually in Mexico, on April 30, parents and teachers plan a special event or treat to celebrate the children. Hmm, I think. Nice date, Cissy's birthday, my youngest.

I walk out, toward the campus cafeteria to meet a group of faculty and staff. And then, unexpected as a quiet zap of lightning, on a campus I'd never attended, in a city I'd only visited, the idea came to me.

What if? What if we, all of us who care about children and literacy, linked the two? What if on April 30, all over the country, we annually celebrated El Día de los niños/El Día de los libros, Children's Day/Book Day? As a mom, I'd heard my three say, "Why do we have Mother's Day and Father's Day and not Children's Day?" This could be our hook.

The kind group waiting for me in the cafeteria, people I did not know well, listened to my babbling and quickly agreed to help. Wasn't I lucky to be with such supportive souls right after the fragile idea fell from above? Día was one of those surprise babies. I didn't deserve her, but there she was. Like all babies, she needed my steady attention. I've told my three grown children that if I'd known how much work Día was going to be, I might have been more cautious. That's parenthood, isn't it? Luckily, members of REFORMA (National Association to Promote Library and Information Services to Latinos and the Spanish-speaking) quickly became her godparents, and others (like Sylvia Vardell) quickly offered to help.

That morning in Tucson was one of the turning points in my adult life. For eleven years I've worked on "Día," as we call it, worked alone and with others. I wrote countless letters that went unanswered and received many promises that never materialized. I've also seen smiling faces, families unfamiliar with libraries enjoying a Día event, feeling at home in a library and thus returning. Those are the treasured moments. Día is a multilingual bridge from the underserved to the library door, and it's great fun for regular patrons too.

Any "what ifs" in your heart, changes you want made in this crazy world? Every waking hour, consciously or unconsciously, we're choosing our actions. If you're like me, you make lists and regularly prioritize. Sometimes the actions we choose are for our own comfort, lunch with a friend, watering plants; sometimes the actions are required by our job description, supervisor, deadlines. Sometimes we choose commitments to meet a need, for others and for ourselves as in the environmental and peace movements.

In collaborative action, we evolve right along with our projects. Good ideas seldom fit in tidy boxes. Like seeds, if well tended, they sprout, flourish, and spread—and spread. My Día partners and I decided that given U.S. literacy challenges, we wanted Día to be completely inclusive and thus we more consciously embraced a commitment to link *all* children to books, languages, and cultures. Then our vision evolved to a need for *family* literacy and for promoting a daily commitment that culminates in an annual, national celebration.

Of course, funding was essential. I'll always be grateful to my friend at the W. K. Kellogg Foundation who became Día's honorary uncle by providing grants for its development and eventual housing at the Association for Library Service to Children (ALSC), a division of the American Library Association (ALA). With them, I'm now always on the lookout for new national funders while amazing librarians and teachers find local funding for the goodies, music, craft and performer expenses, and *free* books for their Día celebrations. Join us! What rewarding emotional gifts Día has for us all, the thrill of sharing bookjoy, of fostering home libraries and more outreach-focused school and public libraries.

Since writing is a form of action and Día is a time gobbler, would my time have been better spent writing more books? We each live with such questions: how best to use our time, talents, energy, resources.

Motivating people and institutions to change, to scrutinize priorities, procedures, and power structures, can be slow and wearying work, but my partners—and that group has grown steadily through the years—emphasize the positive and know the importance of laughter and a hug, even an e-mail hug. We cheer one another on to dust ourselves off, and then we nudge one another upward. Oh yes, making the world fairer or safer is always uphill, but hey, we're building muscles.

I'm proud to be a literacy advocate, but it's not a road I consciously chose. That baby of an idea arrived, and seeing its potential to excite librarians and teachers about reaching out to children and families, I had a job to do. Well, many jobs to do, and I was blessed with partners with strong hearts and arms who shared my vision and sense of urgency. The dream and its urgency pulled me along and pulls me along in spite of regular discouragements. I've fallen in love with the families Día serves. How Día has added meaning to my life.

Thanks to Día, I meet amazing librarians who lure in the unsure and reluctant as did the librarian in *Tomás and the Library Lady*. Such librarians, my good teachers, inspire me with their enthusiasm. They give me hope, and that's a mighty special gift.

Día Resources and Links

http://www.patmora.com
http://www.ala.org/dia
http://www.reforma.org
http://www.texasdia.org

One Book in Action: Tomás and the Library Lady

The Center for the Book in the Library of Congress provides a clearinghouse of information about the "One Book" community-wide reading program first initiated by the Washington Center for the Book in 1998. In addition, the ALA Public Programs Office offers a "One Book, One Community" planning guide as both a PDF file and a CD (http://www.ala.org/programming/onebook). Although this movement started with adults gathering to read and discuss one common book for adults, it has also been modified for multiage communities to focus on children's literature, too. The purpose is to focus on reading and discussion, but it can grow to include special programs, activities, and events, including a visit from the author herself/himself. Teachers also use the "one book" approach in curriculum units that build learning activities in the content areas around a single book. Students read a common book and then engage in discussion, as well as in lessons that develop skill and knowledge in language, math, science, social studies, art, and so on. But middle school librarian Donna MacKinney cautions us to be mindful of balancing reading and activity, however meaningful, with her reminder, "I think that one does have to be very careful not to overdo it and turn a possibly beloved book into just more work."

As we get rolling with "One Book" for each chapter in this text, I chose the picture book *Tomás and the Library Lady* (Knopf, 2000), written by Pat Mora and illustrated by Raul Colón, for our first example. It is an engaging story based on the real life of Tomás Rivera, the child of a migrant working family who went on to become an educator and university president. It's an excellent book to read aloud that also happens to portray a lovely, sympathetic librarian character. It highlights the importance of literacy, story, and books, as well as every child's need for the love and support of family—and others. The book received many recognitions, including the Américas Award for Children's and Young Adult Literature, the Tomás Rivera Mexican American Children's Book Award, and the International Reading Association Teachers' Choices Award, among others. It is also available in both Spanish and English editions and has been performed as a marionette play and as a theatrical production by Childsplay, a nationally recognized professional theater for children and families based in Tempe, Arizona.

When I introduce *Tomás and the Library Lady*, I like to use the "Brown Bag" book report, an idea gleaned from teacher Kim Gale. It is simple and inexpensive, and motivates children to want to read the book being reported about. Plus, children can use this strategy to tell about books that they have read, too, and it provides insight for us into their reading comprehension and oral language skills. Basically, it's a booktalk with props. You gather objects or "book artifacts" that relate to the story, character(s), and main events. You can draw a picture of the item if you can't find the actual item. No need to spend money. Place the book artifacts in a bag. (If you want to get fancy, decorate the bag so it fits the topic of the book.) Then retell the story using the items in the bag, pulling out each book artifact, one at a time, as it is relevant to that part of the story. For *Tomás and the Library Lady*, I have a road map (to show the family's travel from Texas to Iowa), a plastic lemon and orange (to suggest fruit picking), a tree branch (for when Grandpa tells a story), a ball I made out of the stomach of an old stuffed teddy bear (which always generates a lot of discussion), a gift-wrapped dinosaur book (the gift that the "Library Lady" gives Tomás), and finally a graduation cap or mortarboard (to share when reading the epilogue). After sharing the story, the objects can be gathered for a display alongside the book.

A close reading of this book may lead to an honest discussion about the life of the migrant worker and a study of the populations of our own communities. What resources do migrant families have in our neighborhood? How can we help? How can we take what we have learned from Pat Mora's true story and put it into action?

Literature in Action: **Launching Literature and Literacy Celebrations**

One big way that libraries can showcase literature and literacy is by participating in preexisting events that are already planned on a state, regional, or national scale. This includes celebrations such as:

- Read Across America in March
- International Children's Book Day in April
- El día de los niños/El día de los libros in April

- National Poetry Month in April
- National Children's Book Week now in May
- The state lists and programs in your area

These events offer the opportunity to connect with widespread efforts that help you be part of something bigger than any single library can accomplish alone. That's exciting for both librarians and children alike! In addition, their scale means that plans, programs, materials, and resources are often premade and readily available. For example, the National Education Association sponsors what they call "the nation's largest reading event" with the Read Across America campaign. It began as a one-day celebration of Dr. Seuss's birthday on March 2 and has evolved into a yearlong campaign. The NEA website offers extensive information including kits and contests and the opportunities for publicity and interaction.

The International Board on Books for Young People orchestrates a global celebration of reading with International Children's Book Day, in conjunction with Hans Christian Andersen's birthday on April 2. Since 1967, this event has been held "to inspire a love of reading and to call attention to children's books." Each year a different country creates a poster illustrated by a prominent artist from the host country to help promote this worldwide celebration. The IBBY.org website offers more information.

Children's Day/Book Day, also known as El día de los niños/El día de los libros, is a celebration of children, families, and reading held annually on April 30. Sponsored by ALSC (the Association for Library Service to Children) and REFORMA (the National Association to Promote Library Services to Latinos and the Spanish Speaking), this literacy event is focused across languages and cultures, inviting families from all linguistic and cultural backgrounds to encourage their children to read. Guidelines for celebrating this event, including printable brochures and a press kit, are available from the ALSC website.

National Poetry Month is a celebration of poetry first introduced in 1996 by the Academy of American Poets as a way to celebrate poetry and its vital place in American culture. Thousands of organizations participate through readings, festivals, book displays, workshops, and other events.

The Children's Book Council (CBC) sponsors National Children's Book Week in May (formerly in November), a practice that began in 1919. The CBC produces promotional materials for purchase such as posters and bookmarks as well as free digital toolkits and other online resources. In 2008, they launched the Children's & Teen Choice Book Awards and young readers get to vote for their favorite books each year. Check out Bookweekonline.com for more information.

Participating in any of these events is an excellent way to motivate children and adults alike to celebrate the fun of books and reading in our busy, technology-filled world. It provides a model of how we value reading and makes our priorities clear. It is also excellent public relations with the outside world, showing that our library is linked with literacy promotion efforts on a grander scale. We are part of something big and our library is a "happening" place. Plan now to try each one of these events in the next few years. See how the children, their families, and your own colleagues respond. Consider what kinds of individual initiatives you might want to develop for your own library. Think big! This is the kind of thing that often "slips through the cracks" as we work day to day. But with a little bit of forethought, we can reap major benefits by building such celebrations into our planning. Just like holding a special party to celebrate a birthday or anniversary, these moments have a magic all their own and create happy memories that happened in the library.

ONGOING PROFESSIONAL DEVELOPMENT

Keeping up with the field of children's literature is a pleasurable challenge. There are several excellent organizations to participate in, and each offers multiple opportunities for professional development.

- Association of Library Service to Children (ALSC)
- http://www.ala.org/alsc/
- Young Adult Library Services Association (YALSA)
- http://www.ala.org/yalsa/
- American Association of School Librarians (AASL)
- http://www.ala.org/aasl/
- United States Board on Books for Young People (USBBY)
- http://www.usbby.org
- Children's Literature Assembly of the National Council of Teachers of English (CLA/NCTE)
- http://www.childrensliteratureassembly.org
- Children's Literature Association (ChLA)
- http://www.childlitassn.org/

One can begin by simply joining and paying dues. If you're serious about being a professional librarian, you need to be a member of the American Library Association. Period. (Bite the bullet and just do it. It's tax deductible and will reward you many times over.) One colleague I know once said that getting the MLS degree got him the *job* he wanted, but getting involved in professional organizations got him the *career* he wanted. I couldn't have said it better myself! Professional memberships provide very real benefits including newsletters and journals; access to listservs, blogs, and websites that are full of the most current information and resources; plus conferences and other events for ongoing training. You get new ideas, meet colleagues, hear authors and other experts, get "freebies," and you can give back, too, through professional service. If you begin to feel isolated or burned out, you may need to consider reaching out and refueling professionally. Volunteering to serve in a professional organization devoted to children's literature and literacy is just the ticket.

Listservs in the Field of Children's Literature

Electronic mailing lists, discussion lists, or listservs are an excellent tool for the professional who wants to be part of a greater children's literature community. One can sign up to receive communal messages via email on a daily or digest basis. Some organizations host their own listservs for members to maintain contact and dialogue.

CCBC-Net
>   The Cooperative Children's Book Center at the University of Wisconsin–Madison sponsors this listserv that is open to anyone interested in children's literature. For more information: http://www.education.wisc.edu/ccbc/ccbcnet/default.asp

CHILD_LIT
>   CHILD_LIT is an unmoderated listserv maintained by Rutgers University, owned by Michael Joseph, and frequented by librarians, academics, publishers, and writers. For more information: http://www.rci.rutgers.edu/~mjoseph/childlit/about.html

KIDLIT-L
>   KIDLIT-L is a discussion list about children's literature, involving teachers, librarians, students, and others interested in the field. To subscribe, send email to listserv@bingvmb.cc.binghamton.edu

LM_Net
>   LM_Net is a listserv specifically for school library media specialists. For more information: http://lmnet.wordpress.com/

PUBYAC
>   PUBYAC is a discussion list for children's and young adult librarians specifically working in public libraries. For more information: http://pubyac.org/

CONCLUSION

In this chapter, we've considered some of the basic building blocks in creating a culture of reading, beginning with the notion of becoming literate, developing emergent literacy in children, and supporting family literacy. We've touched on the place of reading in the schools via reading aloud, sustained silent reading, and readers' advisory. Tools for selecting and reviewing children's literature were suggested, along with well-known "best" lists, blogs, and awards to watch for. We took a quick tour of the field of children's literature, including bestsellers, historical tidbits, author studies, literature-related websites, and major publishers. And finally, we considered our own professional development and the organizations that can serve as our professional home. This is a good beginning. Next, we'll look at the major genres and formats of children's literature including picture books, traditional tales, poetry, contemporary realistic fiction, historical fiction, fantasy and science fiction, and informational books. Meanwhile, my colleague, Leigh Ann Jones, kindly shared these invaluable tips for developing a reading lifestyle as a library professional. She reminds us that a children's librarian worth her or his salt is *always* reading:

- Read every day.
- Read more than one book at a time.
- Never be without a book.

- Read while waiting (in line, at the doctor's, etc.).
- Listen to audiobooks in the car to double your reading time.
- If possible, download a book on your iPod and listen while you exercise, do housework, and so on.
- Choose books that appear on multiple lists, awards, and with starred reviews to help ensure that your reading time is well spent (but be sure to read at least a smattering of what your students choose to read so you can talk with them about their choices with some familiarity).
- Keep a journal listing the books you read by title and author. Reread your list periodically to keep these titles and authors fresh in your mind for readers' advisory. Consider using online resources like GoodReads .com to document and share your reading and responses.

PROFESSIONAL RESOURCES FOR CHILDREN'S LITERATURE

If you need additional references in the field of children's literature, you may find these comprehensive resource books particularly helpful.

Anderson, Nancy. 2013. *Elementary Children's Literature: Infancy Through Age 13* (Fourth Edition). Boston: Pearson.

Galda, Lee, Lawrence Sipe, L. A. Liang, and Bernice Cullinan. 2013. *Literature and the Child* (Eighth Edition). Independence, KY: Cengage Learning.

Grenby, M. O., and A. Immel. Eds. 2010. *The Cambridge Companion to Children's Literature*. Cambridge, England: Cambridge University Press.

Hillman, Judith. 2002. *Discovering Children's Literature* (Third Edition). Upper Saddle River, NJ: Merrill Prentice Hall.

Kiefer, Barbara Z. 2010. *Charlotte Huck's Children's Literature* (Tenth Edition). Boston: McGraw-Hill.

Nodelman, Perry, and Mavis Reimer. 2003. *The Pleasures of Children's Literature* (Third Edition). Boston, MA: Allyn & Bacon.

Norton, Donna, and Saundra Norton. 2011. *Through the Eyes of a Child: An Introduction to Children's Literature* (Eighth Edition). New York: Pearson.

Russell, David L. 2012. *Literature for Children: A Short Introduction* (Seventh Edition). New York: Pearson.

Short, Kathy, Carol Lynch-Brown, and Carl Tomlinson. 2014. *Essentials of Children's Literature* (Eighth Edition). Boston, MA: Pearson.

Stoodt-Hill, B. D., and L. B. Amspaugh-Corson. 2008. *Children's Literature: Discovery for a Lifetime* (Fourth Edition). New York: Pearson.

Sutherland, Zena. 2004. *Children and Books* (Tenth Edition). New York: Longman.

Temple, Charles, Miriam Martinez, and Junko Yokota. 2011. *Children's Books in Children's Hands: An Introduction to Their Literature* (Fourth Edition). New York: Pearson.

Tunnell, Michael, James Jacobs, Terrell Young, and Gregory Bryan. 2012. *Children's Literature, Briefly* (Fifth Edition). Upper Saddle River, NJ: Prentice Hall.

Standards in Action: ALSC Competencies

As librarians who serve children, we look to our professional organizations for guidance regarding our responsibilities, the expectations of our field, and for help in keeping up with new trends and tools. In the fields of youth services and literacy, we have several professional associations that offer guidance for us and we'll consider several of these in subsequent chapters. But we naturally begin with the Association for Library Service to Children (ALSC), a division of the American Library Association with more than 4000 members and "the world's largest organization dedicated to the support and enhancement of library service to children." In 1989, ALSC developed a set of "Competencies for Librarians Serving Children in Public Libraries" that has been revised and approved on a regular basis (http://www.ala.org/alsc/edca reers/alsccorecomps). They mandate that librarians serving children ages birth to fourteen should achieve and maintain specific "skills, orientations, and understandings to ensure children receive the highest quality of library service as defined in the ALA Library Bill of Rights, and the ALA and Association of American Publishers (AAP) joint Freedom to Read Statement." There are multiple competencies for each of the following key areas.

I. Knowledge of Client Group
II. Administrative and Management Skills
III. Communication Skills
IV. Knowledge of Materials
V. User and Reference Services
VI. Programming Skills
VII. Advocacy, Public Relations, and Networking Skills
VIII. Professionalism and Professional Development
IX. Technology

It is my hope, of course, that reading this book will help you feel better equipped in *many* of these areas. In particular:

IV. Knowledge of Materials
1. Demonstrates a knowledge and appreciation of children's literature, periodicals, audiovisual materials, websites and other electronic media, and other materials that contribute to a diverse, current, and relevant children's collection.

But not only will you build your "knowledge and appreciation" of the world of children's literature, I hope you will also develop your understanding of children and families in all their diversity, learn about planning and problem-solving strategies, refine your reviewing and reference skills, expand your repertoire of programming possibilities, and feel empowered to advocate for children in your workplace and community—all competencies that ALSC values—as do I.

Assignments in Action: Getting Started

1. Quick Quiz

Give yourself the following quiz.

Name one of your favorite books you read as a child.
Name one of your favorite children's books of all time.
Name a book you've recently shared with children.
Name a children's book whose illustrations you especially like.
Name a prize-winning children's book you know.

Stop and think. Discuss your responses with a partner or small group. How many of the children's books that quickly came to mind reflect the experiences of today's diverse population of children? Be honest. Are the books that you remembered published prior to 2000? Do they generally feature only white characters as protagonists? Look for titles and authors of bestsellers and award winners who offer underrepresented perspectives. For example, check out the work of Jacqueline Woodson or Yangsook Choi and the Pura Belpré or Wordcraft Circle award recipients.

2. Going Global

If you want to broaden your horizons and expose children to global literature, how do you find children's books from other countries? It can be a challenge. Fortunately, it's getting easier and easier. Start with the annual list of Outstanding International Books chosen by the United States Board on Books for Young People. This list features books from other countries that are then published (in English) in the United States.

German children's book author and illustrator Hans Wilhelm has written and illustrated over 200 picture books, but unfortunately many are now going out of print. So now he is offering them in their entirety free on the Internet as pdf files, some in English, some in German, and some in multiple versions in twelve different languages. Check it out: http://www.childrensbooksforever.com/index.html

Another excellent tool is the website for the International Children's Digital Library (http://www.icdlbooks.org/), which includes the complete text and illustrations of over 4500 children's books from around the world in 61 different languages.

Using these resources and others, create a scavenger hunt to encourage the exploration of stories from other countries. Who can find a book from South America? A German translation of an American book? Two picture books from different countries about dogs?

3. Teachers as Readers

How do you help the educators that you work with keep current on the latest, wonderful children's books being published? A book club just for teachers can help. The Teachers as Readers movement focuses on teachers reading children's literature and responding personally to the literature as *readers*, an effective tool for teacher renewal and for professional development (Vardell and Jacobson, 1997). Book groups and book clubs can provide an informal atmosphere for reading and talking about books as colleagues. Librarians can be instrumental in starting and organizing such groups. You can booktalk new acquisitions, share titles for teaching units, or just promote recreational reading.

The Cooperative Children's Book Center (CCBC) at the University of Wisconsin–Madison has helpful and longstanding guidelines to assist with leading book discussions. These were developed by Ginny Moore Kruse and Kathleen T. Horning (1989) and are posted on the CCBC website (http://www.education.wisc.edu/ccbc/books/discguide.asp) as well as listed below.

CCBC Book Discussion Guidelines

Look at each book for what it *is*, rather than what it is *not*.

1. Make positive comments first. Try to express what you liked about the book and why (e.g., "The illustrations are a perfect match for the story because . . .").
2. After *everyone* has had the opportunity to say what they appreciated about the book, you may talk about difficulties you had with a particular aspect of the book. Try to express difficulties as questions, rather than declarative judgments on the book as a whole (e.g., "Would Max's dinner really have still been warm?" rather than "That would never happen.").
3. Avoid recapping the story or booktalking the book. There is not time for a summary.
4. Refrain from relating personal anecdotes. The discussion must focus on the book at hand.
5. Try to compare the book with others on the discussion list, rather than other books by the same author or other books in your experience.

All perspectives and vocabularies are correct. There is no "right" answer or single correct response.

1. Listen openly to *what* is said, rather than *who* says it.
2. Respond to the comments of others, rather than merely waiting for an opportunity to share your comments.
3. Talk with *one another*, rather than to the discussion facilitator.
4. Comment to the group as a whole, rather than to someone seated near you.

Look for a preexisting group to sit in on or try a pilot project of your own, launching a book group especially for educators or other adults at your school or public library. Share your experiences with other librarians.

2

Picture Books

"What is the use of a book," thought Alice,
"without pictures or conversations?"
From *Alice's Adventures
in Wonderland* by Lewis Carroll
(Macmillan, 1865)

In this chapter, we will consider the special qualities of the picture book, one of the most popular forms of children's literature. We'll examine both the writing and illustration of picture books, the awards that recognize excellence in picture book creation, and the criteria for evaluating them in print and digital form. You'll learn about all the different kinds of picture books being published and ponder the possibilities for sharing them with older readers and with children learning English as a second language. Finally, we will consider how picture books are commonly shared with children of all ages.

INTRODUCTION

The illustrated book dates back to the Middle Ages, and for many centuries, illustrated books were very rare. The *Orbis Pictus* (1657) was one of the first books that saw the importance of illustration for young people with its woodcuts of images from nature. It was in the 1800s, however, that illustration became a major part of children's books—largely through the use of woodcuts and engravings, although color appeared in the mid 1800s. Randolph Caldecott himself is credited with being one of the first illustrators to put action and humor in his book art; in addition, he was one of the first people to make a living at children's book illustration. The image on the Caldecott seal named after him is taken from his illustrations for the children's book, *The Diverting History of John Gilpin* (1782).

Then came *The Tale of Peter Rabbit* in 1902, a breakthrough in the creation of books for children. Other more child-centered books followed, with *Millions of Cats* in 1928, *And to Think That I Saw It on Mulberry Street* by Dr. Seuss in 1937, *Goodnight Moon* in 1939, and *Make Way for Ducklings* in 1941. Then, in the 1960s, a new age of realism was ushered in with *Where the Wild Things Are* in 1963. The first picture book to show an African American protagonist, *The Snowy Day*, appeared in 1962, and children's books continued to reflect the changing attitudes of society—about what a picture book should look like and about what is appropriate to put in a picture book for children. In recent years, the technology for reproducing art in children's books has revolutionized book publishing. In the 1950s it was not uncommon to alternate printing color pages with black and white illustrations. In the 1970s, artists often had to provide color-separated versions of their art for the printer to use. A picture book like *Interrupting Chicken* by David Ezra Stein (Candlewick, 2010) with its very bright colors, for example, would have cost a fortune to reproduce just fifty years ago.

We are fortunate to be living in a time when the technology, resources, and marketplace are all primed to produce a large volume of children's books of all kinds. (Of course not *all* of that is high quality.) Even nonfiction books are better illustrated now. For example, artists like David Wiesner (one of the biggest award winners in children's book illustration today), Eric Carle (one of the most popular), and Chris Raschka (one of the most prolific) all bring their talent and personality to their work as children's book illustrators. They do careful research when creating the pictures and now exhibit and often sell the original art for their book illustrations in prestigious galleries. Some authors illustrate their own books, like Kevin Henkes and Grace Lin, but most do not. And amazingly, most authors do not choose their own illustrators. It is often an editor who chooses the illustrator for the book. In fact, author and illustrator rarely collaborate. It is felt that each should bring her or his own vision and style to the story. Interestingly enough, it seems that no one artistic style is preferred by kids, and that judgment is rather individual, a matter of taste. That means we shouldn't let our own individual taste get in the way of sharing all kinds of picture books with children. I'm often surprised, in fact, by thinking, "Oh kids will never like that," and they do! Understanding just a little bit more about the art of the picture book might help.

History in Action: The Story of *The Tale of Peter Rabbit*

After over 100 years, *The Tale of Peter Rabbit* by Beatrix Potter (Frederick Warne, 1902) is still one of the bestselling children's picture books of all time according to statistics from *Publishers Weekly* in 2000. Why has it held up as such a classic? Is it the adventure story? The rabbit character stand-ins for young children? The small size and delicate illustrations? The clever, never condescending writing? And how did this special picture book, often considered the first "perfect" picture book, blending story and illustration, come to be?

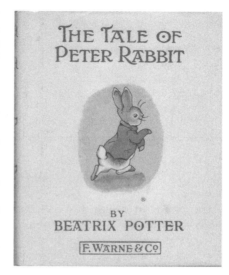

Beatrix Potter grew up a sheltered girl, educated at home in an affluent English household. She studied drawing, painting, and small animals from a very young age and as an adult sold her first paintings as greeting cards to a German firm. She also sent frequent letters filled with drawings to the children in her life and her first book, *The Tale of Peter Rabbit,* started out this way, as a letter to the ailing son of a former governess.

Potter was a single woman of thirty-six when she self-published *Peter Rabbit,* and she used her own money to produce the first 500 copies because six publishers turned it down. She believed that books for children should be easy for little hands to hold and therefore should have a small trim size, be printed on sturdy paper, and have an illustration every time the page was turned. *The Tale of Peter Rabbit* was immediately popular, so she approached the publishing company Frederick Warne again and they offered to publish it if she would produce colored illustrations instead of the original black and white ones. Potter's naturalistic watercolor depictions of animals and their habitats (clothing aside) were a radical departure for children's book illustration of the time. *The Tale of Peter Rabbit* sold 50,000 copies in its first year, an amazing figure for a "first" book, even by today's standards. Over the next ten years, she illustrated twenty more books.

Since its publication in 1902, many others have attempted to illustrate the Peter Rabbit story for various audiences. I'm not sure why, since the originals are so distinctive. An American version was published as early as 1904 with illustrations redone in more vivid colors for American audiences. Many of her books have never been out of print and the merchandising of "Peter Rabbit" items is still a lucrative business 100 years later. Potter herself created a prototype for the first stuffed Peter Rabbit toy.

Beatrix Potter's greatest ambition was to study and paint fungi, but her work was not recognized by the botanists of the day. Potter spent the last half of her life farming and raising sheep and willed 4,000 acres of land to the National Trust, including farm museums she created. She married William Heelis later in life but never had children of her own. Scholars have studied the work of Beatrix Potter for decades, considering everything from a Jungian analysis to a cross-cultural study of *Peter Rabbit* in Japan. Today's authors and illustrators continue to strive for the same blending of wit and intelligence, of fantasy and reality, and of story and art in the creation of masterpieces for children. And young children are still enjoying the adventures of a rabbit named Peter who ventured out into the big world and lived to tell about it.

For even more information about this interesting and historic children's book creator and her work, check these websites:

DEFINITIONS

In the world of children's literature, the picture book is not a genre but rather a form for publishing a book. Usually thirty-two pages in length, it is a marriage of words and pictures working together to create a unique book experience. David Russell said simply, picture books "combine the art of story-telling with the art of illustration" (2012, p. 118).

Children's literature scholar and teacher Charlotte Huck (2000, p. 200) viewed picture books as "art objects . . . books in which images and ideas join to form a unique whole." In the best picture books, the illustrations extend and enhance the written text, providing the reader with an aesthetic experience that is more than the sum of the book's parts. Even the drama of turning the page is an integral part of this unique experience. Barbara Bader (1976, p. 3) maintains, "as an art form the picture book hinges on the interdependence of picture and words, on the simultaneous display of two facing pages." This is essential to the story experience but also critical in picture books that don't tell a story per se, such as alphabet books, counting books, and concept books in which synchronization and accuracy are essential.

For young children, "reading" the pictures is an important part of early literacy. In fact, this can be a helpful barometer of an effective picture book, if the illustrations carry enough narrative to reveal a story thread. Often the pictures include details that are *not* explicit in the words of the story, and kids are typically the first to catch them—like the little mouse in *Goodnight Moon*. This is not to suggest that the pictures are more important than the words,

but rather that a book with only a few pictures that aren't partnered with the text is likely to be an illustrated novel, and not a picture book.

Picture books may be of any genre, including history, fantasy, nonfiction, and poetry. They are usually intended for young audiences, birth through grade 3, but some picture books are so sophisticated and groundbreaking in their content or their art that they are really more appropriate for older readers, even adults.

Whether we're talking about picture books in general (and there are many kinds) or picture storybooks specifically (which tell a story), if you haven't looked at picture books in a while, you may be in for a surprise.

Librarians in Action: Life Imitating Picture Book Art

Xelena González works as a community services specialist for the Little Read Wagon (LRW), the early literacy outreach team of the San Antonio Public Library. She delivers story time programs at various childcare settings and leads hands-on early literacy presentations for teen parents in public schools. She also aids LRW in providing Play & Learn programs throughout the city. Her work is informed by the ten years she spent working as an arts educator and creative writing instructor. Xelena earned her BS in journalism from Northwestern University and her MLS from Texas Woman's University.

Picture Books That Bloom
by Xelena González

Open up your favorite picture book. Imagine an ornate frame surrounding each page. Now see the hundreds of canvases, tapestries, and sculptures that have filled the minds of your youngest readers. . . . It may be years before they begin to browse art on their own. But every time you introduce a picture book, you are putting a piece of art in their tiny hands. In fact, you're exposing them to an entire exhibition that tells a story!

It is the marriage of print and pictures that exercises our brain in beautiful ways. Author-illustrators seem especially adept at working this magic, as they can illustrate their imaginations *and* put the perfect captions on each page. You'll see many such names in this chapter, but I'll spotlight Suzanne Bloom, creator of the popular *Goose & Bear* series. In my work as a community outreach specialist for the San Antonio Public Library, I've had much luck in bringing her stories to life for our youngest readers, who often want to experience exactly what they see in picture books.

They were able to do just that in our Play & Learn program when we featured Bloom's book *Feeding Friendsies* (Boyds Mills Press, 2011) in which children use ingredients from their garden to feed worms, birds, frogs, and other friends. Our program typically begins with a short story time, followed by free play across various activity centers (which promote some aspect of early literacy for our target age group of 0–5). For this particular session, the little ones flocked to the outdoor station where we'd set up a buffet of natural ingredients that could be gathered, stirred, and served up to puppets that mirrored the hungry animals from *Feeding Friendsies.*

Meanwhile our participants were able to play the book's starring roles as they re-created the characters' cuisine—concoctions of leaves, flowers, dirt, sand, seeds, pebbles, twigs, and rainwater. (For less mess indoors, use felt scraps, yarn bits, artificial flowers, etc.) Play is the essential element for our participants, but the added bonus is a rich sensory experience and a chance to tune fine motor skills with spoons, bowls, tongs, pots, cups, and shovels. Then of course there's the story, which has leapt from watercolors and letters into real life.

The Bus for Us (Boyds Mills Press, 2001) is another Bloom book that begs to be reenacted, especially for story times at the start of a new school year. In it, we meet a diverse cast of characters waiting for their school bus to arrive. One child is new to the experience and continually asks, "Is this the bus for us, Gus?" Readers relish this refrain, as they are introduced to a variety of vehicles—taxi, tow truck, backhoe, garbage truck, fire engine, and ice-cream truck. We have extended this experience by offering sets of wheels to roam around the room. Our participants enjoy building roads with masking tape or felt strips (meanwhile vocabulary building is taking place too). The use of hats, road signs, ramps, and other props adds to the dramatic play.

Older readers can tune their creativity after reading Suzanne Bloom's *A Mighty Fine Time Machine* (Boyds Mills Press, 2009). In it, a motley crew of characters attempts to make a time machine from a cardboard box and scattered knick-knacks. Though the time machine never takes off, they succeed in building a book-mobile instead. While an empty cardboard box always incites the imagination, add to the reenactment fun with bottles, canisters, lids, and other recyclables that participants can collect. Allow the group to artfully design a new book nook for the home, library, or classroom.

Return now to that favorite picture book. . . . Allow the art to inspire you. How can the images be re-created or experienced in some way? How can the story come alive for you and your readers so that it is remembered long after the last page? If the ideas don't come right away, your young readers are bound to have some ideas of their own.

TYPES OF PICTURE BOOKS

The rise of the picture book—the slim book equally dependent on illustrations as much as text for the story experience—is *the* literary phenomenon of the twentieth century. With the advent of *The Tale of Peter Rabbit* by Beatrix Potter in 1902 to the most current Caldecott award winner, picture books have found a special niche in the experience of childhood. It's hard for me to imagine a childhood without picture books. Unfortunately, there are still many children who experience only what they read in school—and that is often a steady diet of textbooks. Even Golden Books and other mass market literature available in grocery stores and discount shops are not affordable for every child. That's why public libraries, school libraries, classroom libraries, reading aloud, and story times are doubly important. We also owe it to children to introduce them to the best new books and authors available. As we learn about new books and develop the skills to choose the best quality, we can truly appreciate the artistry of Jerry Pinkney and his paintings of *The Lion & the Mouse* (Little, Brown, 2009) and the *Ugly Duckling* (HarperCollins, 1999) or the zany sense of humor of Mo Willems and his pigeon or *Knuffle Bunny* (Hyperion, 2004). The Caldecott award winners announced each January help us keep up with what the critics say are the best illustrated books for children. And we can ask the children themselves what their favorites are. Meanwhile, let's consider just how diverse the area of "picture books" can be.

The category of picture books refers to a format that includes many different types and topics. The stories may be contemporary or set in the past or entirely make believe. They can be family stories, multicultural stories, nature stories, animal stories, or humorous stories. Folktales, poetry, and nonfiction all appear in the picture book format, too, but we'll consider those three in separate chapters. Generally speaking, picture books are almost always thirty-two pages in length, made of four large sheets of paper that are printed front-to-back, then folded twice and cut and assembled (sewn into hardbacks or glued into paperbacks) to create a book. You can find a helpful description of this process and the basic book components in Harold Underdown's *The Complete Idiot's Guide to Publishing Children's Books* (2008).

By far the most common type of picture book is the picture *story*book, which is simply a picture book that tells a story. It far outnumbers all the other types. These have words and pictures, but no pop-up features, no special counting or listing, no hidden images, and so on. They just tell a story. The classic example of this is *The Tale of Peter Rabbit*. A more modern example might be *Click, Clack, Moo: Cows That Type* written by Doreen Cronin and illustrated by Betsy Lewin (Simon & Schuster, 2000). The other types of picture books sometimes tell a story, but their main feature is not the story itself, but rather the alphabet structure, the predictable refrain, the hidden object, the pull flap, and so on. Clear?

Picture Storybooks

This is the category where you will find most picture books published for children. From the classic *Millions of Cats* by Wanda Gág (Puffin, reissued 2006) to the well-loved *The Polar Express* by Chris Van Allsburg (Houghton Mifflin, 1985), stories in picture book form continue to engage and enthrall young readers and listeners. In addition, recent statistics from *Publishers Weekly* (2000) show that the following ten popular picture books are among the 100 bestselling children's books of all time, among others (in order of sales):

#2 *The Tale of Peter Rabbit* by Beatrix Potter (Frederick Warne, 1902)
#4 *Green Eggs and Ham* by Dr. Seuss (Random House, 1960)
#20 *The Very Hungry Caterpillar* by Eric Carle (Philomel, 1969)
#24 *Are You My Mother?* by P. D. Eastman (Random House, 1960)
#44 *The Polar Express* by Chris Van Allsburg (Houghton Mifflin, 1985)
#48 *Goodnight Moon* by Margaret Wise Brown, illus. by Clement Hurd (HarperCollins, 1947)
#63 *Where the Wild Things Are* by Maurice Sendak (HarperCollins, 1964)

#74 Guess How Much I Love You by Sam McBratney, illus. by Anita Jeram
(Candlewick, 1995)

#77 Kay Thompson's Eloise by Kay Thompson, illus. by Hilary Knight
(Simon & Schuster, 1955)

#96 Make Way for Ducklings by Robert McCloskey (Viking, 1941)

Not only are picture book stories bestsellers, popular favorites, and award winners but many are also not afraid to tackle challenging topics. For example, consider Mordicai Gerstein's homage to Philippe Petit's historic walk in *The Man Who Walked Between the Towers* (Roaring Brook Press, 2003) or Jacqueline Woodson's tribute to her own African American history in *Show Way* (Putnam, 2005). Picture books are not just for little ones; the format is now home to many different kinds of stories for readers of all ages. Bill Martin Jr., author and educator, said that we should be reading at least one book a day to children. Think of what a lovely routine that would be, and what a background of literature children would develop, if this pattern persisted throughout the grades and in families with young children in every community.

Wordless Picture Books

There are some picture books that have no (or very few) words, and the pictures *are* the book. These picture books also generally tell a story, but through the illustrations alone. David Wiesner is the master of this form with Caldecott medal and honor–winning examples such as *Tuesday* (Clarion, 1991), *Sector 7* (Clarion, 1999), and *Flotsam* (Clarion, 2006). This format challenges children to use their imaginations to create or narrate their own text. This can provide an excellent opportunity for storytelling, writing captions, developing oral fluency, assessing visual literacy, and developing ESL vocabulary skills. Who knew a wordless picture book could function in so many ways? Other interesting examples include the Caldecott award books *A Ball for Daisy* by Chris Raschka (Random House, 2011) and *The Lion & the Mouse* by Jerry Pinkney (Little, Brown, 2009), as well as *Zoom* and its sequel by Istvan Banyai (Viking, 1995), *Once Upon a Banana* by Jennifer Armstrong, illustrated by David Small (Simon & Schuster, 2006), and many others by Barbara Lehman, Emily Arnold McCully, Mercer Mayer, Jim Arnosky, John Goodall, Fernando Krahn, and Mitsumasa Anno.

Predictable Books

The predictable picture book really came on the scene with the now-classic *Brown Bear, Brown Bear, What Do You See?* by Bill Martin Jr. (Holt, 1967). So many children have grown up with that book that it has become a staple in kindergartens and daycare centers everywhere. Predictable picture books have a refrain, rhyme scheme, or structure that enables children to "read" the book, even if they are not yet fluent readers. That is, once they have heard the book read aloud or have figured out the pattern, they can join in. In most cases, the structure itself trumps the story. The strength of these picture books is their invitation to participation. Also, they are so formulaic that young children often enjoy imitating them or extending them by writing their own versions. Other popular examples of predictable books include *If You Give a Mouse a Cookie* (and its many sequels) by Laura Numeroff, illustrated by Felicia Bond (HarperCollins, 1985), *Red Sled* by Lisa Judge (Atheneum, 2011), *Where's Walrus* by Stephen Savage (Scholastic, 2011), and *Move Over, Rover* by Karen Beaumont (Harcourt, 2006).

Alphabet Books

Perhaps one of the oldest types of children's books of all kinds, the alphabet book started off as an attempt to teach the alphabet to very young children. That is sometimes still the case, but more often than not, the letters of the alphabet simply form a structure to introduce a variety of objects, images, or terms. For a traditional example designed to reinforce the alphabet letters for young children, look for the song-like *Chicka Chicka Boom Boom* by Bill Martin Jr. and John Archambault, illustrated by Lois Ehlert (Simon & Schuster, 1989, also available with a CD and in board book form). Alphabet books for young children should be clear and explicit, presenting a correlation among letters, words, and objects. For humorous picture books that incorporate the alphabet into the story thread in fresh ways, look for *I Stink!* by Kate McMullan (Harper-Collins, 2002), *AlphaOops! The Day Z Went First* by Alethea Kontis (Candlewick, 2006), or *Zoopa: An Animal Alphabet* by Gianna Marino (Chronicle, 2005).

On the other hand, *The Graphic Alphabet* by David Pelletier (Orchard Books, 1996) or *Alphabet City* by Stephen T. Johnson (Viking, 1995) are two examples of alphabet books that are really more appropriate for older children, as they offer an intriguing look at the design qualities in the shapes of letters. For a more content-rich example of an abecedary, look for David McLimans's *Gone Wild: An Endangered Animal Alphabet* (Walker, 2006) or many of the theme collections by Jerry Pallotta. Here, the alphabet is a way to share information, letter by letter.

Once you're hooked on alphabet books like I am, this makes a great large group writing/drawing activity. Choose a theme. Each child chooses a letter of the alphabet, then decides on a word for that letter and draws a picture and writes a paragraph (or a sentence or whatever is appropriate) for that letter. Put these all together, bind them, and create a homemade alphabet book to share with peers.

Counting Books

Counting books, like alphabet books, have a built-in structure. Often this is simply counting from one to ten, but sometimes counting books include zero, sets, multiples, and so on. For younger children, a clear correspondence between the number or numeral and the quantity of objects is critical, as is the arrangement and sequence of objects and illustrations. Counting books that feature some of children's favorite foods like Cheerios cereal, M&M candies, and Goldfish crackers by Barbara Barbieri McGrath are very popular for younger children. Most counting books take a thematic approach, gathering objects around a unifying topic, such as *One Child, One Seed: A South African Counting Book* by Kathryn Cave (Holt, 2003) or *One Gorilla: A Counting Book* by Anthony Browne (Candlewick, 2013). In addition, making counting books can also be a fun activity for children and can incorporate math skills, too. Reading and creating counting books can be particularly helpful for children who are learning English as a new language.

Concept Books

Concept books are really nonfiction or informational books for very young children. The purpose of a concept picture book is to teach or to present information, not to tell a story. The best ones are very simple, focused, and highly visual. They usually deal with challenging concepts for young children, such as color, direction, time, proportion, and so on. Tana Hoban shaped this form by creating distinctive and useful concept books through the effective use of photographs. Look for *Black and White* (HarperCollins, 2007) for one example by Hoban. *Siesta* by Ginger Guy (Greenwillow, 2005) is a clever bilingual concept book, and *A Second Is a Hiccup* by Hazel Hutchins (Scholastic, 2007) explains the concept of time. For concept books focused on nature and animals, seek out *What Do You Do with a Tail Like This?* (Houghton Mifflin, 2003) or *Move!* (Houghton Mifflin, 2006), both illustrated and written by Steve Jenkins and Robin Page. Other names to know when it comes to introducing concepts in picture book form include Laura Vaccaro Seeger, Lois Ehlert, Zoran Milich, Ben Hillman, Bruce McMillan, and Ann Morris. Each of them has used the picture book format to showcase simple topics like color, foods, clothing, and so forth through vivid collages or photographs and simple, direct language. The concept book format is also ideal for launching discussion and labeling with young children or with older children who are learning English words for familiar concepts in their new language.

Engineered Books

"Paper engineering involves the cutting, folding, or otherwise restructuring of the normal printed or illustrated page" according to experts Tunnell, Jacobs, Young, and Bryan (2012, p. 69). Also called "toy" books, these are probably the least practical of the picture book format for everyday circulation because they may not be as durable for long-term use. Children enjoy the pop-ups, flaps, wheels, pull-tabs, and die-cut pages, but they may not always handle the books as gently as we would like. It is also assumed that these books are for preschool children, but they generally need much sturdier books or close adult supervision. Many authors and illustrators have created delightful picture books using these paper innovations, such as Robert Sabuda's magnificent pop-up masterpieces and Lois Ehlert and Eric Carle's various die-cut creations. At least one "engineered" picture book has even won a Caldecott award: Simms Taback's *Joseph Had a Little Overcoat* (Viking, 1999). The half toy–half book creation actually has a long and surprising history given its apparent flimsy nature, and readers of all ages delight in manipulating the various parts of a cleverly engineered book. In this age of electronic text, the physical appeal of engineered picture books may be an extra special delight.

Board Books

Baby books or board books are everywhere now, but it wasn't until the 1980s that publishers consistently created and marketed this type of picture book widely. With the growing population of book buyers (middle-class and affluent parents waiting to have children later and eager to spend money on books for their children), small, chewable, bendable, and durable cardboard books for very young children became more and more popular. Now many regular format picture books are being reissued in abbreviated form as board books such as *Goodnight Moon; Brown Bear, Brown Bear;* and *The Very Hungry Caterpillar*. In addition, board book versions of simple alphabet books, counting books, concept books, and predictable books are also available. In short, nearly every type of picture book has morphed into board book form. The key is to look for an appropriate adaptation or fresh creation with clear images, a logical sequence, distilled language, and durable, easy-to-turn pages. Although they are intended for babies and toddlers, board books can also be fun and even reassuring for older children to revisit from time to time, like an old friend or teddy bear, or for them to share with younger siblings and other young children.

Easy Readers

At the other end of the picture book spectrum, we have "easy readers" that help children transition from reading picture books to reading novels. Back in the mid-1950s, Dr. Seuss was commissioned to write a children's book using less than 300 different words and the result was the benchmark book *The Cat in the Hat* (Random House, 1957). The result was a trend of creating children's books using a "controlled vocabulary," thinking this would be more manageable for young readers. Some were fun for kids, like *The Cat in the Hat* (although it is rather long by today's standards) and many other Seuss works. But some easy reader or beginning reader books are stilted and dry. It takes a great deal of talent to craft an engaging story using only a handful of quickly recognized vocabulary words. In fact, the Geisel Award was created to recognize this accomplishment and named after Dr. Seuss (Theodor Geisel) to honor the art of the book for beginning readers—including easy readers and picture books. The *Frog and Toad* series manages this beautifully, as does Mo Willems's *Elephant and Piggie* series and Kevin Henkes with his *Penny* books, to name a few.

Easy readers offer a helpful bridge to children who want to read a more "grown-up" book with more words and distinct chapters but who are not quite ready to leave the pictures of picture books behind. These are heavily illustrated with pictures on every page, text in a large font, with limited vocabulary and short sentences, generous white space and margins, simple and direct plots, and generally 40–80 pages long. And kids feel so successful when they finish one! Here are some of the most popular series in this format:

The Cat in the Hat (and more by Dr. Seuss)
Amanda Pig (Jean Van Leeuwen)
Amelia Bedelia (Peggy Parish/Herman Parish)
Anna Hibiscus (Atinuke)
Biscuit (Alyssa Satin Capucilli)
Cat the Cat (Mo Willems)
Cinderella Smith (Stephanie Barden)
Cowgirl Kate and Cocoa (Erica Silverman)
Elephant and Piggie (Mo Willems)
Fly Guy (Tedd Arnold)
Frog and Toad (Arnold Lobel)
Henry and Mudge; Mr. Putter and Tabby; Poppleton (Cynthia Rylant)
Just Grace (Charise Mericle Harper)
Ling & Ting (Grace Lin)
Little Bear (Else Holmelund Minarik)
Mercy Watson (Kate DiCamillo)
Minnie and Moo (Denys Cazet)
Penny (Kevin Henkes)
Zelda and Ivy (Laura Kvasnosky)

Authors and illustrators continue to experiment with the picture book format, creating new variations all the time. Just look at *Casey at the Bat* illustrated by Christopher Bing, based on the classic poem by Ernest Thayer (Handprint, 2000), for a great example of a rule-breaking picture book—part poetry, part history, part scrapbook. Or look for Hervé Tullet's *Press Here* (Chronicle, 2011), the simplest idea perfectly executed, inviting children to press colored dots on the page and participate in a bit of magic as the dots seem to "move around." In chapters that follow, we'll consider how the picture book format also fits into the publishing of traditional tales, poetry, and informational literature.

MAJOR AUTHORS AND ILLUSTRATORS OF PICTURE BOOKS

A picture book may look easy to create with under 1,000 total words and only thirty-two pages, but there is an art to it, despite the proliferation of mediocre picture books churned out by various celebrities. Many authors and artists have developed quite a body of outstanding picture books for children, and their styles range from distinctive and unmistakable to chameleon-like and varying from book to book.

Children's Picture Book Characters from A to Z and Their Creators

The following people have established reputations as authors or illustrators of many distinctive and notable picture books for children. Just for fun, they are presented as creators of picture book *characters* from A to Z. Of course each of these authors or illustrators has also created other notable works and characters. This list is just a sampling.

A   *Arthur* by Marc Brown
B   *Berenstain Bears* by Stan and Jan Berenstain
C   *Chato* by Gary Soto, illustrated by Susan Guevara
D   *David* by David Shannon
E   *Emma Kate* by Patricia Polacco
F   *Frances* (the badger) by Russell Hoban, illustrated by Lillian Hoban
G   *Curious George* (the monkey) by H. A. and Margaret Rey
H   *Henry and Mudge* by Cynthia Rylant, illustrated by Suçie Stevenson
I   *Ira* (in *Ira Sleeps Over*) by Bernard Waber
J   *Jamaica* by Juanita Havill, illustrated by Anne Sibley O'Brien
K   *Knuffle Bunny* by Mo Willems
L   *Lilly* by Kevin Henkes
M   *Madlenka* by Peter Sís
N   *(Fancy) Nancy* by Jane O'Connor, illustrated by Robin Preiss Glasser
O   *Olivia* by Ian Falconer
P   *Pinkerton* by Steven Kellogg
Q   *Queenie* by Bob Graham
R   *Rover* (in *Move Over, Rover!*) by Karen Beaumont, illustrated by Jane Dyer
S   *Sylvester* (*and the Magic Pebble*) by William Steig
T   *Tallulah* by Marilyn Singer, illustrated by Alexandra Boiger
U   *Unhei* (in *The Name Jar*) by Yangsook Choi
V   *Virgie* (in *Virgie Goes to School with Us Boys*) by Elizabeth F. Howard, illustrated by E. B. Lewis
W   *Wild Things* (in *Where the Wild Things Are*) by Maurice Sendak
X   *Xylophone* (the cat in *The Stupids Have a Ball*) by Harry Allard and James Marshall
Y   *Little Yellow* by Leo Lionni
Z   *Zella, Zack, and Zodiac* by Bill Peet

This is just a beginning list of notable authors, illustrators, and characters associated with picture books. In addition, each of these illustrators has created other memorable picture books and book characters worth noting. You could also generate a whole new list of picture book characters from *traditional* literature, such as Aladdin, Beauty, Cinderella, and so on. Since the teaching and learning of the alphabet is such an important element in the primary grades, children's book characters can provide playful support and reinforcement for their learning of the ABCs. For more information about important picture book creators, look for Sharron L. McElmeel's *100 Most Popular Picture Book Authors and Illustrators: Biographical Sketches and Bibliographies* (Libraries Unlimited, 2000).

Authors in Action: Denise Fleming

Denise Fleming is a Caldecott Honor illustrator and author of numerous picture books for young children. Her first book, *In the Tall, Tall Grass* (1991), was well received and its sequel, *In the Small, Small Pond* (1993), won Caldecott honors. Critics have praised her books for the "stunning" spreads and "zippy" language, and for the vibrant hues, bold colors, and dense textures of her pulp painting technique. Plus, teachers and parents appreciate her use of spare, lyrical language and often rhyming, rhythmic text ideal for our youngest readers and listeners. In fact, several of her books are also available as board books for babies and toddlers. Here she talks about the process of creating the unique illustrations in her picture books. This interview first appeared on the comprehensive digital resource TeachingBooks.net and is used with permission.

Interview with Denise Fleming

Bright colors and gorgeous illustrations are what most everyone first thinks about your illustrated books. Yet not everyone sees, or understands, your unique pulp painting technique. Can you please describe the process of creating your pulp painting books?

Let me walk you through the process. First, I have to get the idea—this is the most exciting part—and then somebody buys the idea and we sign a contract. Then, I start working on sketching. I do little scribbles here and there with a china marker, which is like a crayon. That way I don't create too much detail—I can't use a lot of detail in the papermaking. Then I copy the rough sketches, and my husband David scans them into the computer. Then, we put together kind of a loose working dummy to see what's going on. At this point I'm just kind of getting an idea of where I'm headed, and I may make tons of changes. Once I really decide what I want the pictures to look like, I do a much cleaner drawing.

I order my fibers from a papermaking supply company in big five-gallon buckets. Then, I dye the fiber all the different brilliant colors. Next, I cut my stencils. The stencil cutting is probably the most tedious. That just seems to go on and on and on. But it is also the most important stage because that's the point where I'm figuring out what stencil goes next when I'm pouring the paper. In the beginning, that was the hardest thing to figure out, what stencil I put next on the paper to pour the different images. So now I pretend that I'm in the back of the actual piece of art walking toward the front. That's how I figure out what layer goes next. It's a little bit of a puzzle, but that's kind of fun.

And then I pour the paper pulp. It's wet on wet. When I have the picture just the way I want it, I take it and I flip it off and press it. It's a sheet of damp paper. Next, I put it in the vacuum table to draw out all the excess moisture. Then, I put it in the drawing press so that it dries flat. There's a lot of process, and it's time consuming.

You were a successful artist and children's book illustrator working in a variety of media before papermaking. What was the impetus to try papermaking?

The papermaking I discovered just by accident. There was a flyer that came in the mail from the local high school about adult-ed classes, including one on papermaking. So, my sister and I signed up. And that was it. From the first moment I walked into the room and saw all these big vats of beautiful color, I was just hooked.

Do you determine the color schemes for your books before you begin, or do you decide as you go?

In choosing the colors for my books, I have kind of a feeling ahead of time for the basic colors I want the book to be. In *In the Tall, Tall Grass*, I wanted it to feel like a hot summer afternoon, so I use a great deal of yellow in that book because yellow feels hot. In *Time to Sleep* I use the very, very warm colors of fall. But generally, the colors kind of happen as I'm pouring the pulp. It is influenced by the mood I'm in and what music I'm listening to at the time.

I use a lot of complementary colors in my books: colors that are opposite one another on the color wheel, like orange and blue, purple and yellow, red and green, because when you put those colors next to one another, they vibrate. And they make each other stand out more. Complementary colors also give a feeling of more movement and excitement, so I use a lot of them.

You not only write and illustrate all your books, but you even design how the book will look overall. What are some of the challenges you face in book design?

Remembering the "gutter" [where the pages come together in the middle of the book] is one of the most important things in designing the picture book. You don't want to lose words into the gutter; you don't want to lose people's noses into the gutter; you don't want to lose an important part of the picture in the gutter. It's different than when you do a painting that's to be hung on a wall. You don't have to worry about any of that.

Also, making the art for a book is different than a painting because, when you're doing a book, everything has to work together. You have to have continuity. Lots of times I have to take out a picture I really like because it doesn't work with the whole. Sometimes there's a different feeling in a picture that doesn't fit with the rest. So I'll take that piece out or redesign and pour it.

All of the books that you've written and illustrated are read aloud books. What kind of thinking goes into designing a book that is good for reading aloud?

The first books, *In the Tall, Tall Grass* and *In the Small, Small Pond*, are a nice, square, big size. So when you open them up, you have this kind of panoramic view. They are nice books for lap reading. Also, I use big, bold type. The words are part of the pictures in most of my books, because the words are important. I don't want them to just be a little line down at the bottom of a page. I want them to be integrated into the pictures. I also manipulate the words, move the letters around. For instance, in *In the Small, Small Pond*, the word "wiggle" wiggles and the word "jiggle" jiggles, reinforcing what the words mean.

One Book in Action: UnderGROUND

For our "One Book in Action" in the picture book category, let's hone in on Denise Fleming's *UnderGROUND* (Beach Lane, 2012), which *Publisher's Weekly* called an "evocative ode to nature." As a young boy and his dog help plant and water a cherry tree, he explores what he finds above, within, and under the ground including a variety of objects and creatures. With its direct and simple rhythmic language, *UnderGROUND* is a quick and engaging book to read aloud, but young listeners with sharp eyes will enjoy exploring the

cross-section illustrations that reveal many details of the backyard world. It offers multiple opportunities for extending the topic of nature, exploring the art medium used to create the illustrations, and connecting with other parallel works by the same author/illustrator. Let's consider each angle.

More about Nature

This simple picture book offers an excellent opportunity for connecting with the real world in a kinesthetic way—bringing some of the actual objects mentioned in the book (and often found in the dirt) to touch and talk about like old tools, dog bones, a key, a coin, a toy car. Invite children to talk about things they have found on the ground or in the dirt. Then consider the natural elements shown in the story such as seeds, root vegetables, and the underground creatures that appear on the pages, as well as their tunnels, burrows, food sources, and activities. Point out the illustrated "Creature Identification" index that Fleming offers in the back of the book offering information about the underground habits of the insects and other wildlife.

Follow up this book with *All the World* by Liz Garton Scanlon (Beach Lane, 2009), *My Garden* by Kevin Henkes (Greenwillow, 2010), or *The Curious Garden* by Peter Brown (Little, Brown, 2009), or better yet, with a nature walk. Just for fun, consider making "dirt cup" desserts with pudding, crumbled Oreos, and candy Gummi worms.

More about Paper Art

The illustrations that Denise Fleming creates for *UnderGROUND* are an essential part of the book experience and convey much of the story and information visually. She uses her characteristic bold colors and textured pulp paintings to show both what's underneath as well as just above the ground at the same time. *Kirkus Reviews* noted, "Fleming's pulp-painting technique is used to best advantage to capture the textures of coarse dirt, pebbles, roots, and tunnels, and every page-turn offers full-spread cutaway views." With very young children, you might focus on simply identifying each object and animal or creature in repeated "walks" through the pictures. But with older kids, you might try tearing construction paper into animal shapes to recreate some of the book's creatures. For children who want to know how Fleming creates her art, she provides a step-by-step description of her unique papermaking process on her website: http://www.deniseflem ing.com//pages/papermaking.html. Or you can show a demonstration of her artistic process in this video: http://www.youtube.com/watch?v=ngAOeEG5msM.

More about Denise Fleming

When children really enjoy a book, it can be fun to share more by the same author or illustrator. In this case, Fleming has two other books that have a similar, simple focus on natural ecosystems: *In the Tall, Tall Grass* and *In the Small, Small Pond*.

You'll find a complete listing of Fleming's books along with additional interviews, book guides for using her books with kids, audio and video excerpts of interviews and demonstrations, engaging activities, and much more on her very colorful website, http://www.denisefleming.com. With her simple, rhythmic texts and bold, textured illustrations, her books are appealing for our youngest readers and ideal for reading aloud, laptimes, and story times.

CHILDREN'S PICTURE BOOK ILLUSTRATION

A lot has been written about the art of illustrating a children's book, but here we'll simply get a quick bird's eye view to guide our understanding of this unique format in children's literature. In evaluating picture books, it can be helpful to refer to the visual elements including line, shape, color, texture, and composition; to recognize different styles of art (realistic or abstract); and to understand the different artistic media or techniques (painterly or graphic) that illustrators use to create the pictures of a picture book.

Visual Elements

The visual elements of line, shape, color, texture, and composition work together to create art, much as character, setting, plot, theme, and style work together to create literature. When you look at picture book illustrations, think about how the artist is using these "building blocks" to grab your eye, move the story along, or create a certain mood. Some elements stand out as more powerful than others, but all generally have some role.

1. *Line:* Lines can set the mood or convey movement. They provide a feeling of strength, balance, motion, or distance. (Look at Mo Willems's work.)
2. *Shape:* The use of shapes can convey action and includes geometric circles, ovals, squares, rectangles, triangles, and so forth. (Look at Lois Ehlert's work.)
3. *Color:* Color is probably the most obvious element in children's book illustration. It is used to convey emotion and symbolism. Green, blue, and purple, like nature and water, are cool and recede. Warm colors are yellow, orange, and red; like fire and sun, they come forward. (Look at Eric Carle's work.)
4. *Texture:* Texture can be used to enhance the realistic quality of illustrations or to stimulate the imagination. Many contemporary illustrators are experimenting with 3-D and computer graphic effects that make you want to touch the page. (Look at Brian Pinkney's work.)
5. *Composition:* Composition unifies all the elements in an illustration. It is the total arrangement, the balance and symmetry of elements. How are line, shape, color, and texture arranged on the page? Which, if any, dominates? How do they work together to create an impression or mood, to help tell the story?

Artistic Styles

Put it all together and you begin to see how artists through the centuries have used these basic components to create an amazing variety of master-pieces. In addition, the art in a children's book can reflect the different styles usually associated with fine art over the years. It may be very realistic or very abstract, or somewhere in between. Representational art is very realistic and you can recognize the people and images. Think about Michelangelo's paintings in the Sistine Chapel or the wordless books of David Wiesner. On the other hand, naive or folk art is very child-like and two-dimensional like Grandma Moses's art or the illustrations of Barbara Cooney. More abstract art like that of Picasso often breaks images down into basic color, shape, and form. Some children's book artists incorporate aspects of abstract art, like the illustrations of Lane Smith, but most create characters and scenes that have some correspondence with real life that the child reader will recognize.

Illustration Media

How did the artist make that art? The illustration medium is the physical method used to create the illustrations. The technique used by the illustrator is also interesting to consider. In fact, many readers today are fascinated by how the artist made the art, so much so that many illustrators now include information about the illustrations in the back of the book. As you become a connoisseur of children's books, you may soon find yourself reading *all* the small print! And, if you ever get a chance to see the actual art used in children's books, go to a gallery, museum, or exhibit that features original book art. You won't believe the difference. Although the technology for reproducing art is amazing, seeing the art itself is still an incredible experience.

Although illustrators use many different artistic tools and techniques in increasingly creative combinations, illustration media generally fall into two main categories: painterly techniques and graphic techniques. Applying a substance to paper or canvas or some other material is called "painterly" and includes watercolors, tempera, gouache, poster color, oil paint, acrylics, pastels, chalk, pencil, ink, and crayons. Many artists use pen and ink in their illustrations, even if they add other media as well as paint. Look at the work of Chris Van Allsburg, Jerry Pinkney, and Chris Raschka, for example. Whichever "painterly" technique is used, these methods are probably the most popular and prevalent in children's book illustration today.

Graphic techniques do not involve painting as such; instead, they include various methods of printing, cutting, and pasting, including woodblocks, linocuts, scratchboard, and stone lithography. Look at the work of Steve Jenkins and Brian Pinkney, for example. This is where children's book illustration started out several hundred years ago, with woodcuts and copper engravings. But those methods are very expensive and time consuming. Today's artists, however, are experimenting with new "graphic" techniques, especially collage and combination techniques using computers and scanners. One final note: the use of photographs falls somewhere in between these various categories and is another alternative for illustrators of picture books, particularly for concept books and informational picture books.

Bookmaking

Illustrators use all these components, including their knowledge of visual elements, their sense of artistic style, and their preferences for medium and technique to create a memorable picture book. But other artistic and creative decisions go into creating the aesthetic of a picture book from the paper to the binding to the font. Sometimes authors and illustrators offer input into these details, but often they are decided upon by book editors and book designers in the publishing house. Either way, they contribute to our enjoyment and appreciation of the picture book and are worthy of comment. This includes:

Size of book (called the "trim" size)
Shape of book
Endpapers/endpages (at the beginning and end of the book)
Font or typeface
Borders
Paper quality
Cover (and dust jacket)

We know we shouldn't "judge a book by its cover," but every reader does—especially children. Understanding and examining the art of the picture book makes us much better equipped to truly appreciate the picture book as literature. I have found that even kindergarten children can do this with just the littlest bit of discussion and guidance. They recognize a book by Eric Carle or Mo Willems, for example, before they can even read. I believe a closer study of this artistic component deepens our appreciation and enjoyment of the picture book. And on a more pragmatic note, it also helps prepare children for composing their own stories and creating their own art.

I always learn so much from what children see in the illustrations of children's books. You will too. I think you will also begin to appreciate the art and craft behind the best children's books. Do you think that in the future all books will be read on an e-reader or computer screen and we can just forget about all this paper stuff? Maybe. But I think the art form of the picture book still offers a unique experience for the eye, hand, and nose, as well as for the spirit. They're still the most affordable and portable form of book experience (for now). But eBooks also incorporate many of these same visual elements in creating an aesthetic storybook experience, too.

Resources on the Making of Picture Books

These resource books provide information about the picture book illustration process, many from the point of view of the illustrators themselves.

Aliki. 1988. *How a Book Is Made*. New York: HarperTrophy.
Bang, Molly. 2000. *Picture This: How Pictures Work*. New York: SeaStar.
Blake, Quentin. 2003. *Magic Pencil: Children's Book Illustration Today*. London: British Library.
Christelow, Eileen. 1999. *What Do Illustrators Do?* New York: Clarion.
Cummings, Pat. 1992. *Talking with Artists*. New York: Simon & Schuster.
Cummings, Pat. 1995. *Talking with Artists, Volume 2*. New York: Simon & Schuster.
Cummings, Pat. 1999. *Talking with Artists, Volume 3*. New York: Simon & Schuster.
Cummins, Julie and Barbara Kiefer. 1999. *Wings of an Artist: Children's Book Illustrators Talk About Their Art*. New York: Abrams.
Elleman, Barbara. 1999. *Tomie de Paola: His Art and His Stories*. New York: Putnam.
Elleman, Barbara. 2002. *Virginia Lee Burton: A Life in Art*. Boston: Houghton Mifflin.
Elleman, Barbara. 2009. *Drawings from the Heart: Tomie de Paola Turns 75*. Amherst, MA: Eric Carle Museum of Picture Book Art.
Elleman, Barbara. 2009. *Those Telling Lines: The Art of Virginia Lee Burton*. Amherst, MA: Eric Carle Museum of Picture Book Art.
Eric Carle Museum of Picture Book Art. 2007. *Artist to Artist: 23 Major Illustrators Talk to Children About Their Art*. New York: Philomel.
Evans, Dilys. 2008. *Show and Tell: Exploring the Fine Art of Children's Book Illustration*. San Francisco: Chronicle.
Leedy, Loreen. 2004. *Look at My Book: How Kids Can Write and Illustrate Terrific Books*. New York: Holiday House.
Marcus, Leonard. 1999. *A Caldecott Celebration: Six Artists Share Their Paths to the Caldecott Medal*. New York: Walker.
Marcus, Leonard. 2002. *Ways of Telling: Conversations on the Art of the Picture Book*. New York: Dutton.
Marcus, Leonard. 2006. *Pass It Down: Five Picture Book Families Make Their Mark*. New York: Walker.
Marcus, Leonard. 2006. *Side by Side: Five Favorite Picture Book Teams Go to Work*. New York: Walker.
Marcus, Leonard. 2012. *Show Me a Story! Why Picture Books Matter: Conversations with 21 of the World's Most Celebrated Illustrators*. Somerville, MA: Candlewick.
Salisbury, Martin. 2004. *Illustrating Children's Books: Creating Pictures for Publication*. Hauppauge, NY: Barron's Educational Books.
Schiller, Justin, Dennis David, Leonard Marcus, and Maurice Sendak. 2013. *Maurice Sendak: A Celebration of the Artist and His Work*. New York: Abrams.
Shulevitz, Uri. 1997. *Writing with Pictures: How to Write and Illustrate Children's Books*. New York: Watson-Guptill.
Stevens, Janet. 1996. *From Pictures to Words: A Book About Making a Book*. New York: Holiday House.

EVALUATION CRITERIA

When we examine a picture book critically, we need to consider two threads of analysis at the same time. How does the author create an interesting story? And how do the illustrations serve that story and engage the reader/viewer? We rely on the traditional literary elements of character, plot, setting, theme, and style, but we look at them through the lens of words *and* images. In addition, we want to keep in mind our audience and our sense of what is appealing and appropriate for children at various ages and stages. Is this picture book designed for the youngest child to listen to? Or for an older child to enjoy the sophisticated art or complicated structure or mature content? In the classic text *Children and Books,* Zena Sutherland (2004), a highly respected critic of children's literature, suggested that well-written and well-conceived picture books and their illustrations should also build an appreciation of beauty and aesthetics, open up interpretation and imagination, and encourage the child to actively participate in the story. As you read, study, and examine picture books, consider the following elements. Compare what you read and see in the books with these criteria. You will soon see that picture books are far more than "cute" (my pet peeve word), and that the best ones are works of art in every sense of the word.

Characters

The characters in picture books may be teddy bears, talking cars, or tiny tots, but they should be convincing and credible with personalities that emerge as interesting and distinctive. (That's why so many book characters are effective as toys!) Their behavior should be consistent with their ages and background to create believability, so that young children can "grow up" a little with the characters through the book. Often the age of the main character parallels the age of the intended reader, so the perspective should remain true to the less experienced worldview of the young child. In addition, we consider how the character is revealed in the story through narration, description, and dialogue, as well as through the illustrations and images on the page. Think about some of the distinctive characters you've encountered in children's picture books: Olivia (the pig), Lilly (in her red boots), and Max and the Wild Things. What makes them so memorable? Not being cute, sweet, and well behaved, but by being very individual, with a strong sense of self, and a unique way of seeing the world and expressing themselves.

Plot

The plot of a picture book may be very simple, but there should always be some conflict that grows out of a situation that is believable and relevant to the young child. On the other hand, good plots are not just about familiar crises rehashed but are original and fresh even when they cover familiar territory. Max is a "bad boy" like Peter Rabbit, but his rebellion takes him somewhere completely new before leading him back to the comfort of home and a warm meal. Consider how the author constructs the action. Is there a logical series of happenings? Is the climax and resolution clear and satisfying? How do the illustrations move the plot along? Once again, the pictures are also an important part of the plot, so consider how the scenes set the stage and move the action forward.

Setting

The setting of a picture book is often established more through the visuals than through the text. Where does the story take place? Look at the pictures for clues to the time and place. Often the setting is a generalized modern community and is not critical to the story. But sometimes the time or place is an integral element for the story's action or the character's development. For example, in Margaret Wise Brown's famous bedtime book, *Goodnight Moon* (HarperCollins, 1947), the passage of time is the whole construct for the story as the reader says "good night" to each object in the room. Here the setting is so crucial, it's almost a character in the story. Clement Hurd's images of the cluttered room with the green walls, red carpet, and round rug create a self-contained world for the child to enter. The room darkens as time passes and the reader says good night to Brown's litany of objects: red balloon, cow jumping over the moon, kittens, mittens, and bowl full of mush. How does the author indicate the time? Does the story transcend the setting and have universal implications? These are questions to ask about how the setting works in a picture book.

Theme

The theme of a picture book is a sticky area for many of us in the field of children's literature. Your average adult wants a children's book to have a strong message or lesson to impart to children, but experts and scholars see this as didacticism. We want to share stories that have meaning to children, but we want that meaning to emerge naturally out of the characters and actions, and not be imposed as a sermon or moral. In fact, kids are generally rather resistant to sermonizing and enjoy stories for their own sakes. Deeper meanings are gleaned subtly, implicitly, through understanding how the world works, how people behave, and how stories reveal those truths. What is the theme of *Goodnight Moon*, for example? Does the story have a theme? Is it an opportunity for a child to find comfort in the familiar before night comes? Why has this story lasted for over fifty years? In our critical analysis of picture books we look for thematic value, for meaningfulness, for satisfying closure, and we're leery of messages that moralize or overpower the story itself.

Style

The element of style reveals itself in both the language of the author and the artistry of the illustrator in the world of picture books. It's how you recognize a book is by Brian Pinkney, for example, as opposed to Brian Selznick (for either writing *or* illustrating). How does the author use language? Create a mood? Tell the story? Are repetitive patterns used? Is there dialogue? If so, is it suited to the characters in the story?

In *A Critical Handbook of Children's Literature* (2012), Lukens, Smith, and Coffel recommend looking at an author's use of "devices of style" such as imagery, hyperbole, understatement, symbolism, puns and wordplay, figurative language (personification, simile, metaphors, etc.), and features of sound (such as onomatopoeia, alliteration, assonance, consonance, rhyme, and rhythm). And in *From Cover to Cover: Evaluating and Reviewing Children's Books*, K. T. Horning (2010) invites us to "look at each double-page spread and notice what happens" and ask if "surprises (are) balanced with predictable elements" (p. 125). How does the author (and the illustrator) use all the other literary elements (character, plot, setting, and theme) to create a story in a voice that is his or her own? Look for the attributes that characterize a unique storytelling stamp—that's style.

Illustrations

Be sure to look as closely at the illustrations as you do at the writing. How the illustrations create or complement the story is also an essential part of the evaluation of a picture book, of course. Children's literature expert Zena Sutherland (2004) believed that the illustrations in a picture book should have storytelling qualities, a style of art that is appropriate to the story, and reflect warmth and vitality either through rich and harmonious color or appropriate use of monochrome. The illustrations help create the mood of the story, as well as the pacing and tension from page to page. How do the illustrations relate to the words of the story? Horning (2010, p. 101) asks, "Do they complement, extend or highlight the text?" "Do they provide crucial details that are not present in the text, but are an important part of the story?" "Do they clarify in such a way that they take the story beyond its words?" Even the placement of the words and pictures on the page, the design and layout of the book as a whole, affects the story's impact and the entire reading experience. This can be especially true for eBooks as children view book pages on their e-readers.

This is where it is also helpful to know a bit about the art of book illustration itself; to recognize different styles of art (realistic or abstract) and to understand the different artistic media or techniques (painterly or graphic) that illustrators use to create the pictures of a picture book. Even the language of art comes in handy when we discuss picture book illustrations, so we can refer to the visual elements appropriately including: line, shape, color, texture, and composition. Consider Mo Willems's strong use of line in his picture books, for example, and contrast that with Peter Sís's work, which also relies on an extensive use of line from a completely different (crosshatch) approach. You begin to see how the individual artist's style can have a strong and distinctive impact on the creation of a single picture book.

Cultural Markers

It is also important to consider how words and pictures are used to depict culture in children's picture books, as we seek out the very best to share with young readers. In "Making Informed Choices" (1992), children's literature scholar and teacher Rudine Sims Bishop provides guidelines for the close examination of cultural authenticity in children's literature. She also reminds us to include a careful consideration of the traditional literary elements in our analysis of each book. Is it a good story? Cultural accuracy may be rather mechanical if the book's plot does not interest children. For other examples, Reese and Caldwell-Wood (1997) and Slapin and Seale (1998) share their perspectives in relation to Native American children's books. In combination, these authors and scholars offer helpful criteria to guide the novice critic in the careful consideration of multicultural literature for young people.

When considering cultural authenticity in picture books, be sure to pay close attention to the illustrations, as well as the words or text. Look for accuracy and variety in the depiction or description of some of these "cultural markers," including varied skin tones, facial features, body types, hairstyles/hair textures, clothing, homes, language patterns, dialects, names and forms of address, and so on. Do the illustrations avoid stereotypes or rely on only traditional, rather than modern representations, as if people of color live "long ago" or "far away"? Is there variety even within the culture depicted? Bishop (1992, p. 51) challenges us to "Put yourself in the place of the child reader. Is there anything in the book that would embarrass or offend you if it were written about you or the group you identify with? Would you be willing to share this book with a group of mixed-race children? An all-black or all-white group?"

Sample Review

Let's put all these evaluation criteria into action and consider one review and how it uses these criteria. Here's a sample review of a picture book:

Gravett, Emily. 2006. *Wolves*. New York: Simon & Schuster.

Illustrated as a book within a book that brings readers into every page, *Wolves* follows a hapless rabbit as he researches the topic of wolves. After checking a book out at the library, the rabbit walks right into the book, and as the pages turn, into more and more trouble. Readers will delight in the rabbit's wide-eyed surprise as he realizes what they already knew—that the rabbit has managed to walk right out onto the wolf's nose and is about to be dinner. The multimedia illustrations provide visually appealing pages with many different elements, checkout cards from the "West Bucks Public Burrowing Library," and postcards sent to "G. Rabbit" in "Nibbleswick, Great Burrow." Abundant white space provides a more dramatic background for the detailed charcoal drawings of the wolf. For those fearing dead bunny trauma for young readers, an alternate ending is presented wherein the wolf is a vegetarian and the predator and prey share a jam sandwich instead.
[By Tammy Korns for *Librarians' Choices*. Used with permission.]

Notice how this review summarizes the plot of the story, so you have a good sense of what the book is about, but also describes the role of illustration, so you have a feeling for what the book looks like and how the pictures work to help tell the story. The reviewer provides a brief treatment of the key characters in the book (the "hapless rabbit" and the wolf) and the dual settings of the library and the wolf story. The theme of this "cautionary tale" is apparent in the "wide-eyed surprise" the rabbit experiences, but includes an alternative image of collaboration, too (sharing a jam sandwich). There's a nod to the author's style and how she clues the reader into knowing more than the rabbit character. The review addresses several aspects of how the illustrations help create the story from the description of the "book within a book" to how the "multimedia illustrations provide visually appealing pages with many different elements, checkout cards from the 'West Bucks Public Burrowing Library,' and postcards sent to 'G. Rabbit' in 'Nibbleswick, Great Burrow.'" Finally, this brief review still manages to address the variable of child appeal from the pull of the book within a book layout to the visual appeal of the multiple media to the two endings for child readers. All of this in less than 200 words, with a balanced discussion of all the major literary criteria and an inviting approach to describing, discussing, and analyzing this distinctive picture book.

Enjoying Children's Book Art

For a fascinating look at the process one illustrator, Petra Mathers, used to create one picture book, *Kisses from Rosa,* visit Project Eclipse (http://eclipse.rutgers.edu/), an amazing online portfolio developed by Dr. Kaye Vandergrift. You can follow the development of a picture book from its conception through the various revisions of both text and illustration to the published book over a ten-year period. Children who want to explore all kinds of bookmaking will enjoy the blog site *Making Books with Children* (http://www.makingbooks.com/free projects.shtml/), full of information and inspiration for parents, teachers, and kids of all ages. The International Children's Literature Digital Library (http://en.childrenslibrary.org/) also makes it possible to view children's picture book art from around the world via full text versions of their literature online.

It is also possible to see hundreds of examples of children's book illustrations via the websites of several significant special collections, such as the Kerlan Collection (https://www.lib.umn.edu/clrc) at the University of Minnesota or the de Grummond Collection at the University of Southern Mississippi (http://www.lib.usm.edu/legacy/degrum/public_html/html/aboutus-welcome.shtml), which each house a research library of original manuscripts and art that help document the entire creative process of book creation. Two museums of children's book art worth knowing about include the Eric Carle Museum of Picture Book Art (http://www.carlemuseum.org/) in Massachusetts and the National Center for Children's Illustrated Literature (NCCIL; http://www.nccil.org/) in Texas. Both feature regular and rotating exhibits, workshops for kids, and visiting artists and speakers.

For true book art fans, it is possible to invest in original art from children's books from galleries such as the Elizabeth Stone Gallery (http://www

.elizabethstonegallery.com/) or the Child at Heart Gallery (http://childat heartartgallery.com). Or for the next best thing, Peaceable Kingdom Press (http://www.pkpress.com/) creates stationery that features art from classic and modern children's books. And don't forget the book-based promotional products available from ALA Graphics. In addition, the Children's Book Council (http://www.cbcbooks.org) commissions well-known children's book illustrators to create one-of-a-kind posters, postcards, streamers, and bookmarks for National Children's Book Week. A look at these posters across the decades via the book *75 Years of Children's Book Week Posters: Celebrating Great Illustrators of American Children's Books* (Knopf, 1994) by Leonard S. Marcus provides a fascinating glimpse of the history of children's book illustration and artistic techniques.

Evaluating Digital Books

More and more books are available in both print and digital form as eBooks. Already, eBook sales represent almost 13 percent of all children's books sold in 2012, doubled from 2011. And by the end of 2013, it's predicted that 65 percent of U.S. children will have access to an e-reader. Clearly, we need to familiarize ourselves with the digital book format and e-reader boom. Many eBooks are simply electronic versions of the book in print, a PDF file of the book to read screen-by-screen, page-by-page. This can be an efficient way to read a novel, of course, but it can also be a very text-only experience. Some digital novels offer more interactive possibilities with vocabulary help, weblinks, visuals, animation, and even augmented reality features. But with a digital picture book, the visuals are an essential part of the book experience, and the best picture books in eBook form capitalize on that aspect. That said, the availability of digital picture books still varies greatly from simple digital versions of print books to picture books created specifically to maximize the medium—"enhanced eBooks" that incorporate multimedia and interactivity with "hot spots" for pop-up visuals or added sounds and more. Librarian Kiera Parrott provides a very helpful list of "5 Questions to Ask When Evaluating Apps and eBooks," noting that "the good news is that many of the same critical skills used to evaluate physical media are transferable when evaluating digital media" (http://www.alsc.ala.org/blog/2011/07/5-questions-to-ask-when-evaluating-apps-and-ebooks/). Here she presents some basic questions to consider as we select quality digital books.

1. *Does it expand and enhance the traditional reading experience?*
   A great eBook should be interactive and encourage creative thinking and problem solving. It should take the characters, the setting, the themes, or the world of the book and allow the reader to explore them in new ways.
2. *Does it allow a linear reading experience?*
   A well-designed app or eBook should strike a balance between opportunities for exploration outside of the narrative as well as opportunities to lose oneself in the story alone.

3. *Does it engage multiple literacies and learning styles?*
   An excellent eBook should offer the user a dynamic experience that engages the senses and allows for interaction in a variety of ways with visual and auditory and even kinesthetic possibilities.
4. *It is intelligently designed? Is it intuitive, flexible, and customizable?*
   Above all, a good eBook will be user friendly and easy for children to navigate. Beyond that, it may offer customizable features such as the ability to alter the settings (easy/medium/hard) and accessibility options (such as font size or narration speed).
5. *Does it have legs (i.e., longevity)?*
   A good eBook should entice children to enjoy and explore it again and again—what's called "replayability"—just as a good book invites multiple readings.   Reprinted with permission.

In this evolving medium, we are continuing to refine our understanding: asking questions about books vs. apps, e-reading devices, book buying and circulation, and more. But these beginning questions provide a helpful framework as we take "baby steps" into the brave new world of digital books, always focused on connecting kids and books—one way or another.

AWARDS FOR PICTURE BOOKS AND ILLUSTRATION

Which are the very best picture books for children? Awards help us recognize what a variety of experts and others designate as outstanding. Several major awards recognize excellence in the creation of picture books, and many large libraries and state professional organizations issue their own "best" lists of children's books on an annual basis that generally include picture books among them. These are worth consulting, too, for collection development purposes and for finding books that young children are sure to like. On occasion, even the Newbery Medal or Honor distinction may be awarded to a picture book, such as *Dark Emperor and Other Poems of the Night* by Joyce Sidman (Houghton Mifflin Harcourt, 2010); *Show Way* by Jacqueline Woodson, illustrated by Hudson Talbott (Putnam, 2005); *A Visit to William Blake's Inn: Poems for Innocent and Experienced Travelers* by Nancy Willard, illustrated by Alice and Martin Provensen (Harcourt, 1981); or *Doctor DeSoto* by William Steig (Farrar, Straus & Giroux, 1982). And of course you can review circulation statistics and survey kids and parents to find out which picture book authors and illustrators they check out most often. These are all ways to keep looking for those sure-fire classics of the future.

The Caldecott Award

Undoubtedly, the most significant award in the field of children's book illustration is the Randolph Caldecott Medal. Since 1938, it has been presented annually to the artist of the most distinguished American picture book for children published in the preceding year selected by a committee of librarians and other professionals who are members of the ALSC (the Association for Library Service to Children). Recent Caldecott medal artists include Jon Klassen, Chris Raschka, Erin Stead, Jerry Pinkney, Beth Krommes, and Brian Selznick. All award medal and honor recipients are listed on the ALSC website. And don't miss Leonard Marcus's fascinating and richly illustrated picture book biography of this famous illustrator and award namesake, *Randolph Caldecott: The Man Who Could Not Stop Drawing* (Farrar, Straus & Giroux, 2013).

The Coretta Scott King Award and Pura Belpré Award

Other national awards for children's book illustrators include the Coretta Scott King Award given annually to an African American illustrator and the Pura Belpré Award presented biennially to a Latino/Latina illustrator whose work best portrays, affirms, and celebrates the Latino cultural experience. Recent Coretta Scott King Illlustrator Award recipients include Shane Evans, Bryan Collier, Jerry Pinkney, Charles R. Smith Jr., Ashley Bryan, and Kadir Nelson. For the Pura Belpré Illustrator Award, recent recipients include David Diaz, Duncan Tonatiuh, Eric Velasquez, Rafael López, and Yuyi Morales. All award and honor recipients for both awards are listed on the ALA and ALSC websites.

The Geisel Award

In 2006, the American Library Association established the Theodor Seuss Geisel Award, named after Dr. Seuss. It is given annually to the author and illustrator of the most distinguished beginning reader book published in the United States during the preceding year. In particular, the award recognizes creativity and imagination, as well as literary and artistic achievement, in engaging children in reading. This is an important award to note for identifying picture books with strong appeal to young children and emergent readers. Recent recipients have included *Up, Tall and High!*, written and illustrated by Ethan Long (Putnam, 2012) and *Tales for Very Picky Eaters*, written and illustrated by Josh Schneider (Clarion, 2011).

The Gryphon Award

The Gryphon Award, sponsored by the Center for Children's Books at the University of Illinois in Urbana-Champaign, is given annually to a work of fiction or nonfiction for children in kindergarten through grade 4. In particular, the award recognizes books that "successfully bridge the gap in difficulty between books for reading aloud to children and books for practiced readers." The Center for Children's Books also chooses a list of "Blue Ribbon" books each year that includes a sizeable number of picture books worth noting. Recent recipients of the Gryphon Award have included *Island: A Story of the Galápagos* by Jason Chin (Roaring Brook, 2012), *Like Pickle Juice on a Cookie* by Julie Sternberg, illustrated by Matthew Cordell (Abrams, 2011), and *We Are in a Book!* by Mo Willems (Hyperion, 2010).

Ezra Jack Keats Award

The New York Public Library and the Ezra Jack Keats Foundation collaborate to present annual Ezra Jack Keats New Writer and New Illustrator awards to an outstanding new writer and illustrator of picture books for children. The awards are designed to recognize and encourage talented *new* children's book authors and illustrators who "offer fresh and positive views of the multicultural world inhabited by children today." Recent recipients have included authors Julie Fogliano, Meg Medina, Laurel Croza, and Tonya Cherie Hegamin and illustrators Hyewon Yum, Jenny Sue Kostecki-Shaw, Tao Nyeu, and Taeeun Yoo. For more information, check out: http://www.ezra-jack-keats.org/.

SCBWI Golden Kite Award

The Society of Children's Book Writers and Illustrators (SCBWI) also presents an annual award for children's books called the Golden Kite Award, which includes categories for the creators of picture book text and picture book illustration. It is the only major children's book award presented by one's peers and is highly respected in the field of book illustration. Recent recipients have included *Big Red Lollipop* by Rukhsana Khan (Viking, 2010) for text and for illustration, and *A Pocketful of Posies* illustrated by Salley Mavor (Houghton Mifflin, 2010).

The Charlotte Zolotow Award

The Cooperative Children's Book Center at the University of Wisconsin–Madison established the Charlotte Zolotow Award to honor the work of Charlotte Zolotow, a UW alumna, distinguished children's book editor, and author of more than 70 picture books, including such classics as *William's Doll* (Harper, 1972). The award is given annually to the author of the best picture book text for young children (birth through age seven). Recent recipients have included Jacqueline Woodson for *Each Kindness* illustrated by E. B. Lewis (Putnam, 2012) and *Me . . . Jane* by Patrick McDonnell (Little, Brown, 2011).

The Hans Christian Andersen Illustrator Award

The Hans Christian Andersen Illustrator Award, given every two years by the International Board on Books for Young People (IBBY) to a distinguished illustrator for his or her entire body of work, helps us pay attention to artists in other countries who create beautiful, unique picture books for children. Recent recipients include María Teresa Andruetto (Argentina), David Almond (UK), Margaret Mahy (New Zealand), Jürg Schubiger (Switerzland), and Peter Sís (Czech Republic). And while you're looking for good books from other countries, keep an eye on the major awards they present to children's books, such as the Greenaway Medal in the United Kingdom (for Jim Kay's illustrations for *A Monster Calls* by Patrick Ness, Candlewick, 2011, for example), among others.

Media Awards

I think it's also worth mentioning distinctive media awards since they consider picture books and provide alternative modes of delivery that can enrich the picture book reading, listening, and watching experience. This includes the Carnegie Medal for Excellence in Children's Video administered by the American Library Association. The Carnegie Medal is awarded for outstanding video productions for children that "show a respect for a child's intelligence and imagination and take advantage of the special techniques of the medium, including visuals, voices, music, language, and sound effects." Many of the winners are adaptations of picture books, such as *Don't Let the Pigeon Drive the Bus!* produced by Weston Woods, a perfect example of the effective use of media to make a picture book come alive.

Literature in Action: Sharing Picture Books Aloud

Picture books are meant to be read aloud and shared. The practice of one adult holding a picture book out at arm's length to a group of young children sitting rapt at her or his knees is a fixture in children's services. It's one of my favorite times in working with children. But sometimes we get into a rut with our picture book read aloud practices. Let's consider a variety of options for sharing picture books in ways that encourage a deeper understanding.

Think Aloud

In using the "think aloud" strategy, we verbalize our own internal thought processes as we examine a book and begin reading, showing children how fluent readers think. We can involve the children in guessing what the story might be about based on the cover, the title, the author, the dust jacket, and so on. This helps children see that good readers do a lot of thinking while reading; reading doesn't just magically happen. For example, you might hold up the book and say, "I wonder what this book will be about. I see the title is ___ and the author is ___ and it's illustrated by ___. The picture on the cover makes me think that___." This helps children see how readers use all the cues and clues at their disposal to read and interpret a book.

Predicting

Reading experts remind us that good readers are constantly predicting what will happen next. This is another aspect of reading that we can model and encourage from time to time. For example, read the story aloud to the climax of the plot. Pause and ask, "What do you think will happen next?" Invite the children to turn to the child sitting next to them and tell what they think will happen next. This way, all the children get to share their ideas in just a few minutes, everyone stays involved in the story experience, and you don't lose momentum. (Remember, it's the thinking that is important, not necessarily guessing right!) Then continue reading and finish the story. Discuss the ending and why it ended the way it did; what clues helped "predict" this story's ending. It's not as important to guess correctly as it is to learn to understand the story elements. This is a valuable strategy for helping children become familiar with how stories are structured.

Building Visual Literacy

Although children naturally use the illustrations to understand the story, most come to believe that is "cheating." (Some adults think so, too!) It's not. All good readers use all possible sources to understand information, including visuals. Help children see how you do that on purpose, how you see a structure based on the visuals themselves. Flip through a picture book without reading the words, as if the book were a wordless book, telling the story loosely based on the pictures alone. Invite the children to join you. What can be learned from the illustrations only? Point out that readers use all kinds of cues and clues in reading. Sipe and Pantaleo (2008) found that children glean information from many parts of the book, even the endpapers. In fact, readers often learn some things from pictures that are not in the text, giving us an extra layer of the story.

Interactive Read Aloud

Sometimes a book is written in a way that invites the children to participate in the read aloud experience. It may have a repeated phrase or countdown or a sequence. Children can join in on a repeated phrase, take parts with the existing dialogue, complete a predictable sentence, conclude with "The End," and so on. This helps children stay alert to the story read aloud and begin to see the pieces of writing that make up a story. However, you may want to decide beforehand how you want to handle this and alert children to their parts before you begin reading. Sometimes we want a quiet audience to build engagement and even suspense, and sometimes we want a participatory, lively experience. We need to teach the children the difference and set the stage before reading, so they'll know which is which.

Echo Reading

With "echo" reading, we can invite child participation without a great deal of advance preparation, and we can include children who are not yet readers or who are still struggling with learning the English language. Here, children participate as a group, simply repeating key phrases or words after you read them. Choose books with short sentences or rhyming/rhythmic text. Read the line or sentence out loud and have the children "echo" or repeat the line after you. Continue. This strategy only works with some books, like Karen Beaumont's *Move Over, Rover* (Harcourt, 2006), but helps children tune into the rhythm of story language and makes them feel like part of the read aloud experience.

Cloze Procedure

The "cloze" procedure is a technique from the field of reading that helps children learn how to use context clues to figure out a word. Essentially, they have a whole sentence or more to figure out what one missing word within the sentence might be. We can use this strategy to make a read aloud experience more interactive and instructional on occasion. Use Post-it notes to cover key words in the text (one per page). Invite children to figure out what the word should be using the sentence and story context. Also, try using the Post-it cover method with parts of words, showing only the first letter of the word, then consonant blends, then vowels, and so forth. Look especially for simple picture books with many repetitions of sounds. This helps develop children's phonemic awareness. This adaptation of the cloze method can create a guessing game kind of context for reading, if you don't belabor the guessing aspect. This is a way to add variety to reading aloud, while involving children in exercising their decoding and comprehension skills.

Responding

Any time we read a good picture book aloud, we hope for an enthusiastic response. Sometimes the best response is awed silence. Sometimes it's a cry for "read it again!" Either way, it's important to allow a few minutes for a response *after* the reading aloud. You can simply invite the children to share their reactions, feelings, connections, and the like. Allow plenty of "wait time" and avoid being the first one to share your own responses (otherwise kids often think yours is the only correct response). Try to be open to varied responses and opinions. Encourage them to support their opinions; to go back to the book for examples that support their responses. Flip back through the book to ponder a favorite moment, consider a particular illustration more closely, or revisit an appealing phrase. This shows children that good readers are not finished when the book is closed. They often work backward to enjoy parts of the story again or to figure out something they missed or misunderstood. Many children don't realize this and think it's a sign of poor reading; they need guidance and modeling to show otherwise.

Follow-up

Finally, reading aloud a picture book generally calls for more reading. One book is rarely enough. What to do? One of my favorite things is to pair a poem with a picture book, following up on the theme of the book with a poem that echoes the story. For example, the classic picture book *Alexander and the Terrible, Horrible, No Good, Very Bad Day* by Judith Viorst (Atheneum, 1972), can be paired with Karla Kuskin's poem listing the same kind of "bad day" woes in "I Woke Up This Morning" (in Kuskin, 2003). Or consider reading aloud another book by the same author (or illustrator), or about the same topic or theme, or follow up with a related song. Ask the children, "What do you want to read next?" Don't be surprised if they want to hear the same book again. Young children especially find repeated readings comforting and necessary as they develop what's called "story schema," an intuitive understanding of how stories and story language work.

SHARING PICTURE BOOKS

Probably the best place to begin when you decide to start or continue reading aloud is with a picture book. It's the perfect medium for sharing out loud with its blend of watching (the pictures) and listening (to the words). Caldecott artist Mordicai Gerstein called them "little theaters" full of drama with scenes unfolding before a captive audience. Practically speaking, picture books don't take long to read or reread and are available on an incredible array of topics. In addition, picture books can work at a variety of age levels, depending on how you present them, and they are invaluable for helping children who are learning English as a new language.

Books like the classic *Sylvester and the Magic Pebble* (Windmill Books, 1969), for example, are a captivating read aloud about magic and family for the young child but also offer the themes of longing and loss (plus challenging vocabulary) to discuss with older children. See if they detect elements of "Pinocchio" in *Sylvester and the Magic Pebble*, author/illustrator William Steig's favorite story. Play the CD of the book narrated by James Earl Jones. And did I mention this book won the Caldecott award for the best illustrations of the year? (Plus, did you know it was somewhat controversial for its portrayal of the police as pigs? It was the 1960s.) Finally, paint a pebble red and brainstorm wishes that children would make after reading the book aloud. Sharing picture books can involve children in all these ways.

Involving Families

Many picture book story times involve parents and other caregivers as a way to provide a shared experience between children and adults. In addition, this models the read aloud experience for family members who would like to try this with their own children at home. Many public libraries feature "lapsit" programs that provide very young children (birth to two years) with exposure to books, usually beginning with board books. This expansion of the traditional story times for three- to five-year-olds has gained momentum as there is a considerable body of research that links early exposure to books with brain development. Connecting parents and kids via picture books is a natural activity for promoting that early literacy development. Some libraries add book toys to their collections, acquiring dolls, plush toys, and puppets that relate to popular picture books such as Skippyjon Jones, Olivia, Madeleine, Clifford, and Curious George, to pump up the motivation and appeal.

Others create bookbags and book kits that combine the picture book with other items, such as simple props that enable young children to "act out" the story after reading it, or blank paper and art supplies to create response drawings. For the school library setting, this kind of take home activity is often viewed as the most valuable "homework" of all in the early grades. It provides additional minutes of reading, an essential aspect of becoming a fluent and proficient reader. Fortunately, there are many excellent resources for sharing picture books aloud with children including:

Children's Book Corner: A Read-Aloud Resource with Tips, Techniques, and Plans for Teachers, Librarians and Parents, Level Pre-K–K; Grades 1 and 2; Grades 3 and 4; Grades 5 and 6, all by Judy Bradbury (Libraries Unlimited, 2006)

Early Literacy Storytimes @ Your Library: Partnering with Caregivers for Success by Saroj Ghoting and Pamela Martin-Diaz (ALA, 2005)

Rob Reid's books, *Family Storytime* (ALA, 1999), *Cool Story Programs for the School-Age Crowd* (ALA, 2004), *More Family Storytimes* (ALA, 2009), as well as *Reid's Read-Alouds: Selections for Children and Teens* (ALA, 2009) and *Reid's Read-Alouds 2* (ALA, 2010)

The Kids' Book Club: Lively Reading and Activities for Grades 1–3 by Desiree Webber and Sandy Shropshire (Libraries Unlimited, 2001)

Storytimes for Children by Stephanie G. Bauman (Libraries Unlimited, 2010)

Using Picture Books to Help Children Learning English

Imagine that you are a child about to enter a place with a language and cus-toms that may be completely unfamiliar. The sounds and symbols of this new language are completely different, and yet you attend public school and try to pay attention to lesson after lesson, while making friends among the strangers around you. It's challenging and a bit scary, isn't it? How can we help children who are learning English feel comfortable in their surroundings and begin the adjustment to their new language? First, we need to recognize that children are acquiring several different types of proficiency in learning a new language. James Cummins (2003) has highlighted two types of language proficiency that individuals learning a language need—conversational and academic lan-guage. Conversational language does not require formal schooling to develop and grows naturally out of everyday interactions, but academic language is clearly the focus of school, textbooks, and instruction. Research has shown that English learners acquire conversational language in a couple of years as they interact socially, but the academic language so needed for school achieve-ment may take five to seven years to develop. Exposure to quality literature has been shown to be critical in the development of a rich vocabulary for these English language learners.

Where do we begin in helping children function on a day-to-day basis? Carefully chosen picture books can be enormously helpful for children acquiring "survival" language, in particular. Picture books on "school sur-vival" topics chosen with culture and diversity in mind can be helpful for children adjusting to life in the United States or to the routines of American schools. They provide much of the basic vocabulary needed upon initially learning a language. Picture books can provide both text and visuals to make this vocabulary explicit. We can be aware of those teachable moments while reading aloud and be prepared with books and discussion that help English learners maximize their vocabulary acquisition. For older children (and even teens and adults) who are still learning English (as a second or third lan-guage), children's books are essential for providing models of fluid, literary language.

Children's Picture Books for Developing "Survival" Language

We can seek out books that provide basic labels and information that help kids cope with day-to-day life. Here's a handful of titles to get you started based, in part, on *Literature-based Instruction with English Language Learners* (Hadaway, Vardell, and Young, 2002).

Letters of the Alphabet: *Eating the Alphabet: Fruits & Vegetables from A to Z* by Lois Ehlert (Voyager, 1993); *I Stink* by Kate and Jim McMullan (HarperCollins, 2006)

Numbers and Counting: *Feast for 10* by Cathryn Falwell (Clarion, 1996); *100 Is a Family* by Pam Muñoz Ryan (Hyperion, 1996)

Telling Time: *Time To* by Bruce McMillan (Scholastic, 1989); *Somewhere in the World Right Now* by Stacey Schuett (Knopf, 1995); *It's About Time!* by Stuart Murphy (HarperCollins, 2005)

The Calendar: *Today Is Monday* by Eric Carle (Philomel, 1993); *Cookie's Week* by Cindy Ward (Putnam, 1992)

Weather: *Weather* by Seymour Simon (Collins, 2006); *Thunderstorm* by Arthur Geisert (Enchanted Lion Books, 2013); *On the Same Day in March: A Tour of the World's Weather* by Marilyn Singer (HarperCollins, 2000)

The Body: *Here Are My Hands* by Bill Martin Jr. and John Archambault (Henry Holt, 2007); *Two Eyes, a Nose, and a Mouth* by Roberta G. Intrater (Scholastic, 2000)

Clothing: *Shoes, Shoes, Shoes* by Ann Morris (HarperCollins, 1995); *The Jacket I Wear in the Snow* by Shirley Neitzel (HarperTrophy, 1994)

Money: *26 Letters and 99 Cents* by Tana Hoban (Greenwillow, 1987); *Monster Money Book* by Loreen Leedy (Scholastic, 2001)

Family: *Family Pictures* by Carmen Lomas Garza (Children's Book Press, 2005); *The Trip Back Home* by Janet Wong (Harcourt, 2000)

Finding Book-based Apps

Book apps (short for "applications") provide a computerized, interactive experience rooted in a book. Although the line between a digital book and a book-based app can be blurry, they all begin with a book. (And of course there are many fun and appealing apps for kids that are *not* based on books.) Generally, an app differs from an eBook in that children can poke or press various parts of the story, and the iPad (or other device) responds to their actions; it's not simply a story unfolding digitally, and it may go well beyond the story frame or concept. Some book-based apps are very "book-like" and focus greatly on enhancing the experience of the book's story, and some are very "game-like," using the book's story or characters to create a frame for a variety of engaging activities. Mary Ann Scheuer, librarian at Emerson Elementary School in Berkeley, California, and writer of the GreatKidBooks blog, observed, "I've been amazed how iPad book apps can engage children with stories they knew, . . . adding and integrating new content, encouraging children to interact with stories, and enabling young children to read stories by themselves." She identifies six aspects of a successful book app to consider:

1. *Audience and purpose:* Does the app suit the intended age level? Does it reinforce the book nature of the app-reading experience?
2. *Story, plot, information:* Does the app offer a rich story experience or rich nonfiction material that is interesting enough to draw the reader in again and again?
3. *Navigation:* How easy is it to go from section to section? How do users discover how they find their way around the app? How easy is it to start over again?

4. *Narration and audio options:* Does the narration help users interact with the content? Is the narration appropriate for the content? Can you turn the narration off if you just want to read it? Is the narration available in more than one language? How easy is it to listen and relisten to a page or portion of text?

5. *Pacing and chunking:* How is the book divided into part or "chunks" for the user to experience? How does the user control or manipulate the movement of the story and pages? How is the drama of the story and the "page turn" enhanced?

6. *Interactive features:* Do interactive features engage readers but also maintain the narrative focus of the learning experience? Or do you stop thinking about the flow of the story and get sidetracked by the extra features?

Of course all this depends on our purpose for selecting and sharing the app. If we are choosing a book app to introduce a child to a story for the very first time (like Cinderella), the story elements will be particularly important. But if the child is very familiar with the story already (like Cinderella), then perhaps we're choosing the app to provide entertaining and engaging extensions that are rooted in a familiar story. Scheuer notes this is also a very dynamic medium, always changing, and observed, "It's fascinating to watch this new [medium] develop and consider the factors that make these stories work well for children." Apps are not a static format like books; developers often provide updates, new interactive features, and an improved interface. As more digital books include more interactive capabilities, the differences between eBooks and book apps may well disappear and the criteria for evaluating them will converge.

Meanwhile, more and more review sources and professional organizations are giving apps and other digital media thoughtful consideration. *School Library Journal* issues its annual list of "Top 10 Apps" of the year and *Kirkus* does likewise with their list of "Best Book Apps for Kids" each year. In addition, the American Association of School Librarians (AASL) gathered school librarians from around the country to evaluate and select apps to highlight in a list of "Best Apps for Teaching and Learning 2013." Here are those that they identified as the best among recent book-based apps complete with the annotations they provide (from: http://www.ala.org/aasl/standards-guidelines/best-apps/2013), reflecting a surprising variety in content and approach from folktales to nonfiction to Shakespeare:

1. *Bats! Furry Fliers of the Night* layers clear text with interesting diagrams, beautiful photographs, and interactive features that enhance young readers' understanding of the subject. The design elements are top-notch, providing just the right amount of zing to keep kids engaged without distracting them from the essence of the material. This is what a book app should be; it takes you beyond the book with innovative technology related to the topic.

2. Al Gore's *Our Choice: A Plan to Solve the Climate Crisis* is a rich, multimedia app that examines the climate crisis. It will engage both teens and adults alike. Gore published *Our Choice: How We Can Solve the*

Climate Crisis in 2009 as a young readers' edition of *An Inconvenient Truth* (2007). This app updates the book's content, incorporating a variety of compelling information.

3. Nosy Crow's *Cinderella* app engages young readers, encouraging them to explore and play with this original adaptation of the classic fairy tale. Beautiful illustrations draw readers right into the story, but the design keeps readers engaged as they explore the tap-activated dialogue, scenes that extend beyond the screen, and narration that captures the playful tone of the story.

4. The *Shakespeare in Bits: Hamlet* app will appeal to students who want a visual sense of the story as they listen to and read the play. This app combines an excellent full cast narration of the play with a rudimentary animated version enacted on half the iPad screen, while the full text of the play is on the other half. While that may sound cluttered, the design works very smoothly. Each scene is broken into manageable chunks, helping students absorb the original language.

5. *Fam Bam: Got to Have Music* features music and narration by rhythm-and-blues singer Brandy Norwood and her family. This app engages children with its playful tone, love of music, and cartoon animation. This family all loves music, but everybody has their own favorites and doesn't want to listen to the others' music. What's a tight-knit "fam bam" to do? The conflict resolves with a fun twist as everyone learns to compromise.

A variety of children's books have been and continue to be adapted into the app format. As *Kirkus* notes, "Some are adaptations of well-loved classics, others may bring lesser-known, newer books to light and still others are entirely new stories, created to take advantage of the iPad's storytelling capabilities." This is a fascinating area to watch and share with young readers.

Using Picture Books with Older Readers

Picture books are not just for preschool and the primary grades any more. Middle school librarian Donna MacKinney observed, "I think that librarians should be encouraged to read aloud to students of *all* ages—my middle schoolers love it even though they try to pretend that they aren't paying attention. When I read a picture book aloud it's quite amusing to see the 'toughies' want to crane their necks to see the pictures without letting on." Modern printing techniques have enabled artists to experiment more freely with illustration media in creating more complicated and edgy art in the thirty-two–page picture book format. These books may be slim volumes that fit on the "E" shelves, but their content will often be over the head of the usual young audience. Books such as Australian Graeme Base's classic *Animalia* (Abrams, 1987) or *Little Elephants* (Abrams, 2013) or Neil Gaiman's collaborations with Dave McKean, *The Wolves in the Walls* (HarperCollins, 2003) or *Crazy Hair* (HarperCollins, 2009), for example, benefit from the older child's experiences with books and life. Indeed, the lines between the highly visual picture book for young children and the innovative graphic novel for the young adult are blurring. Children are immersed in the visual culture of television and the Web, and thus are often drawn to the visual qualities of art and literature. Illustrated novels and graphic novels are capitalizing on this trend, but picture books have potential here, too.

In addition to the visual and artistic qualities of picture books, they can also offer examples of literary language and spartan phrasing. Indeed, Susan Hall (2007) argues that picture books are the ideal way to provide examples of literary devices such as similes and metaphors to young adults. The context is clear and not intimidating, unlike searching for figurative language in adult fiction and classics that appear daunting. Finally, the picture book is also an example of a book format that older children may try imitating, creating home-made picture books of their own to share with younger readers. They can try various illustration techniques, practice their own oral reading, and develop skills in reading aloud to others. Plus, older children often feel nostalgia for the picture books of their younger days and may recall fond memories of books they read or listened to.

These resources provide guidance in selecting and sharing picture books with older children. They include booklists and strategies for choosing picture books that are particularly effective with older readers.

Ammon, Bette, and Gale W. Sherman. 1996. *Worth a Thousand Words: An Annotated Guide to Picture Books for Older Readers*. Englewood, CO: Libraries Unlimited.

Hall, Susan. 2007. *Using Picture Storybooks to Teach Literary Devices: Recommended Books for Children and Young Adults*, Volumes I, II, III, & IV. Englewood, CO: Libraries Unlimited.

Heitman, Jane. 2004. *Teach Writing to Older Readers Using Picture Books: Every Picture Tells a Story*. Linworth.

Pearson, Molly Blake. 2005. *Big Ideas in Small Packages: Using Picture Books with Older Readers*. Columbus, OH: Linworth.

Pollette, Nancy, and Joan Ebbesmeyer. 2002. *Literature Lures: Using Picture Books and Novels to Motivate Middle School Readers*. Teacher Ideas Press.

Ray, Katie Wood. 1999. *Wondrous Words: Writers and Writing in the Elementary Classroom*. Urbana, IL: National Council of Teachers of English.

Tiedt, Iris. 2000. *Teaching with Picture Books in the Middle School*. Newark, DE: International Reading Association.

Wright, Cora M. 2002. *More Hot Links: Linking Literature with the Middle School Curriculum*. Englewood, CO: Libraries Unlimited.

CONCLUSION

Often people get confused the more they look at all these different kinds of picture books and try to categorize them. But the fundamental key in picture books is the abundance of illustrations and their important role in helping to communicate the story in harmony with the words. This makes them visually appealing for younger children but also offers possibilities for application in the upper grades. This becomes readily apparent when we consider the role of visual literacy, digital literacy, and interpreting signs and symbols, especially in our multilingual world.

As much as I enjoy the Internet and the ease of social media, the spontaneous fun of blogs, and the vast information available via websites, there is still something very satisfying about opening a well-made picture book. From holding the hardback binding, to eyeing the colorful cover, to turning the creamy pages, to poring over the illustrations, it's a very satisfying visual, tactile, and aesthetic experience. Add to that the pleasure of cuddling with a child on your lap to share the story page by page, holding the book together, a kind of totem against the reality of routine life. As a parent, memories of those times with my own children are nearly palpable. As much as I enjoy the opportunities that today's technology provides for quick reading and communication, there is still something about the art of the picture book that feels unique and worthwhile.

In the not-too-distant future, we may not be talking about books in print at all. Our focus may be on eBooks, e-readers, and interactions with digital stories. But human history shows us that there will always be stories in some form and children will always find them and make them their own. Whether children's literature is in print, digital, holographic, or some format yet unknown, there will still be stories to share and characters to believe in and themes to ponder. And we are in the lucky position to be guardians of that legacy—finding, reading, selecting, and sharing those stories with our youngest citizens, guiding them as they shape their destinies molded by the stories they find.

PROFESSIONAL RESOURCES ON THE ART OF PICTURE BOOKS

For more help in learning about picture books and children's book illustration, consult these related professional readings.

Aldana, Patricia. 2004. *Under the Spell of the Moon: Art for Children from the World's Great Illustrators.* Toronto, CA: Groundwood.

Bader, Barbara. 1976. *American Picturebooks from Noah's Ark to the Beast Within.* New York: Macmillan.

Cummins, Julie. Ed. 1997. *Children's Book Illustration and Design II.* Los Angeles, CA: PBC International.

Darling, Harold. 1999. *From Mother Goose to Dr. Seuss: Children's Book Covers 1860–1960.* San Francisco: Chronicle Books.

Gunning, Thomas. 2000. *Best Books for Building Literacy for Elementary School Children.* New York: Allyn & Bacon.

Hearn, Michael Patrick. 1996. *Myth, Magic, and Mystery: One Hundred Years of American Children's Book Illustration.* Lanham, MD: Roberts Rinehart Publishers.

Isaacs, Kathleen T. 2012. *Picturing the World: Informational Picture Books for Children.* Chicago, IL: American Library Association.

Kiefer, Barbara Z. 1995. *The Potential of Picturebooks: From Visual Literacy to Aesthetic Understanding.* Englewood Cliffs, NJ: Merrill.

Lewis, David. 2001. *Picturing Text: The Contemporary Children's Picturebook.* London: Routledge.

Marantz, Sylvia. 1992. *Picture Books for Looking and Learning: Awakening Visual Perceptions Through the Art of Children's Books.* Phoenix, AZ: Oryx Press.

Marantz, Sylvia. 2013. *Artists of the Page: Interviews with Children's Book Illustrators.* Jefferson, NC: McFarland.

Marantz, Sylvia, and Kenneth A. Marantz. 2005. *Multicultural Picture Books: Art for Understanding Others* (Second Edition). Lanham, MD: Scarecrow.

Marantz, Sylvia, and Kenneth A. Marantz. 2006. *Creating Picturebooks: Interviews with Editors, Art Directors, Reviewers, Booksellers, Professors, Librarians and Showcasers.* Jefferson, NC: McFarland.

Marcus, Leonard. 1999. *Margaret Wise Brown: Awakened by the Moon.* New York: Harper.

Marcus, Leonard. 2007. *Golden Legacy: How Golden Books Won Children's Hearts, Changed Publishing Forever, and Became an American Icon Along the Way.* New York: Random House.

Nespeca, Sue McCleaf, and Joan B. Reeve. 2003. *Picture Books Plus: 100 Extension Activities in Art, Drama, Music, Math, and Science.* Chicago, IL: American Library Association.

Nikolajeva, Mari, and Carole Scott. 2006. *How Picturebooks Work (Garland Reference Library of the Humanities).* London: Routledge.

Northrup, Mary. 2012. *Picture Books for Children: Fiction, Folktales and Poetry.* Chicago, IL: American Library Association.

Salisbury, Martin, and Morag Styles. 2012. *Children's Picturebooks: The Art of Visual Storytelling.* London, UK: Laurence King Publishers.

Sipe, Lawrence, and Sylvia Pantaleo. Eds. 2008. *Postmodern Picturebooks: Play, Parody, and Self-Referentiality.* London: Routledge.

Spitz, E. H., and R. Coles. 1999. *Inside Picture Books.* New Haven, CT: Yale University Press.

Standards in Action: Common Core State Standards

The Common Core State Standards (CCSS) for English Language Arts & Literacy are part of the latest national effort to "create the next generation of K–12 standards in order to help ensure that all students are college and career ready." They focus on developing "the close, attentive reading that is at the heart of understanding and enjoying complex works of literature. . . . the wide, deep, and thoughtful engagement with high-quality literary . . . texts" that we so value as librarians.

Most, but not all, of the states in the United States have adopted these standards for the areas of English language arts as well as mathematics. Ideally, the standards provide a framework for informing instruction, so that there is consistency across the country. As librarians, we can provide crucial support in helping teachers understand and meet these objectives. There are standards for reading in grades K–12 in three distinct areas: Literature, Informational Text, and Foundational Skills, as well as in the areas of writing, speaking and listening, and language overall (http://www.corestandards.org/ELA -Literacy). In the "Literature" area, specific skills are identified for each of these four areas:

- Key Ideas and Details
- Craft and Structure
- Integration of Knowledge and Ideas
- Range of Reading and Level of Text Complexity

You were introduced to several activities to use in the "Literature in Action: Sharing Picture Books Aloud" section of this chapter. Each of those could easily be connected with Common Core standards at the primary grades. For example, using the "Think Aloud" strategy with kindergarteners can help them name the author and illustrator of the book and consider what each person does in creating the book (CCSS.ELA-Literacy. RL.K.6). Or inviting first-grade students to try "Predicting" can help them "identify who is telling the story at various points in the text" (CCSS.ELA-Literacy.RL.1.6). With second graders, we can build their "Visual Literacy" skills by guiding them to "use information gained from the illustrations and words in a print or digital text to demonstrate understanding of its characters, setting, or plot" (CCSS.ELA-Literacy.RL.2.7). Finally, at the third-grade level, as we guide students in "Responding" to literature, we can model for them how good readers "refer to parts of stories, dramas, and poems when writing or speaking about a text, using terms such as *chapter, scene,* and *stanza*" (CCSS. ELA-Literacy.RL.3.5).

Good teachers and librarians (and parents) have been "covering the standards" for generations, long before committees came up with lists of subskills and objectives. We should continue to use strategies and activities that have been effective and successful in the past. The new emphasis on the Common Core provides an opportunity to talk about what we've been doing, why we do it that way, and how we can do it even better. In addition, the Common Core materials provide "Exemplars," or lists of recommended books and poems for each grade level. Personally, I find their lists a bit limited, but every list is just one list. Use your judgment, your wide reading, and your knowledge of the children you serve to recommend quality literature that keeps kids motivated and reading.

Assignments in Action: Looking into Picture Books

1. First Lines Quiz

Take the "Children's Literature Literacy Test" on Kaye Vandergrift's website, http:// www.scils.rutgers.edu/~kvander/firstlinesindex.html. How many of these famous first lines do you recognize from well-known picture books? What are some of your own favorite picture books? Are there any favorite lines or first lines that are quote-worthy? Quotes like these make wonderful banners for library walls or doors. You can then challenge children to share their own favorites, too.

2. Picture Book Illustrations as Fine Art

The art of the children's picture book is gradually becoming appreciated in the larger art world. Many of the works of original art that children's book illustrators create for a picture book have become valuable and collectable pieces fetching thousands of dollars for a single work. Several galleries specialize in children's book art, many with images available for viewing on the Web. Look for examples at the following:

R. Michelson Galleries in Northampton, Massachusetts
http://www.rmichelson.com

Child at Heart Gallery in Newburyport, Massachusetts
http://childatheartartgallery.com/

Elizabeth Stone Gallery in Alexandria, Virginia
http://www.elizabethstonegallery.com

Every Picture Tells a Story in Santa Monica, California
http://www.everypicture.com

Many libraries have chosen to adorn their children's areas with original art from children's books, when they can afford the investment. For example, the Betty Brinn Children's Room of the central library in Milwaukee, Wisconsin, is full of the work of Lois Ehlert (who hails from Milwaukee), including 31 different animals designed by Ehlert in a variety of colors, which appear in the floor. Research which children's book illustrators live in your region or area. How might you showcase them and their work in your library? How might you persuade the powers that be to invest in an original piece by a children's book illustrator to be featured in your children's area? Build a case for why art is important in children's lives and books.

3. Promoting Picture Books

A good librarian is always looking for new and innovative ways to share stories and promote reading. One creative approach is using the video features of http://www .YouTube.com, a source of video clips created by viewers themselves. Some librarians are using YouTube, Facebook, and Twitter to feature quick booktalks, digital trailers, and mini story hours for their communities and the public at large. Experiment with various Web 2.0 tools yourself. Partner with a buddy and film a one-minute read aloud (excerpt) or booktalk. If you're brave enough, post it on YouTube, TeacherTube, or another outlet to share. Consider experimenting creatively to feature a favorite picture book with props, commentary, music, and so on.

3

Traditional Tales

"The Mouse Moral: Knowing in part may make a fine tale, but wisdom comes from seeing the whole."
From *Seven Blind Mice* by Ed Young
(Philomel, 1992)

In this chapter, you will learn about traditional tales for children, from picture book folktales to myths, legends, and tall tales. We'll consider the role of the reteller and the storyteller, and look at cultural variants of tale types from around the world. We'll investigate how one evaluates traditional literature and which awards recognize excellence in this genre. From Aesop to modern "fractured" fairy tales, we'll dig deep into the oldest form of children's literature.

INTRODUCTION

Psychologists tell us that traditional literature grows out of our basic human need to explain ourselves and our world. Why are we here? How can we all get along? The knowledge and stories of our ancestors were passed by word of mouth from generation to generation long before this information was recorded in written form. The stories, traditions, customs, and sayings of folk culture are of such long duration—some of them over thousands of years old—that they cannot be traced to one single person. Who was the originator of tales such as "Cinderella"? No one knows for sure. All cultures participate in storytelling and have children's lore, chants, rhymes, riddles, and proverbs. Indeed, folklore in this form served as a means of literacy development for preliterate societies in the past and still functions this way in the present in many ways. (Consider playgrounds and laptime.) So children often bring a wealth of background knowledge of this type of language and activity whatever their level of reading or writing or general education. They may not all be familiar with "Jack and Jill" and "Humpty Dumpty," if they hail from a variety of cultural backgrounds, but they are likely to have heard rhymes, songs, and stories of some kind from their own families, communities, and cultures.

Stories survived for hundreds of years before they were available in written form. We can trace traditional stories to an author or adapter, although this individual is not its true originator. Anthropologists and linguists often spend years studying groups and gathering their folklore. For example, most people are familiar with the brothers Grimm (Jakob and Wilhelm) who transcribed German folktales based on interviews and research and published their *Household Tales* in 1812. Many of the earliest books published for children fall into the category of traditional literature, including *Aesop's Fables* published by William Caxton in England in 1484, and *Tales of Mother Goose* retold by Charles Perrault and published in France in 1697. Can you see why this genre was so quick to become popular with children? The timeless appeal endures even now into the twenty-first century.

Many types of traditional literature published in trade book format are available to today's children. They can read and listen to the entire range from riddles and rhymes to fables, fairy and folktales, myths, and legends. Picture book versions of folktales are one way that children understand the standards of behavior of a culture (Bosma, 1992). Stories help children see what is expected of them as they grow up. For example, it is thought that the underlying caution of "Little Red Riding Hood" is to instill a fear of "stranger danger," but the story also reinforces the importance of caring for one's elders. And for children, of course, the adventure of the story (being alone in the woods) is quite compelling enough, whether they articulate any deeper themes or not. Still, the stories have lasted all this time because both layers are present, the life lesson and the vicarious thrill. Many scholars such as Jack Zipes, Maria Tatar, and Bruno Bettelheim have devoted their lives to the study and analysis of traditional literature from literary, psychoanalytical, and even feminist perspectives, revealing layers of meaning and significance to our adult understanding of the human story.

When we consider a lifetime of reading, we realize that many allusions to traditional literature and folktales appear in longer works of contemporary fiction and nonfiction. Many modern fantasies, for example, borrow or echo literary motifs and patterns found in myths and legends and folktales, such as in the *Percy Jackson* series, *Heroes of Olympus* series, and *Kane Chronicles*, all by Rick Riordan (Hyperion, 2005), or the *Harry Potter* books by J. K. Rowling. Such books have mythic and legendary characters that parallel Prometheus, Aeneas, Odysseus, Jason, and King Arthur. Children can begin to see that many protagonists lack important information about their births, set out on quests to correct wrongs, have access to magic in their fights against evil, and once successful, return home to help others. They will glean even more from the story with a prior knowledge of the root tales from traditional literature.

Finally, traditional literature also has many attributes that appeal to children. It is simple and direct, with a fast-moving plot and stock characters they immediately recognize. The language is generally more informal, and there are motifs and magic that engage their sense of wonder and possibility. Three wishes! Magic eggs! Why not? The predictable endings in which the good are generally rewarded and the evil are punished please their sense of justice. On top of this, traditional tales are a longtime staple of campfires, bedtimes, and story hours, and you can see why this genre is worthy of further study.

History in Action: Aesop

Possibly the very earliest stories for children are the fables attributed to Aesop. They've been retold, adapted, illustrated, animated, filmed, and performed thousands of times over and still hold appeal to children who enjoy animal stories full of characters that exhibit human foibles. However, the roots of the oral fable tradition go back all the way to India and the Panchatantra tales in Sanskrit and were later adopted by early Buddhists as Jataka tales of wisdom. Later, some of these fables made their way to Alexandria where the tales included a moral to sum up the teaching of the fable.

We know very little that is definitive about the actual man who was "Aesop" or whether there ever was such a person at all. Legend has it he was a sixth-century BCE Greek slave, but many scholars believe him to have been African. More than likely the name is a pseudonym for a storyteller noted for animal fables, making the name "Aesop" eventually synonymous with the Western fable tradition. Modern collections list approximately 200 Aesop fables, but there is no way of knowing who invented which tales or what their original roots might have been. Additional fables were added to the Aesop repertoire over the centuries and retold and compiled by the likes of Demetrius of Phaleron, translated into Latin in the fourth century BCE by Phaedrus, a freed slave in the house of the Roman emperor Augustus, and translated into Greek by Babrius in the second century CE. Some say Socrates adapted these fables into verse while he was in prison. Later editions were translated into Arabic and Hebrew, expanding and enriching the repertoire. These fables influenced later writers, notably the seventeenth-century French poet and fabulist Jean de la Fontaine and the nineteenth-century Russian writer Leo Tolstoy.

Aesop's fables have been published in anthologies and individual story collections and adapted and illustrated by a variety of stellar talents in the world of children's books from Arthur Rackham to Randolph Caldecott, Mitsumasa Anno to James Marshall, Jerry Pinkney to Calef Brown. Single tales have also been adapted into graphic novels, as well as film and cartoon versions. The Web is a great source of all things Aesop:

1. For online full-text fables, Project Gutenberg is an excellent source: http://www .gutenberg.org/browse/authors/a#a18
2. The "World Wide School" library offers full-text fables, too: http://www.worldwide school.org/library/books/socl/customsetiquettefolklore/AesopsFables/toc.html
3. This searchable database offers 600 English fables with Latin and Greek texts: http://www.mythfolklore.net/aesopica/
4. Free audio versions of Aesop's fables are also available on LibriVox: https://catalog .librivox.org/
5. An online collection of 650-plus fables, indexed, with morals listed, many with audio: http://aesopfables.com/
6. Child-friendly set of 250-plus fables organized in handy animal categories: http:// aesopsfables.org/

Young children who enjoy animal tales will find fables appealing, and older children may be even better suited to interpret the allegorical meanings of the tales. They can collect multiple versions of a popular tale to compare (like "The Tortoise and the Hare") or seek out fables from other cultures and traditions around the world. Understanding the deep roots of the fable tradition will help them feel connected to an ancient art of storytelling with universal themes and motifs.

DEFINITIONS

The genre of "traditional tales" derives from the oral *tradition*, stories passed down from generation to generation through storytellers, told for hundreds of years before being written down. This could be considered our most basic form of literature, with all other forms built upon this foundation. These are the creation legends and the younger brother challenges and the exaggerated adventure tales that were tried and tested orally for generations before being put into print. One of the distinctive features of the books in this genre is that there are no known authors for these stories. Instead we identify story *adapters* or *retellers.*

In the world of children's literature, traditional tales include a wide range of published variations, including Mother Goose rhymes, folktales, myths, fables, legends, and tall tales. Indeed, even the category of "folktale" includes fairy tales, pour quoi tales, trickster tales, and even modern fractured tales and literary created folktales, such as Hans Christian Andersen's "The Little Mermaid," which is a tale of his own invention, not a retold oral folktale. (Confused? Many people think of Andersen as a folk storyteller when in actuality he created all his stories from his imagination and experience.)

Of all the forms traditional literature can take, folktales make up the bulk of the children's books that are published. These stories are usually produced as individual picture books, with modern illustrators interpreting the traditional tales. Traditional tales have been a very popular niche in the children's publishing market over the years, and many well-written and beautifully illustrated versions can be found that have immense appeal across ages. The best examples read well aloud, reflecting the flavor of an oral tale well told, as well as having distinctive illustrations that make the story fresh and vivid. In addition, the illustrations help cue the reader or listener to important story elements, as well as provide visual cultural details for the story. The art of the folktale should also reflect careful study of the root culture so that the language and illustrations accurately reflect the story's culture for the reader. *Mufaro's Beautiful Daughters*, for example (Steptoe, 1987), is an outstanding example of a "Cinderella" or "good sister/bad sister" tale that is rooted in the flora and fauna of Zimbabwe, and yet it reflects a universality in character and theme that appeals to children in Africa and beyond. In addition, studying folktale variants or versions from other cultures can add depth to our understanding of the basic human characteristics underlying the simple folk story.

Understanding the difference between variants and versions can be tricky since tales continue to evolve with every telling. A *variant* is an example of a tale that comes from a root culture. For example, *Yeh-Shen* by Ed Young (Ai-Ling Louie; Philomel, 1989) is another variant of the Cinderella or good sister/bad sister traditional tale, in this case from China. It is as true to the Chinese tale as possible as interpreted by the artist and reteller Ed Young. On the other hand, *Bubba, the Cowboy Prince* (Scholastic, 2001) by Helen Ketteman is a *version* of the Cinderella tale that comes from Ketteman's imagination and is not attempting to reflect a root culture. There is no age-old "Texan" version of Cinderella; this is a parody of the European variant of Cinderella set in a Texas tall tale realm. Fortunately, there are many types of folktales to choose from with fascinating examples from all around the world to consider, as well as modern versions to share for fun. Professional storytellers and folklore scholars rely on the extensive Aarne-Thompson tale type index to identify the plot patterns, narrative structures, and motifs of folktales in hundreds of numbered categories. For example, Cinderella is tale type #510A with other "persecuted heroines" identified as a multitude of other tale types.

Librarians in Action: Linking Schools and Libraries through Storytelling

Emily Chasse is librarian/storyteller/teacher for the Burritt Public Library, Central Connecticut State University, in New Britain, Connecticut. She earned her master of library science degree from the University of Rhode Island in 1979 and started her library work as a children's librarian with the public library in Plainville, Connecticut. She taught children's literature at Manchester Community College from 1981 to 1983 and has been at Burritt since 1986. She tells tales with all ages, focusing on traditional tales and peace tales. Here, she provides basic steps for any librarian to follow in getting started in the storytelling tradition.

Children's Librarians Telling Tales in the Classroom
by Emily Chasse

I once visited a fifth grade classroom while they were studying Japan and told one of the classic Japanese folktales, "Peach Boy." When I was finished, a small child of Japanese descent spoke up, "Oh, my grandma tells me that story all the time! It's one of my favorites." I saw the other children look at him with admiration, but he seemed embarrassed and got very quiet. I told him how pleased I was to hear that and was glad that his grandma told him Japanese tales. A week later, the classroom teacher stopped me to let me know that in the past she often had to stop other children from picking on that child because he was so small and quiet, but since my storytelling visit when the boy had spoken up, the other children were treating him differently and with newfound respect.

Children's librarians have a wonderful audience waiting for them in the classrooms of local schools. Teachers and students welcome librarians who can give them the gift of stories. Lewis Carroll, author of *Alice's Adventures in Wonderland*, actually called stories "love gifts," which is exactly how children view them. One of the most important gifts children's librarians can give to children in the classroom is through storytelling.

Some people are natural storytellers, while most need to learn the basics of telling tales. Learning to tell tales can be a fun and delightful activity. Librarians interested in learning to tell tales can begin with the following steps.

1. Read and listen to a wide variety of tales. The Dewey Decimal 398 section of books, videos, and DVDs contains many wonderful tales and collections of stories.
2. Find a tale that you really love and would like to share with others.
3. Read the story for sheer pleasure and reread it until you feel you have a sense of the story, characters, setting, mood, and action.
4. Don't try to memorize the story, but as you retell it to yourself, you'll gain a sense of how you'll tell it with your voice, actions, and gestures. In this way you can learn it and practice telling it again and again.
5. Write the key points or an outline of the story onto small index cards that can be reviewed before a performance.
6. Choose a friend or family member for your first performance audience. Let them make comments and suggestions on your presentation and use their ideas to continue working on the story.
7. Consult with other tellers and storytelling groups to work on your tale presentation skills. Consider selecting stories with refrains that invite child participation or using simple props, if you need help feeling less nervous or self-conscious.
8. When you feel comfortable telling a few tales, schedule folktale performances with classrooms in local schools. These can be combined with booktalks to highlight the library collection and new titles of fiction and nonfiction books, too.

Hearing performances of folk and fairy tales by children's librarians provides many benefits to children. By experiencing the same tale simultaneously, the teachers, students, and the librarians share important feelings and emotions. This creates a common bond, which results in positive future encounters. This common bond helps everyone see and realize we are all human beings and can enjoy feelings of kindness, pride, and hope while at the same time seeing our mistakes as we are all also susceptible to feelings of anger, violence, envy, and greed. Storytelling, when done well, can also produce a restful and calm feeling. Ultimately, the stories help all children with some of the psychological and social aspects of growing up. Hearing stories encourages the art of listening and provides a chance to share positive aspects of various cultures and ethnic history and customs. Children from various backgrounds enjoy hearing tales told from their countries or cultures. It can also elevate them in the eyes of their classmates.

Educationally, telling tales can have other advantages. Hearing stories can expand and increase vocabulary and help children understand that there is a beginning, middle, and end to tales. While enjoying entertaining tales, children can form pictures in their minds of the characters, setting, and actions. This visualization is an important part of creativity and imagination. All of these educational benefits can lead directly into support for many areas of classroom curriculum. Children's librarians can collaborate with teachers on instructional units related to folktales. There are also books and websites that offer a variety of classroom activities focusing on folktales, fairy tales, and legends, including:

Garrity, Linda K. 1999. *The Tale Spinner: Folktales, Themes, and Activities.* Golden, CO: Fulcrum Resources.

Polette, Nancy. 2000. *Gifted Books, Gifted Readers: Literature Activities to Excite Young Minds.* Englewood, CO: Libraries Unlimited.

Polette, Nancy. 2006. *Books Every Child Should Know: The Literature Quiz Book.* Englewood, CO: Libraries Unlimited.

Lesson plans and activities:

http://edsitement.neh.gov/view_lesson_plan.asp?id=387

TYPES OF TRADITIONAL TALES

Traditional literature for young people today can be found in both picture book format and in anthologies or collections. The picture book format has particular appeal because of the abundance of illustrations that can help interpret and extend the story. Don't assume all children are familiar with the common "core" of folk literature such as the "Three Little Pigs" or "Jack and the Beanstalk." Many children have missed these classics along the way and enjoy them even as intermediate-level readers. Also, don't assume that all traditional tales are suitable for young children just because they appear in picture book form. Many are complicated or sophisticated and more appropriate for an older child. In addition, sharing variants of a common story from multiple cultures is one way to add interest for older children, or looking for modern references and allusions to ancient tales is another hook for middle graders.

Often children and adults both get confused the more they try to categorize all the different kinds of tales. The thing to keep in mind is this: all of these stories come from the oral tradition and can't be traced to any individual writer. The book should clearly indicate on the cover or on the inside title page who the adapter or reteller or illustrator of the story is. If the *author* is listed, it is not technically part of the traditional literature genre, even if it begins "once upon a time" and has all the usual ingredients. Of course authors today (like Jon Scieszka) are experimenting with this genre formula and breaking all the rules. So don't worry about memorizing literary genre definitions as much as about making sure children have an enthusiastic introduction to traditional literature of all kinds. Not only will you find that children of all ages enjoy the genre immensely, but these stories are also excellent springboards for dramatic skits and for writing activities because they are so predictable and formulaic. And for fantasy-lovers, this genre is an important source of motifs, characters, and themes they will encounter again and again in fantasy fiction as they get older.

Folktales

What is a folktale? Folktales are probably the largest portion of traditional literature for children, rooted in oral tellings and evolving with each retelling and interpretation, yet amazingly resilient and consistent across the ages. They are imaginary stories that embody a simple truth about life. Over the centuries, a handful of individuals have had their names attached to the folktales they've collected, including the Brothers Grimm (in Germany), Charles Perrault (in France), Andrew Lang (*The Red Fairy Book*, *The Blue Fairy Book*, etc.) and Joseph Jacobs (in England), Alexander Afanasyev (in Russia), and Peter Asbjørnsen and Jorgen Moe (in Norway). Many of their written versions have since been retold and adapted in picture book form, such as "Red Riding Hood" (Germany), "Cinderella" (France), "Jack and the Beanstalk" (England), "The Turnip" (Russia), and the "Billy Goats Gruff" (Norway). However, writing the stories down is a relatively recent innovation of the last few hundred years and some cultures have taboos against doing so, even now.

Fortunately, more and more folktales are available in anthologies or single story versions for sharing with children. They contain special conventions and motifs, often with formulaic beginnings and endings, strong repetition and rhythm in the language, and a bit of magic or exaggeration. There are also several subtypes of folktales including cumulative tales, pour quoi tales, beast tales, fairy tales, realistic tales, noodlehead tales, and trickster tales. The Sur-LaLune website is a rich online resource with annotations, illustrations, and histories for nearly 50 different annotated tales, as well as over 1600 folktales and fairy tales from around the world in more than 40 full-text eBooks (http://www.surlalunefairytales.com/). Here are a handful of examples to demonstrate the variety of types and titles of folktales for children.

> *Cumulative tales* are very repetitive with a reiteration of story details or refrains over and over again, as in "The House That Jack Built" or "The Gingerbread Man."
>
> *Pour quoi tales* are called the "why" stories of folklore because they try to examine the animalistic traits or characteristics of human customs. ("Pour quoi" is French for "why" or "how come?") Many Native American folktales are "why" stories, such as *How Chipmunk Got His Stripes* by Joseph and James Bruchac (Puffin, reprinted 2003).
>
> *Beast tales* in which animals act and talk like humans are often considered children's favorites. This includes the classic "The Three Pigs," for example. Many African American stories are "wise beast/foolish beast" tales of how one animal outwits another.
>
> *Fairy tales* are the "and they all lived happily ever after" kind of stories full of magic, and often fairies, such as "Snow White" and "Cinderella."
>
> *Realistic tales* contain no magic or talking animals but rather make their points through humor or irony. The Jewish folktale "It Could Always Be Worse" is an example of this type of tale.
>
> *Noodlehead tales* center around a silly, nonsensical character who does everything wrong and yet all is well in the end as with the character of Anthony in Tomie de Paola's "Strega Nona" stories.
>
> *Trickster tales* revolve around a central character who uses his or her wits, wiles, and sometimes deception to trick other, usually bigger, stronger characters. The "Anansi" stories from Africa are typical of this type of tale.

Myths

Traditional literature has also served to educate the listener/reader about the creation of the world and the history of its peoples. Myths explain, among other things, the creation of the world, the separation of light and dark, the emergence of animals, and so on. They tend to focus on the "big picture" of the natural order of things. Children can also find that different cultures have explained these phenomena in different ways throughout the ages, as in Virginia Hamilton's *In the Beginning* (Harcourt, 1988). Greek, Norse, and Roman mythology also continues to fascinate young people today and the classic collection, Ingri and Edgar D'Aulaire's *Book of Greek Myths* (Delacorte, reprinted 1992), continues to be a staple. Or look for Eric Kimmel's retellings in *The McElderry Book of Greek Myths* (Simon & Schuster, 2008), part of a three-book series that also includes Aesop's Fables and the Grimm fairy tales. These myths are often hero myths that do not seek to explain anything but instead are the grand adventures of the gods. Many high school teachers find that small collections and picture book versions of myths are more readable for their ESL learners and struggling readers. They are also intrigued at the parallels between the supernatural powers of the gods of mythology with the superhuman abilities of the cartoon and television heroes of popular culture, such as Superman, Batman, the X-Men, and so on. Rick Riordan's extremely popular *Percy Jackson* fantasy series of novels, for example, helped fuel interest in the Greek myths once again, with its hero who has superpowers derived from his father, the god Poseidon.

Legends

Legends are stories about the heroic deeds of historical figures, like saints, heroes, or kings, such as King Arthur, or retellings of a heroic event that may be based on some actual happening. The people in legends often really existed, but their lives and deeds may be embellished in the story or there may be a kernel of truth that is much elaborated upon to create a story. "Many people think of them as historical accounts, even though the basic historical facts generally have been embroidered upon and may even be questionable" (Mitchell, 2003, p. 238). Unlike other traditional tales, legends are usually associated with particular times and places in history. One unusual example is the *DK Read & Listen: Robin Hood* by Neil Philip (DK Children, 2000) in the Eyewitness format melding story, background information, and audio recording. Many of these legends are also available in novel-length form as Dover Children's Thrift Classics and in the Puffin classics series, including Robin Hood, King Arthur, the Trojan War, and the like.

Some scholars also include epics and ballads in this category since they serve a similar function, recounting the adventures of a heroic figure like Odysseus, for example, often through poetry or song. According to children's literature professor Barbara Kiefer (2010, p. 269), "an epic is a long narrative or a cycle of stories clustering around the actions of a single hero." For children, one popular example of an epic adaptation is Mary Pope Osborne's "Tales from the Odyssey" series of short novels based on episodes from Homer's *Odyssey.*

Fables

Fables are usually very short stories with just a few animal characters and explicit lessons designed to teach a stated moral. Critic and scholar David Russell (2011) points out that young children frequently miss the intended message of the morals presented in fables because of the abstraction of the message mirrored through animal behavior and attitudes. Yet, children enjoy the fables for their clever animal characters and clear conflicts even if they don't overtly internalize the morals of the stories. And the stories generally make dramatic read alouds and spontaneous skits. Look for Jerry Pinkney's Caldecott medal book, *The Lion and the Mouse* (Little, Brown, 2009), or his *The Tortoise and the Hare* (Little, Brown, 2013), or his picture book collection of *Aesop's Fables* (Chronicle, 2000). Or consider Brad Sneed's picture book collection of *Aesop's Fables* (Dial, 2003), which presents fresh perspectives on fifteen favorite fables, with one additional fable—"told only in the pictures . . . hidden somewhere between these covers" of the book. Or seek out Joseph and James Bruchac's picture book *Turtle's Race with Beaver* (Dial, 2003), for a retelling of the classic "Tortoise and the Hare" fable, but from the Seneca oral tradition.

Tall Tales

The perfect complement to history, geography, or social studies is the tall tale. These are exaggerated narratives containing oversized boisterous characters, humorous actions, and picturesque language, often set in specific regions and sometimes based on a real figure in history. Children can sit spellbound as they listen to stories of Paul Bunyan, Mike Fink, John Henry, and Pecos Bill. Many experts view tall tales as uniquely American, based on the "brag" or "boast" tales told on the frontier of the United States during the westward expansion. A variety of such humorous or hyperbolic tales are available in many excellent picture book or tall tale collections such as Julius Lester's retelling of the *John Henry* tale, illustrated by Jerry Pinkney (Dial, 1994), or *Lies and Other Tall Tales* collected by Zora Neale Hurston, adapted and illustrated by Christopher Myers (HarperCollins, 2005). There are also more and more stories of larger-than-life women from tall tale lore such as Anne Isaacs's *Swamp Angel*, illustrated by Paul Zelinsky (Dutton, 1994); Virginia Hamilton's *Her Stories*, illustrated by Leo and Diane Dillon (Blue Sky Press, 1995); Pat Mora's *Doña Flor: A Tall Tale About a Giant Woman with a Great Big Heart*, illustrated by Raul Colón (Knopf, 2005); and *Granite Baby* by Lynne Bertrand, illustrated by Kevin Hawkes (Farrar, Straus & Giroux, 2005).

Religious Stories

How do you feel about Bible stories as children's literature? Can we share those stories in the library? According to professor and writer Charlotte Huck, the Bible has an important and rightful place in any "comprehensive discussion of traditional literature because it is a written record of people's continuing search to understand themselves and their relationships with each other and their creator. It makes little sense to tell children the story of Jack the Giant Killer but to deny them the stories of David and Goliath. . . . Our fear should not be that children will know the Bible; rather it should be that they will not know it" (2000, p. 334).

Interestingly, in 1963 the Supreme Court asserted "one's education is not complete without a study of comparative religion or the history of religion and its relationship to the advancement of civilization. It certainly may be said that the Bible is worthy of study for its literary and historic qualities." The key is in providing a balanced exposure to multiple religious perspectives and in treating religious stories as literature and not as doctrine. Tricky business in many communities. However, there are many children's books that are based on religious stories, such as these two Caldecott medal–winning books: *Saint George and the Dragon*, retold by Margaret Hodges and illustrated by Trina Schart Hyman (Little, Brown, 1985), and *Noah's Ark* by Peter Spier (Doubleday, 1977). Indeed, there are probably more picture book versions of the story of "Noah and the Ark" than any other Old Testament story. And of course there are "flood" stories in other cultures and religious traditions, too.

Literary Tales

Some authors choose to create completely new tales using traditional folk motifs and styles. These stories are often referred to as "literary tales" since they were not passed on through the oral tradition and have *known* authors. Hans Christian Andersen's stories such as *The Ugly Duckling*, illustrated by Jerry Pinkney (HarperCollins, 1999), is a notable example of a literary tale, not a folktale or traditional tale. It may begin with "once upon a time," but it comes from the imagination of Hans Christian Andersen, not from centuries of oral storytelling. Jane Yolen is also known for creating many lovely literary tales in the style of traditional tales, as well as retellings of oral folktales from around the world. Patricia McKissack has created stories based on the wisdom and rhythms of traditional African American storytellers in her collections, *Porch Lies: Tales of Slicksters, Tricksters, and Other Wily Characters* (Random House, 2006) and the previous companion volume, *The Dark Thirty: Southern Tales of the Supernatural* (Knopf, 1996). One might also consider the "fractured" fairy tale to be a "literary" or created tale with a known author, but since those are generally intentionally humorous and even outrageous, they have earned their own category, which follows.

Fractured Fairy Tales

Older children really enjoy the "fractured" fairy tale in which authors have altered, parodied, or modernized the characters, setting, plots, or language of more traditional well-known tales. These books are especially appealing for more advanced readers or older kids familiar with the basic versions. However, many children have missed the so-called "originals" or know tales from other cultural traditions and not the usual "Three Bears" or "Cinderella" root tales. Thus a parody is less meaningful if they don't understand what is being parodied. You may find it valuable to compare the fractured versions with the traditional European (or other) antecedents that provide opportunities to discuss the differences. Advanced readers may later enjoy creating their own fractured fairy tales.

Jon Scieszka's *The True Story of the Three Little Pigs* (Viking, 1989) remains one of the most popular examples of this "subgenre." Children also enjoy Scieszka's other "folk" story spoofs like *The Stinky Cheese Man* (Viking, 1992) and *Squids Will Be Squids* (Viking, 1998), among others. Other popular examples in picture book form are Diane Stanley's *Rumpelstiltskin's Daughter* (HarperCollins, 1997) or *The Trouble with Wishes* (HarperCollins, 2007), or Mini Grey's *The Very Smart Pea and the Princess-to-Be* (Knopf, 2003). Nowadays, there are probably more humorous fractured tales being published than classic oral-based traditional tales—an interesting shift.

MAJOR RETELLERS OF TRADITIONAL TALES

Since the days of the Brothers Grimm, Joseph Jacobs, and Asbjørnsen and Moe, several individuals have built quite a reputation for retelling or adapting or illustrating traditional oral tales for children. This generally takes the form of a picture book featuring a single folktale, legend, or myth. Some retellers gather stories of a similar type from a variety of cultures and traditions into anthologies, as well. But each is careful to do the research needed to represent the root culture authentically, often including source notes and other documentation.

Retellers Represent the World

The following list of story retellers and adapters highlights one exemplary title of a picture book or anthology by each person. Each of these people has collected, edited, adapted, or illustrated many more tales, too. In addition, these names and books are organized along a map of the earth's continents (except Antarctica). This reveals an ever-growing variety of cultures represented in traditional tales for children with room for many more to come. Some of these authors/retellers hail from the world region they depict in stories and others rely on careful research to lay the foundation for their story retellings.

Asia

Demi, *The Legend of St. Nicolas* (McElderry, 2003)
Yumi Heo, *The Green Frogs: A Korean Folktale* (Houghton Mifflin, 1996)
Jeanne Lee, *I Once Was a Monkey* (Farrar, Straus & Giroux, 1999)

Allen Say, *The Boy in the Garden* (Houghton Mifflin, 2010)
Laurence Yep, *The Dragon Prince: A Chinese Beauty and the Beast Tale* (HarperCollins, 1999)
Ed Young, *The Sons of the Dragon King* (Atheneum, 2004)

Africa

Verna Aardema, *Why Mosquitoes Buzz in People's Ears* (Dial, 1975)
Ashley Bryan, *Beautiful Blackbird* (Simon & Schuster, 2003)
Baba Wague Diakite, *The Pot of Wisdom: Ananse Stories* (Groundwood, 2001)
Nelson Mandela, *Nelson Mandela's Favorite African Folktales* (W. W. Norton, 2004)
John Steptoe, *Mufaro's Beautiful Daughters* (HarperCollins, 1987)
Eleanora E. Tate, *Retold African Myths* (Perfection Learning, 1993)

North America

Jim Aylesworth, *Old Black Fly* (Henry Holt, 1992)
Joseph Bruchac, *Raccoon's Last Race: A Traditional Abenaki Story* (Penguin, 2004)
Paul Goble, *The Girl Who Loved Wild Horses* (Bradbury, 1978)
Virginia Hamilton, *The People Could Fly* (Random House, 2007)
Steven Kellogg, *Pecos Bill* (HarperCollins, 1995)
Julius Lester, *John Henry* (Penguin, 1994)
Gerald McDermott, *Arrow to the Sun* (Viking, 1974)
Pat Mora, *Doña Flor: A Tall Tale About a Giant Woman with a Great Big Heart* (Knopf, 2005)
Yuyi Morales, *Just a Minute: A Trickster Tale and Counting Book* (Chronicle, 2003)
Gayle Ross, *How Rabbit Tricked Otter and Other Cherokee Trickster Stories* (Tandem, 2003)
Robert D. San Souci, *Sister Tricksters: Southern Tales of Clever Females* (August House, 2006)

South America

Alma Flor Ada, *The Rooster Who Went to His Uncle's Wedding: A Latin American Folktale* (Penguin, 1993)
Patricia Aldana, *Jade and Iron: Latin American Tales from Two Cultures* (Groundwood, 1996)
John Bierhorst, *Latin American Folktales: Stories from Hispanic and Indian Traditions* (Pantheon, 2001)
Carmen Diana Dearden, *Little Book of Latin American Folktales* (Groundwood, 2003)

Lulu Delacre, *Arrorró Mi Niño: Latino Lullabies and Gentle Games* (Scholastic, 2004)

Europe

Jan Brett, *Beauty and the Beast* (Putnam, 2011)
Tomie de Paola, *Strega Nona* (Simon & Schuster, 1997)
Paul Galdone, *Rumpelstiltskin* (Book Wholesalers, 2002)
Margaret Hodges, *The Legend of Saint Christopher* (Eerdmans, 2004)
Trina Schart Hyman, *Rapunzel* (Holiday House, 2001)
Eric Kimmel, *The Golem's Latkes* (Two Lions, 2011)
Deborah Nourse Lattimore, *Medusa* (HarperCollins, 2000)
Mary Pope Osborne, *Favorite Greek Myths* (Scholastic, 1989)
Simms Taback, *Joseph Had a Little Overcoat* (Viking, 1999)
David Wisniewski, *Golem* (Clarion, 1996)
Jane Yolen, *Jason and the Gorgon's Blood* (HarperCollins, 2004)
Paul Zelinsky, *Rapunzel* (Dutton, 1997)

Australia

Dal Burns, *The Kookaburra and Other Stories* (PublishAmerica, 2007)
Eric Maddern, *Rainbow Bird: An Aboriginal Folktale from Northern Australia* (Little, Brown, 1993)
Meme McDonald, *The Way of the Birds* (Allen & Unwin, 1996)

Strive to share stories from a variety of cultures as you incorporate traditional literature into your storytime repertoire. Locate the root culture on a map and show the children where the story comes from. Look for other connections to make between the story's culture and other traditions from the culture via arts, crafts, and songs. Many of these story collectors have multiple folktales to their credit, such as Ed Young, Ashley Bryan, Joseph Bruchac, or Jane Yolen, so a "reteller study" could offer multiple tales for telling, comparing, and studying the root cultures. Look for storytelling videos on YouTube and other outlets, such as the Center for Digital Storytelling and Marshall Cavendish's Story Teller, as well as authors' own websites.

Authors in Action: Ashley Bryan

Ashley Bryan grew up in Harlem, served in the U.S. Army, studied art in France and Germany on a Fulbright scholarship, taught for several years at Dartmouth College, and now lives on a small island off the coast of Maine. He has authored and illustrated more than 30 books for children, many of them African folktales, and has won the Coretta Scott King Award for illustration and for writing, as well as several CSK honor citations and ALA Notable distinctions. He is highly regarded as an inspiring presenter and storyteller. Two video documentaries feature his life and work: a National Geographic production (1984) and *Meet Ashley Bryan: Storyteller, Artist, Writer* (American School Publishers, 1992), and several YouTube videos feature his storytelling and poetry reading. Also, check out his inspiring, illustrated autobiography, *Ashley Bryan: Words to My Life's Song* (Atheneum, 2009). Here he addresses the importance of cultural identity in children's books.

Discovering Ethnicity through Children's Books
by Ashley Bryan

There are so many ways in which we learn about life and the self. Each day opens paths to this exploration. For many of us, books play a major role in that adventure.

I grew up in a large family during the Great Depression. The family funds for books were limited, but there were always stacks of books in the home. My brothers, sisters, and I saw to that. We borrowed books from the Public Library. We made bookcases out of discarded orange crates and placed the books on these shelves so that we could share them and keep track of them. It made us feel that we had our own home library, a wonderful feeling.

I read folk tales and fairy tales of many countries, novels, biographies, and poetry. At that time I knew very little about books by or about black people. The books that existed were not assigned in my school classes. Since books meant so much to me, this was unfortunate. I entered the world of books I read, but missed the opportunity of identifying with black people in the stories.

My sense of self and knowledge of black contributions came from the home and the black community in New York City where I was raised. This support is basic, of course, but with the complement of books, one's identity is strengthened and assured.

Today the book world recognizes the need for books that represent the people from all over the world who make up our United States. There is now a growing list of books telling these stories, written and illustrated by the people of these various cultures. Their stories are also told by others who have loved and studied the life and history of cultures other than their own. They offer sensitive works of these cultures as well.

A librarian once told me of a black youngster visiting in her library. He was looking at a painting of the Nativity in my Christmas book of black American spirituals, *What a Morning*. Suddenly he exclaimed, "That the Baby Jesus? Looks just like me! Huh, I could be the Baby Jesus!"

This is an exciting experience for the reader. Children can now see their images in illustrated books and in stories of their people. They make a direct connection to these pictures and stories.

It is important to affirm our ancestry, to learn about our people while learning about others. When we are centered in the gifts our people have offered, we become rooted in who we are and can stand up to any challenge. This gives the balance we need for our daily pursuit of knowledge.

When I meet with audiences, I often begin my program with the poem by Langston Hughes, "My People." In this poem, Langston Hughes sings of the beauty of his people's faces, their eyes, their souls. The poem celebrates the gifts of each person who recites it. When the audience recites this poem with me, I know we have come together.

I now have my own home library. My collection includes the world. I have a growing collection of books on black life. Most are by black authors and illustrators, some by artists of other backgrounds. The illustrated book is my special love. The variety of approaches chosen by the artist keeps me in touch with all that has happened and is happening in the world of art.

My bookshelves are no longer the orange crates I put together as a child. I keep building or buying bookshelves to hold the collection. I am proud of my own home library.

I ask the children at my school programs, "How many of you use the public library?" All hands go up. I ask, "How many of you use the school library?" All hands go up. I then ask, "How many of you are building your own home library?" Fewer hands go up.

I then ask that they promise to keep a jar on hand into which goes the extra coins—for books. When enough coins are saved, a book is added to their own home library. I suggest that sometimes they remember to choose a book about their people.

Used with permission from the Children's Book Council.

One Book in Action: Beautiful Blackbird

To focus on one book of traditional tales, let's look at Ashley Bryan's *Beautiful Blackbird* (Atheneum, 2003), winner of the Coretta Scott King award for illustration in 2004, as a model for folktale study. In this African folktale, the birds of the forest envy Blackbird his unique dark beauty since they are only made of colors, and they beg him to share his blackness with them. As he decorates each of them with a bit of black, he also teaches them about the quality of inner beauty and individuality. This rousing and musical adaptation of a tale of the Ila-speaking people of Zambia begs to be read aloud, chanted, and performed. And obviously the art of the book is prize-worthy with its riot of color in cut-paper collage images of birds of all shapes and sizes.

Reading Aloud *Blackbird*

The true test of a folktale is its read aloud–ability since folktales are all originally oral tales and intended to be passed on from teller to listener. Bryan's *Beautiful Blackbird* is an outstanding example of this quality with strong rhythm and much internal rhyme plus several rousing quatrains for the group to join in on as a whole. As you read the whole story, kids can echo you line by line on the refrains, for example:

Beak to beak, peck, peck, peck,
Spread your wings, stretch your neck.
Black is beautiful, uh-huh!
Black is beautiful, uh-huh!

Dramatizing *Blackbird*

For an even more dramatic and interactive experience, the story can be performed as a readers' theater experience. There are distinct bits of dialogue for two individual characters, Blackbird and Ringdove, plus group parts for the colorful birds and the small birds. A narrator rounds out the cast. Once children have heard and enjoyed the story, they may find it even more engaging to make the story come alive by dramatizing it in this fashion. (No memorization required.) Simple props could be added for extra effect, like feathers or die-cut bird shapes in multiple colors (one black).

The story lends itself beautifully to an old-fashioned flannel board retelling with simple bird shapes in red, green, yellow, purple, orange, blue, pink, and, of course, black. Add a lake, a tree, and Blackbird's medicine gourd bowl and black feather brush, and you can retell the story in a concrete and visible way. (These pieces could then be used as simple props for a readers' theater dramatization, too.) Folktales are ideal for drama and flannel boards because of their oral roots. They were meant to be heard, told, acted out, and interpreted.

Blackbird Art Activities

Beautiful Blackbird could also spawn a variety of fun craft activities, from decorating precut colorful birds with black marker, paint, or yarn, to coloring crayon relief drawings (colorful pictures colored over with black crayon and then scratched to reveal color), to experimenting with cut paper art as Ashley Bryan does in the illustrations for this book (with adult supervision, please). In the book's endpapers, Bryan even includes images of the scissors he used to create the illustrations and notes that they were his mother's sewing and embroidery scissors. Children can investigate what artistic traditions might exist in their own families or share what their own favorite artistic media might be. Blackbird was, of all things, an artist, and the book subtly emphasizes the important place art has in the community.

Music and Dancing with *Blackbird*

This folktale also incorporates dancing as an important part of the bird community, and this provides a wonderful opportunity to invite movement as a follow-up to reading the book. The book specifically mentions four dances: the "Beak and Wing Dance," the "Show Claws Slide," the "Sun-Up Dance," and the "Sun-Down Dance." Bryan provides an explanatory rhyme for the "Show Claws Slide" that begs for physical interpretation:

Tip tap toe to the left, spin around,
Toe tap tip to the right, stroke the ground.
Wings flip-flapping as you glide,
Forward and backward in a Show Claws Slide.

For the other dances, a little interpretation is welcome. And for an added bonus, find or make simple musical instruments modeled after the African kalimba or drum to accompany the dance (http://www.kalimba.co.za/).

> ## More *Blackbird* Connections
>
> Finally, encourage the children to seek out other African folktales, such as the Caldecott winner *Why Mosquitoes Buzz in People's Ears* by Verna Aardema, illustrated by Leo Dillon and Diane Dillon (Puffin, 2004), or the Caldecott honor book, *Anansi the Spider* by Gerald McDermott (Holt, 1972). Older readers may enjoy *In the Beginning: Creation Stories from Around the World* by Virginia Hamilton (Harcourt, 1988), which includes one creation tale from Zambia, or *Favorite African Folktales* edited by Nelson Mandela (W. W. Norton, 2004). Or consider connecting with companion poems about "blackness," such as "Listen Children" by Lucille Clifton from Wade Hudson's *Pass It On, African-American Poetry for Children* (Scholastic, 1993) or Langston Hughes's classic poem "My People" found in his collection *The Dream Keeper and Other Poems* (Knopf, 2007) or in the picture book version of the poem illustrated by Charles R. Smith Jr. (Simon & Schuster, 2009).
>
> Ashley Bryan is also a consummate storyteller and performer, and we are fortunate to have an audio recording of *Beautiful Blackbird* by Bryan himself. Look for *Ashley Bryan's Beautiful Blackbird and Other Folktales* audio CD (Audio Bookshelf, 2004). It also includes stories from his notable collection, *Ashley Bryan's African Tales, Uh-Huh* (Atheneum, 1998), an excellent companion book. Check your area for the availability of other storytellers (http://www.storynet.org/) to bring the live experience of listening to a tale to the children in person. In particular, look for those with knowledge of African stories to connect with *Beautiful Blackbird*.
>
> To learn more about the setting for *Beautiful Blackbird*, lead children in locating Zambia on a world map and in a bit of Internet searching for more information and images of the modern country of Zambia via the Zambia National Tourist Board (http://www.zambiatourism.com/) or the National Homepage of Zambia (http://www.zambia.co.zm/).

EVALUATION CRITERIA

When we select traditional literature for children, we're usually looking for folktales in the picture book format. Thus, we begin with the literary criteria that we applied to the analysis of picture books previously, including plot, character, setting, theme, and style. But how are each of these handled by retellers of traditional tales, in particular? What other characteristics are specific to this genre? Let's take a look.

Characters

The characters in traditional tales are typically archetypes of good or evil, described with a few broad strokes and symbolic of our most basic human traits, both good and bad, such as innocence or integrity, greediness or selfishness. Folktales are full characters that are stereotyped by nature. Some people have even accused traditional literature of being sexist or chauvinistic—it's always the boy who saves the day and the girl who gets saved. But that is not really true. There are many authentic tales with strong and heroic female characters from a variety of cultural traditions. The challenge is digging deeper to find these stories. The single-faceted nature of characterization in folktales provides children with a basis in literature that "distills the essence of human experience" (Kiefer, 2010, p. 234). Folktale characters are not usually dynamic and changing individuals the way they are in nearly every other genre. They're not complicated, introspective, and worried about growing up. They serve more symbolically as representatives for goodness and innocence or wickedness and selfishness. Think about Cinderella and Snow White or Goldilocks and the Big Bad Wolf, for example.

Plot

The plots of traditional tales are usually simple and direct, episodic and full of action. Remember, these were originally oral tales and the teller had to draw the audience in early in the story. Conflicts are crucial to the plot, and there is often a quest or journey with definite obstacles to overcome. Stories move forward logically with a quick ebb and flow of action, often in a formulaic pattern. The final resolution comes quickly, if predictably; it's not necessarily realistic but is very satisfying. Consider the storyline of the three little pigs, for example: pigs leave home, build a house, repeat, repeat, foil the wolf.

Setting

In traditional literature, the settings are generally rather vaguely described and quickly established, and always in the distant past, far away. It is clearly not the real world as we know it, and we instantly accept the "scary forest" or the "magic castle" and understand those parameters. Settings can help us understand the context for our protagonist—royal blood (castle, kingdom, mountain top) or good-hearted peasant (tiny village, small cottage, rice fields). Time passes quickly and often years go by in a matter of sentences, as when baby Rapunzel grows into a lovely long-haired princess, for example.

Theme

The themes of traditional tales are big, global messages with a clear stance on the importance of good triumphing over evil. There's rarely any ambivalence or subtlety in folktales; the evil stepsisters never win the prince's hand. Themes are strongly moral, ethical, and universal, and stories always end happily. Some even contain humor, especially those that skewer human foibles, and some can be tense and suspenseful, such as cautionary tales like *Little Red Riding Hood.*

Style

The reteller's style in capturing a traditional tale is partly based on one individual's unique voice and partly based on the need for capturing the sound of spoken language in print. A well-told tale should reflect the integrity of early retellings and of the culture from which the tale springs. Stories typically have a formalized opening and closing. This also grows out of the cultural basis for the story. Thus many stories in the European tradition begin "Once upon a time," but in other cultures the storyteller begins by extending an invitation. Stories are definitely culturally specific and reveal attributes valued within the culture, many of which cross boundaries, but some of which offer unique insights. Motifs are a big part of the style of folktales and this includes transformations, magic objects, wishes, long sleeps, supernatural helpers or adversaries, and trickery. Numbers may also be significant (in European stories things usually occur in threes; in Native American stories, on the other hand, things often occur in patterns of four). Folktales typically have a strong rhythm in the language, often with repeated patterns or elements. Folktales sometimes even offer help for understanding the dialects and languages of various countries because idiomatic expressions are often used in the storytelling. There is an oral quality to the writing of a good traditional tale that should read well aloud.

Illustrations

Since many traditional tales are published in picture book form, it is also important to consider how the illustrations function as part of the storytelling experience. Once again, we might analyze the artist's style, medium, and use of visual elements to create images that serve to complement and extend the narrative. We look for examples of artistic excellence, for art that elevates the story to another level. In addition, the illustrations should reflect the cultural heritage of the tale. It's in the pictures that we often get the clearest indications of the context for the story, the setting, the clothing, the foliage, and so on. Winters and Schmidt (2001) remind us to ask how the book's illustrations present the parent culture. Where can you see use of a culture's artistic traditions?

Culture

Since traditional tales are oral stories that grow out of long-held cultural traditions and beliefs, the cultural quotient in this genre is very high. Thus, we also need to consider the cultural authenticity of a tale and seek out stories that are representative of the root culture. Much material written about cultures is by people who are *not* part of that culture and thus it can be stereotyped or nonauthentic. Folktales come from the people themselves—they are part of the culture, not something written about the culture. Through folktales, children can gain insight into the customs and values of many nations and cultures. Most of today's retellers and adapters and illustrators conduct careful research to be sure they capture the cultural traditions relevant to the story in rich and accurate ways. Look for the cultural markers mentioned earlier to assess whether the story and illustrations are grounded appropriately.

Of course, individual storytellers add their own interpretations, as do the illus-trators who help create the picture book versions. But unless it's a modern parody or spoof, we trust that the language and images of the story are true.

Just a note: It is also important to go beyond traditional literature and folk-tales when we're teaching children about culture. Contemporary realistic liter-ature (as well as other genres) is also needed to provide a well-rounded picture of the "parallel cultures" of our world. Otherwise, we grow up thinking Japa-nese people lived "once upon a time" instead of right down the block! Remem-ber that many elements in folktales are stereotypes or archetypes and thus not multidimensional representations of a culture. Folktales can be a beginning point to study the cultural roots of various kinds of tales, but we need to go beyond traditional literature to understand the complexity of contemporary cultures today.

Evaluating Anthologies

The criteria for evaluating anthologies of traditional stories also begins with the literary elements of plot, characterization, setting, theme, and style—par-ticularly the oral flavor of the storytelling. In addition, consider the organiza-tion of the collection overall.

Which stories are represented?
Are they generally familiar or unfamiliar to young readers?
Is background information on the stories provided?
Is there a table of contents? Source notes?
If there are illustrations, do they suit the varied stories and their root cultures?
Is the collection child-friendly or intended for adults to share with children?

Choose one or two stories as exemplars of the style and tone of the collection and read them out loud to assess their storytelling quality and "kid appeal."

Sample Review

Let's put these evaluation criteria into action and consider one review and how it uses these criteria. Here's a sample review of a traditional tale:

Pinkney, Jerry. 2006. *The Little Red Hen.* New York: Penguin.

When the little red hen finds some strange seeds, she scoops them up and takes them home. Learning the seeds are wheat seeds, the little red hen plants them. Before she does this though, she asks the other animals, the short brown dog, the thin gray rat, the tall black goat, and the round pink pig, if they will help her. All of the animals decline to help with a "Not I." The little red hen tends the seeds, harvests the wheat, and takes the grain to the mill, each time asking the animals for help and being rejected. "A very busy hen was she!" In this classic telling of *The*

Little Red Hen, the Golden Rule message rings as loudly as ever. What gives this story a freshness are the beautiful illustrations. Five-time Caldecott Honor winner Jerry Pinkney delivers another book with page after page of intricately detailed illustrations that bring the story to life. With graphite, ink, and watercolor, *The Little Red Hen* is a "joy of joys."

[By Mary D. Buckalo for *Librarians' Choices*. Used with permission.]

This review begins with a quick and helpful overview of the plot and the sequence of story activities from finding to planting to harvesting the seeds. It introduces the major characters with a nod to the illustrations by noting their colors (red, brown, gray, black, and pink) and acknowledges the storytelling style of this particular version with references to the repeated response, "not I," the strong protagonist, "A very busy hen was she!" and the strong concluding, "joy of joys." Although the setting is not directly acknowledged (beyond noting "home" or the mill), the theme is characterized explicitly as "the Golden Rule message." Note that nearly half of the review addresses the importance of the illustrations, appropriate since this is a retelling of a familiar tale with new art.

AWARDS FOR TRADITIONAL TALES

As we look for input to guide our collection development, award lists can be helpful in providing a measure of excellence in the genre. In the area of traditional tales, the Caldecott award is one distinction to note, since traditional tales are often recognized with this award or honor citations. The Aesop Prize is specific to the area of folklore, so it's a helpful source of information here, too.

Caldecott Award

The Caldecott medal for illustration presented by the Association for Library Service to Children is one to consider when searching for the very best examples of traditional tales in picture book form. Many picture book adaptations of traditional tales have been Caldecott award recipients or honor books for "the most distinguished American picture book for children," including these titles:

The Lion & the Mouse by Jerry Pinkney (Little, Brown, 2009)
Noah's Ark by Jerry Pinkney (SeaStar, 2002)

The Three Pigs by David Wiesner (Clarion, 2001)
Joseph Had a Little Overcoat by Simms Taback (Viking, 1999)
Rapunzel by Paul O. Zelinsky (Dutton, 1997)
There Was an Old Lady Who Swallowed a Fly by Simms Taback (Viking, 1997)
Golem by David Wisniewski (Clarion, 1996)

Aesop Prize

The Aesop Prize is conferred by the Children's Folklore Section of the American Folklore Society for the most outstanding book or books incorporating folklore, published in English, for children or young adults. Recent recipients and "accolade" selections have included several folktale collections as well as picture book retellings:

- *Which Side Are You On?* by George Ella Lyon, illustrated by Christopher Cardinale (Cinco Puntos Press, 2011)
- *Mouse & Lion* retold by Rand Burkert, illustrated by Nancy Ekholm Burkert (Scholastic, 2011)
- *The Matatu* retold by Eric Walters, illustrated by Eva Campbell (Orca 2012)
- *Walking on Earth & Touching the Sky: Poetry and Prose by Lakota Youth at Red Cloud Indian School* compiled by Timothy P. McLaughlin, illustrated by S. D. Nelson (Abrams, 2012)

Literature in Action: Featuring Folktale Variants

Sharing multiple versions or variants of one story is an excellent way to approach traditional tales. Here, one *story* becomes the focus, rather than a single book title. By highlighting the basic story elements or motifs in one tale, like the mistreated girl, the obnoxious sister(s), the magical task, we can help children see the building blocks of stories, while developing their awareness of the similarities and differences across cultures. In studying something so familiar, children have the opportunity to learn more about basic story elements, unique cultural markers, and their own personal responses. I recommend using the Cinderella tale for a sample study of traditional tales because there are probably more picture book versions of this story available than any other, including examples with boy "Cinderellas."

It is also important to recognize that the label "Cinderella tale" is a European one, with other cultures referring to this type of tale as a "good sister/bad sister" tale. Folklorists have identified more than 3,000 stories that qualify as Cinderella variants worldwide; almost every culture, every nation, has at least one variant (Sloan and Vardell, 2004). The story of Cinderella has endured for more than 1,000 years, rooted first in ninth-century China in the T'ang dynasty. In 1891, the Folk-Lore Society in London published Marian Roalfe Cox's *Cinderella: Three Hundred and Forty-Five Variants of Cinderella, Catskin, and Cap o' Rushes*, the first modern, scientific study of the Cinderella body of work.

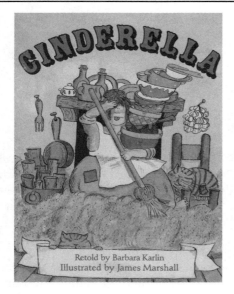

Retold by Barbara Karlin
Illustrated by James Marshall

A literary approach to the Cinderella tale is simply to take two or more examples of the tale and read, analyze, and compare them, looking for similarities and differences in both the narrative and the illustrations in these picture book versions. Children may be surprised to discover that in some Cinderella tales, there is no glass slipper or fairy godmother. Nevertheless, the story is considered a version of the Cinderella story. You and the children can work together to generate a list of story characteristics and decide which or how many elements must be present in order to say, "That's a Cinderella story." Then, once a clear understanding of Cinderella elements is in place, children can apply their knowledge by reading and responding to other variants from a variety of world cultures.

European Variants

Brown, M. 1954. *Cinderella, or the Little Glass Slipper*. New York: Atheneum.
Craft, K. Y. 2001. *Cinderella*. New York: Seastar.
Daly, J. 2005. *Fair, Brown, and Trembling: An Irish Cinderella Story*. New York: Farrar, Straus & Giroux.
Manna, Anthony, and Christodoula Mitakidou. 2011. *The Orphan: A Cinderella Story from Greece*. New York: Random House.
Mayer, M. 1994. *Baba Yaga and Vasilisa the Brave*. New York: Morrow.
Sanderson, Ruth. 2002. *Cinderella*. New York: Little, Brown.

Latin American Variants

Coburn, J. R. 2000. *Domitila: A Cinderella Tale from the Mexican Tradition*. Arcadia, CA: Shen's Books.
San Souci, D. 2002. *Cendrillon: A Caribbean Cinderella*. New York: Aladdin.
San Souci, R. D. 2000. *Little Gold Star: A Spanish American Cinderella*. New York: HarperCollins.

Native American Variants

Martin, R. 1998. *The Rough-face Girl*. New York: Philomel.
Pollock, P. 1996. *The Turkey Girl: A Zuni Cinderella*. New York: Little, Brown.

Rural American Variants

Hooks, W. 1987. *Moss Gown*. New York: Clarion.
San Souci, R. D. 1998. *The Talking Eggs*. New York: Dutton.
Schroeder, A. 2000. *Smoky Mountain Rose: An Appalachian Cinderella*. New York: Puffin.

African Variants

Climo, S. 1992. *The Egyptian Cinderella*. Minneapolis, MN: Econo-Clad.
Onyefulu, O. 1994. *Chinye: A West African Folktale*. New York: Viking.
Sierra, J. 2000. *The Gift of the Crocodile*. New York: Simon & Schuster.
Steptoe, J. 1987. *Mufaro's Beautiful Daughters*. New York: Lothrop, Lee, & Shepard.

Asian Variants

Climo, S. 1996. *The Korean Cinderella*. New York: HarperTrophy.
Coburn, J. R. 1998. *Angkat: The Cambodian Cinderella*. Arcadia, CA: Shen's Books.
Coburn, J. R., and T. C. Lee. 1996. *Jouanah: A Hmong Cinderella*. Arcadia, CA: Shen's Books.
Louie, A. 1996. *Yeh-Shen: A Cinderella Story from China*. New York: Puffin.

Middle Eastern Variants

Climo, S. 2001. *The Persian Cinderella*. New York: HarperTrophy.
Hickox, R. 1999. *The Golden Sandal*. New York: Holiday House.

Three collections of less familiar Cinderella versions include *Cinderella Tales from Around the World* collected by Heidi Anne Heiner (2012) and part of the SurLaLune Fairy Tale Series, Judy Sierra's *Cinderella* (1992), from the Oryx Multicultural Folk Tale series, and *Cinderella Tales from Around the World* (LEAP's Global Understanding Book Series) by Ila Lane Gross (LEAP, 2001). Studying folktale variants from a variety of cultures opens an avenue to understanding basic characteristics underlying the simple folk story. Folktales extol the qualities of goodness, mercy, courage, and love, which children can see are valued in all cultures. However, children's literature professors Tunnell, Jacobs, Young, and Bryan (2012) remind us of the importance of going beyond using only traditional literature and folktales to teach children about cultures. We also need to teach children to read critically, looking for cultural details that add authenticity to the folktale and avoiding those that reflect negative or inaccurate stereotypes.

Once children have encountered a variety of Cinderella tales from different cultures, they may also begin to notice the different ways the heroine herself is portrayed. In some Cinderella tales, the protagonist takes responsibility for herself and doesn't look to others for help. This contrasts with the classic Perrault heroine waiting for the prince to find her and the Disney Cinderella with whom children are usually most familiar. This basic attribute of Cinderella as an active or passive figure can be a subtle and interesting area to address with children. Traditional stories can be useful tools for learning about gender roles (Mello, 2001). Several modern interpretations of Cinderella provide heroines with attributes usually credited to male heroes. These characters are not "modern revisionist creations by contemporary authors, but rather authentic folk heroines of the past whose stories are finally being put in book form" (Sloan and Vardell, 2004).

Studying Cinderella

For engaging children in a close study of these tales, Worthy and Blood-good (1993) provide an excellent outline of a "Cinderella unit" in their article, "Enhancing Reading Instruction through Cinderella Tales." Other helpful resources for guiding activities include *Teaching with Cinderella Stories from Around the World (Grades 1–3)* by Kathleen Hollenbeck (Teaching Resources, 2003) and *In Search of Cinderella: A Curriculum for the 21st Century* by Katharine F. Goodwin (Shen's Books, 2003). I would suggest the following progression of possible activities.

- Have children get into groups and brainstorm everything they know or associate with "Cinderella" and its sister tales.
- Introduce variants and versions of Cinderella; show children the covers of books, read the titles, and note the names of adapters and illustrators.
- Discuss with children any unfamiliar vocabulary, particularly any unusual names for Cinderella and other characters (e.g., Cenerentola, Cendrillon, Aschenputtel, Shih Chieh, Ella, Ash-boy, etc.).
- As children read the books, create and maintain a chart that compares the stories, using the following headings:

  > Title
  > Author/Adapter
  > Illustrator
  > Country of Origin/Setting
  > Main Character (Name)
  > Secondary Character(s) (Relationship to Main Character)
  > Supernatural Helper

- Children can research topics relevant to the story, such as geography, climate, or flora and fauna (begin by studying the book illustrations closely).
- Children can investigate some aspect of the culture that emerges in the story, such as courtship and weddings, holidays, religion, clothing, or food.
- And, of course, there are many animated and live action films based on the Cinderella story available on video and DVD, including Disney's animated *Cinderella* (1950) as well as the Rogers & Hammerstein musical version (1965 and 1997) or a contemporary remake, *Ever After* (1998) or *A Cinderella Story* (2004) or *Another Cinderella Story* (2008). Seek permission before sharing these media adaptations, of course.

Other possible Cinderella connections include linking with poems, novels, parodies, and websites, as follows. Look for Paul Fleischman's picture book *Glass Slipper, Gold Sandal: A Worldwide Cinderella* (Henry Holt, 2007), an interesting compilation of attributes and motifs from Cinderella stories from many cultures all woven together into a single story.

Cinderella Poems

It might also be appealing to connect the Cinderella story with poem versions and parodies of the tale.

- Dahl, Roald. 2002. "Cinderella." In *Revolting Rhymes* (Q. Blake, Illus.). New York: Knopf.
- Maccarone, Grace. 2013. *Princess Tales: Once Upon a Time in Rhyme with Seek-and-Find Pictures.* New York: Feiwel & Friends.
- Silverstein, Shel. 1981. "In Search of Cinderella." In *A Light in the Attic.* New York: HarperCollins.
- Viorst, Judith. 1981. ". . . And Then the Prince Knelt Down and Tried to Put the Glass Slipper on Cinderella's Foot." In *If I Were in Charge of the World and Other Worries.* New York: Atheneum.
- Whipple, Laura. 2002. *If the Shoe Fits: Voices from Cinderella.* New York: McElderry. (This is a collection of 32 poems representing many "voices" from Cinderella—even that of the glass slipper.)

Cinderella Novels

Modern versions of "Cinderella," such as the novels *Ella Enchanted* by Gail Carson Levine (1997) or *Just Ella* by Margaret Peterson Haddix (1999), could be read and compared to more traditional folktale picture book Cinderella tales with older children.

Burnett, Frances H. 1886. *Little Lord Fauntleroy.* New York: Scribner's.
Haddix, Margaret P. 1999. *Just Ella.* New York: Pocket.
Levine, Gail C. 1997. *Ella Enchanted.* New York: HarperCollins.
Maguire, Gregory. 1999. *Confessions of an Ugly Stepsister.* New York: HarperCollins.
Mah, Adeline Yen. 2001. *Chinese Cinderella: The True Story of an Unwanted Daughter.* New York: Laurel Leaf.
Meyer, Marissa. 2012. *Cinder.* New York: Feiwel & Friends.
Stanley, Diane. 2006. *Bella at Midnight.* New York: HarperCollins.

Cinderella Parodies

It can be very appealing to share versions of "Cinderella" that parody the traditional story elements, particularly once children are familiar with the traditional tale.

Brett, Jan. 2013. *Cinders: A Chicken Cinderella.* New York: Putnam.
Buehner, Caralyn. 1996. *Fanny's Dream.* New York: Dial.
Cole, Babette. 1999. *Prince Cinders.* Minneapolis, MN: Econo-Clad.
Edwards, Pamela D. 1999. *Dinorella: A Prehistoric Fairy Tale.* New York: Hyperion.
Hazen, Lynn E. 2008. *Cinder Rabbit.* New York: Holt.
Jackson, Ellen. 1998. *Cinder Edna.* New York: Mulberry.
Johnston, Tony. 2000. *Bigfoot Cinderrrrella.* New York: Puffin.

Ketteman, Helen. 2001. *Bubba, the Cowboy Prince*. New York: Scholastic.

Lattimore, Deborah N. 2002. *Cinderhazel: The Cinderella of Halloween*. New York: Scholastic.

Lowell, Susan. 2001. *Cindy Ellen: A Wild Western Cinderella*. New York: HarperTrophy.

Minters, Frances. 1999. *Cinder-Elly*. Minneapolis, MN: Econo-Clad.

San Souci, Robert. 2000. *Cinderella Skeleton*. San Diego, CA: Harcourt.

Cinderella Websites

Many examples of variants and versions of the Cinderella tale can be found on Russell Peck's website (http://www.lib.rochester.edu/camelot/cinder/cinintr.htm), which has a lengthy bibliography with a wealth of information. Other websites that offer Cinderella resources include:

http://www.surlalunefairytales.com
http://www.acs.ucalgary.ca/~dkbrown/cinderella.html
http://www.nationalgeographic.com/grimm/cinderella.html
http://www.northcanton.sparcc.org/~ptk1nc/cinderella/

Also look for Cinderella apps, like Nosy Crow's *Cinderella* app mentioned in Chapter Two.

To conclude their study of Cinderella, children can create their own versions of the Cinderella tale or a sister tale. This also provides an excellent opportunity to point out the difference between a fictional story with an author (e.g., their own stories) and a preexisting story that an adapter has retold authentically (a folktale). Cinderella is only one of several popular folktales available in multiple versions. You might also consider bringing in different picture book versions of one of these stories:

- The Three Little Pigs
- The Three Bears
- Little Red Riding Hood
- Jack and the Beanstalk
- Rumpelstiltskin
- Rapunzel

SHARING TRADITIONAL TALES

Whether we focus on one traditional tale like Cinderella, the sister tale, or bring children's folklore from the playground to the library, or try our hands at storytelling ourselves, this genre is a natural for sharing with children in many active and engaging ways. With its oral roots, it is *meant* to be read aloud and retold, which invites participation. In addition, the archetypes, formulas, and motifs seem almost intuitive and familiar to children, even across cultures, so that it seems natural to dramatize these scenes and scenarios. Fortunately, there are also many resources available for guiding our selection and implementation of traditional tales.

Children's Playground Lore

There is a rich lore of stories, traditions, and customs unique to childhood, passed on by word of mouth from generation to generation of children on the playground or in nursery school and daycare (Thomas, 2007). Children often learn their ABCs, numbers, days, and months from rhymes and riddles we share from memory. Children also play with variations of the same songs, dances, and games that generations did before them.

The oral traditions of childhood studied in depth by scholars Iona and Peter Opie in their seminal *The Lore and Language of Schoolchildren* (Oxford University Press, 1959) include lullabies, nursery rhymes, playground chants, street rhymes, and more, which exist in nearly every culture. However, there is not necessarily a common set of lore familiar to everyone. Children may grow up knowing many rhymes, chants, and songs, but those may not be in English, for example. Fortunately, many published versions of childhood rhymes and poetry from around the world are readily available to share with children today. Children of all ages often find tremendous enjoyment in discovering that the rhymes and chants of their playtime can often be found in books. This medium helps validate children's experiences, connect written and oral expression, and invite active, physical participation (Vardell & Jacko, 2005).

Whether it's the active handclapping and ball bouncing rhymes such as those found in Stephanie Calmenson and Joanna Cole's collections, like *Miss Mary Mack* (Morrow, 1990), or the finger plays, chants, and cheers in Judy Sierra's *Schoolyard Rhymes* (Knopf, 2005), or the chants and riddles gathered in *Juba This and Juba That* edited by Virginia A. Tashjian (Little, Brown, 1995), or the jokes, songs, tongue twisters, and nonsense verse of Alvin Schwartz's *And the Green Grass Grew All Around* (HarperCollins, 1992) and many others, children's folklore is full of fun connections for participation. Invite kids to share a favorite riddle or joke as they line up, pack up, or during other transition moments. Sharing folklore aloud is excellent practice for building oral fluency and speaking skills. Children can collect other examples via audio or video recording and explore neighborhood, cultural, and language variations (Hadaway, Vardell, & Young, 2002). They can translate their English favorites into other languages represented in their communities. Older children may enjoy exploring the historical roots of childhood rhymes, discovering the second and third verses of familiar songs, or writing down new and unfamiliar examples. Connecting with children's playground lore is an opportunity to take literacy outside and to invite the outside in. We can demonstrate that the library is a place where children's own literary traditions are valued and welcomed.

Storytelling

We all tell stories every day. If you talk to someone about your day, share a childhood memory, or describe an event, you are very likely framing it as a story. Translating this natural narrative ability into more formalized storytelling with an audience takes a bit of practice but can be very rewarding. For many librarians, in particular, it becomes a staple of their library programs. The resources noted below are invaluable, and a mini-course or workshop can help get you started.

Bauer, Caroline Feller. 1995. *Caroline Feller Bauer's New Handbook for Storytellers.* Chicago, IL: American Library Association.

de Las Casas, Dianne. 2006. *Kamishibai Story Theater: The Art of Picture Telling.* Englewood, CO: Libraries Unlimited.

de Las Casas, Dianne. 2011. *Tell Along Tales!: Playing with Participation Stories.* Englewood, CO: Libraries Unlimited.

Greene, Ellin, and Janice M. Del Negro. 2010. *Storytelling: Art and Technique* (Fourth Edition). Englewood, CO: Libraries Unlimited.

Haven, Kendall, and MaryGay Ducey. 2006. *Crash Course in Storytelling.* Englewood, CO: Libraries Unlimited.

Livo, Norma J., and Sandra A. Rietz. 1991. *Storytelling Folklore Sourcebook.* Englewood, CO: Libraries Unlimited.

MacDonald, Margaret Read. 2006. *Storyteller's Start-Up Book.* Atlanta, GA: August House.

MacDonald, Margaret Read. 2006. *Ten Traditional Tellers.* Urbana, IL: University of Illinois Press.

MacDonald, Margaret Read, and Brian W. Sturm. 2001. *Storyteller's Sourcebook: A Subject, Title, and Motif Index to Folklore Collections for Children, 1983–1999.* Farmington Hills, MI: Thomson Gale.

Norfolk, Sherry, Jane Stenson, and Diane Williams. 2006. *The Storytelling Classroom: Applications Across the Curriculum.* Englewood, CO: Libraries Unlimited.

Ohler, Jason B. 2013. *Digital Storytelling in the Classroom: New Media Pathways to Literacy, Learning, and Creativity* (Second Edition). Thousand Oaks, CA: Corwin.

Pellowski, Anne. 1991. *The World of Storytelling.* New York: H. W. Wilson.

Pellowski, Anne. 2005. *Drawing Stories from around the World and a Sampling of European Handkerchief Stories.* Englewood, CO: Libraries Unlimited.

Sawyer, Ruth. 1977. *The Way of the Storyteller.* New York: Penguin.

Sierra, Judy. 2002. *Can You Guess My Name?: Traditional Tales Around the World.* New York: Clarion.

Sometimes teachers, parents, or grandparents have a knack for storytelling and are willing to share their gifts. Invite a guest teller to share his or her story repertoire. And there is nothing quite like hearing a story told by a professional storyteller. The National Storytelling Network (http://www.storynet .org) of the National Storytelling Association can help you locate storytellers and storytelling festivals in your area. Of course, it would be a special treat to invite a professional storyteller to perform, if the budget allows. You'll also find a "Story Tellers' Handbook" along with information on how to tell a folktale, where to find a storyteller, and how to develop and present a story at http:// www.storyarts.org. Instructional ideas for science, math, and social studies as well as extensions for drama and literature are also available here. If nothing else, there are excellent audio sources (from August House at http://www .augusthouse.com/ and other companies) of stories told by professional storytellers that can be very effective for storytimes.

CONCLUSION

Parents, teachers, librarians, and children all delight in the oral qualities of folk literature for reading, sharing, and enjoying together. An entire range of traditional tales is available for reading and listening, from riddles and nursery rhymes to fables, fairy tales and folktales, myths and legends. This genre provides engaging reading experiences for children, since they enjoy the wit, humor, clever word choice, and the fact that the good characters are rewarded and misfortune falls upon the bad. Traditional literature is a rich genre that provides many language growth opportunities for children as they absorb story structures, story language, and story motifs. And the potential for increasing personal and cultural awareness for all children is an added benefit of folklore study. Whether we tell stories from our own cultures, read aloud old favorites, or invite children to participate in dramatic, puppet-based, or flannel board retellings, traditional tales are essential for grounding children in the literary heritage we all share as human beings.

PROFESSIONAL RESOURCES FOR TRADITIONAL LITERATURE

For more help in learning about traditional literature for young people, consult these related professional readings.

Bettelheim, B. 2010. *The Uses of Enchantment: The Meaning and Importance of Fairy Tales.* New York: Vintage Books.

Bosma, Bette. 1992. *Fairy Tales, Fables, Legends, and Myths: Using Folk Literature in Your Classroom.* New York: Teachers College Press.

Cashdan, Sheldon. 2000. *The Witch Must Die: The Hidden Meaning of Fairy Tales.* New York: Basic Books.

Tatar, Maria. 1992. *Off with Their Heads!: Fairy Tales and the Culture of Childhood.* Princeton, NJ: Princeton University Press.

Tatar, Maria. 1998. *The Classic Fairy Tales: Texts, Criticism (Norton Critical Editions).* New York: W. W. Norton.

Tatar, Maria. 2003. *The Hard Facts of the Grimms' Fairy Tales. Revised.* Princeton, NJ: Princeton University Press.

Wolf, J. 1997. *The Beanstalk and Beyond: Developing Critical Thinking through Fairy Tales.* New York: Teacher Ideas Press.

Yolen, Jane. 2005. *Touch Magic: Fantasy, Faerie and Folklore in the Literature of Childhood* (Expanded Edition). Atlanta, GA: August House.

Young, Terrell A. 2004. *Happily Ever After: Sharing Folk Literature with Elementary and Middle School Students.* Newark, DE: International Reading Association.

Zipes, Jack. 1994. *Fairy Tale as Myth, Myth as Fairy Tale.* Lexington, KY: University Press of Kentucky.

Zipes, Jack. 1997. *Happily Ever After: Fairy Tales, Children, and the Culture Industry.* London: Routledge.

Zipes, Jack. 2000. *The Great Fairy Tale Tradition: From Straparola and Basile to the Brothers Grimm (Norton Critical Editions).* New York: W. W. Norton.

Zipes, Jack. 2002. *Breaking the Magic Spell: Radical Theories of Folk and Fairy Tales.* Lexington, KY: University Press of Kentucky.

Zipes, Jack. 2003. *The Brothers Grimm: From Enchanted Forests to the Modern World* (Second Edition). New York: Palgrave Macmillan.

Zipes, Jack. 2006. *Why Fairy Tales Stick: The Evolution and Relevance of a Genre.* London: Routledge.

Zipes, Jack. 2011. *Fairy Tales and the Art of Subversion.* London: Routledge.

Zipes, Jack. 2012. *The Irresistible Fairy Tale: The Cultural and Social History of a Genre.* Princeton, NJ: Princeton University Press.

Standards in Action: AASL Standards for the 21st-Century Learner

The American Association of School Librarians (AASL) has been a division of the American Library Association since 1951 and is the only national professional association for school librarians in the United States. In 2007, the AASL released the Standards for the 21st-Century Learner to "guide instructional programs" in school libraries, followed by an "action plan" in 2009 that provides benchmarks and indicators for each standard (http://www.ala.org/aasl/standards). There are four major areas of emphasis delineated in the standards:

Learners use skills, resources, and tools to:
1. Inquire, think critically, and gain knowledge.
2. Draw conclusions, make informed decisions, apply knowledge to new situations, and create new knowledge.
3. Share knowledge and participate ethically and productively as members of our democratic society.
4. Pursue personal and aesthetic growth.

They also identify skills, "dispositions in action" or beliefs, responsibilities, and self-assessment strategies for each of these four areas. In this chapter, we have certainly focused on Area #4, encouraging children to "pursue personal and aesthetic growth" by sharing traditional literature with them orally and encouraging them to read, discuss, and dramatize favorite folktales. This specifically addresses two skills:

1.1.1. Read, view, and listen for pleasure and personal growth.
1.1.2. Read widely and fluently to make connections with self, the world, and previous reading.

In addition, when we involve students in drawing conclusions (Area #2) using the Cinderella tale, for example, we can consider variants of the tale from differing cultures and explore new vocabulary, cultural attributes and traditions, geographical and historical contexts, and multimedia representations. This addresses another skill:

2.1.3. Use strategies to draw conclusions from information and apply knowledge to curricular areas, real-world situations, and further investigations.

Whether we work in the school setting or in the public sector, these standards offer a helpful reference point for emphasizing the value of libraries in educating our children. We can use them to make that case and incorporate them as we document our successes.

Assignments in Action: **Celebrating Traditional Tales**

1. **Building Storytelling Muscles**

Although we tell "stories" about our lives on a daily basis, sometimes we feel shy about storytelling before an audience. Yet children are so captivated by the story listening experience, it is worth building our storytelling skills to give it a try. Consult some of the storytelling resources shared previously, check out the related websites, visit a storytelling festival, or talk with a librarian experienced at storytelling. Then choose a favorite story and challenge yourself to master the telling of it. Use audio or video recording to help you improve your delivery. Then gather a sympathetic group and give it a try.

2. **Capturing Stories**

Culture is an important variable when it comes to what makes traditional tales distinctive. What are your own cultural roots? Did you grow up with any folktales particular to your culture? If so, look for picture book versions of those stories and see how they compare with your memories of the tales. Or try your hand at retelling your favorite tales. You could polish your delivery of one or two of these tales as part of your regular repertoire of storytime activities. Or if you speak a language other than English, consider taking a popular traditional tale like *The Three Little Pigs, The Three Bears,* or *Little Red Riding Hood* and translating it into another language. Or involve a group of children in collecting, writing down, and illustrating traditional tales and playground folklore from their own families, neighborhoods, and communities.

3. **Violence in Traditional Tales**

When we look at many of the traditional tales that are part of children's literature, we can find some rather scary and grim events—wolves devouring pigs, grandmothers, or children, for example. How have various retellers and adapters handled issues of violence, vengeance, or other harsh subject matter in a manner appropriate to a child reader? How do *you* feel about these issues? Gather several versions of a single tale that generally contains a violent event, like *Little Red Riding Hood* or *The Three Little Pigs* and examine how these events are handled. Does the wolf eat the grandmother? The first two pigs? Is the wolf himself killed in the end? Think about how you might present these stories to children and at what age. Librarian Donna MacKinney warns us that it's possible that "*too* much to worry about in a story is a tell-tale sign that it needs to wait for a more mature audience."

4

Poetry for Children

"Poetry and Hums aren't things which you get, they're things which get *you*. And all you can do is to go where they can find you."
From *The House at Pooh Corner*
by A. A. Milne (Methuen, 1928)

In this chapter, we will investigate the state of contemporary poetry for children with an eye to the different types of poetry books being published, including current examples of each. Major poets writing today will be highlighted as well as creative ways to share their poetry with children. You'll learn more about poets and poetry on the Web and in the schools, about poetry awards and evaluation, and about performing and promoting poetry in the library with kids. We'll even look at the role of Mother Goose nursery rhymes in getting started with poetry for kids. Welcome to the most musical genre of literature for children.

INTRODUCTION

In survey after survey, we find nearly every library holds multiple copies of Shel Silverstein's poetry collections. Who has not heard of Shel Silverstein? His first poetry anthology, *Where the Sidewalk Ends*, published in 1974, sold more than four million copies to become the bestselling children's poetry book ever. His work is a staple of children's poetry and has now been enjoyed by several decades of children. Jack Prelutsky follows as a close second in being represented in most library collections. His zany humor and musical rhythms continue to engage children. But that's where the list often stops. And if you're a new poet writing for children, it can be challenging to get your name out there in the Silverstein-Prelutsky stratosphere. "After all, the way Prelutsky and Silverstein became household words to many readers was through promotion by teachers and librarians" (Wilson & Kutiper, 1994, p. 277). In my research on the poetry holdings of school and public libraries, I have found that poetry collection development is often uneven and inconsistent. Many people are unfamiliar with poetry awards, with contemporary poets writing for children today, and with multicultural poets, in particular.

How do we know which poetry books to choose? Poetry for young people can have many different faces, from familiar folk rhymes to sophisticated verse novels, from songs and fingerplays to standard anthologies, from traditional Mother Goose rhymes to poem picture books. Where do we begin in sharing poetry with children? I recommend humorous poetry, based on studies of children's preferences, as well as on my own personal experiences with poetry. I think we can all benefit from the leaven of laughter through poetry. But I also believe that if you are steeped in poetry and have your own more serious favorites to share, please do. Success depends so much on our own positive presentation of poetry, so begin with what you enjoy. But if don't know where to begin, rest assured that there is plenty of poetry variety to choose from.

Did you know that generally speaking in the field of children's literature, fewer poetry books are published than books in any other genres? Poetry books go out of print more quickly, too. Thus, as you learn about the different kinds of poetry books that are published and what to look for in selecting quality poetry, be aggressive about adding them to your collection to catch these gems before they go out of print. Indeed, consider purchasing multiple copies, because popular poetry books seem to disappear off the shelves, too. Would one copy of *Where the Sidewalk Ends* be adequate for your library? As we learn new ways of promoting and sharing poetry for children, we can create that same level of interest in new and up-and-coming poets and poetry books. With only a handful of poetry published for children each year (some fifty titles per year of poetry books for young people), acquisition can be relatively simple once you make poetry a priority.

History in Action: Mother Goose

Over the years, I have found that many children are missing the traditional exposure to Mother Goose nursery rhymes and they know very few of them. Children who are new to learning English may know rhymes from their home cultures but not be familiar with "the house that Jack built," for example. That's unfortunate, because in popular culture and adult literature there are constant references to Mother Goose rhymes and characters (e.g., ever heard of Robert Penn Warren's Pulitzer Prize–winning novel, *All the King's Men*, with a title that references "Humpty Dumpty"?). Even with older children, it can be fun to share Mother Goose rhymes and the history behind them. For example, check out *The Annotated Mother Goose* (by William Baring-Gould and Ceil Baring-Gould; Random House, 1988), which is full of the stories *behind* the rhymes.

Peter and Iona Opie spent a lifetime together collecting and gathering children's rhymes in a variety of historic collections worthy of study with older children. Their seminal work, *The Oxford Dictionary of Nursery Rhymes* (Oxford University Press, 1952), established a serious study of children's rhymes and folklore. They also assembled one of the richest collections of children's literature, toys, and games, some 20,000 pieces from the sixteenth to the twentieth centuries now held at the Bodleian Library at Oxford University in England. Three of their more contemporary collections of nursery rhymes are very appealing: *My Very First Mother Goose* (Candlewick, 1996), *Here Comes Mother Goose* (Candlewick, 1999), and *Mother Goose's Little Treasures* (Candlewick 2007), all illustrated by Rosemary Wells, and *I Saw Esau: The Schoolchild's Pocket Book* (Candlewick, 1992/2012) illustrated by Maurice Sendak. Individual Mother Goose rhymes are also available in board book form illustrated by Rosemary Wells.

What do we know about the woman who was "Mother Goose"? There was probably no such person. Most of the rhymes included in any Mother Goose collection originated in the distant past as folk stories told to children. The name of "Mother Goose" was first associated with nursery rhymes in an early collection of *Songs and Lullabies of old British nurses, Mother Goose's Melody; or, Sonnets for the Cradle* (1781), published by successors of John Newbery. The name is said to have come from Charles Perrault's fairy tales, *Contes de ma mère l'oye* (1697; *Tales of Mother Goose*). The legend that Mother Goose was an actual woman from Boston is false. In 1787, Isaiah Thomas published the first American edition, entitled *Mother Goose's Melody: or Sonnets for the Cradle*, which included such favorites as "Jack and Jill."

Mother Goose collections have been illustrated by various artists over the years including Jessie Wilcox Smith, Marguerite De Angeli, Michael Hague, Sylvia Long, Arnold Lobel, Tomie de Paola, Richard Scarry, Mary Engelbreit, David McPhail, and many others. In fact, the classic Blanche Fisher Wright anthology, *The Real Mother Goose* (Rand McNally, 1916), has sold five million copies and remains one of the 100 bestselling children's books of all time. There are countless examples of contemporary collections, including a few of my favorites: *You Read to Me, I'll Read to You: Very Short Mother Goose Tales to Read Together* by Mary Ann Hoberman (Little, Brown, 2005), Ruth Sanderson's *Mother Goose and Friends* (Little, Brown, 2008), *The Neighborhood Mother Goose* by Nina Crews (Amistad, 2003), *Mother Goose: Numbers on the Loose* by Leo and Diane Dillon (Harcourt, 2007), and *This Little Piggy: Lap Songs, Finger Plays, Clapping Games, and Pantomime Rhymes* by Jane Yolen (Candlewick, 2006).

For younger children, Jack Prelutsky created a kind of "American Mother Goose" with nursery rhymes that reference cities and places in the United States, rather than European sites such as "London Bridge" or "Banbury Cross" in his collections, *Ride a Purple Pelican* (Greenwillow, 1986) and *Beneath a Blue Umbrella* (Greenwillow, 1990).

Alice Schertle adapted English versions of Spanish rhymes for young children in *¡Pío Peep!: Traditional Spanish Nursery Rhymes* by Alma Flor Ada and F. Isabel Campoy (HarperCollins, 2003), followed by *Muu, Moo! Rimas de animales/Animal Nursery Rhymes* (HarperCollins, 2010). For additional rhymes in Spanish/English and in other languages, look for Jose-Luis Orozco's *Diez Deditos: Ten Little Fingers and Other Play Rhymes and Action Songs from Latin America* (Dutton, 1997) or Jane Yolen's *Street Rhymes from Around the World* (Boyds Mills/Wordsong, 2000) and *Sleep Rhymes Around the World* (Boyds Mills/Wordsong, 1994). It certainly bears remembering that all cultures have rhymes shared in the nursery and that gathering and comparing them can be very meaningful for children and their families.

Mother Goose also has a massive presence online, and you can find a variety of different resources on the Web:

Links to games, crafts, activities, songs, clip art, and an alphabetical directory of hundreds of nursery rhymes from A to Z:
http://www.mothergoose.com/

Nursery rhymes grouped by theme:
http://www-personal.umich.edu/~pfa/dreamhouse/nursery/rhymes.html

The official Mother Goose Society, which celebrates May 1 as Mother Goose Day:
http://www.librarysupport.net/mothergoosesociety/

Mother Goose rhymes in rebus form (pictures + words):
http://www.enchantedlearning.com/Rhymes.html

There are also several helpful professional resources for planning Mother Goose–based programs with children including *Mother Goose on the Loose* by Betsy Diamant-Cohen (Neal-Schuman, May 2006) and *Baby Rhyming Time* by Linda Ernst (Neal-Schuman, 2007).

DEFINITIONS

It is important to recognize what is unique and special about poetry, particularly poetry for children. Children's literature scholars Winters and Schmidt (2001) remind us that children's poetry, like children's literature, is not poetry simplified. It is poetry that is accessible to a child audience, that speaks to children, and that is able to convey meaningfully the experiences and perceptions of the child. Kiefer notes, "Fine poetry is this distillation of experience that captures the essence of an object, a feeling, or a thought" (2010, p. 341). Poetry is concise and full of beautiful language, but it is the emotion or experience that gives poetry its special power. Poetry also does this in fewer words than any other genre. In addition, we often return to the same poems over and over and over again in the course of our lives. We can cherish one poem throughout our lives, gaining new meaning from it as life experiences shape our understanding.

Children's poetry includes many different kinds of things: Mother Goose, rhymes, verse, jingles, doggerel, songs, lyrics, and so on. Unfortunately, many people have negative associations with the very word "poetry" based on prior school experiences memorizing or analyzing poetry. It is unfortunate how universal some of these negative experiences with poetry can be. The role of adults can be pivotal in shaping these attitudes toward poetry (or in keeping children away from poetry). Personally, I believe the key is sharing poems out loud and getting the kids to participate. More on that later. First, let's look at the state of children's poetry publishing today.

Librarians in Action: Visiting Poets Make a Difference

Hilary Haygood earned her master of library science degree at Texas Woman's University and served as the librarian at San Andres Elementary School in Andrews, Texas. An assignment for a graduate class motivated her to write a grant proposal that was unfortunately rejected. Undaunted, she revised and resubmitted it, it was accepted, and she has since launched a popular series of author visits. She writes about that pivotal experience here.

Granting Wishes
by Hilary Haygood

"Can you find me a book of poems with Spanish words by that lady that came to our school when I was in third grade?" Two years after children's poet and author Pat Mora visited our school district, I am often greeted with that question as my fifth grade students enter the library in search of just the right book.

For years I noticed the enthusiasm and increase in circulation of the books that visiting regional authors generated in my students. When my local school district formed an Education Foundation to fund innovative teaching ideas through grants, I saw a potential source of funding that would fulfill my dream of bringing a renowned children's author to my small west Texas town.

The majority of the students in my school district come from homes where Spanish is the primary language. After much deliberation and research, I decided that Pat Mora would be the perfect author to satisfy my goal of stimulating interest in reading quality literature through personal interaction with a critically acclaimed author and to meet the needs of my students by instilling a sense of pride in being bilingual.

Initially I wrote two grants, one to purchase additional books to supplement my library's poetry collection for use in collaboration with one of the fifth grade teachers to enrich student learning across the curriculum, and the second to bring Pat Mora to my campus as a culminating activity to address the student body and to work with the class that was going to be involved in daily poetry activities.

When the "prize patrol" of our local Education Foundation arrived at my campus in late September of 2005 to award grants, I was thrilled as I saw them approach the library. They awarded the grant to purchase the additional poetry books, but no mention was made of the grant for Pat Mora's visit.

Grant recipients are traditionally recognized at the school board meeting immediately following the announcements. When I was recognized at the board meeting, I was informed that the Education Foundation committee loved the idea of bringing Pat Mora to visit our school district but would prefer that all students in our district benefit from her presentations. I was asked to rewrite the grant with the cooperation of all the librarians in the district and resubmit it in January of 2006.

I wasted no time in enlisting the support of the other librarians and rewriting the grant to bring Pat Mora to our school district for three days instead of the one-day visit that I had originally proposed. The grant was funded in January of 2006 and Pat Mora visited our school district in April of that year, speaking to every campus in our district. She also spent over an hour working with the class that had been immersed in a poetry-rich curriculum throughout the school year.

As Pat spoke with pride of being bilingual, I watched students begin to sit up straighter and saw shoulders rise with a newly found sense of ethnic pride. She mesmerized them with her poetry and stories of her youth. Everywhere we went, Pat's message inspired and captivated students.

Presently, my students are looking forward to a visit by children's nonfiction author Kathleen Krull that was also made possible through grant funding of the Education Foundation. I have already seen an increase in the circulation of her books in anticipation of her arrival.

Author visits can inspire students to read books that might otherwise have gone unnoticed and motivate them to aspire to heights that they might have thought were beyond their reach. After Pat Mora's visit, I received this letter of thanks from a former student. "I might have told you last year, but I have wanted to be an author since the second grade. Pat Mora definitely inspired me to work *even harder* for that goal."

Note: Unfortunately, since implementing this successful program, Hilary's school library position was eliminated due to budget cuts. She taught fifth grade science, then worked for a book company, and has now moved to the public library setting where she works as Youth Services coordinator and has big plans for future poetry programs.

TYPES OF POETRY BOOKS FOR CHILDREN

What kinds of poetry books are available for children and young adults? Here we will examine five general categories of poetry books for children: general anthologies, topical collections, individual poet compilations, poem picture books, and verse novels. Each has its unique attributes with examples of each format now published on a regular basis.

General Anthologies

General anthologies include many different kinds of poems on many different topics by many different poets. Collections like these are usually very global but may be organized by subthemes or subcategories (such as the seasons, emotions, childhood experiences, etc.). This kind of poetry collection has probably been around the longest of all the types and is a practical resource for finding a variety of poems by many different poets. Indeed, this is probably the easiest way for new poets to get their work published and their names known. It is also an easy way to gather poems that are in the public domain. In days gone by, anthologies tended to be comprehensive and lengthy, often 200–300 pages long, but newer anthologies are usually shorter and often richly illustrated. They are still probably most often accessed by adults who share them with children, rather than by child readers themselves. And they can be a helpful beginning point for librarians or teachers who want one place to start for selecting a variety of quality poems.

One of the most popular collections continues to be *The Random House Book of Poetry for Children* compiled by poet Jack Prelutsky and illustrated by Arnold Lobel (Random House, 1983). It's a good example of the poem variety and friendly format that characterizes many contemporary anthologies. Prelutsky also compiled two other noteworthy general anthologies, *The 20th Century Children's Poetry Treasury* (Knopf, 1999) and *The Beauty of the Beast*, both illustrated by Meilo So (Knopf, 1997). Another gem is Lee Bennett Hopkins's *Days to Celebrate: A Full Year of Poetry, People, Holidays, History, Fascinating Facts, and More* (HarperCollins, 2005). *Poetry Speaks to Children* edited by Elise Paschen (Sourcebook, 2005) and *Poetry Speaks: Who I Am,* also edited by Paschen along with Dominique Raccah (Sourcebooks, 2010), both include audio CDs of many of the poets featured in the book reading their own work. And I'm proud to say I collaborated with poet Janet Wong and several other prominent poets to publish the first digital anthologies of original poetry for young people in eBook form: the Poetry Tag Time series (*PoetryTagTime*, *P*TAG, Gift Tag*, all in 2011).

For prize-winning poets, look for *Another Jar of Tiny Stars* edited by Bernice Cullinan and Deborah Wooten, which contains poems by the NCTE Poetry Award recipients (Wordsong/Boyds Mills Press, 2009). Other general anthologies often include classics, Mother Goose, nursery rhymes, and even poems written by children themselves such as you'll find in *Soft Hay Will Catch You: Poems by Young People* compiled by Sanford Lyne (Simon & Schuster, 2004) and *Walking on Earth and Touching the Sky: Poetry and Prose by Lakota Youth at Red Cloud Indian School* edited by Timothy McLaughlin (Abrams, 2012).

Topical or Thematic Collections

The special topical or thematic anthology is becoming one of the most popular forms of poetry, offering librarians and teachers who enjoy thematic collections poems to supplement the curriculum or connect with specific topics and themes. These are collections gathered around a single topic such as animals, holidays, family, and so on. They still include poems by a variety of poets, so they provide a good introduction to a variety of poetic styles and voices all selected to provide different perspectives on the unifying theme or subject.

Specialized anthologies offer a more concentrated exposure to poems on a single topic, thus appealing to a reader's prior interest in a topic like dogs, or providing an introduction to a topic unfamiliar to readers, such as outer space. These slimmer, specialized collections are usually more visually inviting and are also very popular among *both* adults and children. Lee Bennett Hopkins set a Guinness Book of World Records for compiling 113 poetry anthologies, many of them thematic collections, such as *I Am the Book* (Holiday House, 2011), poems about books and reading. For an even more comprehensive collection, look for *The National Geographic Book of Animal Poetry* edited by Children's Poet Laureate J. Patrick Lewis (2012), full of poems about all kinds of animals by a variety of poets old and new and illustrated with amazing full-color photographs from National Geographic sources.

For two other lovely examples, look for Pat Mora's collection, *Love to Mama* (Lee & Low, 2001), a gathering of poems about mothers and grandmothers by a variety of poets, or its companion book, *In Daddy's Arms I Am Tall* compiled by Javaka Steptoe (Lee & Low, 1997). Since all the poems are similar in subject, but by different poets, these are excellent examples of "topical collections" and lovely for sharing with parents and families.

Individual Poet Compilations

Poets like to publish their own work in single collections featuring only their writing too, of course. This is also the best way to get a feeling for the unique voice and style of the poet. These collections may also have a topical connection, such as animals or holidays or sports, but all the poems in the collection are authored by one person, the featured poet. These collections are also very popular with both children and adults once they have had some introduction to the writer of the collection. *A Light in the Attic* (1981), for example, is one of the most circulated books of children's poetry ever because there are now several generations of Shel Silverstein fans. Readers seek out Silverstein's anthologies of poetry year after year. If you're not familiar with the poet, however, you may not pick up a book of poetry by names such as X. J. Kennedy, John Ciardi, or J. Patrick Lewis, for example. Unless the book topic, cover art, or interior illustrations intrigue you, you may not realize that both Ciardi and Lewis, for example, are as clever and humorous as Silverstein in their writing.

As with all readers' advisory work, of course, this is where the poetry-savvy librarian can really make a difference, guiding children (and adults) to collections by poets who may become new favorites. Start with two classic collections of individual poetry, Langston Hughes's landmark work, *The Dream Keeper and Other Poems* (seventy-fifth anniversary edition, Knopf, 2007), or the "color poems" of Mary O'Neill's *Hailstones and Halibut Bones: Adventures in Color* (Doubleday, 1989). Follow up with *We Are America: A Tribute from the Heart* by Walter Dean Myers (HarperCollins, 2011) or *Red Sings from Treetops: A Year in Colors* by Joyce Sidman (Houghton Mifflin, 2009). Children may also find new favorites in the many collections of Douglas Florian (*Unbeelievables: Honeybee Poems and Paintings*; Beach Lane, 2012) or Kristine O'Connell George (*Emma Dilemma: Big Sister Poems*; Clarion, 2009).

Poetry on the Web

Poetry-related sites on the Web offer actual poems for and by children, audio recordings of poems, biographical information about poets, teaching activities, and some even welcome child participation. Be sure to look for poets' personal websites, too.

The Academy of American Poets
http://www.poets.org
This site offers sample poems, poet biographies, audio archives, National Poetry Month celebrations, curriculum resources, teacher discussion forums, teaching tips, and more.

Giggle Poetry
http://www.gigglepoetry.com/
This kid-friendly website offers poems to read, with new ones posted regularly, as well as opportunities for child interaction.

Potato Hill Poetry
http://www.potatohill.com/
This wonderful Web resource suggests many unusual and innovative ways to celebrate poetry reading and writing with children.

The Library of Congress Poetry and Literature Center
http://www.loc.gov/poetry/
This site may interest older children who are interested in learning about the poet laureates of the United States, national prizes in poetry, special poetry events, and audio archives.

Favorite Poem Project
http://www.favoritepoem.org/
This site features Poet Laureate Robert Pinsky's project to have average citizens audiotape their favorite poems.

Poem Picture Books

Another format for poetry books is the poem picture book that showcases an individual poem, often a classic poem, as the only poem in the book. The text of the poem is spread out line by line across the pages of a standard thirty-two–page picture book. These poem picture books offer the benefit of extensive illustrations to help understand and interpret or even reinterpret each line of the poem. The picture book version of Robert Frost's "Stopping by Woods on a Snowy Evening" illustrated by Susan Jeffers (Dutton, 2001) is one of my favorites in this format. The literal portrayal of the snowy path is refreshing after many of us have been forced to analyze its deeper meaning. "The Owl and the Pussycat" by Edward Lear has received this treatment by several artists, as have the classic poems "Casey at the Bat," "A Visit from St. Nicholas" (or "'Twas the Night Before Christmas"), "Jabberwocky," "The Midnight Ride of Paul Revere," and many individual Mother Goose rhymes.

This format of the poem picture book is not to be confused with poetic or rhyming picture books, such as Dr. Seuss's books with their strong rhythms and frequent rhymes. In a poem picture book, the poem can stand alone—without the book format or even the illustrations. In the usual picture book, text and illustrations work together to convey a story. In a poem picture book, the illustrations help provide one vision of the poem's meaning. This can help introduce young readers to longer, narrative poems or classic works. It can also be a helpful medium for older students who may be familiar with the classic poem but haven't found it moving or meaningful until they see it as a visually rich experience. They might even enjoy choosing a favorite poem and creating their own simple picture book, interpreting the lines through their own illustrations.

Verse Novels

A relatively new poetic form with roots in ancient epic poetry, the verse novel or novel in verse is a form that is growing in popularity, particularly with middle school readers and older. Indeed, the majority of verse novels currently available are probably best suited to young adults. However, there are several examples that children ages nine or ten and up may enjoy, such as *Amber Was Brave, Essie Was Smart* by Vera Williams (Greenwillow, 2001), or *Minn and Jake's Almost Terrible Summer* by Janet Wong (Farrar, Straus & Giroux, 2008), or *Summerhouse Time* by Eileen Spinelli (Knopf, 2007), or *Diamond Willow* by Helen Frost (Farrar, Straus & Giroux, 2008), among others.

Newbery-winning novelists Karen Hesse and Sharon Creech have also authored several interesting novels in verse, including *Out of the Dust* (Scholastic, 1997) by Hesse and *Love That Dog* (HarperCollins, 2001) and *Hate That Cat* (HarperCollins, 2008) by Creech. The best verse novels are built on poems that are often lovely "stand alone" works of poetry. A narrative unfolds poem by poem, often with multiple points of view and in colloquial, conversational language. This format is wooing many middle grade children both to poetry and to reading in general and provides a fun format for dramatic read alouds or readers' theater–style performances.

Other Sources of Poetic Language

There are even more types of books that are written in rhyme and might loosely be considered "poetry." They certainly hold a great deal of appeal to children who enjoy the music of the language when these books are read aloud. In fact, once you start looking you may be surprised at all the different places poetry is appearing.

- Rhyming picture books (for example, *Move Over, Rover* by Karen Beaumont; Harcourt, 2006)
- Rhythmic picture books (for example, *Goodnight Moon* by Margaret Wise Brown; Harper, 1947)
- Predictable books (for example, *Brown Bear, Brown Bear* by Bill Martin Jr.; Holt, 1967/2007)
- Alphabet books (for example, *Chicka Chicka Boom Boom* by Bill Martin Jr. and John Archambault; Simon & Schuster, 1989)
- Counting books (for example, *Counting Crocodiles* by Judy Sierra; Gulliver, 1997)

- Dr. Seuss (for example, *Oh, the Places You'll Go!*; Random House, 1990)
- Nonfiction picture books (for example, *Flush: The Scoop on Poop Throughout the Ages* by Charise Mericle Harper; Little, Brown, 2007)

Technically, many of these in the list above would not be considered "poetry." They may be written in rhyme (like Dr. Seuss's books, for example), but the words probably would not stand alone published as a poem. However, these books do make the point that poetry, rhyme, and verse are all around us.

MAJOR POETS

In the United States today, there is a great deal of renewed interest in poetry for young people with new poets and poetic forms emerging all the time. In addition, greater openness to new voices has encouraged multicultural poetry to flourish. And more and more international poetry is finding its way into the United States as well. Seeking out the poetry of parallel cultures that reflects many diverse viewpoints such as the works of Francisco X. Alarcón, Michio Mado, and Monica Gunning enables us to show children firsthand both the sameness and the differences that make the human landscape so dynamic and fascinating. We need to seek out poetry books by new voices as we expand our poetry collections and keep them relevant to today's young readers and listeners.

Calendar of Poets' Birthdays

One way of celebrating poets is by acknowledging their birthdays and sharing a sample poem or poetry book by him or her on that special day. Here's a beginning calendar of birthdays of contemporary poets who write for children to get you started. These featured poets are known predominantly for specializing in writing poetry for children, and they include major award winners, popular bestsellers, and multicultural voices.

January

2 Jean Little
5 Monica Gunning
7 Minfong Ho
18 A. A. Milne; Grace Nichols
19 Pat Mora
29 Tony Johnston

February

1 Langston Hughes
2 Judith Viorst

11 Jane Yolen
20 Kenn Nesbitt
21 Francisco X. Alarcón
26 Allan Wolf
27 Laura E. Richards

March

1 Alan Katz
4 Craig Crist-Evans
12 Naomi Shihab Nye
13 David Harrison
17 Lilian Moore
18 Douglas Florian
26 Robert Frost

April

7 Alice Schertle
12 Gary Soto
13 Lee Bennett Hopkins
20 April Halprin Wayland
22 William Jay Smith
25 George Ella Lyon
28 Barbara Juster Esbensen

May

2 Bobbi Katz
5 J. Patrick Lewis
6 Kristine O'Connell George; José-Luis Orozco
8 Constance Levy
12 Edward Lear, Limerick Day
17 Eloise Greenfield
25 Joyce Carol Thomas

June

1 Bruce Lansky
6 Nancy Willard; Cynthia Rylant
8 Judy Sierra
16 Kalli Dakos
20 Nancy Wood
24 John Ciardi
26 Nancy Willard

July

6 Kathi Appelt
10 Rebecca Kai Dotlich; Patricia Hubbell
13 Anna Grossnickle Hines
16 Arnold Adoff
17 Karla Kuskin
19 Eve Merriam
27 Paul Janeczko

August

12 Mary Ann Hoberman; Walter Dean Myers
15 Betsy Franco
17 Myra Cohn Livingston
19 Ogden Nash
21 X. J. Kennedy
29 Karen Hesse
31 Dennis Lee

September

5 Paul Fleischman
8 Jack Prelutsky
9 Aileen Fisher
15 Sara Holbrook
25 Shel Silverstein
30 Janet Wong

October

3 Marilyn Singer
20 Nikki Grimes
27 Lillian Morrison
29 Valerie Worth
31 Joan Bransfield Graham

November

2 Ted Scheu
13 Robert Louis Stevenson
15 David McCord
22 Brod Bagert

December

1 Carol Diggory Shields
5 Christina Rossetti
10 Emily Dickinson
13 Georgia Heard
21 Susan Pearson
27 Juan Felipe Herrera

Creating a "featured poet" display or hosting a real or "virtual" visiting poet are two excellent ways to showcase the people behind the poems we enjoy. Choosing a variety of poets to highlight on a rotating basis can provide children with more in-depth exposure to their poems and poetry writing. You might consider:

- Gathering the poet's works and making them prominent and available
- Creating a bulletin board, poster, or display featuring the poet (include a photo, a printout of their website home page, a few "fun facts" about their lives)
- Reading the poets' works aloud often
- Looking up biographical information about the poet and sharing with children
- Looking for autobiographies, video/audio interviews, and poet websites to share
- Setting up an online chat with a poet or even a guest appearance by a poet, being sure to prepare the children beforehand with extensive reading
- Involving children in choosing poets to study and in developing featured poet centers
- If funds allow, setting up a Poet-in-Residence program, inviting a poet to work with children on an ongoing basis for a short period of time

We typically feature popular fiction writers with booktalks and displays in our book promotion activities, but have we considered giving poets the same publicity and close study? Creating time and space for featured poets helps introduce their work and encourages children to read more poetry. In addition, it can be inspiring for young would-be poets to see that there are successful adults who have made poetry writing their career.

Based on Vardell, Sylvia. (2007). *Poetry People: A Practical Guide to Children's Poets*. Englewood, CO: Libraries Unlimited.

Authors in Action: J. Patrick Lewis

After serving as a professor of economics at Otterbein College for over two decades, J. Patrick Lewis turned to writing children's poetry. His first book of poems for children, *A Hippopotamusn't*, was published in 1990, and he has followed with over eighty-five children's books since then, most of them poetry. He makes over thirty elementary school visits a year and is a frequent speaker at workshops and conferences. He received the National Council of Teachers of English (NCTE) Excellence in Children's Poetry Award for his body of work and was chosen as Children's Poet Laureate in 2011. Here he answers a few questions about his poetry writing for young people.

A Circus for the Brain: The 2011 Children's Poet Laureate Speaks (excerpt) by J. Patrick Lewis with Sylvia Vardell

Why do you think poetry is important for children?

Children spend their whole lives talking, listening, reading, and dreaming in one language (or more, if they are lucky), so why not encourage them to do all those things in the most pleasurable possible way—with poetry. Great poetry is a circus for the brain. It's ten pounds of excitement in a nine-pound bag. But children won't know what that means unless we offer them the best. Soon, they'll be asking for second and third helpings. Even though few children will become poets, poetry helps them realize that one of the most phenomenal gifts humans get free of charge is the English language. And there is nothing in any language more beautiful, more inspiring and thought-provoking than poetry.

How did you come to the writing of poetry for children when you're also a scholar of economics and Russian history?

My usual answer (a joke) is that an economist can become a children's poet only after a very delicate operation. Actually, I wanted to be a writer first, and so I wrote for nearly 30 years in economics. But very few people read economics unless they are roped to a chair. Happily, when I was still a pup (but almost 40!), I discovered poetry—"the road not taken . . . and that has made all the difference."

What part did poetry play in your own childhood?

Where was the magical teacher when I was in second, fifth, eighth, or sixteenth grade who would say, "I'm going to do you a favor, sonny. Read Emily Dickinson or Robert Frost, and tell me if you don't come down with a fever of delight." Alas, it never happened. So I'm sad to say that poetry played no part in my childhood. I'm a walking, talking example of "It's never too late." Good things happen to those who wait.

Do you follow a regular process in creating your poetry? Care to share?

Writers are odd folk; peccadilloes abound. Each one of us has a unique way of answering this question. When I'm not making school visits, I spend at least eight hours a day, seven days a week working. By working I mean reading (which always comes first), then writing, rewriting, doing research.

Your poetry is often grounded in history or historical topics. How did you come to that focus? Why is that important to you?

My objective, as I've always said, is to range across the curriculum and all ages. My choice of subjects—the Civil War, extraordinary women, notable black Americans, famous monuments, geography, Galileo, Michelangelo, and the like—stems from a sense that I might be able to add my own small voice, with a heavy dose of humility, to these well-traveled themes, and not repeat what others have done. I'm always searching for a new untouched—or insufficiently touched—subject.

You seem to delight in experimenting with poetic form. Which are your favorite forms? Are there any you would still like to try?

Ballad stanzas or common measures are overused in children's poetry, I think. A whole book of ballad stanzas, even if it's a very funny collection, gets to be monotonous. There are hundreds of other forms, most foreign born, just begging to be tried. I think children's poets should be willing to take more risks. Unfortunately long forms seem to have fallen out of favor with publishers and parents. So short forms are winning the day. I can't choose a favorite form since so much depends upon the subject, whether it's nonsense verse, nonfiction topics, biographical poetry. I invented a new verse form, the zeno, but it has almost no chance of finding a stall in the redoubtable stable of verse forms, simply because its rhyming requirements are too strict.

What is your favorite part about visiting kids in schools and libraries?

Having done over 520 author visits here and abroad, I think I can safely say that the children's appreciation of books is the most rewarding part of author visits. That and the obvious pleasure they take in hearing poetry spoken. Riddles are always great favorites, simply because they are interactive. And they treat you like a rock star! (Which my wife has thus far refused to do.) I hasten to add that being with those amazing beings called teachers and librarians is another reason why school visits are so rewarding. Without seeming to curry favor, I don't think most people appreciate the hard work and imagination of the shepherds of our youth.

Source: The Poetry Foundation http://www.poetryfoundation.org/article/242020. Used with permission.

One Book in Action: The National Geographic Book of Animal Poetry

For our focus book of poetry, let's consider *The National Geographic Book of Animal Poetry* (National Geographic, 2012), edited by U.S. Children's Poet Laureate J. Patrick Lewis and beautifully illustrated with full-color nature photographs from National Geographic. It's an amazing anthology full of 200 poems about all kinds of animals written by the best poets writing for young people now and in the past. And it is also one of the most popular books of poetry for children that I have shared in recent years. Teachers, librarians, families, and children of all ages are just blown away by the beautiful photographs when they browse through the book and then completely captivated when they pause to ponder the poems, too. From the first oversized image of a mother and baby polar bear nuzzling each other, to the final photograph of an elephant against a vivid red sunset, this book is a rich resource worth exploring in depth.

Animal Poetry

This collection features 200 poems about animals of all kinds organized in categories like "the big ones," "the little ones," "the winged ones," "the water ones," "the strange ones," "the noisy ones," and "the quiet ones," with twenty or more animals depicted in each section. Using the table of contents or the index, invite children to look up poems about their favorite animals. They can prepare to read their selection aloud to the whole group or work with a partner to prepare a paired or choral reading of their chosen poem. If time allows, they can copy and post their favorite poems in an animal poem collage alongside drawings or photos of their own. Then encourage students to explore the 811 shelf for more animal poems. You'll find a comprehensive list of animal poems in general and specific animal categories in *The Poetry Teacher's Book of Lists* (Vardell, 2012). Here are just a few excellent titles to gather:

Ehlert, Lois. 2008. *Oodles of Animals*. San Diego, CA: Harcourt.
Elliott, David. 2012. *In the Sea*. Somerville, MA: Candlewick.
Florian, Douglas. 2005. *Zoo's Who*. San Diego, CA: Harcourt.
Schwartz, David M., and Schy, Yael. 2010. *What in the Wild? Mysteries of Nature Concealed . . . and Revealed*. Berkeley, CA: Tricycle.
Singer, Marilyn. 2012. *A Strange Place to Call Home: The World's Most Dangerous Habitats and the Animals That Call Them Home*. San Francisco: Chronicle.
Wong, Janet. 2011. *Once Upon a Tiger: New Beginnings for Endangered Animals*. OnceUponaTiger.com.
Worth, Valerie. 2007. *Animal Poems*. New York: Farrar, Straus & Giroux.
Zimmer, Tracie Vaughn. 2011. *Cousins of Clouds: Elephant Poems*. New York: Houghton Mifflin.

Poetic Form

In the backmatter for *The National Geographic Book of Animal Poetry*, J. Patrick Lewis provides a two-page guide to "Writing Poems About Animals" that briefly explains different forms of poetry including the couplet, shape poem, haiku, limerick, and free verse. Work with the kids to find a poem in the book that is an example of each form and talk about why the poet may have chosen that form to describe that animal. For example, share Myra Cohn Livingston's poem "Crickets" on p. 130 and talk about how she uses two columns of words to suggest the rhythm of the cricket's sound. Then challenge them to work with a partner to create a new, original animal poem in the form of their choice. For more guidance on poem forms, check out the "Resources" page Lewis also provides in the back and look for Avis Harley's alphabet of poetry: *Fly with Poetry: An ABC of Poetry* (Wordsong/Boyds Mills Press, 2000) and *Leap into Poetry: More ABCs of Poetry* (Wordsong/Boyds Mills Press, 2001).

Pairing Poetry and Nonfiction

When the topic is animals, it's a great opportunity to pair animal poems with informational books about animals, particularly highly visual nonfiction picture books. The images grab the kids first and you can talk with them about the animals and what they know about them. Look up details in the nonfiction books and work together to create "found" poems based on the key words and details gleaned from the nonfiction text. For examples of "found" poems, check out Georgia Heard's *The Arrow Finds Its Mark: A Book of Found Poems* (Macmillan, 2012). Then share and compare with the animal poems they like in the poetry books you have gathered. Show them how both poets and scientists observe closely, describe natural phenomena, and use well-chosen words.

More by the Poet

Children who enjoy poems about nature, animals, and science will likely respond to other works by J. Patrick Lewis such as:

Ridicholas Nicholas: More Animal Poems (Dial, 1995)
The Little Buggers: Insect and Spider Poems (Dial, 1998)
Swan Song: Poems of Extinction (Creative Editions, 2003)
Scientrickery: Riddles in Science (Harcourt, 2004)
Galileo's Universe (Creative Editions, 2005)

These poems explore the natural world in fresh and playful imagery and clever language. Find a shady spot outside to read these poems or research insect or animal sounds online and play them in the background while you read selected poems aloud.

EVALUATION CRITERIA

Clearly poetry is different from prose in its form and structure. Thus, we don't typically use the usual literary criteria of characterization, plot, setting, theme, and style to evaluate poetry (except for some verse novels). Poetry has its own unique elements that give it distinctiveness: rhythm, sound, language, imagery, and emotion. In addition, we usually consider both individual poems as well as whole poetry books as we decide which poetry books are best for our needs.

Evaluating Poems

As you read poems, you can probably say whether you like them or not. Saying *why* you like them can be more challenging. This is where the poetic elements of *rhythm, rhyme, sound, language, imagery,* and *emotion* are helpful. Short, Lynch-Brown, and Tomlinson remind us that poetry is "the concentrated expression of ideas and feelings through precise and imaginative words carefully selected for their sonorous and rhythmical effects" (2014, p. 84). This combination of ideas + feelings + rhythm + words + sounds adds up to a powerful package. Let's consider each of those poetic elements briefly.

Rhythm.   The use of *rhythm* refers to the beat or meter of the poem, whether it's rhyming or free verse. Does the poet use short lines to create a staccato rhythm or long couplets to create a flow? The arrangement of lines and verses is a deliberate decision by the poet to create a rhythm that is apparent in the read aloud. It should fit the words and meaning of the poem and seem to fall naturally without forced syllables or beats.

Rhyme.   *Rhyme* is the obvious parallel of matching sounds, usually at the ends of lines of poems, although it can also occur elsewhere in a poem as internal rhyme. Rhyming is an appealing part of poetry for younger children as you see in many Mother Goose nursery rhymes. But it is challenging to rhyme well in contemporary poetry without feeling forced or sacrificing word meaning for rhyme. Does it seem natural and appropriate as you read the poem aloud? Does it move the poem easily forward or does it bring the poem to a stop and overwhelm the words of the poem?

Sound.   The *sound* of poetry depends greatly on the rhythm and rhyme of the poem, but it is also built upon each letter and word, chosen carefully by the poet for its individual and collective effect. This is where alliteration, assonance, consonance, onomatopoeia, and the like come in. Is one sound repeated in a sequence of words? Like "s" or "l," for example? That creates a certain effect that should add to the impact of the poem. Or is a long vowel sound in the middle of words used repeatedly, like "a" or "o"? Again, read the poem aloud and listen for these sounds. They add to the drama or music of the poem.

Language.   The *language* of the poem refers to the poet's choice of each and every word. Are there surprising choices? Is figurative language used in fresh and unusual ways in similes, metaphors, personification? Are words and phrases chosen and arranged in ways that seem vivid and meaningful? As Mark Twain put it, "The difference between the right word and the almost right word is the difference between lightning and the lightning bug."

Imagery.   Of course the language helps create the *imagery* of the poem, the visual picture you have in your mind when you read a poem. Good poems use sensory words to create this mental picture; great poems provide surprising and unexpected images that grow from a creative and unique use of language.

Emotion.   Finally, poems also have an *emotional* impact, making us laugh or sigh or feel what the poet might have felt in capturing this moment. Does this grow naturally out of the poem's language and the poet's use of poetic tools? Or does it feel flat or forced or completely absent?

These labels are not an essential part of sharing poetry with children, although kids often notice these elements even when they don't know the terminology. Instead these components help us understand which poetic elements are "hooking" us as readers and listeners. Poets can help us see, smell, hear, taste, and even feel that we can touch things through their powerful use of language. We often rely on these poetic elements to guide us in discussing the genre. Which seem most prominent? How does the poet use particular poetic elements to special effect? The poet Emily Dickinson claimed, "If I feel physically as if the top of my head were taken off, I know that is poetry."

Evaluating Poetry Books

Don't forget to look at the book as a whole, too. Consider the theme or topic, organization and design, length and breadth, balance and variety of poems, use of illustrations, inclusion of reference aids, and appeal to audience. Are the poems in the collection appropriate for young people? What age range? Does the theme or topic "grab" kids or will it need to be more actively promoted? Is the overall length of the collection appropriate? Is there a balance and variety of poems? Are they current or classic? Is the book well organized and designed? Do the illustrations complement or overpower the poems? Does the book make you want to read more poems by this poet (or anthologist)? We look at the book in terms of the balance of illustration and text, if it's a picture book, but also in terms of the individual poems and poets represented.

The construction and organization of anthologies is also important to consider. For example, I think a poetry collection is also enhanced when there is a bit of background information on the poets or poems provided. Or when reference aids are included such as a table of contents, subject index, and/or first line index. How are the poems grouped or organized and accessed? Are the themes or categories appropriate and meaningful to children? We should consider these aspects of anthology design and organization, since many poetry collections are browsed, rather than read from cover to cover. Is it easy to find a specific poem? Does the book's design invite further reading as well?

These variables can help us look critically at the poetry books we encounter. They can help us break down the process to look at the language, the book's organization and layout, and its appeal to children. But ultimately, some trial and error is involved, too. It's not as mathematical as simply ticking off a checklist. Some elements will not apply in some cases and others may emerge as more important. One weighs the overall combination of poems, poem types, tone, look, and accessibility while looking for books that will appeal to young readers.

Sample Review

Let's put these evaluation criteria into action and consider one review and how it uses these criteria. Here's a sample review of a book of poetry:

Myers, Walter Dean. 2006. *Jazz*. Ill. by Christopher Myers. New York: Holiday House.

Jazz is a vibrant picture book poetry collection that is both a celebration of jazz music and history and a tribute to the city of New Orleans. The language is vivid and participatory and the art is sprawling and expressive in Mardi Gras colors of wild greens, purples, and oranges. The fifteen poems celebrate the jazz band, vocalists, various instrumental combinations, and even a traditional New Orleans funeral procession, each with words and phrases highlighted for emphasis and for children reading along. A helpful introduction, glossary of terms, and a timeline provide additional background. This father and son team has once again collaborated to create a masterpiece that magically captures the spirit and rhythms of music on the printed page. It's a visual treat, but one that also begs to be shared out loud to bring the music and the music of language to life again. One example poem, "Stride," contrasts eight long lines in rhyming couplets with short two-word phrases juxtaposed after each line, providing an echo of the key words and ideas and inviting children to shout or chant along: "jiving/bones; pride/stride; driving/tones; glide/ride." Follow up with playing piano, drum, horns, or homemade instruments while saying the lines together, or adding marching, movement or dance, or listening to recordings of jazz greats.

[From *Librarians' Choices* and http://poetryforchildren.blogspot.com/. Used with permission.]

This review of a poetry book considers both the poetic elements apparent in the poems as well as the construction of the book as a poetry resource. As it considers the poetry, it mentions that the language is "vivid and participatory" and captures the "spirit and rhythms of music." It addresses the emotional power of the poetry in portraying the "celebration of jazz music" and in its "tribute to the city of New Orleans." A sample poem, "Stride," is highlighted to note the structure the poet creates for one poem, the words he chooses, and how this emphasizes sound and music in both the language and content. The book as a whole is discussed, too, with particular attention to the illustrations since this is a "visual treat" of a picture book: "the art is sprawling and expressive in Mardi Gras colors of wild greens, purples, and oranges." The unifying theme (jazz) is explicit as are the contents including "fifteen poems" that "celebrate the jazz band, vocalists, various instrumental combinations, and even a traditional New Orleans funeral procession." The inclusion of reference aids is also mentioned with a nod to "a helpful introduction, glossary of terms, and a timeline." The appeal to the child audience is discussed with particular emphasis on how the book "begs to be shared out loud" with "words and phrases highlighted for emphasis and for children reading along." Suggestions for child participation and follow-up activities are even included ("shout or chant along"; "Follow up with playing piano, drum, horns, or homemade instruments . . . marching, movement or dance, or listening to recordings of jazz greats"). One comes away with a sense of what this poetry book is about, what it looks like, and how to share it with kids.

Perhaps more than any other genre, poetry knows no age level or bias. Although poems may appear short and simple on the surface, they may be deceptively complex. The more poetry we know and the more ways we share it, the more likely we are to experience success in selecting poetry and sharing it with children. The more we share it with children, the more their understanding of these poetic elements grows.

AWARDS FOR POETRY

How do we select the best poetry for our library collections? One of the best places to begin is by looking at award winners. Just as we eagerly anticipate the announcement of the Newbery and Caldecott award recipients and add those titles to our collections, we can use the poetry awards to guide our selections. In fact, a handful of poetry books have even been recognized with Newbery and Caldecott distinctions, too, such as Paul Fleischman's *Joyful Noise* (1988) and Laura Amy Schlitz's *Good Masters! Sweet Ladies!* (2007) or Joyce Sidman's *Red Sings from Treetops: A Year in Colors* illustrated by Pamela Zagarenski (Houghton Mifflin, 2009). But when we're looking for poetry recommendations on an ongoing basis, more poetry-specific awards can be very helpful for scoping out the very best poetry being published for children.

NCTE Award for Excellence in Poetry for Children

One major award for poetry for children is given by the National Council of Teachers of English entitled the NCTE Award for Excellence in Poetry for Children. This award is given to a poet for her or his entire lifetime of poetry writing for children. Previous recipients include David McCord, Aileen Fisher, Karla Kuskin, Myra Cohn Livingston, Eve Merriam, John Ciardi, Lilian Moore, Arnold Adoff, Valerie Worth, Barbara Juster Esbensen, Eloise Greenfield, X. J. Kennedy, Mary Ann Hoberman, Nikki Grimes, Lee Bennett Hopkins, and J. Patrick Lewis.

Lee Bennett Hopkins/International Reading Association Promising Poet Award

It is also helpful to watch for promising "up-and-coming" poets writing for young people via the Lee Bennett Hopkins/International Reading Association Promising Poet Award established by Hopkins along with the International Reading Association in 1995. These awardees have only published two books (to qualify for the award), but their work has already been judged to be of high quality. Recipients of this award are poets to watch for future works as well as current worthy titles and include Deborah Chandra, Kristine O'Connell George, Craig Crist-Evans, Lindsay Lee Johnson, Joyce Lee Wong, Gregory Neri, and Guadalupe Garcia McCall.

The Lee Bennett Hopkins Award

It is also useful to know about awards for specific titles of poetry books. The Lee Bennett Hopkins award, established in 1993, is presented annually to an

American poet or anthologist for the most outstanding new book of children's poetry of the year. Recent awardees include *Won Ton: A Cat Tale Told in Haiku* by Lee Wardlaw (Holt, 2011), *The Ink Garden of Brother Theophane* by C. M. Millen (Charlesbridge, 2010), *Button Up* by Alice Schertle (Houghton Mifflin, 2009), *Diamond Willow* by Helen Frost (Farrar, Straus & Giroux, 2008), and *Jazz* by Walter Dean Myers (Holiday House, 2006).

Other Poetry Recognitions

Other awards for children's poetry include the Claudia Lewis Award given by Bank Street College in New York and the Award for Excellence in North American Poetry, established in 2005 by the distinguished journal *The Lion and the Unicorn*. You can also count on the *Boston Globe/Horn Book* "Fanfare" list to specify poetry titles in their "best" list of children's literature each year. As we strengthen the poetry holdings in our library collections, one extra step that may help patrons find more award-winning poetry is to mark the circulation records of these titles with poetry awards received. This can also assist us in compiling bibliographies and recommended reading lists.

Poems about Libraries

To celebrate National Poetry Month, National Library Week, or use as an open invitation to the library, share any of these poems about libraries, books, and reading.

Alarcón, Francisco X. 1999. "Books" from *Angels Ride Bikes: And Other Fall Poems/Los Angeles Andan en Bicicleta: Y Otros Poemas de Otoño*. San Francisco, CA: Children's Book Press.

Bagert, Brod. 1999. "Library-Gold" from *Rainbows, Head Lice and Pea-Green Tile: Poems in the Voice of the Classroom Teacher*. Gainesville, FL: Maupin House.

Dakos, Kalli. 2003. "When the Librarian Reads to Us" from *Put Your Eyes Up Here: And Other School Poems*. New York: Simon & Schuster.

George, Kristine O'Connell. 2002. "School Librarian" from *Swimming Upstream: Middle School Poems*. New York: Clarion Books.

Greenfield, Eloise. 2006. "At the Library" from *The Friendly Four*. New York: HarperCollins.

Grimes, Nikki. 1998. "42nd Street Library" from *Jazmin's Notebook*. New York: Dial.

Grimes, Nikki. 2005. "At the Library" from *It's Raining Laughter*. Honesdale, PA: Boyds Mills Press.

Gunning, Monica. 2004. "The Library" from *America, My New Home*. Honesdale, PA: Wordsong/Boyds Mills Press.

Holbrook, Sara. 2012. "The Library" in Sylvia Vardell and Janet Wong, Eds. *The Poetry Friday Anthology K–5*. Princeton, NJ: Pomelo Books.

Hopkins, Lee Bennett. Ed. 2000. "Good Books, Good Times" from *Good Books, Good Times!* New York: HarperTrophy.

Katz, Alan. 2001. "Give Me a Break" from *Take Me Out of the Bathtub and Other Silly Dilly Songs.* New York: Scholastic.

Lewis, J. Patrick. 1999. "Read . . . Think . . . Dream" from *The Bookworm's Feast: A Potluck of Poems.* New York: Dial.

Lewis, J. Patrick. 2005. "Please Bury Me in the Library" and "Necessary Gardens" from *Please Bury Me in the Library.* San Diego, Harcourt.

Lewis, J. Patrick. 2009. "#66 The Hippopotabus," "#174 The Librarian," "#116 Library Fine," and "#89 New York Public Library" from *Countdown to Summer: A Poem for Every Day of the School Year.* New York: Little, Brown.

Lewis, J. Patrick. 2009. "Librarian" from *The Underwear Salesman: And Other Jobs for Better or Verse.* New York: Simon & Schuster/Atheneum.

Livingston, Myra Cohn. 1994. "Quiet" in Lee Bennett Hopkins, Ed. *April Bubbles Chocolate: An ABC of Poetry.* New York: Simon & Schuster.

Lottridge, Celia Barker. 2002. "Anna Marie's Library Book and What Happened" in Deborah Pearson, Ed. *When I Went to the Library.* Toronto, Canada: Groundwood Books.

McLoughland, Beverly. 1990. "Surprise" in Lee Bennett Hopkins, Ed. *Good Books, Good Times!* New York: HarperTrophy.

Medina, Jane. 1999. "The Library Card" from *My Name Is Jorge on Both Sides of the River: Poems.* Honesdale, PA: Boyds Mills Press.

Merriam, Eve. 1998. "Reach for a Book" in Mary Perrotta Rich, Ed. *Book Poems: Poems from National Children's Book Week, 1959–1998.* New York: Children's Book Council.

Nye, Naomi Shihab. 2005. "The List" from *A Maze Me; Poems for Girls.* New York: Greenwillow.

Prelutsky, Jack. 2006. "It's Library Time" from *What a Day It Was at School!* New York: Greenwillow.

Silverstein, Shel. 1981. "Overdues" from *A Light in the Attic.* New York: HarperCollins.

Soto, Gary. 1992. "Ode to My Library" from *Neighborhood Odes.* San Diego, CA: Harcourt.

Worth, Valerie. 1994. "Library" from *All the Small Poems and Fourteen More.* New York: Farrar, Straus & Giroux.

Zimmer, Tracie Vaughn. 2009. "Librarian" from *Steady Hands: Poems About Work.* New York: Clarion.

Based, in part, on Vardell, Sylvia M. 2006. "A Place for Poetry: Celebrating the Library in Poetry." *Children and Libraries* 4 (2), 35–41; and Vardell, Sylvia. 2012. *The Poetry Teacher's Book of Lists.* Princeton, NJ: Pomelo Books.

Literature in Action: Leading Choral Reading and Poetry Performance

Poetry is meant to be read aloud. As poet Brod Bagert (1992) said, just as songs are not just sheet music, poetry is not just text. The poem's meaning is more clearly communicated when it is both read and heard. When children participate in the oral reading, they have the opportunity to develop their own oral fluency and understanding of language. Experimenting with various vocal arrangements can also help provide an outlet for self-expression and build student confidence.

Caroline Feller Bauer takes a similar approach with her book *The Poetry Break* (1995). She proposes a wandering poetry presenter who drops in to share a poem throughout the school throughout the day. Her book is an excellent resource for creative ways to present poetry. The "poetry break" is an outstanding way to infuse poems throughout a school or library program.

As you invite children to participate in reading poems aloud with you, there are a few guidelines and strategies that may be helpful. First, always read the poem aloud yourself so children can hear how the words and rhythm sound. Then, get children involved in participating, first as a whole group, then in smaller groups, and finally as individual volunteers. Don't be surprised if children want to hear poems over and over again and try different arrangements of their own creation. Here are some of my favorite techniques for reading poetry out loud with children. They're listed more or less in order of difficulty, providing a sequence for easing you and the kids into a more participatory poetry performance. For more ideas and examples, see *Poetry Aloud Here 2: Sharing Poetry with Children* (Vardell, 2014).

1. *Modeling.* The adult reads the poem aloud to the class. Choose poems *you* like and read them slowly, but expressively. Show the poem using the eBook version or a projector or on a poster while you read it so the children can follow along with the words.
2. *Unison.* The adult still reads the poem out loud first. But then, everyone joins in on repeated reading to read the poem in unison. Once the children have heard a poem read aloud, they usually enjoy joining in. You can adapt this approach with "echo" reading of some poems, in which children repeat lines after you read each one, echoing your reading.
3. *Refrain.* The adult leads the poem reading, but children participate in a word or phrase or refrain that is reoccurring, much like the classic Greek chorus joining in for repeated lines.
4. *Movement.* Children read the poem in unison using simple motions or gestures. Motions can be as simple as alternating standing and sitting, clapping at key intervals, or gesturing with hands. It is also possible to incorporate basic American Sign Language into poetry readings.
5. *Groups.* The class or large group is divided into two or more groups for multiple stanzas. This takes some practice with timing but creates a "wave" effect with the poem flowing across the room.
6. *Solos.* Individual children volunteer for individual solo lines. "Volunteer" is the key word. Do not put children on the spot. If you continue sharing poetry orally every day, eventually nearly everyone will want a turn to shine. Many "list" poems work well in the line-around read aloud format.
7. *Two Voices.* This is the most complex form of choral reading. It takes a bit of practice but is very powerful. Two individuals volunteer to practice and perform poems for two voices (often with overlapping lines). It can be effective with two groups, rather than with two individuals, but it does take practice. (Underline the lines that are spoken simultaneously to help cue the children. Be aware that they may be saying different words at the same time.) Paul Fleischman's *Joyful Noise* is the perfect example of poems written specifically for this strategy.
8. *Singing Poems.* Perhaps the silliest form of choral reading is singing poems. It's not especially difficult, but it is irresistible fun and does require a bold adult (or child) to get it started. You simply sing poems by adapting those that have a strong, rhythmic beat to familiar tunes that have the same beat or meter, such as "Mary Had a Little Lamb," "Row, Row, Row Your Boat," "Ninety-Nine Bottles of Pop," "On Top of Old Smoky," and so on.

Now that you've begun, experiment with other ways to make poetry come alive. Try chants (jump rope rhymes, sidewalk chants, cheerleader chants, etc.), pantomime, puppetry, and props. For elementary-age children, I prefer to emphasize choral reading, readers' theater, poetry jams, poetry café readings, puppets and poetry, and so on à la Sara Holbrook's approach in *Wham! It's a Poetry Jam: Discovering Performance Poetry* (2002) and *Outspoken: How to Improve Writing and Speaking Through Poetry Performance* (2006). These spoken word events allow children to participate with the support of a partner or group and help them gain confidence as they share poetry with an audience. Two anthologies that focus on guiding children in learning poetry by heart include Caroline Kennedy's *Poems to Learn by Heart* (Hyperion, 2013) and Mary Ann Hoberman's *Forget-Me-Nots: Poems to Learn by Heart* (Little, Brown, 2012).

Other ideas include inviting guests to read poetry aloud, particularly professional actors in your area who can offer a polished delivery of poetry, or welcoming bilingual members of your community who can read poems in languages other than English. Consider inviting a traveling poetry troupe from the national organization Poetry Alive! (http://www.poetry alive.com). You might also try making poetry available in a listening center. Many excellent collections of poetry are available on tape, CDs, or as downloadable audio, many read by the poets themselves, such as Shel Silverstein and Jack Prelutsky. Some websites even offer audio clips of poems read aloud by the poets. Children might also want to choose to enlarge their favorite poem on a poetry poster for easy choral reading or create their own anthologies or podcast recordings of favorite poems for frequent sharing.

Fun with Poetic Form

Children may enjoy discovering unusual forms of poetry or even trying their hands at writing them. Or working as a group, children can create their own alphabet books of poetry with each child responsible for a letter to build a poem upon. Paul Janeczko has a wonderful resource book for children filled with both serious and wacky poetry forms in *Poetry from A to Z: A Guide for Young Writers* (1994), including clerihews, how-to poems, letter poems, and others. Another lovely Janeczko anthology that offers additional guidance to budding poets is *Seeing the Blue Between: Advice and Inspirations for Young Poets* (Candlewick, 2002). And in his picture book guide to poetic form, *A Kick in the Head: An Everyday Guide to Poetic Forms* (2005), children will encounter examples of twenty-nine different kinds of poems from tankas to pantoums accompanied by Chris Raschka's energetic illustrations. Janeczko and Raschka also paired up to create *A Poke in the I: A Collection of Concrete Poems* (Candlewick, 2001), an inviting introduction to "shape" poetry, and *A Foot in the Mouth: Poems to Speak, Sing, and Shout*, a ready-to-read-aloud set of poems (Candlewick, 2009).

SHARING POETRY

Finding time for sharing poetry can be challenging, until you realize that just a few minutes can be a good beginning. One teacher, Tonya Rodriguez, tried a project she called "Three Minutes a Day Can Make a Difference." It was her contention that she could share a poem effectively and even invite the children to participate or respond to it in just three minutes. So for about a month, she took three minutes a day to do just that. Within a week, children were reminding her when she had forgotten their three-minute poetry break. By the end of the month, they were asking to hear favorite poems over again. Three minutes a day *had* made a difference. It had shown these children that poetry was enjoyable, even memorable.

Poetry Fridays

In 2006 blogger Kelly Herold brought the concept of Poetry Friday to the "kidlitosphere" on the Internet. Much like "casual Friday" in the corporate world, there is a perception in the world of literature that on Fridays we can relax a bit and take a moment for something special. We can capitalize on the Poetry Friday concept in the library or classroom and take five minutes every Friday to share a poem and explore it a bit, connecting it with children's lives and capitalizing on a teachable moment to reinforce literacy learning. We can share poetry on other days of the week too, of course. But for those who are not already teaching poetry regularly, planning for Poetry Friday makes poetry sharing intentional and not incidental.

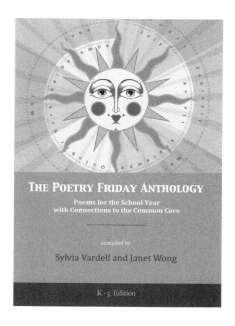

THE POETRY FRIDAY ANTHOLOGY
Poems for the School Year
with Connections to the Common Core

compiled by
Sylvia Vardell and Janet Wong

K-5 Edition

When it comes to sharing poems with children, there is no magic formula for success. Over the years, however, I have found a few key steps make it easy to engage students and integrate some basic language skill reinforcement. In our book, *The Poetry Friday Anthology*, poet and collaborator Janet Wong and I borrowed the phrase "Take 5" from the great jazz musician Dave Brubeck to propose that teachers and librarians take five minutes every Friday to introduce and share a poem. We collaborated with many popular poets writing for young people today to publish *The Poetry Friday Anthology* (one edition for grades K–5 and one for middle school, grades 6–8) featuring a poem a week written by more than seventy different major poets for the whole school year for every grade level. For each poem we provide "Take 5" activities tied to the new Common Core standards (or the TEKS standards in Texas). These are strategies that can be applied to sharing any poem. So, what are the five components of the "Take 5" approach to poem sharing?

Take 5: Steps for Poetry Sharing

1. Read the poem aloud (vary your approach in multiple readings).
2. Read the poem aloud again with student participation and involvement.

3. Take a moment to invite students to discuss the poem; have an open-ended question ready as a prompt.
4. Make a subtle skill connection with the poem—just one.
5. Connect with other poems and poetry books that are similar in some way.

These steps are quick and simple and begin with the adult leading the poem sharing, then involve children in active poem rereading, followed by brief discussion and skill connections, and if time allows, another related poem—all in approximately five minutes. *The Poetry Friday Anthology* makes it easy to find and share a poem at each grade level with activities provided, but certainly any book of poetry can jumpstart Poetry Friday poem sharing. You've already been introduced to choral reading and poetry performance techniques; now let's consider strategies for guiding poetry discussion.

Discussing Poetry

When we read a poem aloud to children, we're often hesitant about how to talk with them about poetry. We need to give a few moments for the poem to sink in, but the silence sometimes seems uncomfortable. Plus, we'd like to know what kids are thinking: Did they enjoy the poem? Understand the poem? Want to hear it again? How do we ask them without being too pushy or ruining the magic of the moment? Following up on poetry reading is not a lock-step process: Read poem. Ask questions. Finished. It's more intuitive, following the lead of the children, the poem, and the moment. This becomes clearer and more natural the more often you share poems with children. However, there are a few guidelines that can help.

When we read a poem aloud, we may find that children still seem unsure of what is expected of them afterward and may be more concerned about offering "correct" answers than about sharing opinions or responses. Our questions should be as open-ended as possible and we need to stay open to all kinds of responses from children. They may not give you the answer you expect to hear, but it will help you understand how they see the poem and perhaps help you perceive the poem itself in new ways. Try one or two of the following questions, based on questions from McClure (1990), Fitch and Swartz (2008), and O'Connor (2004). Vary which ones you use from time to time.

What did you think?
How did this poem make you feel?
What did you see or imagine when we read this poem?
What did you like about this poem?
Does this remind you of anything you know about?
Why do you think the poet wrote this poem?
Did the things in this poem ever happen to you? Will you tell about it?
Are there any words or lines that you think are interesting? Why?

Celebrating National Poetry Month

In 1996, the Academy of American Poets inaugurated the observance of National Poetry Month to celebrate poetry and its place in American culture. Since then, the movement has continued to gain momentum with a focus on poetry slams as the centerpiece for Teen Read Week in 2003 sponsored by the American Library Association, and the inauguration of the Poetry Blast in 2004, a concert of children's poets held at the annual ALA conference. For ideas for celebrating Poetry Month or Poetry Week, check out Potato Hill Poetry: http://www.potatohill.com/npm.html.

Poetry across the Curriculum

There are several ways that poetry can also enhance learning in every subject area. Poetry lends itself to integration across the curriculum in language arts, science, mathematics, and social studies. It can serve to jumpstart or introduce a lesson or topic, offer a transition between activities, provide closure, and extend the topic further. Three helpful resources full of strategies for connecting poetry with each of these major curricular areas (math, science, social studies) are Barbara Chatton's book *Using Poetry Across the Curriculum* (2010); Bernice Cullinan, Marilyn Scala, and Virginia Schroder's collaboration *Three Voices: An Invitation to Poetry Across the Curriculum* (1995); and poet Sara Holbrook's *Practical Poetry: A Nonstandard Approach to Meeting Content-Area Standards* (2005). There is such a variety of poetry being published that connections with science or social studies, in particular, are abundant. For example, consider *Seeds, Bees, Butterflies, and More!: Poems for Two Voices* by Carole Gerber (Holt, 2013), a close-up view of the plant and insect worlds, or *Rutherford B., Who Was He?: Poems About Our Presidents* by Marilyn Singer (Disney-Hyperion, 2013), a clever poetic introduction to our nation's leaders. There is also a Poetry Friday anthology available with 100+ poems focused on STEM: science, technology, engineering, and math (Vardell and Wong, 2014).

Pairing Poetry

Another way to begin incorporating poetry is to inject poems into the activities that are already a part of your schedule. If you regularly read a picture book out loud, try following up with a poem that has a similar subject or theme. If you enjoy reading aloud novels in excerpts or installments, try sharing a poem before the book to set the stage. If you field regular questions about "classic" poems, suggest contemporary poems as a bridge to understanding these older works.

Start with a familiar story or book you share often and look for a matching poem. For example, share Judith Viorst's now classic picture book,

Alexander and the Terrible, Horrible, No Good, Very Bad Day (1972) and follow this story with Karla Kuskin's poem listing the same kind of "bad day" woes, "I Woke Up This Morning" (in Kuskin, 2003). If you introduce novels to young readers in booktalks or through reading aloud in installments, consider sharing a poem to whet their appetites for the story that follows. For example, Langston Hughes's "Poem" (Knopf, 2007), which begins "I loved my friend. / He went away from me," can help introduce Katherine Applegate's Newbery medal–winning *The One and Only Ivan* (HarperCollins, 2012); and Eloise Greenfield's poem "Education" (Greenfield, 1988) can set the stage for Louis Sachar's Newbery medal award book *Holes* (Frances Foster, 1998). Or in honor of National Library Week, connect Patricia McKissack's *Goin' Someplace Special* (Simon & Schuster, 2001), about a welcoming library, with Nikki Grimes's poem "At the Library" from *It's Raining Laughter* (Boyds Mills Press, 2004). For more examples, look for the *Book Links* article, "Linking Picture Books and Poetry: A Celebration of Black History Month" (Vardell, 2007) at http://www.ala.org/ala/booklinksbucket/linkingpoetry.htm. And once you make these connections, don't be surprised if children come to you with poems they feel match stories they are reading or books you are sharing.

Promoting Poetry

We all know that a good visual display generates interest in library materials. Highlighting new poetry books, low-circulating poetry book gems, books by featured poets, and children's favorite poetry books are all ways to make poetry for children more visible in the library. Poet Georgia Heard encourages children in the schools to create a "living anthology." She says, "Instead of collecting poems we love and putting them in a book, we'll make an anthology out of the walls and spaces around the school. It will be our jobs to make sure poetry is all around the building so that other students and teachers can have a chance to read some poetry" (Heard, 1999, p. 23). New or favorite poems can also be displayed via mobiles and other three-dimensional displays. One librarian created a "poet-tree" by using rolled-up brown paper to create a tree trunk and branches and invited children to write their favorite poems on green paper cut into leaf shapes, which were attached to the "tree limbs." Consider creating a "Hall of Poets" and featuring children's favorite poems or original poems, the writing of local poets, the work of favorite or featured poets, or a combination of these. If you have access to a school or library website, consider adding a poetry quote, or children's original poems (with their permission), or information about new poetry book acquisitions, lists of children's favorite poems or poetry books, or a featured poet of local or national stature. Children themselves can participate in creating this poetry presence, particularly in preparation for National Poetry Month in April.

Poetry Practice Checklist

Here is a checklist that might be helpful in guiding a reevaluation of your poetry collection holdings. Consider these questions as you assess your poetry collection and common practices.

Are the poetry books as easy to find as the fiction and nonfiction?

Are the poetry books in a child-friendly location, easily reachable, with the area well labeled and quickly identified?

Do poetry posters and poetry book displays invite children to browse through poetry even if they're not immediately seeking it?

Do you have special plans for National Poetry Month?

Are some poetry books displayed face out?

Is there room on the poetry shelves for expansion?

Are the poetry books on the shelf current?

Are the poetry award winners represented and highlighted?

Do you actively seek out poetry books from diverse perspectives?

Are there multiple copies of the most current and popular poetry titles?

Do you mention children's poetry choices when general subject requests come up?

Do you include children's poetry books on your recommended reading lists and bibliographies?

Do you feature children's poets in displays, materials, and booktalks?

Do you incorporate poems for children in your story times and read alouds, openings and closings?

Do you seek out opportunities for linking poems with picture books, novels, and nonfiction?

Do you provide opportunities for children to participate actively in the choral reading and performance of poetry?

Based, in part, on Vardell, Sylvia M. 2006. "Don't Stop with Mother Goose." *School Library Journal* (April), 40–41.

CONCLUSION

If we build it, they will come. If our library has a current and relevant poetry collection and we promote it actively, children can discover the pleasures of poetry at an early age. Indeed, our youngest children tend to respond readily to poetry in the early years based on the enduring appeal of Mother Goose, nursery rhymes, and playground verse—all a natural part of childhood. Why does our appreciation for this genre often end with Mother Goose? We need to provide children with a bridge from "Ring Around the Rosie" to the classics they'll likely encounter in high school and college. They need to experience the words and images of poets who specialize in writing just for children. As children's literature scholars Perry Nodelman and Mavis Reimer (2003) remind us, "If adults want children to enjoy poetry, they need to provide them with knowledge of the possibilities of poetry and of helpful attitudes toward the experience of it, and with techniques and strategies for deriving both understanding and pleasure from that experience" (p. 272). Poetry books today are short and focused, often richly illustrated. They are visually inviting, and they contain more new poets than ever before, including poets of color and international poets from around the world. Fortunately, the variety and quality of poetry for children that is available now is tremendous. Finding poems that children will enjoy is easier than ever.

PROFESSIONAL RESOURCES IN CHILDREN'S POETRY

If you've been "bitten" by the poetry "bug," these resources will provide additional background you'll find helpful.

Ada, Alma Flor, Violet Harris, and Lee Bennett Hopkins. 1993. *A Chorus of Cultures: Developing Literacy through Multicultural Poetry.* Carmel, CA: Hampton-Brown Books.

Barton, Bob, and David Booth. 2004. *Poetry Goes to School: From Mother Goose to Shel Silverstein.* Markham, Ontario, Canada: Pembroke.

Bauer, Caroline Feller. 1995. *The Poetry Break: An Annotated Anthology with Ideas for Introducing Children to Poetry.* New York: H. W. Wilson.

Booth, David, and Bill Moore. 2003. *Poems Please! Sharing Poetry with Children* (Second Edition). Markham, Ontario, Canada: Pembroke.

Chatton, Barbara. 1993. *Using Poetry Across the Curriculum.* Phoenix, AZ: Oryx Press.

Franco, Betsy. 2005. *Conversations with a Poet: Inviting Poetry into K–12 Classrooms.* Somers, NY: Richard C. Owen.

Glover, M. K. 1999. *A Garden of Poets.* Urbana, IL: National Council of Teachers of English.

Holbrook, Sara. 2002. *Wham! It's a Poetry Jam: Discovering Performance Poetry.* Honesdale, PA: Wordsong/Boyds Mills Press.

Hopkins, Lee Bennett. 1995. *Pauses: Autobiographical Reflections of 101 Creators of Children's Books.* New York: HarperCollins.

Kennedy, X. J., and D. Kennedy. 1999. *Knock at a Star.* New York: Little, Brown.

Livingston, Myra Cohn. 1990. *Climb into the Bell Tower: Essays on Poetry.* New York: HarperCollins.

Vardell, Sylvia M. 2007. *Poetry People: A Practical Guide to Children's Poets.* Englewood, CO: Libraries Unlimited.

Vardell, Sylvia M. 2014. *Poetry Aloud Here 2: Sharing Poetry with Children* (Second Edition). Chicago, IL: American Library Association.

Standards in Action: Texas Essential Knowledge And Skills (TEKS) for English Language Arts and Reading

The Common Core State Standards have been adopted by the vast majority of states in the United States, but not all. My own home state of Texas, for example, did not adopt the Common Core standards. I mention this here and provide an example of how the

Texas standards connect with instruction to demonstrate how we need to be knowledgeable about the standards in our area whatever they may be. Check and see what standards are in place in your area—at the state, district, or local level. In Texas, the TEKS (or Texas Essential Knowledge and Skills) guide our planning and instruction (http://ritter.tea.state.tx.us/rules/tac/chapter110/ch110a.html). The standards for 110.11. English Language Arts and Reading address skills for reading, writing, speaking, and listening specific to each grade level, K–12. The list is extensive and comprehensive, so for this chapter on poetry, let's focus specifically on the TEKS for poetry learning.

What are the expectations outlined in the TEKS related to poetry for children?

In sharing poetry with *kindergartners*, we capitalize on their developing knowledge of language, their joy in learning and playing with words, and their emerging understanding of how words should be spoken, spelled, read, and written. First we focus on enjoyment and understanding, then we guide students in responding to the rhythm and beat of poems as well as the power of rhyme and similarities in word sounds. [110.11(b)(7)]

With *first graders*, we shift slightly to help students respond to the rhythm of poetry and recognize how rhyme is used in poems. We explore the sounds of poetry, particularly the repetition of sounds used in alliteration. [110.11(b)(8)]

In *second grade*, we then examine the rhythm of poetry and lead students in recognizing how rhyme is used in various ways. We can also explore how repetition helps shape a poem and how images emerge. [110.11(b)(7)]

In *third grade*, we guide students in responding to poetry in various forms, exploring narrative poems that tell stories, lyrical poems that explore questions and emotions, and humorous poems that make us groan or laugh. We can also consider how some poems such as free verse do not rhyme and how images emerge in each form. [110.11(b)(6)]

In *fourth grade*, we also help students understand how structural elements such as rhyme, meter, stanzas, and line breaks help shape a poem. We guide students in understanding poetry in various forms including free verse poems and lyrical poetry. [110.11(b)(4)]

In *fifth grade*, the emphasis is on helping students understand how sound effects such as alliteration, internal rhyme, onomatopoeia, and rhyme scheme help reinforce meaning in a poem. In a variety of playful, meaningful, and participatory ways, we can celebrate poetry while gently introducing and reinforcing key skills. [110.11(b)(4)]

Finally, in *grade six*, we focus on helping students understand the structure and elements of poetry, how figurative language contributes to meaning, and how a poet uses sensory language to create imagery. We guide them in making inferences and drawing conclusions and challenge them to support their opinions with examples from the poem. We can help them understand how poets create meaning through figurative language and stylistic elements including alliteration, onomatopoeia, personification, metaphors, similes, and hyperbole, as well as the use of refrains, line length, and line breaks. [110.18. (b) (4); (8); (15 B i, ii, iii)]

Do you see how many of the activities described in this chapter address these skills described above? Targeting the sound of poetry through reading it aloud? Or guiding children in understanding how poets use rhyme or free verse for different effects? In addition, the Common Core State Standards for poetry are very similar to these standards in Texas. For more poetry resources tied to the TEKS as well as the Common Core, look for the following resources:

Heard, Georgia. 2013. *Poetry Lessons to Meet the Common Core State Standards: Exemplar Poems with Engaging Lessons and Response Activities That Help Students Read, Understand, and Appreciate Poetry*. New York: Scholastic.

Janeczko, Paul B. 2011. *Reading Poetry in the Middle Grades: 20 Poems and Activities That Meet the Common Core Standards and Cultivate a Passion for Poetry*. Portsmouth, NH: Heinemann.

Vardell, S. M., and Janet Wong. 2012. *The Poetry Friday Anthology K–5: Poems for the School Year with Connections to the Common Core*. Princeton, NJ: Pomelo Books.

Vardell, S. M., and Janet Wong. 2012. *The Poetry Friday Anthology K–5: Poems for the School Year with Connections to the TEKS*. Princeton, NJ: Pomelo Books.

Vardell, S. M., and Janet Wong. 2013. *The Poetry Friday Anthology for Middle School, Grades 6–8: Poems for the School Year with Connections to the Common Core*. Princeton, NJ: Pomelo Books.

Vardell, S. M., and Janet Wong. 2013. *The Poetry Friday Anthology for Middle School, Grades 6–8: Poems for the School Year with Connections to the TEKS*. Princeton, NJ: Pomelo Books.

Assignments in Action: Exploring Poetry Possibilities

1. Creating Anthologies

Pull a handful of Mother Goose or nursery rhyme collections and examine the variations you discover. Which nursery rhymes are familiar to you? Which are new? Work with a partner or small group to create a homemade anthology of nursery rhymes from languages and cultures represented in your group or community. Invite children to illustrate it for you and bind, self-publish, and share it in your library.

2. Performing Poetry

Sharing poetry out loud is becoming more and more popular, and many libraries now hold open mic (microphone) sessions for children and teens to read aloud their own original or personal favorite poems. Attend an open mic poetry event in your area. How is it advertised? How is the session conducted? What arrangements and equipment are needed? Take notes on which poems children choose as their favorites and how their sharing is acknowledged and celebrated. Congratulate the kids who present and talk to them about their experiences with poetry.

3. Poetry on the Web

Poetry has quite a strong presence on the Internet, which offers many resources for planning poetry-related events or gathering ideas for sharing poetry with children.

Start by checking out the personal websites of children's poets such as Nikki Grimes, Janet Wong, Kristine O'Connell George, Jack Prelutsky, J. Patrick Lewis, or April Halprin Wayland. Consider sending your favorite poet some fan email. Investigate some of the Internet resources mentioned previously including the websites for the Academy of American Poets, Giggle Poetry, and Potato Hill Poetry. Or select a favorite activity from one of the websites below and try it with a small group of children you know.

Favorite Poem Project
http://www.favoritepoem.org/
This site features videos of average citizens reading their favorite poems—something you could imitate by making your own group of homemade videos of kids reading their favorite poems.

Magnetic Poetry
http://www.magneticpoetry.com/
Here you will find a multitude of kit options including Shakespeare, haiku, and foreign language kits as well as kits designed especially for children, and the opportunity to publish poetry created by adult or child "magnetic" poets.

5

Contemporary Realistic Fiction

"It often takes more courage to be a passenger than a driver."
From *The View from Saturday*
by E. L. Konigsburg (Atheneum, 1996)

In this chapter, you will learn about current trends in writing and publishing contemporary realistic fiction for young people. We'll consider a range of books from the classics like *Little Women* to popular series books, major authors writing in this genre and their presence online, and how to handle book challenges. You'll examine the criteria for reviewing fiction, including cultural authenticity, awards for highlighting excellence in writing realistic fiction, and strategies for promoting reading of contemporary realistic fiction, one of the most popular genres among young readers.

INTRODUCTION

This is the genre of "reality" or the "accurate reflection of today's life and people," according to critic Zena Sutherland (2004, p. 317). Contemporary realistic novels reflect the society of the times. Unfortunately, there are different views about how much or whose reality should be included in literature for young people. Until the 1960s, authors who wrote for children did not usually portray the negative aspects of society. But with the publication of *Harriet the Spy* by Louise Fitzhugh in 1964 (Harper & Row), a more authentic and complex genre began to emerge. Authors today now often tackle major societal taboos in their writing, including divorce, death, illness, sexuality, violence, and profanity. The argument is often given that books that portray these elements are suggesting tacit approval or making more acceptable these negative aspects of society. The counterargument, however, is that writers are simply reflecting society, not creating or promoting negative circumstances such as child abuse or homelessness. For many children, this *is* their reality and sugar-coating it or denying it is unrealistic. It is this very realism that makes this genre a frequent target of book challenges and potential censorship.

As we look at contemporary novels for young people, our audience is generally children in fourth grade and up. Of course, there are exceptions, and many good contemporary novels can be read aloud to children of any age, but the sophistication level of many of the books in this genre is more appropriate for older children, ages 10 and up, for independent reading. In addition, children's silent reading ability usually kicks into high gear in the fourth grade and they can sustain interest in much longer books. Of course, this is not a hard and fast rule, but I am not a fan of pushing novels down into the lower grades. Usually this means their reading slows way down and they read fewer books all around. Personally, I would rather third graders pore over 100 picture books than struggle through one long novel, but so many adults put a premium on children reading "chapter" books.

For those intermediate grade readers who want stories that seem true-to-life and characters with whom they can identify, contemporary realism is just the ticket and is easily the most popular genre with this age group. They typically enjoy reading about protagonists who are a year or two older than they are, ostensibly giving them a glimpse of the growing up years ahead. Since they identify so readily with peers and age-mates, the protagonist's age is a major factor in readers' involvement in the story.

Studies of children's preferences reveal their penchant for stories about friends and friendship, for mysteries, and survival stories. They enjoy animal and sports stories, too, and humorous writing all around. In addition, as children move into reading these longer novel-length works, sustaining interest in more complex narratives, we seek to provide books that function as "windows" or "mirrors" for their consideration (Bishop, 1992). That is, books can offer a mirror, holding up their own experiences for thoughtful scrutiny or a window into other ways of being, a vicarious experience of life outside their own particular norm, fostering empathy for others. Since individual readers come to particular books at different moments in their lives, books may help children discover insights they might otherwise not have experienced in their personal lives. Kiefer (2010, p. 397) reminds us, "Childhood is not a waiting room for adulthood, but the place where adulthood is shaped by one's family, peers, society, and most importantly, the person one is becoming."

History in Action: Little Women

Widely considered one of the most influential books of American literature for children, Louisa May Alcott's *Little Women* stands out as a landmark work on family life and coming of age. *Little Women* revolutionized the domestic tale of the day by creating believable characters and lifelike situations, with children seen as people rather than as examples of good and bad moral character. It marked a departure from the stiff and authoritarian stereotype of family life so prevalent at the time with an honest focus on the daily routines of childhood and the human foibles of children growing up. Although we consider it a historical novel now, it was a fresh and contemporary slice of life after the Civil War in the United States.

In 1867, Thomas Niles, Alcott's editor and publisher, requested that she write a story for girls and her first reaction was negative, but she remarked in her journal, "But I work away and mean to try the experiment for lively, simple books are very much needed for girls, and perhaps I can supply the need" (Alcott, 1868). She published *Little Women or, Meg, Jo, Beth and Amy* in 1868. It was autobiographical in nature and based somewhat on Alcott's experiences growing up with her three sisters. According to Alcott's sister Anna, "although nearly every event in the book is true, of course things did not happen exactly as they are there set down" (Pratt, 1903).

The novel was an instant success and sold more than 2,000 copies. Her publisher begged her for a second volume. It was published in 1869 and more than 13,000 copies sold immediately (Durbin, 1997). The two volumes were eventually published as one book with two parts, and *Little Women* was firmly established as a commercial and critical success.

Little Women was Alcott's masterpiece, but she followed its success with seven more novels often grouped under the *Little Women* series. The novels include *An Old-Fashioned Girl*, *Little Men*, *Eight Cousins*, *Rose in Bloom*, *Under the Lilacs*, *Jack and Jill*, and *Jo's Boys and How They Turned Out*. The subsequent novels follow the lives of the March sisters and their families as they grow older.

Little Women has never been out of print since its first publication. The novel has been translated into numerous languages and is read by children and adults around the world. There are numerous websites that provide book discussion guides, lesson plans, and more information about Alcott, her life, and her literature. Many scholars have studied her life and work in great depth (e.g., see Kim Wells's master's thesis available online chapter by chapter at http://www.womenwriters.net/domesticgoddess/thesis.htm), and there's a Norton Critical Edition of *Little Women* for the truly dedicated.

The Orchard House, home of the Alcotts from 1858 to 1877, is now a museum in historic Concord, Massachusetts. There have been no major structural changes to the house and 75 percent of the furnishings displayed were originally owned by the Alcotts. Visitors can tour the house, attend educational programs and living history events, and visit the museum shop. For details, see http://www.louisamayalcott.org/. A documentary film about Alcott herself was also filmed there (http://www.alcottfilm.com/).

Copies of the classic *Little Women* are available in multiple formats, including print and electronic versions:

It is available in e-text form at Bibliomania and Project Gutenberg:
http://www.bibliomania.com/0/0/5/4/frameset.html
http://www.gutenberg.org/etext/514

You can listen to *Little Women* being read aloud one chapter at a time by volunteer readers at Librivox.com.

The World Wide School Library provides an electronic full-text version that includes book decorations and a large font, making it very child-friendly for reading:
http://www.worldwideschool.org/library/books/youth/youngadult/
LittleWomen/toc.html

The University of Virginia offers a hypermedia presentation (including full text) with links to many resources related to *Little Women:*
http://xroads.virginia.edu/~hyper/ALCOTT/LWHP.html

Over the years, the story of *Little Women* has been adapted for the stage, as a Broadway play, as an opera, and even in several anime and graphic novel productions. Film adaptations have been immensely popular, featuring major stars of several different eras (the 1930s, 1940s, 1950s, 1970s, and 1990s), most recently with Winona Ryder as Jo (1994). The success of this engaging "family story" helped pave the way for many works to come, including the popular *American Girl* books and the *Dear America* series, among others.

DEFINITIONS

Novels in the genre of contemporary realistic fiction are set in the present time (contemporary), could really happen (realistic), but are still created and imagined by the author (fiction), rather than being true stories about actual people (nonfiction). Because the label is rather long, you will often see it shortened to "contemporary realism" or "realistic fiction." You get the idea. Please note, we are talking about *novels* here, not picture books.

Novels in this genre all contain events that could really happen; even if they're animal stories or survival adventures, they seem real and believable. That is part of their appeal to young readers. Situations are often familiar and children can relate to them. They live vicariously through the characters as they deal with the pressures of growing up. In fact, if the stories veer to the extreme and include talking animals or fantasy rescues, the book becomes a fantasy novel, rather than contemporary realistic fiction. Of course, some contemporary novels become historical fiction over the years, particularly if there are many time and place "markers" in the story. Many contemporary novels are also excellent for reading aloud, full of conversational dialogue, built upon real-life experiences that are relevant to most children, which can lead to thoughtful discussions of important issues afterward.

Some contemporary novels or "problem novels" can even become overwhelmed by the reality quotient and lose sight of the importance of simply telling a good story. This modern "didacticism" is a flaw that makes a story less appealing to the young reader, even if authors and publishers intend to address these tough issues for the sake of the child. Some of the more familiar problems to be found in many contemporary novels include the need for acceptance, conflict with siblings and/or parents, and conquering fears and egocentrism. These are issues nearly every child copes with in the process of growing up. More unfamiliar problems that are increasingly common, though not necessarily universal, are coping with divorce, dealing with drugs or alcohol abuse, and the effects of violence, abuse, aging, disease, disability, and death, even the death of a child. This expanding range of life experiences is part of our global society in the twenty-first century. Good literature reflects these complexities and portrays children coping with them in realistic settings; great literature weaves these elements seamlessly throughout a compelling story.

Librarians in Action: The Readers' Theater Club

Mia Steinkamp is the Learning Commons Director at Houston Christian High School in Texas. Her BS degree in elementary education was earned in 1987, an MLS in library science from Texas Woman's University in 2004, and a postgraduate certificate in Instructional Media in the Classroom in 2009. Her professional passion is helping teenagers navigate the increasingly chaotic and complex world of information, and promoting literacy by instilling a lifelong love of reading for enjoyment. Here she writes about her efforts with an elementary afterschool club featuring readers' theater. This was offered as an afterschool club in the lower division of a diverse American International School in Penang, Malaysia, where she lived and worked for seven years.

Readers' Theater and the School Library Media Center
by Mia Steinkamp

While working at Dalat International School on the island of Penang, Malaysia, I offered elementary students an afterschool club focused on readers' theater. The student body at this American school abroad is a vibrant mix of North American, European, and Asian children. My club was comprised of Taiwanese, American, Canadian, Korean, and students from India. We had a blast together! Children were surprised to find that reading aloud in groups was . . . fun! Parents were thrilled that their children were excited about reading. One enthusiastic club member, Grace, took the initiative to write her own script outside of school hours. We performed it together, boosting her confidence level and rewarding her effort.

Readers' theater is a group of people who read aloud from a script based on a children's book or story. In my club we used minimal props, costumes, and simple classroom staging. Of course, children love to play dress up; I did have a large basket of dress up clothes that they were free to go through to create a costume. However, we didn't invest a lot of time on this aspect. We found that readers' theater and the library go hand-in-hand as we focused on building literacy in a nonthreatening, collaborative environment. Even though I could be tired by the end of the school day, I looked forward to hosting this weekly club. It was enjoyable for me too.

The beauty of readers' theater is that it yields such an enthusiastic response, yet is so very easy to do. You can relax knowing that the primary focus is building literacy; the aesthetics come from the children's sweet voices. They create the magic that is readers' theater. I found the bulk of my time was spent on finding appropriate scripts, but once those were in place it was quicker from year to year. Many scripts are freely available from sites on the Internet. Generous teacher friends and colleagues shared their scripts for my cause as well.

My logistics for operating the club follow. When I found a script that looked interesting and was an appropriate reading level for my club, I made a print copy of the script for each club member. (However, experiment with the latest technology that you have available at your school; there is a lot of potential for the use of tablet devices and readers' theater.) I had a fairly large club that was split into two groups, reading two different scripts. Determining which child got which role in the script was determined by the fair process of "lucky duck pulls." I wrote club members' names on Popsicle sticks and randomly pulled these out to match people to character parts. This worked well for me, as I wasn't showing favoritism and the more advanced readers weren't dominating the longer, and possibly more interesting, roles. After I passed out the script and parts were assigned, each person then would highlight his or her part and read it silently. I made myself available to help with pronunciation and clarification of words. Each group would then huddle together and read the entire script aloud. I encouraged them to find a "voice" and to use accents that were appropriate to the character. We had many laughs together over this. Finally, "It's show time!" One group would perform their readers' theater for the audience, which usually was comprised of the other half of the club. We were always happy to perform for others too, and would invite people to listen. Club members were greatly motivated to do their best, knowing they had an audience.

My club was open to second through fourth graders with a wide range of ability. Laying the ground rules early on in the club helped the children understand that members would be kind at all times; there would be no eye rolling or snickering at slow readers. I was proud of members' patience when some of the children struggled through passages. I nurtured a positive atmosphere and it paid off, benefiting struggling readers. I would encourage you to work closely with teachers to see how you can tie in curricular objectives; however, not if it threatens to drown out the aspect of fun and enjoyment. Learning to read for enjoyment was my primary goal with this club.

Document how your club meets state and national standards. The library should be a vital part of every school. When teachers and administrators see the value we bring with our passion for building literacy and supporting educational objectives by infusing engaging connections to the curriculum, we can't be ignored. Publicize your efforts. We can't be quiet about the value we add to education for the sake of our children and a literate nation.

TYPES OF CONTEMPORARY REALISTIC FICTION

Many different subjects have been featured in contemporary realistic fiction, including survival, the search for identity, the roles of family and peers, growing up, animals, and sports. The tone of the story can range from serious and tense to humorous and even outrageous. Authors like Beverly Cleary, Judy Blume, and Betsy Byars are at the top of their game writing humorous stories for the middle grades with important points subtly tucked inside. They are frequently on lists of children's favorites across the globe. Judy Blume is probably one of the few children's authors who is also a millionaire because her books have sold so well for so many years. Her novel *Tales of a Fourth Grade Nothing* is a hilarious read aloud (and followed by several sequels with the same funny family of characters). And of course, the little girl who has given several generations of girls (and boys) permission to be themselves, Ramona Quimby, the creation of Beverly Cleary, is also the subject of several excellent novels for reading aloud across the grades. Each of these novelists has created many excellent novels that are real, contemporary, and pleasurable to read and ushered in many more humorous growing up stories such as those by Sara Pennypacker, Lisa Yee, Andrew Clements, and more. Blume is sometimes somewhat controversial in that her books for older readers (such as *Are You There, God? It's Me, Margaret,* Yearling, 1970) also deal with young people's questions about their developing sexuality in ways that are frank and honest, but never sensational. And her ear for natural dialogue and the woes of growing up is unmistakable.

Contemporary Realistic Fiction Subtopics (Self, Family, Friends)

When it comes to realism, many authors have tackled tough topics that today's children face in their daily lives. This includes searching for a sense of self, exploring one's place inside and outside the nuclear family, and coping with the growing importance of relationships with friends, even budding romances. In addition, these stories may be set in the context of modern urban life or a more rural community, surrounded by people who don't understand you or engaging with people from diverse backgrounds who do. Characters may be gifted, isolated, abused, abandoned, loved, disabled, and more. All these variables add shading to the essential growing up story that makes up the vast majority of contemporary realistic fiction for young people.

For one example of a family story that seems almost old-fashioned in its focus on sisterly summer fun, look for Jeanne Birdsall's National Book Award–winning *The Penderwicks* (Knopf, 2005) and its sequels. The family (with four daughters) rents a cottage on a grand estate and befriends the young, lonely son of the main house for a summer full of innocent adventures reminiscent of Louisa May Alcott's *Little Women.* For a more hip and comic take on family life, look for Sharon Creech's novel *Replay* (HarperCollins, 2005). Presented in thirty-nine short scenes, the book introduces readers to Leo's chaotic extended family and all his constant worries squeezed in between them. Many of Creech's works offer a lighter look at family life, always grounded in a meaningful theme.

Another, more serious view of family life is presented in Nikki Grimes's Coretta Scott King honor book *The Road to Paris* (Putnam, 2006). Removed from her home and her alcoholic mother, Paris has bumped from one foster home to another and finally becomes comfortable with the Lincolns, despite being separated from her beloved brother. A hopeful ending has Paris reunited with her brother and trying life together with their mother once again. Katherine Paterson tackled similar themes with her Newbery honor book *The Great*

Gilly Hopkins about a foster child and her struggles with accepting love as well as loss (Crowell, 1978). The Russian writer Leo Tolstoy reminds us that "happy families are all alike, but every unhappy family is unhappy in its own way." This is true even in children's novels.

In Pam Muñoz Ryan's Pura Belpré honor book *Becoming Naomi León* (Scholastic, 2004), eleven-year-old Naomi Soledad Leon Outlaw lives with her Gram, who is her great-grandmother, and her anxious younger brother, Owen, until their mother shows up and fights for custody for selfish reasons. Naomi's talent for soap carving and a trip to their birth father in Mexico merge to provide a satisfying conclusion. Beverly Cleary's Newbery Medal book *Dear Mr. Henshaw* (Morrow, 1983) echoes similar themes with a lonely young boy coping with newly divorced parents and estrangement from his father.

Notice that multiculturalism is also reflected in more and more titles of contemporary realistic fiction, with authors of color telling stories that come from their own growing up experiences. More of the same shines through Grace Lin's novels, *The Year of the Dog* (Little, Brown, 2006), *The Year of the Rat* (Little, Brown, 2009), and *Dumpling Days* (Little, Brown, 2012), in which a young girl copes with everyday childhood concerns (like finding her own talents, coping with a friend moving away) while parallel stories from her mother's and grandmother's experiences growing up Taiwanese are sprinkled throughout. Candace Fleming writes about a boy's worries about fitting in and making friends in *Lowji Discovers America* (Atheneum, 2005). He is a new immigrant from India and his #1 desire is to own a pet. Perspectives from various cultures add leaven and richness to the usual family story. In Julia Alvarez's Pura Belpré medal–winning novel *Return to Sender* (Knopf, 2009), a family of undocumented Mexican laborers helps a Vermont family farm survive and their lives intertwine in unexpected ways.

Unfortunately, children are also coping with grave and serious issues, too, all around the world and right here at home. In Jacqueline Woodson's award-winning novel *Locomotion* (Putnam, 2003), young Lonnie Collins Motion (nicknamed "Locomotion") tells his story in poems and prose as he copes with the death of his parents in a fire, adjustment to a foster home setting, and separation from his younger sister, revealing a resilient spirit throughout. In Gigi Amateau's *Claiming Georgia Tate* (Candlewick, 2005), Georgia Tate Jamison has lived with her Nana and Granddaddy Tate in Mississippi since she was an infant. When her birth father wants her to visit and then abuses her, she convinces Nana that she must come home immediately. The loving relationship between Georgia and her grandparents helps this novel transcend its frightening subject. Cynthia Rylant's Newbery medal novel *Missing May* (Orchard, 1992) tells a parallel story of a young girl raised by an elderly couple but coping with the devastating death of one of them. And in Kevin Henkes's serious story *Olive's Ocean* (Greenwillow, 2003), a Newbery honor book, the protagonist faces the death of a classmate she barely knew, but who admired *her*.

Characters in contemporary novels are also living with disabilities that have an impact on them and those around them. In R. J. Palacio's novel *Wonder* (Knopf, 2012), Auggie Pullman strives for a normal life in a new school despite a significant facial deformity, but with a sense of humor and strength of spirit that make him both admirable and engaging. As the story is filtered through multiple points of view (family, friends, Auggie), we see a community struggling with empathy and acceptance. Cynthia Lord gives us the sister's point of view in *Rules* (Scholastic, 2006), about a girl who loves her autistic brother and tries to help him cope with the rest of the world by creating rules to guide him (about whom to hug, for example), but is equally frustrated by the cost to herself and her family. In Sarah Weeks's novel *So B It* (HarperCollins, 2004), Heidi, the twelve-year-old protagonist, has a kind of role reversal relationship with her mother, So B. It, a severely mentally disabled woman. The bond is close and authentic, however, and propels Heidi on a journey of self-discovery. In Esmé Raji Codell's novel *Sahara Special* (Hyperion, 2003), a fifth grader with "special needs" struggles with insecurities, including a secret desire to

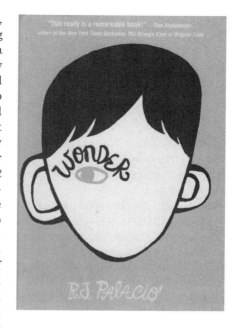

be a writer. And Jack Gantos's series about a young boy with attention deficit issues, *Joey Pigza* (e.g., *Joey Pigza Swallowed the Key*; Farrar, Straus & Giroux, 1998), is equal parts honestly painful and hysterically funny—and never at the expense of stereotyping the different characters.

We need more and more realistic stories with contemporary characters living with disabilities. As Temple, Martinez, and Yokota remind us, "When child readers recognize something in a story that is similar to their own feelings or thoughts, they realize they are not alone" (2011, p. 295). Esmé Raji Codell (2007), teacher, librarian, "readiologist," and author of *How to Get Your Child to Love Reading: For Ravenous and Reluctant Readers Alike* (Algonquin, 2003), as well as *Sahara Special*, explains, "My wish was that this story would help children be hopeful that no matter where they live or how they live or what's in their file . . . a lot of kids are lonely, even when they are standing right next to someone else who might be lonely, too. That's a bad situation, but it can be fixed in real life and in stories."

Contemporary Realistic Fiction Subgenres (Adventure, Mystery, Animals, Sports)

A variety of contemporary novels for young people may involve families and friendships in the background, but the special emphasis of the story—such as survival or adventure, mystery, animals, or sports—is the driving force of the story. These "subgenres" of realism are also very popular with young readers, particularly during the 'tween years when children are beginning to take on more responsibility for themselves, for their problems, for animals, for a team or group, and for society, as they head toward adulthood.

Adventure. Adventure stories are strong on plot and action with survival often the focus of the book. One standout author of these action-filled realistic novels for kids is Gary Paulsen. Not only is he a prolific author with more than 100 books to his credit, he writes novels full of conflict, with crisp dialogue, and protagonists who often go it alone. He is also the name to know when it comes to luring *boys* into reading longer works. Unfortunately, many boys seem to stop reading fiction by fifth grade or so, and they are often reluctant readers altogether. Gary Paulsen's writing can grab even these reluctant readers. In his now classic survival novel *Hatchet* (Bradbury, 1987), a Newbery honor book, Brian is on his way to spend the summer with his dad after his parents' divorce. The small plane that he is on crashes in the Canadian wilderness and he must survive alone for over a month. I love the fact that Brian is *not* well versed in survival lore and learns what *not* to do through trial and error, rather than being an instant survivalist. It makes the book even more believable. *Hatchet* continues to be very popular, and there are several sequels to it.

Carl Hiaasen, known for his writing for adults, has carved out a name for himself with eco-adventures for young people that are also in demand, like *Chomp* (Knopf, 2012), about a boy whose father wrangles alligators. Hiaasen's "save the owls" story, *Hoot* (Knopf, 2002), was also made into a successful feature-length film. For more realistic adventure novels, look for the works of Will Hobbs, Jean Craighead George, Graham Salisbury, and Louis Sachar.

Mystery. Mysteries emerge as a very popular choice with children in the middle grades that are stretching their problem-solving skills. This is often where the interest in mystery series like *Nancy Drew* and the *Hardy Boys* blossoms. Look for the popular series featuring girl detective *Sammy Keyes* by Wendelin Van Draanen or the interactive series *39 Clues* by various authors including Rick Riordan, Gordon Korman, Linda Sue Park, among others. Art shapes the backdrop for the mysteries of Blue Balliett, such as *Hold Fast* (Scholastic, 2013), as well as the classic mystery by E. L. Konigsburg, *From the Mixed-Up Files of Mrs. Basil E. Frankweiler* (Atheneum, 1967), a Newbery medal book. Other Newbery-winning mysteries include *The Westing Game* by Ellen Raskin (Dutton, 1978). The mystery format is so popular, you will also encounter this "subgenre" in other major genres, including *historical* mysteries by authors such as Zilpha Keatley Snyder and Avi, as well as mysteries in *fantasy* such as the ghost stories of Betty Ren Wright or John Bellairs.

Animals. Animal stories maintain their hold on children's imaginations even into the older grades. However, in novel form they usually involve adventure and serious conflict. Here, an animal plays a major role in the story, often serving as a major character. The relationship between the protagonist and the animal acts as the crux of the story and serves to help the child grow up a bit. *Because of Winn-Dixie* by Kate DiCamillo (Candlewick Press, 2000), a Newbery honor book, is an excellent example of this kind of story, with a stray dog adopting a lonely girl and helping her connect with her father and the people in her community. Phyllis Reynolds Naylor's Newbery medal book *Shiloh* (Atheneum, 1991) is another "dog" story in which the protagonist's relationship with the dog, Shiloh, is a key element in helping him to grow up, even forcing him to make important moral and ethical choices. The characters were so compelling that Naylor wrote several *Shiloh* sequels. It's interesting to note that both *Because of Winn-Dixie* and *Shiloh* have also been adapted into feature-length films, capitalizing on the appeal of people and their pets stories. Keep in mind that these pets never talk in contemporary novels (that would make it a fantasy novel). They consistently behave as animals would, but their relationship with the child is the key, echoing the experiences of so many children who care for beloved animals. In addition, you may also find animals as characters in many popular *historical* fiction novels (and book-based movies) such as the classics, *Old Yeller* (Harper, 1956), a Newbery honor book by Fred Gipson, and *Where the Red Fern Grows* (Doubleday, 1961) by Wilson Rawls.

Sports. For many children, sports and recreation are an important part of their growing up experiences, and several authors have captured this in their writing of contemporary realism for young people. For years, Matt Christopher has been the go-to guy for sports novels for children, with over 100 titles depicting nearly every competitive sport that children might encounter from baseball to soccer, skateboarding to wheelchair basketball. Gradually, even girls have been portrayed as athletes and "wannabes." In more recent years, John H. Ritter has also authored appealing sports novels for young readers, often using the themes of competition and cooperation to mirror other struggles in the protagonist's life, as in *Fenway Fever* (Philomel, 2012). Mike Lupica, well known for his writing for adults, has also made a successful transition to writing sports books for kids with several novels including the *New York Times* bestselling basketball story *True Legend* (Philomel, 2012). Also look for sports-themed novels by Gary Soto or Dan Gutman. Sports fiction appeals to young athletes, of course, but offers all readers a deeper understanding of the beauty of a game well played and a validation of the life lessons to be learned from discipline and teamwork.

Short Stories for Children

Authors are also tackling contemporary issues in the literary format of the short story. Short story collections are particularly helpful for reading aloud since their length is often just right for one sitting. They also lend themselves to discussion afterward. Story collections by Gary Soto, such as *Baseball in April* (Harcourt, 1990), or Cynthia Rylant, such as *Every Living Thing* (Atheneum, 1985), offer powerful writing for young people on a variety of topics. Other examples of short stories for children include:

Chicken Soup for the Kid's Soul by Jack Canfield (Vermilion, 2001)
Guys Read: Funny Business edited by Jon Scieszka (Walden Pond, 2010)
Guys Read: Other Worlds edited by Jon Scieszka (Walden Pond, 2013)
Guys Read: The Sports Pages edited by Jon Scieszka (Walden Pond, 2012)
Guys Read: Thriller edited by Jon Scieszka (Walden Pond, 2011)
Hey! Listen to This: Stories to Read Aloud by Jim Trelease (Penguin, 1992)

Out of Bounds: Seven Stories of Conflict and Hope by Beverley Naidoo (HarperCollins, 2003)

Sideway Stories from Wayside School by Louis Sachar (HarperCollins, 1998)

Tripping Over the Lunch Lady and Other School Stories edited by Nancy Mercado (Dial, 2004)

When I Went to the Library: Writers Celebrate Books and Reading edited by Deborah Pearson (Groundwood, 2001)

Children's magazines and periodicals (such as *Stone Soup* and others) can also be an excellent source of current short fiction for children by both popular and up-and-coming authors. And don't forget that there are also collections of short stories in other genres, especially fantasy (e.g., ghost stories, scary stories, etc.) and nonfiction (e.g., true stories, sports vignettes, etc.).

Transitional Novels

Somewhere between the novel and the short story lies the short novel or transitional novel, a natural bridge from the highly visual "easy readers" first created by Dr. Seuss (with the "I Can Read" series) to longer novels without any illustrations. Today's "transitional novels" are often decorated in strategic places (like chapter headings and endings) or illustrated with doodles, cartoons, and sketches. Many of these transitional "chapter books" are generally 100 pages long or longer with short chapters to structure the story. Small sketches or illustrations appear regularly throughout the narrative, at least every few pages. They offer visual interest, but unlike "easy readers," these are not as essential to understanding the story as illustrations usually are when reading picture books. These shorter illustrated novels provide visual cues, larger fonts, and more white space to assist the developing reader in building fluency and confidence. Horning (2010) identifies four major attributes of this format:

- A simple vocabulary without too many surprising descriptors or multisyllabic words
- Sentences that are relatively short, direct, and uncomplicated
- Brief episodes, chapters, or intervals that stand out to the reader
- Content compelling enough to hold a child's interest but not so complicated that it's hard to follow (pp. 133–136)

Many of these transitional novels also emerge as popular series books with central characters that have continuing adventures. Look for some of these popular examples:

Amber Brown (Paula Danziger)
Bink & Gollie (Kate DiCamillo)
Calvin Coconut (Graham Salisbury)
Captain Underpants (Dav Pilkey)
Charlie Joe Jackson (Tommy Greenwald)
Clarice Bean (Lauren Child)

Clementine (Sara Pennypacker)
Creature from My Closet (Obert Skye)
Diary of a Wimpy Kid (Jeff Kinney)
Dork Diaries (Rachel Renée Russell)
Hank Zipzer (Henry Winkler)
Ivy and Bean (Annie Barrows)
Judy Moody and *Stink* (Megan McDonald)
Junie B. Jones (Barbara Park)
Justin Case (Rachel Vail)
Marvin Redpost (Louis Sachar)
My Life (Janet Tashjian)
Ruby Lu and *Alvin Ho* (Lenore Look)
Sam and *Gooney Bird* (Lois Lowry)

Series

Series books for young people have been popular for over 100 years, and the continuing appeal to young audiences of today is undeniable. Whether it's the long-running *Nancy Drew*, *Hardy Boys*, *Encyclopedia Brown*, or *Boxcar Children* series, young readers enjoy the familiarity of reading about the same characters in each story. (By the way, did you know that the Nancy Drew books were written by a variety of hired authors? There's no such person as author "Carolyn Keene.") Like transitional novels, series books meet an important need for the developing reader. They may be somewhat predictable, but they provide a structure and instant context that help build reading fluency. Much like adults' enjoyment of soap operas or other television programs, young readers find the series books satisfying, if formulaic. In fact, studies have found that many proficient adult readers were once voracious readers of series books as children.

Of course, series books have enormous appeal, even if they'll never win any literary awards for writing. But over time, various literary characters have become so popular that the authors who created them have continued their stories in additional novels. These literary sequels or "series" can be very satisfying reading, too. Check out the continuing adventures of these timeless characters created by Newbery medal and honor authors:

Alice (by Phyllis Reynolds Naylor)
Anastasia (by Lois Lowry)
Brian (by Gary Paulsen)
Cammy (by Virginia Hamilton)
Joey Pigza (by Jack Gantos)
Pacy Lin (by Grace Lin)
Ramona Quimby (by Beverly Cleary)
Shabanu (by Suzanne Fisher Staples)
Teddy and Bobby (by Laurence Yep)

Another new trend is offering series books in graphic novel format, such as the enormously popular *Babysitter's Club*, now a graphic novel series. And of course there are many memorable characters whose adventures are serialized in *fantasy* and *historical fiction* novels, too, but those are other chapters.

CONTROVERSY AND CONTEMPORARY REALISM

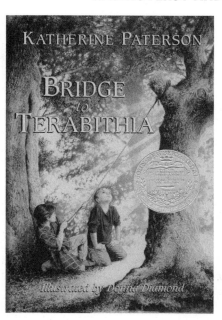

This genre can also be very controversial in that the content is current and contemporary and often reflects the challenges of urban life and global issues today. Book characters may be coping with the death of a loved one; the divorce of parents and family separations; personal sexuality issues; physical, mental, or emotional disabilities; war and persecution; and other real-life crises that touch us all in one way or another. In addition, some contemporary novels include some violence or profanity that many adults feel is not appropriate for children to encounter in books. Thus, this is the genre that may be subject to more book challenges. Read for yourself and see what you think. This is some of the best, most thought-provoking writing for kids, but it also can be edgy and disturbing—like real life for many kids, unfortunately.

For example, author Judy Blume is sometimes somewhat controversial in that her books for older readers (such as *Are You There, God? It's Me, Margaret*) also deal with young people's questions about their developing sexuality in ways that are frank and honest, but never sensational. Because her writing has often been challenged, she is quite a vocal and effective speaker on the subject of books. Check out her website for more information (http://www .judyblume.com). The ALA list of "The 100 Most Frequently Banned/Challenged Books of 2000–2009" includes several landmark books of contemporary fiction for children (as well as other genres) including *Bridge to Terabithia* and *The Great Gilly Hopkins,* both by Katherine Paterson; *Blubber* and *Are You There God? It's Me, Margaret* by Judy Blume; the *Alice* series by Phyllis Reynolds Naylor; *Olive's Ocean* by Kevin Henkes; the *Junie B. Jones* series by Barbara Park; and the *Anastasia* series by Lois Lowry. Each of these has been immensely popular with children but has also been challenged by someone somewhere along the way.

Book Challenges and Censorship

Book challenges and potential censorship are a fact of life in libraries, particularly for those of us who work in children's and youth services. We are all concerned about the experiences we provide for our children and want to be sure they grow up in a safe and healthy environment. However, what we deem appropriate for children is a highly subjective judgment and varies greatly from person to person. When it comes to children's literature, the genres of contemporary realistic fiction and fantasy are generally the most frequent targets of challenges today.

Those who work in the book field believe strongly in open access to books. I believe families should be involved in reading and talking about books and can decide what might not be appropriate for their own children. Libraries and schools, however, are public institutions with a responsibility to the community at large. Communities are not usually homogeneous, and often an outspoken minority wants to decide what is appropriate for the whole community. Here we must be careful. As the American Library Association recommends, we need calm procedures in place for people to raise their questions about appropriate reading material. We need representative committees that can discuss and decide these issues in an open and democratic forum where differences of opinion can be respected.

Our first priority should be to have a good book selection and collection development policy in place. How do we select books for the library? Is this process documented in writing? Next, it's critical to have a protocol for book challenges or grievances in place—again in writing. How are grievances reported and handled? Be sure that is clear and in writing. Third, this is not a "fight" to take on alone. Often a separate committee is formed for each stage: selection and grievance. Tunnell, Jacobs, Young, and Bryan (2012) also recommend dealing with *one* book at a time to keep the situation manageable and remind us that we need to recognize the emotional quotient in this process, and as we listen calmly "we should also get someone else to listen: (like) another librarian. . . . Having someone else present helps keep everyone honest and serves to reduce tension" (p. 213). Inform the library director, utilize the committees in place, muster your resources, including the ALA's Office for Intellectual Freedom (OIF) and their many excellent tools including the online *Intellectual Freedom Manual* (ifmanual.org).

The ALA defines a book challenge as "a formal, written complaint, filed with a library or school, requesting that materials be removed because of content or appropriateness." Challenges can be based on a variety of reasons, the most common being for sexually explicit material, offensive language, unsuitability to age group, presence of occult themes or promoting the occult or Satanism, violence, homosexual themes, or promoting religious viewpoints. Among the most challenged authors (2005–2012) of books for young people are Alvin Schwartz, Judy Blume, Lois Lowry, Phyllis Reynolds Naylor, and Peter Parnell and Justin Richardson. One irony: Often banned books become the most sought after. There is nothing more irresistible to kids than something a grown-up has said you can't have. (Maybe we should ban math textbooks!)

Of course, the greatest danger may well be our own caution working against us. Will we avoid purchasing or promoting Blume or Lowry because we *anticipate* challenges? This kind of self-censorship is also a problem. We need to be aware of our community demographics, but hold to our goal of providing a quality collection. In addition, we need to reflect on our own biases and prejudices and consider how they might be affecting our acquisition decisions. It gets sticky! As Amy Hielsberg (1994) observed, "Some of the best books are those that disturb us, challenge our complacency. Nobody tries to ban bland books."

Banned Books Week (every September):
http://www.ala.org/ala/oif/bannedbooksweek/bannedbooksweek.htm

Additional Resources

Adams, Helen R. 2013. *Protecting Intellectual Freedom and Privacy in Your School Library.* Englewood, CO: Libraries Unlimited.

Asheim, Lester. "Not Censorship but Selection." http://www.ala.org/ala/oif/basics/notcensorship.htm

Bishop, Kay. 2007. *The Collection Program in Schools: Concepts, Practices, and Information Sources* (Fourth Edition). Englewood, CO: Libraries Unlimited.

Donelson, Kenneth L. 1974. "What to Do When the Censor Comes." *Elementary English, 51* (3), 410–414. (EJ097697)

LaRue, James. 2007. *The New Inquisition: Understanding and Managing Intellectual Freedom Challenges.* Englewood, CO: Libraries Unlimited.

Morris, Betty J. 2004. *Administering the School Library Center* (Fourth Edition. Revised and Expanded). Englewood, CO: Libraries Unlimited.

Scales, Pat R. 2001. *Teaching Banned Books: 12 Guides for Young Readers.* Chicago: American Library Association.

Scales, Pat R. 2009. *Protecting Intellectual Freedom in Your School Library: Scenarios from the Front Lines.* Chicago: American Library Association.

MAJOR AUTHORS OF CONTEMPORARY REALISTIC FICTION

In recent years, most children's book authors have established their own Web presence on the Internet with personal websites. In fact, new authors who are just getting started are finding using Web tools and social media an essential aspect in reaching out to readers and promoting their work. Most author website URLs or addresses center around their names, with a few notable exceptions (like Katherine Paterson's website, for example). Thus it's sensible to begin the search for an author on the Web by typing in his or her name, as well as by "Googling" him or her. If they don't have a personal website, however, it is still possible to find out information about them through the research that others have conducted about these authors. This includes Professor Kaye Vandergrift's website, author interviews on Cynthia Leitich Smith's website, videos on YouTube, databases like TeachingBooks.net, publishers' websites, the Internet Public Library (IPL), and Wikipedia, as well as "old school" reference resources like *Something About the Author* and the *Tenth Book of Junior Authors and Illustrators* (2008), for example.

Authors Online

Here's a partial list of some established authors of contemporary realistic fiction who maintain consistent websites. In addition, many authors also maintain blogs with weekly, even daily entries such as Cynthia Leitich Smith, Grace Lin, Lois Lowry, Linda Sue Park, and Lisa Yee, among others. (Keep in mind that some of these authors listed below also write books in other genres, and that many authors in other genres also maintain helpful websites. This is just a sampling.) More children's author websites are popping up all the time.

Avi	http://www.avi-writer.com
Blue Balliett	http://www.blueballiettbooks.com
Jeanne Birdsall	http://www.jeannebirdsall.com
Judy Blume	http://www.judyblume.com/
Betsy Byars	http://www.betsybyars.com/
Matt Christopher	http://www.mattchristopher.com
Beverly Cleary	http://www.beverlycleary.com
Andrew Clements	http://www.andrewclements.com
Esmé Raji Codell	http://www.planetesme.com/
Sharon Creech	http://www.sharoncreech.com/
Candace Fleming	http://www.candacefleming.com/
Jack Gantos	http://www.jackgantos.com/
Nikki Grimes	http://www.nikkigrimes.com/
Virginia Hamilton	http://www.virginiahamilton.com/
Kevin Henkes	http://www.kevinhenkes.com/
Carl Hiaasen	http://www.carlhiaasen.com/
Grace Lin	http://www.gracelin.com/
Lois Lowry	http://www.loislowry.com/
Linda Sue Park	http://www.lspark.com/
Katherine Paterson	http://www.terabithia.com/
Sara Pennypacker	http://www.sarapennypacker.com
John H. Ritter	http://www.johnhritter.com/
Pam Muñoz Ryan	http://www.pammunozryan.com/
Louis Sachar	http://www.louissachar.com
Cynthia Leitich Smith	http://www.cynthialeitichsmith.com/
Jerry Spinelli	http://www.jerryspinelli.com/
Sarah Weeks	http://www.sarahweeks.com
Lisa Yee	http://www.lisayee.com/

Of course, this is just a partial list of some of the outstanding individuals who have created engaging contemporary realistic fiction for young readers. These folks are some of the many authors you can find online. An author's website usually offers a photo of the author, brief biographical information, a list of his or her books, awards won, downloadable audio and video clips, and often much more. Many authors' sites go well beyond presenting their own works to include recommendations for additional reading, tips for children about writing, and other fun literacy-related activities. Many even include a "contact" link so that children can write to the author directly if they want to.

Authors in Action: Janet Tashjian

Janet Tashjian is the author of acclaimed books for young adults, including *The Gospel According to Larry, Vote for Larry, Larry and the Meaning of Life, Fault Line, Tru Confessions, For What It's Worth, Multiple Choice,* as well as the extremely popular "My Life" series for younger readers including *My Life as a Book, My Life as a Stuntboy, and My Life as a Cartoonist* illustrated with cartoons and drawings by her son, Jake Tashjian. She lives in California and has a rich website with a blog, videos, and extensive "teacher resources" complete with downloadable discussion guides and bookmarks. Here she writes about the impetus for writing the first "My Life" book and on collaborating with her son on this series.

My Life as a Book
by Janet Tashjian

The *My Life as a Book* series is very personal for me—a real blend of my life as a children's book author and my life as a mom. As a writer, I do a lot of school visits where I see firsthand the struggle many students have with reading. Teachers and librarians constantly ask me to address the "reluctant readers" in my presentations and several of my other books—especially *Tru Confessions* and *The Gospel According to Larry* series—have long been used to connect with students who have reading issues.

On the home front, my house has always been filled with lots of kids—mostly boys—who often struggle with reading. I am fascinated with how many children love books but hate reading, and I wanted to explore that struggle in a novel.

Almost every kid I know learned to read by devouring Bill Watterson's *Calvin and Hobbes* comic strips. Even though the concepts and vocabulary can be challenging, the visual support helped pull these "reluctant readers" through. My son, Jake, has always had reading issues and taught himself his vocabulary words by illustrating them on index cards all through elementary school. Friends would see the drawings around our house and laugh at his interpretation of difficult words like "anxious" or "colleague." So I decided to write a book that would appeal to kids like Jake and his friends, a next step for kids who loved *Calvin and Hobbes* but were being urged to start reading "real" books—that is, books without cartoons.

I based the story in Los Angeles before we decided to uproot our Boston life and move here—one of those life/art coincidences that constantly fascinate me. I also wanted to write a "boy and his dog" story, so gave Derek a loving mutt like our family dog, Cinder. A few of the incidents in the book—sliding under a security gate at the DVD store or criss-crossing a room with fishing line—are straight from the exploits of Jake and his friends. (Although I admit the security gate spy thing might have been my idea . . .)

Jake's illustrations just kill me—the drawing for "overwhelmed" almost made me burst into tears when I first saw it. Jake does between 200 and 250 illustrations for each book; he was completely professional—even through the rigorous rewriting and redrawing process. He was and is my favorite collaborator, a kid who exercises his imagination muscles every day.

Parents and teachers always ask me where I stand on the subject of summer reading lists—our character Derek's main bone of contention in the book. On the one hand, several of my books are on such lists so I'm obviously for them. On the other hand, I've seen Jake and his friends run screaming from the room as if on fire when forced to read a book someone else chose for them during summer vacation. It's a conundrum I still haven't figured out yet; that being said, I'm for *any* kind of reading—comic books and cereal boxes included—that a kid chooses on his or her own terms.

I had so much fun exploring Derek's world with my son that the series keeps growing. What started out with *My Life as a Book* continues with *My Life as a Stuntboy, My Life as a Cartoonist,* and the upcoming *My Life as a Joke.* We also just collaborated on a new series coming out this year called *Einstein the Class Hamster,* based on a comic strip Jake drew in middle school. I have a lot of stories inside me; he has a lot of images. We make a pretty good team.

Just today, we had an hour's drive ahead of us and I asked Jake to entertain me with a story. He made up the escapades of a lovelorn frilled lizard that had me howling with laughter as I drove. As Derek comes to realize in *My Life as a Book,* reading may sometimes be challenging, but stories are something we can't live without.

One Book in Action: My Life as a Book

When it comes to contemporary fiction, children enjoy a story they can identify with, one that reflects kids like themselves. For our "one book" for close study in this genre, we'll focus on Janet Tashjian's novel *My Life as a Book* (Holt, 2010), the hilarious story about a boy who hates reading books, but is pulled into solving a family mystery—and learns

a few things along the way. It's a fun and engaging story, as well as a great example of the new illustrated novel that blends drawings and doodles with the narrative in a book designed with wide margins and a large font. It also launched an entire "My Life" series featuring the further adventures of twelve-year-old Derek Fallon, along with his friends, family, and beloved dog, Bodi, all told from his spunky, snarky, and authentic first-person point of view. Look for *My Life as a Book, My Life as a Stuntboy, My Life as a Cartoonist,* and *My Life as a Joke.* Our featured book, *My Life as a Book,* is even available in a Spanish edition, *Mi vida es un cuento.*

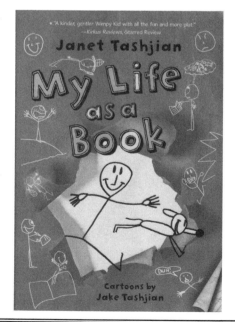

Making Connections

Tashjian's true-to-life novel features so many details of contemporary children's lives that young readers can relate to.

Derek has a much-loved family dog (named Bodi), is an avid skateboarder, and is quite adept at drawing, even trying digital animation. Although our hero, Derek, is not always successful in the usual ways (in school, in particular), his sense of humor and adventure is very appealing. In addition, he has a loving family—an understanding mother who is a successful veterinarian and a kind father who works at home as an illustrator and shares Derek's affinity for art. Plus, Derek has a good friend (who is away for most of the summer) and a new friend, a competitive girl from school who becomes more sympathetic as they survive "learning camp" in the summer. These elements provide discussion points as children think about the connections with their own lives: their family, friends, hobbies, talents. In particular, while Derek struggles with reading, he flourishes with drawing and doodling. Talk with children about their own hobbies and talents and encourage them to explore various possibilities. Provide nonfiction books on hobbies that they can browse through like Lee Ames's "How to Draw" titles as well as fun books referenced in *My Life as a Book* like the *Calvin and Hobbes* comics that Derek just loves.

As you consider how to introduce the *My Life* books, you will find a great deal of support for sharing this book on Tashjian's informative website http://www.janettashjian .com, especially the hilarious video blog entries created by Tashjian and her son and the *My Life* illustrator, Jake Tashjian.

Also consider incorporating poetry about family experiences to go along with *My Life as a Book:*

Harrison, David. 2009. *Vacation, We're Going to the Ocean!* Honesdale, PA: Wordsong/ Boyds Mills Press.
Hoberman, Mary Ann. 2009. *All Kinds of Families.* New York: Little, Brown.
Hopkins, Lee Bennett. Ed. 2010. *Amazing Faces.* Ill. by Chris Soentpiet. New York: Lee & Low.

Read-Alikes

My Life as a Book captures the persona of the misfit child who sees things a little differently and gets in (and out of) trouble on a regular basis. Children may enjoy continuing this thread by reading more humorous, illustrated chapter books featuring kids like this. Some of my favorites include:

Calvin Coconut (Graham Salisbury)
Charlie Joe Jackson (Tommy Greenwald)
Creature from My Closet (Obert Skye)
Diary of a Wimpy Kid (Jeff Kinney)
Dork Diaries (Rachel Renée Russell)
Hank Zipzer (Henry Winkler)
Marvin Redpost (Louis Sachar)
Ruby Lu and *Alvin Ho* (Lenore Look)

Developing "read-alike" lists (in bibliographies or bookmark form) is always a good practice for recommending books on favorite topics or for various age levels.

Vocabulary Drawings

The visuals that appear throughout *My Life as a Book* are drawings created by the author's son, Jake Tashjian. They represent what the book's character, Derek, might be doodling himself as the story progresses. Each is a small sketch to visualize a new vocabulary word (like "unison" or "goatee"). These stick figures and simple cartoons in the book's margins provide examples of what you and the kids can sketch together yourselves as you talk about unfamiliar words encountered while reading.

Author Janet Tashjian writes about the value of the vocabulary drawings that are featured throughout the *My Life* books, "Embedded in . . . (the) . . . books are techniques from Lindamood Bell's Visualizing and Verbalizing as well as Reading Specialist Maryanne Wolf's Rave-O program. . . . One of the things we see in our travels is that students are illustrating their own vocabulary words much the way Derek does in the books." Children are even encouraged to send their vocabulary drawings to Tashjian's website for posting there.

EVALUATION CRITERIA

In evaluating contemporary realistic fiction, we rely on the traditional literary elements of characterization, plot, setting, theme, and style to help us analyze these novels. We're looking for a story that feels current, that could happen today in the world as we know it. It's a work of imagination, not fact, but it rings true to our understanding of modern life. Believability is the hallmark of contemporary realism, often labeled as "verisimilitude," meaning "similar to truth" or true to life. Kiefer (2010) demands that realism be factual, situational, emotional, and social, recognizing the many layers that contribute to the fabric of realistic fiction. Child readers, in particular, want a book that is *realistic* and will often discard novels that are overtly didactic or moralistic in favor of stories with strong characters, exciting plots, and subtle themes. Next we'll consider each literary element that contributes to creating quality contemporary realistic fiction, citing Newbery medal books that exemplify each element beautifully.

Characters

The characters in a realistic novel are absolutely critical, particularly to the child reader, who often identifies with the main character or protagonist and experiences life vicariously through this character's perspective. In fact, in some books, particularly for older readers, the character's internal journey and emotional growth are far more significant than the plot or action of the story. Do we see both their strengths and their weaknesses? We expect characters to be dynamic and three-dimensional, to change and grow a bit in the course of the story. For example, in E. L. Konigsburg's second Newbery medal book, *The View from Saturday* (Atheneum, 1996), there are multiple main characters coming together as a team competing for a prize, and we follow each one individually, as well as the interactions between them, from multiple points of view. Their developing relationships as well as their emerging self-knowledge are more significant than the competition itself. Thus, in this genre, dialogue becomes especially important as a window into the characters and their relationships and can quickly "date" a book as "old-fashioned" if it relies too much on slang or colloquialisms. The language in the book should feel fresh and believable and reflect the way children really think and talk at that age and stage of life.

Plot

In contemporary novels, the plot is a "slice of life" built upon events that must seem plausible and true to life. Although young readers identify with the characters, they also want an engaging story. In fact, some reading experts believe the action must grab the child from the very first page. In addition, we look for plots that seem fresh and original and perhaps even surprise us with unexpected twists and turns. Yet the plotline must be logical and prepare the reader, if indirectly, for the cause and effect of the story's happenings. The climax and conclusion of the story are also critical and should seem inevitable, but not obvious; hopeful, if not always happy. A good writer avoids coincidence and pat resolutions while leading the reader to a satisfying resolution without obvious moralizing. For example, in her Newbery medal book *Walk Two Moons* (HarperCollins, 1994), Sharon Creech weaves a fairly complex plot with the use of flashbacks to piece together the story of a girl who is coping with moving and adjusting to a new home and new friends, while longing for her missing mother, whose story is revealed bit by bit.

Setting

Obviously, the settings for novels in this genre are contemporary, set in a time we recognize as the present. Consequently, some contemporary novels become historical with the passing of the years, particularly if they are anchored in specific details of time and place. Again, it is important that the novel's setting be believable and, if a place is acknowledged, the description of it is accurate. In addition, the author should consider how the setting affects the action, the characters, and even the theme. Is the story set in a small town? A school? A foreign country? All those factors will influence other aspects of the story. In Susan Patron's Newbery medal book *The Higher Power of Lucky* (Simon & Schuster, 2006), for example, the California desert is a crucial backdrop for the story's action, as is the small, nuclear community of forty-three that Lucky finds herself in. It shapes her sense of herself in specific ways as she looks for examples of how to be. Often the settings of contemporary novels are generalized and nonspecific, simply suggesting modern-day life in a small community; either way, the story should transcend the setting and have universal implications for readers in many different situations.

Theme

Most contemporary realistic novels for young people focus on the search for an independent identity, the desire for an understanding of one's role within families, friendships, blossoming romances, and other landmarks of growing up into adulthood. These themes and topics have a personal resonance for the child reader in a way that is meaningful and worthwhile. And yet, the theme should emerge naturally from the story, from the conflicts in the plot, and from the nature of the characters. If it is stated too obviously, it overpowers the story and veers into moralizing and didacticism. For example, in the Newbery medal book *Missing May* (Orchard, 1992), Cynthia Rylant manages to deal with death, grief, and isolation while underscoring the importance of reaching out for love from family and friends in unexpected ways. Never is it heavy-handed or manipulative; instead, the quirky personalities of the character group help us recognize ourselves in their foibles.

Style

Once again, style is the element that is most individualistic for each genre. For contemporary realistic fiction, an author may leave his or her distinct stamp on the writing in a multitude of ways. The language may often be very conversational, even colloquial. Or it may be filled with figurative language and literary devices, such as symbolism, allusion, similes, and so on. Look at the use of dialogue in the story. Does it seem natural and believable, as if you could imagine children talking to each other? Is there a balance of narration and dialogue? The point of view is also important to the story. Who is telling the story? Is the point of view from which the story is told appropriate to the purpose of the book? The tone and mood of the book is another hallmark of an individual author's style. Is it humorous? Serious? Mysterious? How did the author create a mood? Even the physical and organizational aspects of the novel can reflect an author's personality. Are the chapters especially short? Are there interesting chapter titles? A foreword or an afterword? Look at Lynne Rae Perkins's Newbery medal book *Criss Cross* (Greenwillow Books, 2005), for example, for some very unique stylistic innovations such as the inclusion of small sketches, doodles, and poems throughout the narrative, in addition to changing points of view among multiple characters. Today's authors often enjoy experimenting with style and narrative, so watch for additional variations to come.

Gender and Culture

Finally, it is also important to consider the depiction of gender and culture in the creation of high-quality contemporary realistic fiction, particularly since this genre is a reflection of today's society and current attitudes and mores. For many years, it was boys who dominated nearly every novel, serving as the protagonist of the story and taking the most active, problem-solving roles. Girls were there, but they served as sisters, friends, or girlfriends and rarely as the one who stepped up to the challenge or saved the day. That has gradually changed and girls' voices are heard more and more often as the main character that takes the lead. That has also led to an acceptance of more sensitive boy characters who are in supporting roles and who can be depicted struggling with emotional issues and identity questions. The same can be said of adult characters in contemporary novels, with mothers and fathers, women and men, portrayed in more varied ways and with family structures more variable and wide-ranging as well, from single-parent families to blended families and everything in between. Consider the gender quotient as you analyze contemporary novels and reimagine the story as if the gender of the protagonist were reversed (male to female or vice versa). Would it make a difference? Why or why not?

Like gender, our understanding of culture and its impact on the lives and stories of individuals has also changed and evolved over the years. It is important to take this into consideration when assessing the depiction of contemporary life in fiction for young people. However, once again Rudine Sims Bishop reminds us, in "Making Informed Choices" (1992), to include a careful consideration of the usual literary elements in our analysis of each book, since cultural accuracy may be rather mechanical if the book's story does not interest children. In addition, our understanding of culture is limited to our own education and life experiences, so we may feel ill-equipped to spot the cultural stereotypes. As Pang, Colvin, Tran, and Barba (1992) wrote in "Beyond Chopsticks and Dragons: Selecting Asian-American Literature for Children," everyone is diminished when stereotypes of various groups are reinforced in children's literature." This includes:

- Tokenism and typecasting offering a one-sided, rather than multidimensional character of color
- Positive stereotypes such as the "polite, intelligent, cooperative Asian child" or the "Indian environmentalist" that still pigeonhole a person of color as being only one type
- Prevalent ethnocentrism suggesting the myth of Anglo superiority, often with a "sidekick" of color
- Cultural overloading with a "cultural parade" of details, rather than a good story
- Romanticism; a story that presents a "tourist approach" to culture, rather than real people and real problems (Harris, 1997)

Instead, we look for accurate "cultural markers" such as the description of the characters, their homes, language patterns, dialect, names and forms of address, as well as issues and concerns that grow out of the characters and their cultures. Are these modern characters you could imagine meeting or people who seem to have lived "long ago" or "far away"? Is there variety even within the culture depicted? Even within a single micro-culture, there are major cultural differences, class distinctions, and even prejudices. One quickly begins to see the complexity behind the issues. It's a task that challenges us to keep reading, learning, and growing with an open mind.

As you read, select, and critique novels in this genre, remember to consider these elements in your process. Compare what you read in the novel with these criteria and with "benchmark books" of realistic fiction that are considered outstanding. You will soon find some of the most memorable books ever written for children in this genre and discover that this can be pivotal reading in the lives of kids as they mature. Do you remember how you felt when you read *Are You There, God? It's Me, Margaret* (Yearling, 1970) or *Hatchet* (Bradbury, 1987) or *Shiloh* (Atheneum, 1991)? How it felt to read about someone like you? With the same worries that you had? Contemporary realistic fiction offers young readers a literary experience that validates their own searching and honors their questions, concerns, and crises.

Sample Review

Let's put these evaluation criteria into action and consider one review and how it uses these criteria. Here's a sample review of a novel of contemporary realistic fiction:

Greenwald, Tommy. 2011. *Charlie Joe Jackson's Guide to Not Reading*. Ill. by J. P. Coovert. New York: Roaring Brook Press.

Charlie Joe, a smart, self-effacing and endearing middle school underachiever, will go to any length NOT to read a book. This chronicle of his efforts to write the dreaded seventh grade Position Paper without actually cracking a book involves the strategic use of friends, cliques, deception, and romance. Revelations at the school dance demolish these well-laid plans, and Charlie has to choose between two punishments that truly fit the crime. Reading tips ("Never read a book by someone whose name you can't pronounce") interspersed throughout the book contribute to Charlie Joe's case against reading and to the reader's enjoyment. Written in first person, Charlie Joe's keen observations on middle school life are both hilarious and insightful. Clever line drawings and the twenty-five exclusive nonreading tips contribute to the story's humor and energy. Avid and reluctant readers alike should find Charlie Joe's account of his middle school year a thoroughly enjoyable story. [By Susi Grissom from *Librarians' Choices*. Used with permission.]

Notice that this review begins with a clear focus on the protagonist character (Charlie Joe), often the central element of a contemporary realistic novel. The reviewer deftly captures his personality, as well as the humorous tone of the writing of the novel (he "will go to any length NOT to read a book"). Then the plot is communicated briefly ("write the dreaded seventh grade Position Paper . . . strategic use of friends, cliques, deception, and romance. Revelations . . . demolish these well-laid plans"), concluding with an allusion to the theme. ("Charlie has to choose between two punishments that truly fit the crime.") The reviewer includes an excerpted sentence ("Never read a book by someone whose name you can't pronounce") as an example of the book's "Reading Tips," an essential part of *Charlie Joe Jackson's Guide to **Not** Reading*. Then the rest of the review focuses on the style, format, and appeal of the novel, noting the first person point of view, the humor in the book, and the presence of visuals ("clever line drawings"). She acknowledges that this novel may appeal to both "avid and reluctant" readers, considering possible audiences for this book. This review models how literary analysis can integrate all the usually literary elements along with a discussion of "kid appeal" in a way that acknowledges the importance of both, without starting with the usual "This book is about. . . ."

AWARDS FOR CONTEMPORARY REALISTIC FICTION

In the genre of contemporary realistic fiction, many books receive recognition from many different sources for their themes, characters, culture, and writing. Since this is also a very popular genre among young readers, you will find that realistic fiction is frequently on lists of their favorites, too. In fact, young people often enjoy participating in selecting award titles, including holding their own "mock" Newbery discussions.

The Newbery Award

When you look for the best examples of contemporary realistic fiction, you may also be surprised to find the best of children's literature. Period. Many of the Newbery award winners presented by the Association for Library Service to Children for the "most distinguished contribution to children's literature" for a given year have been examples of contemporary realistic fiction. They've tackled tough subjects like homelessness, death of a family member or friend, mental illness, and abuse, but they've also shown writing that is fresh and powerful, with memorable characters and distinctive plots. It is said that children do not generally choose Newbery books to read on their own, and that adults may need to read them aloud to lead children to discover them. That has often been true in the past, but many of the winners of the last 20 years have also emerged as the favorites of children, too, such as these books:

The Higher Power of Lucky by Susan Patron, illus. by Matt Phelan (Simon & Schuster, 2006)
A young girl struggles with finding her own identity and sense of family in a community of a motley group of people.

Criss Cross by Lynne Rae Perkins (Greenwillow Books, 2005)
Four young teens "criss cross" paths one summer as they grow up in a small town.

The View from Saturday by E. L. Konigsburg (Atheneum, 1996)
Through multiple characters and points of view, a team comes together to compete for a prize.

Walk Two Moons by Sharon Creech (HarperCollins, 1994)
A girl misses her mother, moves, and adjusts to a new home and friends; flashbacks tell us the whole story.

Missing May by Cynthia Rylant (Orchard, 1992)
  An older gentleman and his young adopted daughter mourn the passing of his wife, as they look for answers and some kind of a future.

Shiloh by Phyllis Reynolds Naylor (Atheneum, 1991)
  A boy befriends, then hides an abused dog and compromises his own integrity and that of his family; in the end, he must make it right again.

Maniac Magee by Jerry Spinelli (Little, Brown, 1990)
  A homeless white boy, innocent of racism, is bullied by whites, befriended by blacks, and bumps from place to place until he finds his way "home."

What an interesting and varied list, isn't it? Marianne Follis (2010) studied the diverse winners of the Newbery medal for a ten-year period looking for evidence of strong trends and found some interesting surprises. Her dissertation, *Newbery and Notables 2000–2009: Investigating Trends*, examined the subject headings of a decade's worth of Newbery award–winning books as well as the American Library Association's Notable books for these same years. Her study explored 758 titles, collecting and evaluating 2,814 Library of Congress subject headings for each book. Results indicated that although there were six years (out of ten) in which there were shared subject headings, the percentage of associated subject headings was less than 7 percent. When examining specific Newbery titles in detail, it was apparent that there was a great gap in similarity in the content of the Newbery award–winning books and the Notable books. So while these books may represent exceptional children's literature, they were not very similar to one another or to the majority of other books being published, as a whole. It is ironic that we take something distinguished and recognize these works for outstanding quality, but then also erroneously assume that these books are typical of the publishing of the same period. They are not only distinguished, but they are unique, too.

Other ALA Awards

Other national awards for children's contemporary fiction given by the American Library Association include the Coretta Scott King Award given annually to an African American author and the Pura Belpré Award presented biennially to a Latino/Latina author whose work best portrays, affirms, and celebrates the Latino cultural experience. Recent Coretta Scott King author honors have gone to Nikki Grimes for *The Road to Paris* (Putnam, 2006), and the Pura Belpré author medal has been awarded to Julia Alvarez for *Return to Sender* (Scholastic Press, 2009).

In addition, the ALA Schneider Family Book Awards include an author of a book for middle school that embodies an artistic expression of the disability experience for child and adolescent audiences. *Rules* by Cynthia Lord (Scholastic, 2006) is a Schneider award recipient for its depiction of a young girl's struggle to find her place in a family absorbed by the needs of her autistic brother.

The Batchelder Award presented by the Association for Library Service to Children honors an American publisher for an outstanding children's book originally published in a foreign language in a foreign country, and subsequently translated into English. Often a work of contemporary fiction is selected, providing an interesting glimpse into other settings across the globe, such as *Samir and Yonatan,* a story about an injured Palestinian boy recovering in a Jewish hospital, written by Daniella Carmi, translated from the Hebrew by Yael Lotan (Scholastic Press, 2000), or *Son of a Gun* by Anne de Graaf about a kidnapped brother and sister forced to become child soldiers in Liberia's civil war (Eerdmans, 2012).

The Hans Christian Andersen Award

The Hans Christian Andersen Award, also known as the "Nobel Prize" of children's literature, is given every two years by the International Board on Books for Young People (IBBY) to a living author whose complete works have made a lasting contribution to children's literature. Many are novelists known for writing contemporary stories that cross boundaries, such as Uri Orlev (Israel), Katherine Paterson (United States), Ana Maria Machado (Brazil), Martin Waddell (Ireland), and Margaret Mahy (New Zealand). And while you're looking for good books from other countries, keep an eye on the major awards they present to children's books including the Governor General's Literary Awards in Canada and the Carnegie Medal in the United Kingdom, among others.

Literature in Action: Guiding Responses

As we guide children in their reading of longer works, encouraging them to verbalize their responses after reading a book can be both helpful and therapeutic. They may benefit from confirming their understanding with an outsider or may want to speculate about questions they have with a good listener. The emphasis should be twofold:

- Promote extensive reading and responding to books to build comprehension and reading skill
- Promote pleasure in reading, thinking, and talking about books in order to build a lifetime habit of reading

The research of Louise Rosenblatt in *Literature as Exploration* (MLA, reissued 1996) on the interactive nature of reading (between reader and text) has taught us a great deal about this reading, interpreting, and responding dynamic. Being an adult who is a reader, one who openly invites discussion, who is in tune with children's interests, who listens to their opinions, is an important beginning in developing confident and articulate young readers.

Which activities best facilitate children's thoughtful responses? There's no magic formula. As adult readers, we simply enjoy talking with other readers in informal conversations and book group discussions. As librarians, we should try to create an atmosphere where these informal conversations and discussions can also occur. However, in more formal organized settings, particularly in schools, we're often called upon to create more concrete response activities. Here are a few that I have found most effective for children in these middle grade years.

Brown Bag Book Reports

The brown bag book report is an idea I gleaned from a teacher, and I mentioned it in Chapter One in conjunction with Pat Mora's picture book *Tomás and the Library Lady* (Knopf, 1997). I have used it with many groups of all ages and found it to be very appealing and successful. It is simple, inexpensive, and extremely low-tech, and helps readers build their oral skills and confidence while you assess their comprehension. To top it off, it motivates other children to want to read the book being reported about. It is a strategy generally used with fiction and is particularly effective for summarizing novels. Here are the steps (for you and for kids):

1. Read a book (preferably one you have chosen yourself).
2. Think about the book, the characters, and the main events.
3. Gather objects or "book artifacts" that relate to the story, character, and main events. You can draw a picture of the item and color it or find an image online and print the page, if you can't find the actual item. *(Discourage children from buying the items. No need to spend money for this project.)*
4. Gather the book and all the book artifacts in a bag. (If you want to get fancy, decorate the bag so it fits the book.)
5. Orally retell the book using the items in the bag, pulling out each book artifact, one at a time, as it is relevant to that part of the story.
6. Should you reveal the ending? Decide beforehand if you will leave the audience hanging, eager to read the book themselves!

Here's a sample "Brown Bag" book report for one of my all-time favorite dog stories, *Shiloh* by Phyllis Reynolds Naylor (Atheneum, 1991).

Shiloh is a Newbery award–winning novel about an eleven-year-old boy named Marty Preston who lives in West Virginia *(show bag decorated with rural scene)*. One day he finds a dog *(show beagle puppet)* that seems to be very neglected. He falls in love with the dog, names it "Shiloh" after the bridge where he finds it, and decides it must belong to cruel Judd Travers. Judd is so mean, he hunts deer out of season *(show hunting magazine)* and neglects his dogs so they'll be meaner. Marty can't stand this, so he decides to hide Shiloh from Judd and from his family. This sets up some serious deception, however, that makes Marty very uncomfortable. His mom becomes suspicious and reminds him of the time Marty ate his sister's chocolate bunny *(show chocolate bunny)* and then lied about it. Marty even begs for old, expired groceries *(show fake food and empty sour cream container)* at the local market, arousing sympathy for his family. He keeps his younger sisters away from Shiloh's hidden pen by reminding them there are snakes *(show rubber snakes)* up on the hill. It all comes to a crisis point, however, when Shiloh is attacked by a vicious neighbor dog and has to be taken to the vet, and everyone finds out what Marty has been up to *(show chain dog collar)*. Does Marty get to keep Shiloh? Does Shiloh go back to live with Judd? You'll have to read the book to find out!

Other more informal approaches to guiding children's responses to their reading include using thoughtful questioning and discussion, conducting follow-up research, and encouraging creative extensions.

Questions and Discussion

Asking good questions is a bit of an art and may take some trial and error. The key is often to wait long enough after asking the question to allow children time to come up with responses. Avoid answering your own questions! Author Gary Paulsen says to ask the *second* question—the why behind the why. And of course we have to be open to different responses. Children don't always see things the way we see them and often catch things that we never notice. Be open to a discussion balanced between the book and the child (what happens in the book vs. how they feel about it). Try to subtly guide discussion with higher level questions that stretch children to speculate, support their guesses, and make connections to other literature and other life experiences. Lead children to compare responses, to compare books, and to compare book events to their own experiences. Often a climate that encourages discussion is one that also nurtures book clubs for regular gatherings of readers. Children's librarian Marianne Follis holds regular book club meetings for her 'tween and teen readers. She remarked, "The members of the group do not read the *same* book, but they simply discuss what they are reading. It has been a great way for the kids to promote books to each other. There are some amazing readers at my library, and I could never read as much as they all do. I usually walk out of our session with a new title I *have* to read. Recently, we talked about what books they read, what languages they speak, and how they feel about people of color in books."

Follow-Up Research

Children often enjoy taking a book to the next level, reading more books by the same author or more books on the same topic (often called "read-alikes"). Help them research related books, poems, short stories, picture books, movies, songs, and so on. Make a list of these and share them with other interested readers. This is especially helpful when there is a huge demand for a particularly popular title but not enough copies to circulate to everyone at once. I'm a real fan of pairing poetry with fiction, digging up a poem or poems that express similar feelings, responses, experiences, or even a similar idea or story as the book. It's a very meaningful way to get at the heart of a story and can open or close a good book discussion.

It can also be meaningful to research the time and place of the book's setting or other factual details presented in a good book. For example, is there really a town called "Hard Pan" in California as described in the 2007 Newbery winner, *The Higher Power of Lucky* by Susan Patron (Simon & Schuster, 2006)? Does it really boast a "Found Object Wind Chime Museum & Visitor Center"? What community resources can you think of that might help us learn more? Are there Internet sites that might be useful? Digging into book details can lead to more reading and further discussion and sharing. Often the author's website will provide a back-story on the writing of favorite titles.

Creative Extensions

What creative activities might a book inspire? Does it mention particular songs or music? Or art activities like drawing, painting, or sculpture? Are there cooking activities or recipes to try? Are there dance or games or movement in the story? Make a list. Find examples, if possible. Encourage children to visualize their feelings, responses, and experiences in drawings and art and craft projects: drawing a scene from the book, or a book character's portrait; creating a book jacket, a bookmark, cartoons, and so forth. Invite students to use digital tools to create their projects, if they have those skills, too. Extend the reading by acting out a scene from the book, or by acting out a character, the book's climactic ending, or a significant conflict or turning point in the book for others to guess "charades" style; try converting the text into a readers' theater script in which dialogue becomes character parts (not memorized, but simply read aloud with expression); or children might even prepare and present a sequel skit. If you're comfortable offering children more artistic outlets for responding to favorite books, the sky's nearly the limit when it comes to possibilities that kids can dream up. For some children, this mode of response is right up their alleys, allowing them to connect with their reading while exercising their artistic and creative sides.

Readers' Theater

Readers' theater is a group method of reading a story aloud that is informal but still dramatic. Basically, you take a story or excerpt with plenty of dialogue and turn it into a kind of script with parts, once the story has been read or read aloud and is familiar to the children. No props or costumes are needed, no lines are memorized. All "acting" is accomplished through voices and expression. Many realistic and fantasy novels lend themselves to dramatic interpretation or a readers' theater presentation, although it's a technique that can be applied to any genre. Readers' theater can be a perfect way to "hook" students into reading the whole book or to follow up a favorite book with a memorable experience. Choose one chapter or excerpt that can serve as a fun culmination of the book, or an early chapter that might "lure" the students into reading the rest of the book.

Begin by choosing a suitable excerpt, generally 10 minutes in length for reading aloud. Children each volunteer to read aloud a character's lines. Exposition or narration can be assigned to one or more narrators. Purists stick as closely to the original text as possible, others adapt the text or interpret the text in their own words. Older children can choose and format stories into scripts themselves. When children create the script, they have many opportunities to read and reread, think, edit, and practice their fluency. The final result is an unintimidating form of theater that makes the story come alive and promotes deep comprehension. (Warning: they'll want to do each script over and over again, so everyone can have a "major" part!)

For a different twist, consider a professional alternative, Authors Readers Theatre, founded in 2006 by authors Avi, Sharon Creech, Walter Dean Myers, and Sarah Weeks. Here, these authors themselves (and others) are the actors, reading from their works with zest and panache—but again, with no costumes or props, just a podium and a mike. It's a fantastic model and an affordable program for many libraries. You'll also find video clips of live performances on YouTube—a model of what you can try with kids yourself.

For more information about readers' theater, check out readers' theater guru Aaron Shepard's website: http://www.aaronshep.com/ as well as these helpful resources:

Black, Alison, and Anna M. Stave. 2007. *A Comprehensive Guide to Readers Theatre: Enhancing Fluency and Comprehension in Middle School and Beyond.* Newark, DE: International Reading Association.

Campbell, Melvin, and Joann V. Cleland. 2003. *Readers Theatre in the Classroom: A Manual for Teachers of Children and Adults.* New York: iUniverse.

Jenkins, Diana R. 2004. *Just Deal with It!: Funny Readers Theatre for Life's Not-So-Funny Moments.* Englewood, CO: Libraries Unlimited.

Jenkins, Diana R. 2007. *All Year Long!: Funny Readers Theatre for Life's Special Times.* Englewood, CO: Libraries Unlimited.

Shepard, Aaron. 2004. *Readers on Stage: Resources for Reader's Theater (or Readers Theatre), with Tips, Play Scripts, and Worksheets, or How to Do Simple Children's Plays That Build Reading Fluency and Love of Literature.* Olympia, WA: Shepard Publications.

Worthy, Jo. 2005. *Readers Theater for Building Fluency: Strategies and Scripts for Making the Most of This Highly Effective, Motivating, and Research-Based Approach to Oral Reading.* New York: Scholastic.

A Caveat

Although I have had many memorable experiences with children in encouraging and formalizing their unique responses to books, I want to make it clear that we can take this too far and make even fun creative activities too much like dry assignments that kill the joy of reading. Sometimes we just like to read a good book. Period. It's been said that adult readers don't rush out to create dioramas of favorite novels. Very true. We just enjoy mulling over our thoughts and possibly sharing them with trusted friends. Try to keep that in mind as you promote postreading activities and strive to be that trusted book-loving friend and guide for the kids in your life.

"Unlucky Arithmetic: Thirteen Ways to Raise a Nonreader"

Dean Schneider and Robin Smith wrote the following tongue-in-cheek piece for *Horn Book* (March/April 2001). Think about what it tells us about nurturing a love of reading, in a backward way.

1. Never read where your children can see you.
2. Put a TV or computer in every room. Don't neglect the bedrooms and kitchen.
3. Correct your child every time she mispronounces a word.
4. Schedule activities every day after school so your child will never be bored.
5. Once your child can read independently, throw out the picture books. They're for babies.
6. Don't play board games together. Too dull.
7. Give little rewards for reading. Stickers and plastic toys are nice. Money is even better.
8. Don't expect your children to enjoy reading. Kids' books are for teaching vocabulary, proper study habits, and good morals.
9. Buy only 40-watt bulbs for your lamps.

10. Under no circumstances read your child the same book over and over. She heard it once, she should remember it.
11. Never allow your child to listen to books on tape; that's cheating.
12. Make sure your kids only read books that are "challenging." Easy books are a complete waste of time. That goes double for comic books and *Mad* magazine.
13. Absolutely, positively no reading in bed.

Copyright 2001 by Dean Schneider and Robin Smith. Reprinted by permission of *The Horn Book Magazine*, http://www.hbook.com.

SHARING CONTEMPORARY REALISTIC FICTION

As we consider how to share contemporary realistic fiction with young readers, we've examined organized activities like readers' theater and book reports, as well as more informal response options including discussion and research. Let's pause for a moment and look briefly at gender and its role in promoting reading in the middle grades, and at the place of reading incentive programs and booktalking.

Boys and Books

According to most studies of reading habits and reading preferences, right around fifth grade we begin to "lose" many readers, especially boys. Until then, boys and girls seem to like reading in equal measure and enjoy a wide variety of books. But as children mature, societal pressures and other factors impact their reading choices more and more. Even as these middle grade readers choose contemporary realistic fiction, girls tend to choose more stories about growing up, families, and friends, and boys tend to choose more survival, sports, and adventure stories. Many boys stop choosing to read fiction altogether, preferring nonfiction, magazines, and graphic novels. Of course, this is a big generalization and there are many girls who enjoy adventure and boys who read stories about friendship, but we need to be aware of the prevalence of this pattern. In addition, another piece of the puzzle is the programming we plan in conjunction with books for middle grade and 'tween readers. As they hit this sensitive stage, girls generally enjoy opportunities to talk, talk, talk about books, their responses, and their feelings, but boys generally prefer more activity-based programs. That's something to consider, too.

In addition, our library collections and their arrangement can also be a factor in creating a reading climate that welcomes boys (and girls) with differing interests. Where are the audiobooks? Sports books? Most children's services librarians are (middle-aged) women and may not realize that their own experiences and tastes as girl readers are influencing their selections and programs. We all have to step outside of our comfort zone from time to time to consider the needs of a variety of patrons and how to serve them better. When it comes to working with boys, in particular, author Jon Scieszka has launched a special program to promote reading among boys called "GuysRead" (http:// www.guysread.com/) with helpful booklists and guidelines, as well as printable posters, stickers, and bookmarks. Check out the audio component of this program too at http://www.guyslisten.com. Let boys help you with your collection development, scanning online sites to make suggestions of books to consider. There are also several professional books that are helpful for learning more about serving boy readers, including:

Brozo, William. 2002. *To Be a Boy, to Be a Reader: Engaging Teen and Preteen Boys in Active Literacy.* Newark, DE: International Reading Association.

Maynard, Trisha. 2002. *Boys and Literacy: Exploring the Issues.* London: Routledge.

Scieszka, Jon. Ed. 2008. *Guys Write for Guys Read: Boys' Favorite Authors Write About Being Boys.* New York: Viking.

Smith, Michael, and Jeffrey D. Wilhelm. 2002. *"Reading Don't Fix No Chevys": Literacy in the Lives of Young Men.* Portsmouth, NH: Boynton/Cook.

Sullivan, Michael. 2003. *Connecting Boys with Books: What Libraries Can Do.* Chicago: American Library Association.

Sullivan, Michael. 2009. *Connecting Boys with Books 2: Closing the Reading Gap.* Chicago: American Library Association.

Reading Incentive Programs

Another alternative for promoting wide reading is the use of "reading incentive programs," such as the popular "Accelerated Books" program from Renaissance Learning or the "Reading Counts" program sponsored by Scholastic. These are essentially programs that provide computerized tests for thousands of popular children's books from which children can choose. The idea is that we can quickly discern whether a child has read the book or not by virtue of a test score, which is provided instantly for us. Unfortunately, it does not tell us whether the child truly read the book, understood the book, or enjoyed the book. In addition, the incentive factor can be mixed, with some children motivated by the climate of competition and others discouraged by the prospect of tests following the reading. So these programs also offer "rewards," extrinsic motivation like stickers, small toys, and class parties. Sure, those are fun, but there is little evidence that these elements promote a lifelong habit of reading. Making reading a competition has always had mixed results, but check out the program for yourself.

Reading advocate Jim Trelease (http://www.trelease-on-reading.com/) and reading and language learning expert Stephen Krashen (http://www .sdkrashen.com/) each have written extensively about the subject of reading incentives. For example, in his book *The Read-Aloud Handbook*, Trelease mentions that the positive results found by reading incentive programs "have been accomplished in various places without electronic incentive programs, places where there are first-class school and classroom libraries, where the teachers motivate children by reading aloud to them, give booktalks, and include SSR/ DEAR time as an essential part of the daily curriculum. And the money that would have gone to the computer tests went instead to building a larger library collection" (2013, p. 3). Children's librarian Marianne Follis noted the impact of incentive programs on the parents who regularly visit the public library where she works. They often ask, "Where are the points listed for the books? Why don't you have them grouped by reading and point level?" and comment, "We don't have time to read for pleasure, we have to get these points taken care of." That's certainly not the goal of any reading program.

We can consider creative alternatives for building enthusiasm for reading such as the "Book It" program from Pizza Hut (http://www.bookitprogram .com/) in which children read for pizza gift certificates or other similar short-term programs. Your own community may include other restaurants, as well as theme parks, sports teams, and businesses that offer support for encouraging reading. But no prize can take the place of the "book culture" created by book-loving librarians, teachers, and parents. An effective librarian can create book memories second to none.

Reading Is Fundamental (RIF, http://www.rif.org/) does not offer "incentive programs," per se, but the organization does sponsor book giveaway programs for schools and communities that qualify. RIF is the oldest and largest nonprofit literacy organization in the United States focused on children and reading and relies on a vast network of volunteers to get free books and resources to millions of kids. We know from research that book *ownership* is a major factor in building lifelong reading habits, so working with organizations such as RIF can help create readers that keep coming back to the library for more.

Booktalking

It's tempting to turn to technology for overseeing kids' reading. It seems tidy and mathematical. But no computer program can substitute for having a conversation with a person who has read what you're reading and knows more great books just like that one. The best alternative to a canned program that manages children's reading behavior is the well-read librarian who cares about kids. This is where booktalking comes in. Talking about books comes rather naturally to people who enjoy books, but presenting books orally in "booktalks" takes some practice. How does one convey enough information about the book to motivate someone to want to read it, but not so much information that they feel they have already read it? How do you keep it fresh and varied when you booktalk on a regular basis? How do you booktalk to groups of varying sizes from 1 to 100? Fortunately, there are several resources that provide guidance:

Blass, Rosanne J. 2002. *Booktalks, Bookwalks, and Read-Alouds: Promoting the Best New Children's Literature Across the Elementary Curriculum.* Englewood, CO: Libraries Unlimited.

Blass, Rosanne J. 2005. *Celebrate with Books: Booktalks for Holidays and Other Occasions.* Englewood, CO: Libraries Unlimited.

Diamant-Cohen, Betsy, and Selma K. Levi. 2008. *Booktalking Bonanza: Ten Ready-to-Use Multimedia Sessions for the Busy Librarian.* Chicago: American Library Association.

Langemack, Chapple. 2003. *The Booktalker's Bible: How to Talk About the Books You Love to Any Audience.* Englewood, CO: Libraries Unlimited.

Pearl, Nancy. 2007. *Book Crush.* Seattle, WA: Sasquatch Books.

Thomas, Cathlyn, and Carol Littlejohn. 2003. *Still Talking That Book!: Booktalks to Promote Reading Grades 3–12.* Columbus, OH: Linworth.

The art of booktalking becomes more and more essential in working with kids in the middle grades and above. Novels don't always "sell" themselves, so we have to help them move off the shelves. That requires regular reading of all kinds of books, keeping a record or journal of our reading, and doing a bit of planning to "spin" the books in ways that are appealing to our young readers. We can employ a variety of approaches and resources, including the latest digital tools like PowerPoints, videos, podcasts, and so on. The homework is worth it, however, when you see the light in kids' eyes when you've led them to a book they come to love. An added bonus is the relationship you develop with children through booktalks and conversations about books. They come to view you as someone who cares about reading and *them*—something no computer can communicate.

CONCLUSION

Of course, all genres can show a slice of the world, and contemporary realism certainly doesn't have a monopoly on this. Historical fiction and fantasy novels also reveal truths about the human condition couched in settings that may seem far away by comparison to today's reality. The genre of contemporary realistic fiction often feels especially relevant to young readers who want to read about kids like themselves coping with issues of growing up like they are. What's tricky, however, is recognizing that young people experience a wide variety of growing up issues. For some children, topics such as family, friends, mystery, and sports are favorite topics. For others, they may face challenges in coping with the death of a loved one, personal disability, family violence, or sexual confusion. We want children to have access to books that are relevant to their lives and reading needs, but many adults get nervous about who reads what. Thus, this chapter also addressed the importance of having collection development and book selection policies in place, as well as systematic procedures for challenging book holdings. We also considered the importance of cultures and cultural markers in diverse literature by authors of color and the presence of today's authors on the Web and online. Finally, it's helpful to investigate options for following up the reading of realism, including response activities, readers' theater, and other activities.

PROFESSIONAL RESOURCES IN CONTEMPORARY REALISTIC FICTION

For more help in learning about contemporary realistic fiction written for young people, consult these related professional readings.

Becker, Beverly C., and Susan M. Stan. 2002. *Hit List for Children 2: Frequently Challenged Books.* Chicago: American Library Association.

Cavanaugh, Terence W. 2006. *Literature Circles through Technology.* Columbus, OH: Linworth.

East, Kathy, and Rebecca L. Thomas. 2007. *Across Cultures: A Guide to Multicultural Literature for Children.* Englewood, CO: Libraries Unlimited.

Hadaway, Nancy, and Marian McKenna. 2007. *Breaking Boundaries with Global Literature: Celebrating Diversity in K–12 Classrooms.* Newark, DE: International Reading Association.

Inness, S. 1997. *Nancy Drew and Company: Culture, Gender, and Girls' Series.* Bowling Green, OH: Bowling Green State University Popular Press.

Knowles, Elizabeth, and Martha Smith. 2007. *Understanding Diversity Through Novels and Picture Books.* Englewood, CO: Libraries Unlimited.

Kolencik, Patricia Liotta, and Carianne Bernadowski. 2007. *Teaching with Books That Heal: Authentic Literature and Literacy Strategies to Help Children Cope with Everyday Problems.* Columbus, OH: Linworth.

Kuharets, Olga R. 2001. *Venture into Cultures: A Resource Book of Multicultural Materials & Programs.* Chicago: American Library Association.

Larson, Jeanette. 2004. *Bringing Mysteries Alive for Children and Young Adults.* Columbus, OH: Linworth.

McDaniel, Deanna J. 2007. *Gentle Reads: Great Books to Warm Hearts and Lift Spirits, Grades 5–9.* Englewood, CO: Libraries Unlimited.

Perry, Phyllis J. 1998. *Exploring the World of Sports: Linking Fiction to Nonfiction.* Englewood, CO: Libraries Unlimited.

Peterson, R., and M. Eeds. 1990. *Grand Conversations: Literature Groups in Action.* New York: Scholastic.

Rochman, Hazel. 1993. *Against Borders: Promoting Books for a Multicultural World.* Chicago, IL: American Library Association.

Roser, Nancy L., and Miriam G. Martinez. 1995. *Book Talk and Beyond: Children and Teachers Respond to Literature.* Newark, DE: International Reading Association.

Trites, Roberta S. 1997. *Waking Sleeping Beauty: Feminist Voices in Children's Novels.* Iowa City, IA: University of Iowa Press.

Volz, Bridget Dealy, Cheryl Perkins Scheer, and Lynda Blackburn Welborn,. 2000. *Junior Genreflecting: A Guide to Good Reads and Series Fiction for Children.* Englewood, CO: Libraries Unlimited.

York, Sherry. 2005. *Ethnic Book Awards: A Directory of Multicultural Literature for Young Readers.* Columbus, OH: Linworth.

Standards in Action: NCTE/IRA Standards for the English Language Arts

The two largest professional organizations in the area of reading, English language arts, and literacy learning and instruction are the National Council of Teachers of English (NCTE) and the International Reading Association (IRA). These two groups collaborated to publish jointly *The Standards for the English Language Arts* in 1996, reaffirmed in 2012 (http://www.ncte.org/standards/ncte-ira). They are "designed to complement other national, state, and local standards and contribute to ongoing discussion about English language arts classroom activities and curricula."

These standards focus on helping children "develop the language skills they need to pursue life's goals and to participate fully as informed, productive members of society." They are not intended to be prescriptive and should leave "ample room for the innovation and creativity essential to teaching and learning"; "they are not distinct and separable; they are, in fact, interrelated and should be considered as a whole." Here are the standards, in brief:

The Standards

1. Students read a wide range of print and nonprint texts to build an understanding of texts, of themselves, and of the cultures of the United States and the world; to acquire new information; to respond to the needs and demands of society and the workplace; and for personal fulfillment. Among these texts are fiction and nonfiction, classic and contemporary works.
2. Students read a wide range of literature from many periods in many genres to build an understanding of the many dimensions (e.g., philosophical, ethical, aesthetic) of human experience.
3. Students apply a wide range of strategies to comprehend, interpret, evaluate, and appreciate texts. They draw on their prior experience, their interactions with other readers and writers, their knowledge of word meaning and of other texts, their word identification strategies, and their understanding of textual features (e.g., sound-letter correspondence, sentence structure, context, graphics).
4. Students adjust their use of spoken, written, and visual language (e.g., conventions, style, vocabulary) to communicate effectively with a variety of audiences and for different purposes.
5. Students employ a wide range of strategies as they write and use different writing process elements appropriately to communicate with different audiences for a variety of purposes.
6. Students apply knowledge of language structure, language conventions (e.g., spelling and punctuation), media techniques, figurative language, and genre to create, critique, and discuss print and nonprint texts.
7. Students conduct research on issues and interests by generating ideas and questions, and by posing problems. They gather, evaluate, and synthesize data from a variety of sources (e.g., print and nonprint texts, artifacts, people) to communicate their discoveries in ways that suit their purpose and audience.
8. Students use a variety of technological and information resources (e.g., libraries, databases, computer networks, video) to gather and synthesize information and to create and communicate knowledge.
9. Students develop an understanding of and respect for diversity in language use, patterns, and dialects across cultures, ethnic groups, geographic regions, and social roles.
10. Students whose first language is not English make use of their first language to develop competency in the English language arts and to develop understanding of content across the curriculum.
11. Students participate as knowledgeable, reflective, creative, and critical members of a variety of literacy communities.
12. Students use spoken, written, and visual language to accomplish their own purposes (e.g., for learning, enjoyment, persuasion, and the exchange of information).

[Standards for the English Language Arts, by the International Reading Association and the National Council of Teachers of English, copyright 1996 by the International Reading Association and the National Council of Teachers of English. Reprinted with permission.]

You'll find further details, vignettes, and even a glossary at the website. In contrast with the Common Core State Standards or standards at the state level, these standards are not broken down by grade level or into further subskills. As we look at the genre of contemporary realistic fiction, we are clearly supporting Standard #1, particularly when we guide students in reading widely, build an "understanding of texts, of themselves, and of the cultures of the United States and the world," and read for personal fulfillment. In addition, the standards also provide guidance in what professionals in this area value overall, as well as further "ammunition" for collection development and seeking instructional collaboration opportunities.

Assignments in Action: **Checking Out Contemporary Realistic Fiction**

1. Policies and Challenges

Think back about some of the novels you enjoyed most as a young reader. Was it Judy Blume's *Are You There, God? It's Me, Margaret?* Or did you sneak into the adult section to read Stephen King's stories? Which books are "right" for children? Why do you think contemporary realistic fiction is so controversial? Why is it also so tremendously appealing to middle grade readers? Have you had any experiences with parents (or others) raising concerns about these books? Which books and what kinds of concerns? How were they handled? Check your library or district center for the presence of collection development policies and book challenge protocols. Familiarize yourself with these procedures. Interview the library director or other library colleagues about their experiences with book challenges in the past.

2. Children with Special Needs

In recent years, more and more authors of color are writing contemporary novels for young people reflecting the diverse experiences of children in a variety of settings. We are *also* on the lookout for books for young readers that portray the experiences of kids with special needs or disabilities in ways that are balanced and authentic. Books like Esmé Raji Codell's *Sahara Special* are essential for providing the same "mirrors" and "windows" for young readers who live with disabilities or who don't, but can deepen their understanding of this life. Look at the recipients of the ALA Schneider Award given for books that embody an artistic expression of "the disability experience." Seek out teachers who work with children with special needs and get their input on the reading preferences of their students. Read more about serving kids with special needs in the library:

Akin, Lynn, and Donna MacKinney. 2004. "Autism, Children and Libraries: The 3 R's: Repetition, Routine, and Redundancy." *Children and Libraries, 1* (2), 57–63.

Akin, Lynn, and Erin O'Toole. 2000. "The Order of the Public Library and the Disorder of Attention Deficit." *Public Library Quarterly, 18* (3/4), 69–80.

Banks, Carrie Scott, Sandra Feinberg, and Barbara Jordan. 2013. *Including Families of Children with Special Needs: A How-to-Do-It Manual for Librarians* (Revised Edition). Chicago: American Library Association.

Farmer, Lesley. 2013. *Library Services for Youth with Autism Spectrum Disorders*. Chicago: American Library Association.

Jarombek, Kathy, and Anne Leon. 2010. "Leadership at Its Best: Library Managers Spearhead Successful Special Needs Programming." *Children & Libraries, 8* (2), 54–57.

Ross, Virginia, and Lynn Akin. 2003. "Texas Public Libraries and Children with Learning Disabilities." *Public Library Quarterly 21* (4), 9–18.

3. Practice Booktalking

The art of booktalking becomes more and more essential in working with kids in the middle grades and above. For practice, write a booktalk for a favorite novel, then audio or video record yourself giving the booktalk and have a friend critique your delivery. Is your summary concise and captivating? Is your enthusiasm obvious? Are you clear and easy to understand? Are you looking at your audience? Librarian Donna MacKinney offers this advice, "One of my favorite (and I think most effective) strategies is to set up a scene or describe the book *very* briefly, and then read an excerpt from the book. Let it speak for itself." Consult the resources mentioned previously for additional assistance. What makes a great booktalk really stand out?

6

Historical Fiction

"Baby, we have no choice of what color we're born or who our parents are or whether we're rich or poor. What we do have is some choice over what we make of our lives once we're here."
From *Roll of Thunder, Hear My Cry* by Mildred Taylor (Dial, 1976)

In this chapter, you will learn about historical fiction for young people in all its variety, including series books, blended formats, historical picture books, and poetic history. You'll also read about the unique criteria for evaluating historical fiction and the professional resources available in this area for sharing this genre with kids. You will be introduced to major authors and awards worth noting in this genre, as well as creative ways to connect kids, history, and the world outside the library. We'll look at examples of historical fiction–based activities related to the novel *Hattie Ever After*, learn about the chocolate drop during World War II, and consider the place of the classic *Robinson Crusoe* for today's readers.

INTRODUCTION

Historical fiction may be one of the most difficult genres to promote. Nearly all children respond to the immediacy of contemporary realistic fiction and many avid, imaginative readers seek out fantasy novels that are hundreds of pages long. But history? For many children, it's as strange and hard to understand as fantasy, only boring. To them, the distant past feels as remote as a make-believe future. Those of us who love the genre are crushed and want to be sure children discover these gems, but why? Is it simply for the didactic reason that "those who cannot remember the past are condemned to repeat it"? We must also recognize that just like other novels of fantasy or contemporary fiction, well-written historical fiction contains compelling characters, engaging plots, and meaningful themes. As the critic Zena Sutherland put it, "The historical novel clothes the bare historical facts with trappings of a thousand details, bringing emotion and insight to scholarship" (2004, p. 384).

Historical fiction definitely offers meaty content that has "teachable" value. Historical novels can supplement the history or social studies curriculum with human stories that bring events to life. They can help develop an appreciation of our historical heritage and provide the reader with a vicarious experience of the past through literature. A well-written historical novel can give children a sense of participation in the past, a sense of continuity, of our place in the sweep of human destiny. These are big ideas that are worth considering. Just as fantasy encourages children to imagine an alternative reality, so does historical fiction. If you choose carefully and share enthusiastically, children can learn a lot about history without even knowing it, while engaging in a story with a hero just like them, struggling with important decisions and trying to grow up to become an independent person. Ultimately, historical novels not only show us that change is inevitable but also that some things (such as the human need for love and connection) are unchanging through time.

History in Action: Robinson Crusoe

Nearly every "classic" by definition becomes historical fiction with the passage of time, since a contemporary setting is often made historical as time goes by. An author may base a novel on a current event, but one hundred years later, that novel is historical fiction. One of the most famous examples of this may be Daniel Defoe's *Robinson Crusoe*, published in 1719 and based loosely on the true story of Scottish sailor Alexander Selkirk, who was put ashore on an uninhabited island in 1704 (at his own request after a quarrel with his captain). The book's full title is *The Life and Strange Surprizing Adventures of Robinson Crusoe, of York, Mariner: Who Lived Eight and Twenty Years, All Alone in an Uninhabited Island on the Coast of America, Near the Mouth of the Great River of Oroonoque; Having Been Cast on Shore by Shipwreck, Wherein All the Men Perished but Himself. With an Account how he was at last as Strangely Deliver'd by Pyrates. Written by Himself.*

Robinson Crusoe is often regarded as the first novel to be published in English. It was considered a "fictional autobiography" of the title character or a "false document," presenting an account of supposedly factual events that provided a realistic frame story and a commercial "hook" for sales that was ahead of its time. The book was an immediate success in England and across Europe, and Defoe wrote a sequel (*The Farther Adventures of Robinson Crusoe*) that was also published in 1719. *Crusoe* reflects the Puritan ideology of the time while presenting an adventure story that children adopted as their own (although it was published for adults, of course).

By the end of the nineteenth century, no book in the history of Western literature had generated more editions, translations, and spin-offs, with more than 700 alternative versions, including children's adaptations such as *The Swiss Family Robinson* by Johann

D. Wyss (J. R. Wyss, 1812). The term "Robinsonade" was even coined to describe the various permutations of the Robinson Crusoe formula. You don't have to look far to find more examples of similar "survival" stories in children's literature, from *Island of the Blue Dolphins* by Scott O'Dell (Houghton Mifflin, 1960) to *Hatchet* by Gary Paulsen (Bradbury, 1987). It's an immensely popular subgenre of adventure story, sometimes contemporary, as in *Hatchet*, and sometimes historical, as in *Island of the Blue Dolphins*. Children also enjoy stage and film adaptations such as *The Swiss Family Robinson* or *Castaway*.

Fans of the survival formula may enjoy digging deeper into the original Crusoe ancestry and will find multiple versions available as eBooks, e-texts, audiobooks, and more. *Robinson Crusoe* is available:

As an e-text from Project Gutenberg and Bibliomania:
http://www.gutenberg.org/etext/521
http://www.bibliomania.com/Fiction/defoe/robin/index.html

In the digitized version of the 1719 book with cover art:
http://www.pierre-marteau.com/editions/1719-robinson-crusoe.html

As a downloadable audiobook available from LibriVox:
http://librivox.org/robinson-crusoe-by-daniel-defoe/

As a children's adaptation with illustrations by N. C. Wyeth (more than a dozen individual illustrations can even be sent as e-postcards):
http://wyeth.artpassions.net/

Two children's books that are particularly intriguing for bringing this classic to today's readers are:

Eyewitness Classics: Robinson Crusoe by Daniel Defoe with commentary by Julek Heller (Penguin, 1998), is part of the DK Classics series that is illustrated, abridged, and annotated with "the classic adventure and its real-life world in information and photographs." Here children can read an abridged version of the Defoe story, alongside nonfiction tidbits and photographs about places and details in the story.

Marooned: The Strange but True Adventures of Alexander Selkirk, the Real Robinson Crusoe written by Robert Kraske, illustrated by Robert Andrew Parker (Clarion, 2005) describes Alexander Selkirk's solitary survival, rescue, and return to Scotland, as well as Daniel Defoe's attempt to use the man's records to create a literary work.

DEFINITIONS

Defining historical fiction seems easy. It refers to fiction in which the story's setting is historical. But what is historical? That is not a fixed date. Clearly a book set in the World War II era is historical. A novel about the Vietnam War is also considered historical (even though it is within my own lifetime, for example). Very shortly, however, stories occurring in the 1990s will also be judged as historical fiction, especially if they are clearly linked to world events of the time. This is partly because we should also consider the age of the child who will be reading these books. For example, consider your typical ten-year-old fifth grader, a good age for promoting historical fiction. A book set twenty to twenty-five years before his or her birth is historical to that child reader. It is his or her parents' generation. Do the math. Does that make you feel old? But it is important to consider the child reader when we look for historical fiction to share with children. It also helps us gauge what seems "historic" to the children who are the audience for the books we select. What seems like history to *them*? We generally say that historical fiction is set at least one generation in the past. That bar is movable as time keeps moving on and new children are born.

Historical fiction dramatizes and humanizes the past for us, giving us the "virtual experience" of living in another time. Historical fiction typically consists of novels set in a historical period before the author's lifetime (most historical novels fall here) or novels that become historical with the passing of time (like Mark Twain's *Tom Sawyer*). It is the genre that tells fictional stories while weaving in historical facts, people, and places. For many readers it is the best way to learn about history. But, unfortunately, for many more readers, it is also associated with boring history textbooks. Before age nine, most children have little concept of history. Their cognitive abilities are still developing. To them, last summer or last Christmas seems like ancient history. But typically by age ten or so, historical stories can help provide young readers a context for beginning to learn more about human history, as well as a source of reading that involves exciting adventures and engaging characters—just set in a different time.

Librarians in Action: Making History Come Alive

After earning a degree in business administration, Marleen Gould Horsey changed directions, became a teacher, and then turned to school librarianship. Working full-time at Nathan Adams Elementary School in Dallas, Texas, she earned her master's degree in library science from TWU. She was awarded the Texas PTA (Parent Teacher Association) Lifetime Membership, their highest honor, and was named the Dallas Association of School Librarians (DASL) Elementary Librarian of the Year. In her very first year as an elementary school librarian she tried something different, and it just happened to mushroom into a major event covered in the newspapers, on radio, and on television. Here's the story.

A Sweet History Lesson
by Marleen Horsey

When I think of the phrase "literature in action," I think of making a story *come to life* for children, especially if it's the story of a historical episode that will link their lives with literature and social studies. I found such a story in *Mercedes and the Chocolate Pilot* by Margot Theis Raven (Sleeping Bear Press, 2002). The story takes place in Germany after World War II, during the Berlin airlift. One American pilot bringing food and supplies to the city under siege began to drop parachutes made of handkerchiefs and candy to the children of Berlin. A young girl named Mercedes wrote a letter to Lieutenant Gail S. Halvorsen, whom the children called "The Chocolate Pilot," asking him to drop candy at her house, because she was too small to catch the candy at the airfield. Touched, Lt. Halvorsen mailed a letter and a package of candy to Mercedes. Years later, now-Colonel Halvorsen returned to Germany and met Mercedes, who had saved his letter and was now a pilot herself. They remain friends today.

After meeting with the principal, the PTA president, and the Reading Department faculty of our school, we decided to reenact the story on our elementary school campus. The PTA rented a helicopter and purchased the supplies, the language arts teachers and parent volunteers made 600-plus parachutes with Hershey candy bars attached, while I read and discussed the story with every class in the school. Students created Venn diagrams, learned new vocabulary and geography, and wrote letters of their own. Some classes even created dioramas of the story.

Early in November, the principal announced that in honor of Col. Halvorsen and Veterans' Day, we were going to have a "Spirit Rally." The students were to gather around the soccer field and have a contest to see which class could yell "U-S-A" the loudest. As the children were chanting "U-S-A, U-S-A!" the helicopter appeared and started dropping the parachutes and candy. I was standing beside a preschool class and knew the project was successful when I heard one of the children say, as she gazed up at the falling candy, "It's just like in the story."

I thought that was the end of the project. But I started to hear from military veterans who said they had been there in Berlin during WWII. One came to the school to give me a signed poster picturing Col. Halvorsen. The *Dallas Morning News* ran a full-page article showing a book discussion with our students and a group of veterans, including Col. Halvorsen himself (on speakerphone), who is now living in Utah. People called to offer photos and videos to share their personal war stories with the students. The Dallas Independent School District featured a piece about the project on their television show, *School Zone Dallas*.

What I envisioned had taken place—and more. Not only did the children make a personal connection between their lives, literature, and history, but they also learned the far-reaching effect of one person's act of kindness.

TYPES OF HISTORICAL FICTION

What are some of the current trends in the writing and publishing of historical fiction for young people? There has always been a rather ethnocentric focus in historical fiction published in this country. Most historical novels published here are set in the United States. This includes the New World (pilgrims, colonialism, the American Revolution), the American frontier (slavery, the Civil War), and World War II. But that is changing. More books are appearing about the Middle Ages, for example. And more history with a multicultural focus is being published with former taboos discussed openly in an appropriate historical context. In addition, authors are experimenting with the genre's boundaries, mixing historical fiction and fantasy, as well as poetry and history.

U.S. History

There are many, many titles of historical novels set in various eras of American history. In fact, the majority of historical fiction for young people is set in the United States prior to 1950. You will also notice that many such titles have also been Newbery award recipients as the most distinguished book of the year selected by the Association of Library Service to Children, including this sampling:

Johnny Tremain by Esther Forbes (Houghton Mifflin, 1943)
The Witch of Blackbird Pond by Elizabeth George Speare (Houghton, 1958)
Island of the Blue Dolphins by Scott O'Dell (Houghton, 1960)
Sounder by William H. Armstrong (Harper, 1969)
The Slave Dancer by Paula Fox (Bradbury, 1973)
Roll of Thunder, Hear My Cry by Mildred D. Taylor (Dial, 1976)
Jacob Have I Loved by Katherine Paterson (Crowell, 1980)
Sarah, Plain and Tall by Patricia MacLachlan (Harper, 1985)
Bud, Not Buddy by Christopher Paul Curtis (Delacorte, 1999)
A Year Down Yonder by Richard Peck (Dial, 2000)
Kira-Kira by Cynthia Kadohata (Atheneum, 2004)
Moon Over Manifest by Clare Vanderpool (Random House, 2010)
Dead End in Norvelt by Jack Gantos (Farrar, Straus & Giroux, 2011)

In recent years, historical novels have also tackled sensitive issues such as poverty and prejudice. Authors are grappling with challenging issues and are not afraid to include them in a story for children, particularly when *not* to include these issues makes a book *less* authentic. For example, race and slavery are powerfully depicted in *Jip* by Katherine Paterson (Scholastic, 1997), an author who consistently produces acclaimed historical fiction. Ellen Klages frames her story around the research on the atomic bomb at Los Alamos during World War II in *The Green Glass Sea* (Viking, 2006) and its sequel, *White Sands, Red Menace* (Viking, 2008). And *Bull Run* by Paul Fleischman (HarperCollins, 1993 or *Soldier's Heart* by Gary Paulsen, Delacorte, 1998) will make you see the horror of the Civil War in a way you may never have experienced before. Using multiple viewpoints, Fleischman creates a vivid scene depicting one important battle. For example, did you know that ladies and gentlemen of fashion rode their carriages out to see the battle of Bull Run as if it were a spectator sport?

In addition, we are fortunate to see more authors from a variety of backgrounds and cultural perspectives write historical novels for children and receive distinctions for their work. For example, in recent years Coretta Scott King author awards have gone to Rita Williams-Garcia for her engaging coming-of-age story set in the volatile 1960s, *One Crazy Summer* (Amistad, 2010); to Christopher Paul Curtis for his story about a young boy discovering for himself the conditions of slavery that his own family had escaped in *Elijah of Buxton* (Scholastic, 2007); and to Julius Lester for his powerful novel about a slave auction (based on actual characters), *Day of Tears: A Novel in Dialogue* (Jump at the Sun, 2005). And recent Newbery medals were awarded to *Kira-Kira* by Cynthia Kadohata (Simon & Schuster, 2004), which deals with prejudice and discrimination, as well as family bonds and sisterhood, and to Linda Sue Park for her compelling growing up story about a young apprentice in ancient Korea in *A Single Shard* (Clarion, 2001). These perspectives enrich our literature and invite even more readers to see themselves in our history.

Not all historical fiction is serious, however, and several authors offer a wry or humorous voice in the telling. For example, look for the Newbery award–winning *A Year Down Yonder* (and others) by Richard Peck (Dial, 2000), a hilarious read aloud with an unlikely heroine, feisty Grandma Dowdel, and others featuring this same cast of characters like *A Long Way from Chicago* (Dial, 1998) and *Fair Weather* (Dial, 2001). Speaking of hilarious, don't miss Jack Gantos's autobiographical *Dead End in Norvelt* (Farrar, Straus & Giroux, 2011), detailing a summer of impromptu nosebleeds and typing unorthodox obituaries. Or consider Gennifer Choldenko's novel about a young boy living on Alcatraz Island in 1935 and his reluctant friendship with the warden's "entrepreneurial" daughter in *Al Capone Does My Shirts* (Putnam, 2004), a Newbery honor book, and its sequels, *Al Capone Shines My Shoes* (Dial, 2009) and *Al Capone Does My Homework* (Dial, 2013).

World History

Although U.S. history dominates much of historical fiction, there are many significant works with settings outside the United States that children will enjoy. Once again, a surprising number of them are Newbery medal books. Consider Karen Cushman's Newbery-winning novel, *The Midwife's Apprentice* (Clarion, 1995). It tells of a dirty, homeless girl in medieval England who learns self-respect as well as midwifery in this short, excellent read aloud. In fact, Cushman has authored several outstanding historical novels for young readers including *Catherine, Called Birdy* (Clarion, 1994), *Matilda Bone* (Clarion, 2000), and *Will Sparrow's Road* (Clarion, 2012), among others. Other Newbery titles that feature a larger worldview include Lois Lowry's novel depicting Danish resistance during World War II, *Number the Stars* (Houghton, 1989); Linda Sue Park's story of an orphan boy trying hard to become a craftsman in twelfth-century Korea, *A Single Shard* (Clarion, 2001); and *Crispin: The Cross of Lead* by Avi (Hyperion, 2002), a medieval adventure about a boy's search for his true identity. In addition, Park and Avi have each written many other excellent historical novels worth sharing and exploring.

Though these novels are generally for the intermediate grades (sixth grade and up) where world history is more of a curricular focus, another Newbery winner, *The Whipping Boy* by Sid Fleischman (Greenwillow, 1986), is a great choice even for the younger grades. It's a hilarious novel similar to *The Prince and the Pauper*. Here, the prince has a boy who takes his place for spankings—what a premise for the children to discuss. The novel is also a hilarious read aloud, with short, action-packed chapters, full of fun dialect and odd vocabulary.

Historical Series

Another way of promoting historical fiction is to seek out historical series books. The *American Girl* series, for example, is a series of short historical novels designed for young children (ages eight and up). Although they are marketed in conjunction with dolls and other materials, the books do rely on solid research and include notes and sources and historical photos in the backmatter. For older children, Scholastic has published the *Dear America* series of books (and *The Royal Diaries* series, *My Name Is America* series, and others). Although there has been some criticism of the series in that they *appear* to be authentic recovered diaries, when in actuality they are simply fiction written in a diary format, they have been very popular with young readers. The child point of view is a big draw, and most of the books even include source notes to help substantiate their authenticity. Of course series books may suffer from unevenness or worse, but for children who do enjoy the format, they provide an avenue for continued reading.

Historical Picture Books

Another interesting development in the publication of historical fiction for young people is the historical (usually thirty-two–page) picture book. Previously, few picture books were set in a historical era because it was believed that young audiences were not interested in or could not fully understand history. I still believe that six- and seven-year-olds have a limited perspective on what history is. It is difficult for them to conceptualize their parents as children, much less George Washington as a boy. That said, however, I do believe historical picture books are worth sharing with young children if they contain a good story, simply to share a good story and lay the historical groundwork for later. Even better, however, is the usefulness of the historical picture book with older children. The shorter format is unintimidating, the clear focus of the story is memorable, and the illustrations help them visualize the historical era.

The best historical picture books tend to be focused on one person or a specific event—a story that can be told in the span of a few pages. Generally, these stories are already somewhat familiar through the popular culture (for example, knights, pirates, soldiers, pioneers, etc.), making less exposition or background building necessary. And finally, the illustrations should be maximized to provide a visual window into history, portrayed authentically and accurately. Some recent examples that are lovely models of this format include *The Wall* by Peter Sís (Farrar, Straus & Giroux, 2007), an autobiographical story about life behind the Iron Curtain; *The Cats in Krasinski Square*, a powerful Holocaust story by Karen Hesse (Scholastic, 2004); or the family history portrayed in Jonah Winter's *Born and Bred in the Great Depression* (Random House, 2011). For powerful stories of African American history, look for the lyrical *Moses: When Harriet Tubman Led Her People to Freedom* (Hyperion, 2006) or *Freedom on the Menu: The Greensboro Sit-Ins*, a glimpse into the civil rights struggle, both by Carole Boston Weatherford (Dial, 2005), and compare these with *Minty: A Story of Young Harriet Tubman* by Alan Schroeder (Dial, 1996) and *Sit-In: How Four Friends Stood Up by Sitting Down* by Andrea David Pinkney (Little, Brown, 2010), respectively. All are based on real people and actual occurrences in history. Patricia Polacco has also created several historical picture books including the popular *Pink and Say* (Philomel, 1994), a deeply moving Civil War story, along with the companion books, *January Sparrow* (Philomel, 2009) and *Just in Time, Abraham Lincoln* (Putnam, 2011), among others. These are each good examples of picture books that are very appropriate for sharing with older, independent readers because of their historical content.

Blending Genres

Some authors are using historical fiction in conjunction with other genres in new, creative ways, such as historical fantasy. Jon Scieszka, for example, has created a *Time Warp Trio* series that takes three boy characters throughout history via a magic book. Mary Pope Osborne has similar adventures for a brother and sister duo in the *Magic Tree House* series. Here we have a blend of history and fantasy. These often make for humorous, action-packed read alouds guaranteed to entertain while they weave in historical information.

Karen Hesse, on the other hand, has blended poetry and history to create novels in verse that qualify as beautiful historical fiction, beginning with the Newbery medal–winning *Out of the Dust* (Scholastic, 1997). These spare poems serve as dated journal entries and perfectly capture the tough, dust bowl days of Oklahoma in the 1930s. Many more excellent poetry/history books have been published since then including *Witness* (Scholastic, 2001) and *Aleutian Sparrow* (Margaret McElderry, 2003), also by Karen Hesse; and the Newbery winner *Good Masters! Sweet Ladies!* (Candlewick, 2007), portraits of multiple players in a medieval village by Laura Amy Schlitz. Other writers who have used poetry to create historically rich novels in verse include Helen Frost with *The Braid*, the tale of two Scottish sisters who immigrate in the 1850s (Farrar, Straus & Giroux, 2006); *Crossing Stones* (Farrar, Straus & Giroux, 2009), set against the backdrop of World War I; and *Salt* (Farrar, Straus & Giroux, 2013), set in Indiana Territory in 1812. Margarita Engle plumbs Cuban history for powerful stories rooted in fact such as *The Surrender Tree* (Holt, 2008), *Tropical Secrets: Holocaust Refugees in Cuba* (Holt, 2009), *The Firefly Letters: A Suffragette's Journey to Cuba* (Holt, 2010), *Hurricane Dancers: The First Caribbean Pirate Shipwreck* (Holt, 2011), and *The Lightning Dreamer* (Houghton Mifflin Harcourt, 2013). Poet Paul Janeczko created powerful historical stories in *Worlds Afire*, chronicling a horrific circus fire that took place in 1944 (Candlewick, 2004) and *Requiem: Poems of the Terezín Ghetto* (Candlewick, 2011), a gut-wrenching look at a concentration camp during World War II.

Here we have history and poetry woven together. For poetry lovers, it's a way to absorb history, and for all readers, the poetic format provides a unique entrée into stories of the past. The novel-in-verse form also lends itself to reading aloud, particularly for dramatic readings in parts for multiple voices that help bring history to life.

Connecting Poetry and Historical Fiction

Poetry can also capture the people, places, and emotions of the past in vivid images and language. As Cullinan, Scala, and Schroder (1995) observe, "Reading poetry about other cultures allows our students' minds to travel to the four corners of the universe." Consider linking poems and poetry books with historical literature before or after reading a historical novel. This helps children make connections and remember the people, places, and times more vividly. You may be surprised how many connections are possible—and how much children enjoy it. Here is a sampling of history-related poetry to get you started.

Cheng, Andrea. 2013. *Etched in Clay: The Life of Dave, Enslaved Potter and Poet*. New York: Lee & Low.

Clinton, Catherine. Comp. 1993/1998. *I, Too, Sing America: Three Centuries of African American Poetry*. Boston: Houghton Mifflin.

Corcoran, Jill. Ed. 2012. *Dare to Dream . . . Change the World*. San Diego, CA: Kane Miller.

Grady, Cynthia. 2012. *I Lay My Stitches Down: Poems of American Slavery*. Ill. by Michele Wood. Grand Rapids, MI: Eerdmans.

Hopkins, Lee Bennett. Comp. 1994. *Hand in Hand: An American History through Poetry*. New York: Simon & Schuster.

Hopkins, Lee Bennett. Comp. 1999. *Lives: Poems about Famous Americans*. New York: HarperCollins.

Hopkins, Lee Bennett. Comp. 2005. *Days to Celebrate: A Full Year of Poetry, People, Holidays, History, Fascinating Facts, and More*. New York: HarperCollins.

Katz, Bobbi. Comp. 2000. *We, the People*. New York: Greenwillow.

Lewis, J. Patrick. 2005. *Monumental Verses*. Washington, DC: National Geographic.

Lewis, J. Patrick. 2005. *Vherses: A Celebration of Outstanding Women*. North Mankato, MN: Creative Editions.

Lewis, J. Patrick. 2013. *When Thunder Comes: Poems for Civil Rights Leaders*. San Francisco: Chronicle.

Lewis, J. Patrick, and Rebecca Kai Dotlich. 2006. *Castles, Old Stone Poems*. Honesdale, PA: Wordsong/Boyds Mills.

Myers, Walter Dean. 2011. *We Are America: A Tribute from the Heart*. Ill. by Christopher Myers. New York: HarperCollins.

Nye, Naomi Shihab. Comp. 1992. *This Same Sky: A Collection of Poems from around the World*. New York: Four Winds Press.

Paul, Ann Whitford. 1999. *All by Herself: 14 Girls Who Made a Difference: Poems*. San Diego: Harcourt.

Philip, Neil. Comp. 1994. *Singing America: Poems That Define a Nation*. New York: Viking.

Rochelle, Belinda. Comp. 2000. *Words with Wings: A Treasury of African American Poetry and Art*. New York: HarperCollins.

Shields, Carol Diggory. 2002. *American History, Fresh Squeezed.* New York: Handprint.

Siebert, Diane. Comp. 2006. *Tour America: A Journey Through Poems and Art.* San Francisco: Chronicle.

Singer, Marilyn. 2013. *Rutherford B., Who Was He?: Poems About Our Presidents.* New York: Disney-Hyperion.

Volavkova, Hana. Comp. 1993. *I Never Saw Another Butterfly.* New York: Schocken Books.

Weatherford, Carole Boston. 2002. *Remember the Bridge: Poems of a People.* New York: Philomel.

For more great ideas, see:

Chatton, Barbara. 2010. *Using Poetry Across the Curriculum.* (Second Edition). Santa Barbara, CA: ABC-CLIO.

Holbrook, Sara. 2005. *Practical Poetry; A Nonstandard Approach to Meeting Content-Area Standards.* Portsmouth, NH: Heinemann.

Vardell, Sylvia. 2012. *The Poetry Teacher's Book of Lists.* Princeton, NJ: Pomelo Books.

MAJOR AUTHORS OF HISTORICAL FICTION

Historical fiction has long been an important part of children's literature. Authors are branching out with more different kinds of settings and characters than ever before. Some authors are even experimenting with genre conventions. However, one of the things that sets authors of historical fiction apart is research: conducting careful research, citing sources, offering recommendations for further reading, and generally grounding their fictional story in an authentic, believable setting. Fortunately, several individuals have made this their domain, so we have many wonderful works to seek out, including many Newbery medal and honor titles.

Authors across the Eras

Look for historical fiction by the following noteworthy authors, among others. Just for fun, their names are arranged along a historical timeline based on one exemplary work of historical fiction for which each is known. The year that is listed is the setting for the novel. Each of these authors has written many other works of historical fiction that fall in other eras, as well. This is just a sampling.

125: Rosemary Sutcliff, *The Eagle of the Ninth* (Oxford, reissued 1987)
1100s: Linda Sue Park, *A Single Shard* (Clarion, 2001)
1300s: Avi, *Crispin: The Cross of Lead* (Hyperion, 2002)
1492: Michael Dorris, *Morning Girl* (Hyperion, 1992)

pre-1500: Sid Fleischman, *The Whipping Boy* (Greenwillow, 1986)

pre-1500: Karen Cushman, *The Midwife's Apprentice* (Clarion, 1995)

1681: Paul Fleischman, *Saturnalia* (HarperCollins, 1990)

1687: Elizabeth George Speare, *The Witch of Blackbird Pond* (Houghton, 1958)

1700s: Ann Rinaldi, *The Color of Fire* (Jump at the Sun, 2005)

1775: James and Christopher Collier, *My Brother Sam Is Dead* (Four Winds, 1974)

1797: Margarita Engle, *The Poet Slave of Cuba* (Holt, 2006)

1835: Scott O'Dell, *Island of the Blue Dolphins* (Houghton, 1960)

1840: Paula Fox, *The Slave Dancer* (Bradbury, 1974)

1850: Gary Paulsen, *Nightjohn* (Delacorte, 1993)

1858: Kathryn Lasky, *True North* (Scholastic, 1996)

1859: Julius Lester, *Day of Tears* (Jump at the Sun, 2005)

1865: Laurence Yep, *Dragon's Gate* (HarperCollins, 1993)

1866: Louise Erdrich, *Chickadee* (HarperCollins, 2012)

1867: Laura Ingalls Wilder, *Little House in the Big Woods* (HarperCollins, 1953)

1880s: Patricia MacLachlan, *Sarah, Plain and Tall* (Harper, 1985)

1918: Kirby Larson, *Hattie Big Sky* (Delacorte, 2006)

1930: Yoshiko Uchida, *A Jar of Dreams* (McElderry, 1981)

1930s: Christopher Paul Curtis, *Bud, Not Buddy* (Delacorte, 1999)

1930s: Mildred Taylor, *Roll of Thunder, Hear My Cry* (Dial, 1976)

1935: Gennifer Choldenko, *Al Capone Does My Shirts* (Putnam, 2004)

1935: Jennifer Holm, *Turtle in Paradise* (Random House, 2010)

1937: Richard Peck, *A Year Down Yonder* (Dial, 2000)

1940s: Katherine Paterson, *Jacob Have I Loved* (Crowell, 1980)

1941: Graham Salisbury, *Under the Blood-Red Sun* (Delacorte, 1994)

1943: Lois Lowry, *Number the Stars* (Houghton, 1989)

1944: Patricia Reilly Giff, *Lily's Crossing* (Delacorte, 1997)

1946: Ellen Klages, *White Sands, Red Menace* (Viking, 2008)

1950s: Cynthia Kadohata, *Kira-Kira* (Atheneum, 1994)

1960s: Virginia Hamilton, *M. C. Higgins, the Great* (Macmillan, 1974)

1967: Gary D. Schmidt, *The Wednesday Wars* (Clarion, 2007)

1968: Rita Williams-Garcia, *One Crazy Summer* (Amistad, 2010)

Each of these authors has written multiple works of outstanding historical fiction, often set in different historical eras and locations. Reading historically can help children understand how events and issues of the time affected different people. For example, simply gathering and reading the six books set in the 1930s from this list reveals interesting details about Depression-era life in the United States as experienced by Japanese Americans, African Americans, children in rural settings, and children with disabilities. This can lead to an interesting discussion about how our perceptions are formed in part by where we are "planted." Study guides for many of these novels are also available at Sparknotes.com, among other sources.

Authors in Action: Kirby Larson

Kirby Larson has written both picture books and novels, winning a Newbery honor citation for *Hattie Big Sky*, the novel inspired by her great-grandmother who did indeed homestead in Montana as a young woman. Using extensive research and a gift for creating memorable characters, Larson has since authored several other works of historical fiction including the sequel, *Hattie Ever After*, as well as *The Friendship Doll*, *The Fences Between Us* (in the *Dear America* series), and *Duke*, as well as the picture books *Two Bobbies: A True Story of Hurricane Katrina, Friendship, and Survival* and *Nubs: The True Story of a Mutt, a Marine, and a Miracle* in collaboration with her good friend Mary Nethery. Here she shares some of the background in telling Hattie's continuing story in an interview on KidsRead.com.

Interview with Kirby Larson

Hattie Brooks had a great adventure in Hattie Big Sky, *and here she is in another quest to find a connection to her family. Why did you want to revisit Hattie and bring her to San Francisco?*

I had no intention of revisiting Hattie! I thought I'd completed her story with *Hattie Big Sky*; however, a stampede of readers did not agree with me and wrote to tell me so. I'm a firstborn and hate to disappoint people. So after getting all of those letters and emails, I began to think about what might make me want to write more about Hattie. Several summers ago, I reread *Hattie Big Sky* and found I really enjoyed Hattie's company. And I saw where I'd (unintentionally) left myself a little story breadcrumb in the guise of Hattie's "scoundrel" uncle, Chester. And why San Francisco? Because Hattie was ready for Adventure, with a capital A.

What were the feathers that Hattie picks up around San Francisco supposed to mean for her?

I'm an amateur bird watcher but a professional bird appreciater. At our beach cabin, I watch huge eagles circling above the bay, tiny kingfishers diving for dinner, and all sizes of birds in between. I am in awe of birds' ability to do something that it took mankind thousands of years to imitate: to fly. In my mind, those feathers signaled an affirmation of Hattie's decision to spread her wings, and to soar where others couldn't or wouldn't.

Female relationships are especially important for Hattie. What makes relationships between girls and women so special?

I was lucky to have been supported and mentored from a young age (youth groups, Campfire Girls, etc.) by caring women. Female friendships have made a huge difference in my life, so I suppose it's not surprising they make a difference in Hattie's.

What interests you about this time period after WWI, when women were unwilling to leave the workforce?

To be accurate, we should point out that some women were happy to get back to their pre–WWI lives. However, I am especially intrigued by the women who found something new and surprising in themselves because they'd stepped out and taken a risk by working as mechanics or in hospitals or even department stores. Frankly, stick-in-the-muds don't make for interesting reading.

Hattie took quite a number of risks: she moved to San Francisco almost on a whim and even played baseball to win a story for the Chronicle. *Is there something about Hattie's personality that makes her successful in taking these risks?*

Like her creator, Hattie is a terminal optimist; what else is there to say?

What is the biggest risk you ever took?

Four big risks: getting married, having kids, daring to write, and going to Beirut in 2009 to speak to students at the International College (middle/high school).

What I really appreciated about Hattie Ever After *is that although women were support systems for Hattie, not all were to be trusted. Why did you choose a woman to become Hattie's threat instead of a man?*

What a great question! It wasn't a deliberate decision on my part as I sat down to write this book. Elements converged: Uncle Chester's mysterious love interest; my learning about women con artists of that time period; and Hattie's longing for a true friend like Perilee there in San Francisco. Novels are all about conflict, and what better conflict than a threat from a trusted source?

Many of the characters in Hattie Ever After *were based on real people, whether they were reporters or thieves. Who is your favorite historical person that you found in your research for this book?*

I knew very little about President Wilson before this book and came to admire his grit and determination—can you imagine traveling by train around this entire country, trying to win folks over to your way of thinking? The man was a saint! But, I have to be honest, I most admire the people who don't end up in the history books: the women like Hattie and Tinny and Perilee, who did their very best to make a difference in their own small ways.

What do you want people to take from this story?

I want them to take away whatever means most to them.

Will there be any more adventures for Hattie?

I hope this doesn't sound cruel or that I don't love Hattie, because I do, but this book is the end of the adventures I will create for Hattie. Readers are welcome to take her wherever they care to!

This interview appeared first on KidsReads.com and is used with permission (http://www.kidreads.com/authors/kirby-larson/news/interview-020513).

One Book in Action: Hattie Ever After

A focus book for historical fiction allows us to provide an entry into history through a work of appealing fiction. In schools, it offers the opportunity to link reading with the teaching of history or the social studies. And in general, it helps us nudge children backward, so to speak, to take a glimpse into the past and see how people before us lived, learned, believed, and thought. In my experience, this genre is often the hardest "sell" with children, perhaps because they associate history with rote learning or dry facts, or perhaps because their young worldview can be somewhat limited. Whatever the reason, we sometimes have to be creative in introducing kids to historical fiction, keeping the focus on the universality of human emotion and experience, whatever the setting.

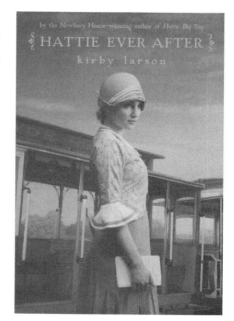

Our "one book in action" for this chapter is Kirby Larson's *Hattie Ever After* (Delacorte, 2013), the sequel to her Newbery honor book, *Hattie Big Sky* (2006). Both books focus on an orphan girl, Hattie Inez Brooks, who strikes out on her own—first to prove her uncle's claim in Montana, and then to strive for a job as a journalist in San Francisco. Here we'll focus on her latter adventures as she experiences life in this big city in 1919, on her dreams of being a writer, and her quest to solve the mystery of her uncle's "crime."

Setting the Stage

If time allows, *Hattie Ever After* is a very engaging book to read aloud. Or play an excerpt from the excellent unabridged audiobook adaptation of the book produced by

Listening Library/Books on Tape. You can even download an excerpt from the audio-book at the author's website, http://www.KirbyLarson.com. In fact, this site is rich in resources, with access to Chapter One of the book, a video of Larson speaking on a Newbery author panel, "Hattie's Playlist" of favorite musical selections with links to more than a dozen tunes popular during this time period, links to other interviews and essays with and by Kirby Larson, and a gallery of fun photos and images. Larson's attention to detail is further explained in her author's note at the back of the novel, where she also describes some of the back stories for plot elements in the book.

Understanding Time and Place

Next, work with students to understand the setting (time and place) for the story, locating Great Falls, Montana, and San Francisco, California, on a map of the United States and tracing possible routes between the two cities. Look up images for each locale in an atlas, via Google maps, or other resources. Then, challenge young readers to research images of these places in 1919 (or thereabouts), the year the story takes place. Look up what was happening in the world during this time, particularly World War I, an important part of the backdrop to this story. Both PBS and the BBC offer resources with images and footage from WWI (http://www.pbs.org/greatwar/ and http://www.bbc.co.uk/history/worldwars/wwone/), and the Presidential Library of Woodrow Wilson (Hattie's presidential interview) includes a photo gallery too (http://www.woodrowwilson.org). At Jackdaw.com you can obtain kits of facsimiles of historical documents and photo collections that include broadsheets, timelines, maps, political cartoons, advertisements, posters, telegrams, and documents on the topics of World War I, urbanization in the early twentieth century, and the struggle for women's rights in the United States.

For more background information and period photographs of San Francisco, the story's vivid setting, consult the Virtual Museum of the City of San Francisco (http://www.sfmuseum.org), for example, or the San Francisco Museum and Historical Society (http://www.sfhistory.org), or the San Francisco History Association (http://sanfranciscohistory.org). Often when reading historical novels, children will want to learn more about the facts behind the story, an ideal opportunity for recommending research and reading nonfiction. For example books, look for works by these authors who often write about women's history: Tanya Lee Stone (e.g., *Who Says Women Can't Be Doctors? The Story of Elizabeth Blackwell*, 2013) and Cheryl Harness (e.g., *Remember the Ladies: 100 Great American Women*, 2003).

Goals and Connections

Hattie's goal is to become a journalist and write stories for a big-time newspaper. Investigate the news outlets in your community and invite a guest speaker to talk about her or his training and work experiences. Or collaborate with a journalism teacher or yearbook sponsor to review the basics of reporting like the Five Ws (who, what, when, where, why) and the "inverted pyramid" style of writing (with the most important information shared at the "top" of the story). Hattie finally gets a chance to move from cleaning lady to bona fide journalist at the city newspaper, the *San Francisco Chronicle*. Check out their contemporary website now at http://www.sfchronicle.com. Newspapers were *the* media outlet of 1919. If Hattie's story occurred today, would she be a blogger? Or have her own Twitter feed? Talk with students about her desire to be a writer and invite them to share their own plans and career possibilities.

Read On

Finally, children who enjoyed this glimpse into American history may want to read more historical novels by Kirby Larson. They certainly may want to read *Hattie Big Sky*, the novel that precedes *Hattie Ever After*, and its extensive website (http://www.hattiebigsky.com). Avid readers may also enjoy Larson's other historical fiction titles: *The Friendship Doll,* a Depression-era story about four girls and a Japanese Friendship Doll; *The Fences Between Us* (in the *Dear America* series), set in Seattle in 1941 about a girl whose brother is off fighting the war, but whose Japanese neighbors are being incarcerated; and *Duke,* the story of a boy and his beloved German shepherd whom he shares with Dogs for Defense, an organization that allowed Americans to "loan" their pets to the military during WWII. Or they can connect with similar books by other authors like Helen Frost's *Crossing Stones* (Farrar, Straus & Giroux, 2009), a novel in verse that deals with themes of war, women's rights, and romance. Through one of these several avenues, surely children can find some spark of personal connection with history and historical fiction.

Examining Historical Significance

In her book *Making Sense of History: Using High-Quality Literature and Hands-On Experiences to Build Content Knowledge,* Myra Zarnowski offers a helpful set of questions to guide children's discussion about the historical significance of the stories and events they encounter in historical fiction (2006, p. 81). Consider using these question prompts to discuss the five criteria of historical significance or work together to create a simple table with answers to each question for the book under discussion. Identify the seminal event in the story under discussion. Then ask each of the following questions and guide students in considering each one as they think about the book they read.

Criteria	Questions
1. Contemporary Significance	How important was it to people at the time?
2. Profundity	How deeply were people affected?
3. Quantity	How many people were affected?
4. Durability	How long lasting were the effects?
5. Relevance	How does it help us understand current issues and events?

Questions and criteria like these can help children peel away the layers of significance in the history they encounter. They may begin to realize the way events help shape people and develop more thoughtful reading and responding abilities.

EVALUATION CRITERIA

In evaluating works of historical fiction, we use all the usual literary elements: characterization, plot, setting, theme, and style. However, with this genre, the key in choosing high-quality historical fiction is *authenticity*. Writers must thoroughly research the time period for the setting of the story: the times, the people, the values, the language. They must then, however, create a story that draws readers in without overwhelming us with historical details and long descriptions. A balance of fact and fiction is essential. Then, we look to see how the author uses the traditional literary elements of plot, characterization, setting, theme, and style as all these pieces are woven together to create a compelling and authentic story.

Characters

Even though the story is set in the past and may even include famous people from history, the reader should still be able to identify with the story's protagonist and other major characters. The characters should seem real and believable, even if they speak a dialect full of "thees" and "thous." They should be doing things that could actually have happened (no talking animals, please). Historical validity rests in recreating accurately the social fabric of the times and the patterns of daily life. Historical novels usually reveal history through the eyes of a young protagonist, so the narrative should stay true to a youthful point of view. Although we look for characters that "seem like us," they should still be grounded in the clothing, attitudes, and language appropriate to their times. Which characters from historical novels seem most vivid to you? Richard Peck's irascible Grandma Dowdel? Mildred Taylor's spunky Cassie? Each of these is a well-rounded individual, dynamic, imperfect, and completely memorable.

Plot

In historical fiction for young people, history should not be sugar-coated, but be presented accurately in terms that children can understand. Historical accuracy concerning events, places, and other facts is required to set up an authentic story. The plot should not be overwhelmed by details, but should be realistic to the time period. It should grow out of the characters and how they would really behave given the circumstances of their setting. In Lois Lowry's Newbery medal–winning Holocaust story, *Number the Stars* (Houghton, 1989), for instance, it is both thrilling and believable that a child might be thrust into a brave and dangerous act by simply taking a walk with a basket to deliver a handkerchief.

Setting

In historical novels, setting is integral; time and place should be explicit and vividly described, because this influences everything else. Much of the authenticity in the writing of a good historical novel rests in the re-creation of the time and place of the story. It's what makes the fiction *historical* fiction. In Linda Sue Park's Newbery award book *A Single Shard* (Clarion, 2001), for example, medieval Korea is the backdrop for the story, and we are given details throughout the novel that help us picture the Korean landscape, from the humble village to the emperor's palace and the long road in between. We come to see the poverty of many people during this time and the special relationship of craftsman and apprentice that provides an outlet for the protagonist, Tree-ear.

Theme

The theme of a good historical novel should reflect the attitudes, values, and morals of the times, but still be relevant to today. This is a bit of a balancing act, since our beliefs and attitudes change and evolve over time. However, universal themes that still speak to readers of today carry as much weight as ever. For example, readers can identify with the importance of standing up for what one believes in, or the power of family love and commitment, or coming to know oneself and being responsible for one's choices. These are all timeless ideas that are still relevant today. In *The Midwife's Apprentice*, the Newbery medal book by Karen Cushman (Clarion, 1995), for example, the protagonist grows from a filthy, homeless girl with no name into a resourceful young woman with choices in life. Her recognition of this fact and her quandary in choosing what's best for herself provides a timeless parallel for young readers today wondering where their own paths will lead.

Style

The style of writing embodied in a historical novel is also particularly important. It should reflect the author's own voice and manner, while capturing the flavor of the times and the dialect or language patterns peculiar to the characters in that setting. Dialogue should be used judiciously and should always capture the speech patterns of the era. Careful research should be apparent in the details but not overwhelm the pull of the story. All of the other literary elements mentioned above should be woven together to create a seamless story that just happens to be set in a previous historical time. Consider the differences in style between Avi's medieval story *Crispin* (Hyperion, 2002) and Christopher Paul Curtis's Depression-era novel *Bud, Not Buddy* (Delacorte, 1999), for example, both told from the point of view of a young boy seeking his identity. The voice and cadence of each telling is quite unique, due in part to the time and place of the setting, and due in part to the author's individual approach to telling the story.

Beware Stereotyping

One final note as we consider what makes a good historical novel. Things change. That's obvious, but it becomes truly apparent when one examines historical fiction from previous eras. For example, frontier life is lovingly captured in Laura Ingalls Wilder's *Little House* novels; however, they reflect her own upbringing and the antagonistic and superior attitudes commonly held toward Native Americans and other people of color at that time. Wilder wrote these stories based on her own life years later from memory during the 1930s with her daughter. This does not justify the negative depiction of the Native characters in her work; however, it does present a dilemma. Do we simply get rid of books that contain negative images of people or cultures? We certainly don't want to offend, exclude, or alienate children whose culture is represented in this way. Imagine it was *your* family heritage that was being slammed in a book. How eager would you be to read it aloud at story time? We have no easy answers here. But we can proceed with sensitivity, constantly seeking out *more* accurate and authentic representations of all people, looking for the cultural markers in a novel that suggest a richer portrayal based in reality. This is a continuing issue in the appreciation and evaluation of historical fiction and one we need to consider carefully. As author Patricia McKissack (2000) wrote, "We must talk about these things or we will never get a full understanding of what really happened, and without understanding there can be no healing."

Sample Review

Let's put these evaluation criteria into action and consider one review and how it uses these criteria. Here's a sample review of a novel of historical fiction:

Klages, Ellen. 2006. *The Green Glass Sea*. New York: Viking.

Dewey Kerrigan's life consists of one change after another. Her mother has disappeared, her father has been gone for months working for the army, and when the grandmother she is staying with has a stroke, Dewey is shipped across the country to her father. Set in 1943, against the backdrop of a town that supposedly doesn't exist, and the creation of a "gadget" that no one can discuss, this story focuses on an eleven-year-old-girl's need for human connection during difficult times. Readers may not understand the feeling of living in a country at war, but those who have been the new kid in town will recognize Dewey's anxiety masquerading as false bravado, and her obsession with the one thing she feels connected to, her treasured radio. Dewey's façade crumbles when her father is suddenly killed, and she is forced to acknowledge that she needs a family. The significance of the setting in Los Alamos, New Mexico, and the fact that "the gadget" is the atomic bomb will intrigue historical fiction readers and Dewey's emotional journey will resonate with those struggling to find connection in their own lives.
[By Tammy Korns for *Librarians' Choices*. Used with permission.]

Notice how this review gives you enough factual information to understand the who, what, when, where, and why, while letting a sense of the story's significance and the author's style unfold at the same time. For example, we immediately learn the protagonist's name, "Dewey Kerrigan," and gradually find out that she is motherless, than grandmother-less, then fatherless, all at age eleven. We are told that the time is 1943 but learn the specific location, Los Alamos, New Mexico, only at the end, when the presence of the atomic bomb is revealed in the final sentence. These details help ground the necessary underpinnings of historical authenticity. The plotline is briefly described in terms of various story milestones: the disappearance of her mother, her father's work in the army, her grandmother's stroke, Dewey's subsequent move, and her father's eventual death. These are then connected with the story's theme and the character's "need for a family," "emotional journey," and struggle to "find connection." The review acknowledges the author's handling of "a town that supposedly doesn't exist, and the creation of a 'gadget' that no one can discuss," setting up a tension that underscores the difficult situation the child without a family faces. Finally, this reviewer also acknowledges the challenge of appealing to the child reader perhaps unfamiliar with the history of Los Alamos and the atomic bomb with these words: "Readers may not understand the feeling of living in a country at war, but those who have been the new kid in town will recognize Dewey's anxiety masquerading as false bravado, and her obsession with the one thing she feels connected to." This review helps us get a glimpse of the story and the history, as well as how to promote it with kids.

AWARDS FOR HISTORICAL FICTION

It has already been pointed out that many works of historical fiction have been awarded the Newbery medal, so be sure to watch that award announcement every January for possible recommendations of quality historical novels. In addition, there are a few other awards and lists that help us in our search for good books set in the past.

Scott O'Dell Award for Historical Fiction

Probably the best-known barometer of excellence in historical fiction for children is the Scott O'Dell award. First presented in 1984, the award was originated and donated by Newbery award–winning historical author Scott O'Dell himself. The award committee was headed by children's literature scholar and critic Zena Sutherland for many years and is now chaired by Roger Sutton, editor-in-chief of *The Horn Book*. The winning book must be published in English in the United States and must be set in the "New World" (North, South, or Central America). Recent recipients have included *Chickadee* by Louis Erdrich (HarperCollins, 2012), *Dead End in Norvelt* by Jack Gantos (Farrar, Straus & Giroux, 2011), *One Crazy Summer* by Rita Williams-Garcia (Amistad, 2010), *The Storm in the Barn* by Matt Phelan (Candlewick, 2009), *Chains* by Laurie Halse Anderson (Simon & Schuster, 2008), *Elijah of Buxton* by Christopher Paul Curtis (Scholastic, 2007), and *The Green Glass Sea* by Ellen Klages (Viking, 2006).

Notable Social Studies Trade Books for Young People

For a helpful list of books focused on social studies that includes many works of historical fiction, watch for the annual annotated book list "Notable Trade Books for Young People," created by the National Council for the Social Studies (NCSS) in cooperation with the Children's Book Council (CBC). The list is published every spring in the journal *Social Education* and is posted by the Children's Book Council on their website, http://www.cbcbooks.org, and at the NCSS site at http://www.socialstudies.org.

Jane Addams Book Award

The Jane Addams Children's Book Award recognizes books for young people that promote the cause of peace, social justice, world community, and the equality of the sexes and all the races. The committee seeks out "beautifully crafted, compelling books, telling complex stories that delight, inspire, and deepen the understanding of young people." The award has been presented annually since 1953 by the Women's International League for Peace and Freedom (WILPF) and the Jane Addams Peace Association. The award is announced on April 28, the anniversary of the founding of WILPF. Recipients have included many outstanding titles of historical fiction (as well as other genres) including *Elijah of Buxton* by Christopher Paul Curtis (Scholastic, 2007) and *Weedflower* by Cynthia Kadohata (Simon & Schuster, 2006), as well as the historical novels in verse *The Surrender Tree: Poems of Cuba's Struggle for Freedom* by Margarita Engle (Holt, 2008) and *Inside Out and Back Again* by Thanhha Lai (HarperCollins, 2011).

Literature in Action: Using Community Resources

As we invite children to dip into the past, envisioning a world before they were born, it can be powerful to make this abstraction more tangible for them through hands-on and participatory activities. We can look beyond our doors to utilize the resources, organizations, and people in our own communities who have links with history—inviting guest speakers, utilizing available museum resources, and researching primary source documents and artifacts. Use a favorite historical novel as a jumping-off point or make a booklist or bookmark of historical novels available as you provide encounters with these community resources.

Guest Speakers

Inviting guest speakers who can share their own experiences in connection with a work of literature can also be very meaningful. Check with your PTA/PTO, local college or university, Chamber of Commerce, Rotary, League of Women Voters, and so on to see who might be available on topics of relevance to your events and programs. Even local experts, such as students' own parents and grandparents, can be valuable resources for connecting literature with real-life experiences. For example, the Dallas (Texas) Holocaust

Museum has a list of Holocaust survivors who live in the area and are willing to make classroom/library visits. (There is a nominal fee.) I've seen unruly sixth graders sit silently glued as they hear about the atrocities of war from someone who was really there. Look for local experts to provide a human dimension to their historical reading. Then be sure to do some preparation with students, reading and discussing historical fiction, and researching relevant resources, so the visit with this special speaker will be more meaningful and contextualized for students.

Museum Resources

Using the museum resources available outside the classroom can add so much to children's learning of historical content and reading of historical fiction. Many cities and communities have excellent museums, civic centers, and resource people. Check to see what local history museums or children's museums might be available where you live. Do they have personnel who can visit the library? Exhibits or materials they will loan out? With a little planning, you can provide children first-hand experience with objects and artifacts or with listening to people sharing their own lives and experiences. It is also possible to take advantage of traveling exhibitions and bring the museum resources to you. Link these tools with the books children are reading and collaborate with teachers about units of historical study for maximum relevance.

Traveling Exhibits
Smithsonian Institution Traveling Exhibition Service
Curriculum materials and links to additional Smithsonian resources
http://www.sites.si.edu/education/teachers_res2.htm
Featuring topics such as civil rights, the First Ladies, family folklore, Latino life, and so on.

Holocaust Museum Houston
Curriculum Trunk
http://www.hmh.org/ed_cur_trunk.shtml
All trunks are a compilation of multimedia tools including videos, posters, CDs, CD-ROMs, artifact kits, maps, classroom sets of books, lessons plans, and student activities.

U.S. National Library of Medicine
National Institutes of Health
History of Medicine Exhibition Program
http://www.nlm.nih.gov/hmd/about/exhibition/booktraveling.html
This includes a wide variety of available exhibits such as "Harry Potter's World: Renaissance Science, Magic, and Medicine" and "Life and Limb: The Toll of the American Civil War," for example.

Web Resources

We can use the Internet to locate and share resources that go well beyond what is available in our own local communities. There are excellent websites that provide easy access to historical documents, photographs, and other visual aids that can expand our understanding of historical fiction. Two of my favorite resources are U.S. government websites offering treasures from American history via images on the Internet.

The National Archives
Today's Document
http://www.archives.gov/historical-docs/todays-doc/
> Provides a visual image of an actual historical document stored in the U.S. National Archives, plus links to related documents, more information, and lesson plans

The Library of Congress
American Memory project
Today in History link
> Provides a visual image tied to a historical event for each date, with embedded links to additional sources and information
> http://memory.loc.gov/ammem/index.html

In addition, the Biography television channel (http://www.biography.com/) and the History television channel (http://www.history.com/) both offer a wealth of information and visuals to supplement historical study that children may find surprising.

Primary Sources

Sharing primary source documents, maps, timelines, artifacts, and Jackdaws helps children visualize and conceptualize historical times through hands-on materials. Even audio resources can provide a connection with the voices of the past. For example, the American Rhetoric website offers an Online Speech Bank with audio recordings, transcripts, and visuals for over 5,000 important speeches at http://www.american rhetoric.com/. When children can hear, see, or touch the "stuff" of history, it becomes so much more real and memorable for them. Mine your local archives for materials to display and consider collaborating with teachers to supplement curricular units of study. My favorite resource for purchasing facsimiles of historical documents is Jackdaws Publications (http://www.jackdaw.com/), a company that bills itself as "the world's largest educational primary source materials company" with materials that support the study of both American history (and economics, government, and social issues) and world history (including the Greeks and Romans, ancient civilizations, explorers, etc.). As they describe it, "a Jackdaw is a treasure chest of primary source materials . . . full-size reproductions of actual letters, diaries, telegrams and newspapers, study maps and many other authentically reproduced documents . . . with full descriptions of the documents and their sources . . . and transcripts and translations of difficult to read documents." Each portfolio focuses on a specific time in history and offers a goosebump experience like seeing a passenger manifest for an immigrant ship that might have carried our ancestors, for example. For a model of how to use primary sources and "do history" with kids, check out http://www.dohistory.org, a website that "shows you how to piece together the past from the fragments that have survived" with one case study, a working midwife in 1807.

SHARING HISTORICAL FICTION

There are many creative ways to bring historical fiction to life for young readers. Whether through drama activities, or investigating online resources, simulations, and games, children can begin to understand the people, places, and events of the past in ways that make their reading even more meaningful. When we "play" with history, it becomes a little less intimidating and helps children take on the personas of people in the past.

Drama

Consider drama as a follow-up to history, involving local drama teachers and coaches, if possible. Bring the historical period of a novel to life through readers' theater, dressing up and speaking as a historical figure, and other dramatic skits and interpretations. Readers' theater (as described in the previous chapter) is a fun and meaningful way to read an excerpt of a favorite historical novel aloud in parts (for dialogue and narration) without elaborate preparations. If children really enjoy this experience, simple costumes and props can be borrowed or created to add a dimension of authenticity to the presentation. Challenge children to do the research to get the details right in dramatizing a sequence from a favorite historical novel—perhaps in preparation for a Presidents' Day program or a Thanksgiving or seasonal celebration. Connecting drama with history makes the people and places real to children through first-hand experience, almost like participating in a living history museum. In fact, Carol Otis Hurst provides helpful guidelines for involving children in creating and participating in their own informal "Living History Museums" at http://www.carolhurst.com/subjects/history/livinghistory.html. Video record their presentations to save and share (with parent permission). Look for local reenactors, individuals who participate in historical reenactments and might want to share their experiences. Even local actors who perform in community or professional theater can be recruited as guests to share their insights on costuming, dialect coaching, and character research for historical dramas. Follow up with reading lists of additional historical novels that might be interesting and relevant.

Virtual Travel

We live in a time when we can have visual and virtual access to many other places on the planet and we can see some of the settings we read about in books. One website, in particular, offers virtual travel to book-related places. Google Lit Trips (http://www.googlelittrips.com/GoogleLit/Home.html), created by educator Jerome Burg, offer free downloadable files that "mark the journeys of characters from famous literature on the surface of Google Earth." He has created several virtual literary field trips that offer "pop-up windows containing a variety of resources including relevant media, thought-provoking discussion starters, and links to supplementary information." Many historical novels are included in the roster of options such as *Number the Stars* by Lois Lowry, *A Family Apart* by Joan Lowery Nixon, *Journey to Topaz* by Yoshiko Uchida, *Blood on the River* by Elisa Carbone, *Hard Gold* by Avi, *The Watsons Go to Birmingham 1963* by Christopher Paul Curtis, and *The Slave Dancer* by Paula Fox. Jerome Burg, the site creator, says his goal is to "three-dimensionalize" the reading experience by placing readers "inside the story," and he has even posted student-created Google Lit Trips, too—something your own students might want to try creating.

School librarian Cynthia Alaniz uses other technological tools to make books come alive for her students. She has incorporated SoundCloud to record oral readings and share them with others, plus she notes, "Skype has enlarged our reading community because it's allowed us to connect with librarians and teachers from around the country. Also, through our class Twitter account, we can share our learning with others." Using social network tools helps us connect with one another as readers as well as explore the books we love more deeply.

Historical Simulation Games

"Playing history" can also be a fun way to explore the people and events of the past in interactive and participatory ways. Many years ago, I remember trying the Oregon Trail simulation with students—and loving it! Now that game is available for the Wii—and many more historical simulations and games with a rich historical backdrop are available free on the Internet. Start with Playinghistory.org, a resource that offers a database of more than 100 shared games that is searchable and rich in community member reviews. Jeremiah McCall, teacher and author of *Gaming the Past: Using Games to Teach Secondary History*, noted, "Historical simulation games have the power to immerse students in a world of conflicting goals and choices where they have the power to make decisions and experience (virtually) the consequences of those decisions" (http://teachinghistory.org/nhec-blog/25117). Or go retro and offer old-fashioned board, book, and card games that also have a historical focus, like these:

Board, Book, and Card Games
- Axis & Allies; military strategy bookshelf game set during World War II
- Britannia; historical board game featuring the millennia-long struggle for control of England, Scotland, and Wales
- Chrononauts; card game of time travel
- A House Divided; strategy game set during the American Civil War
- Samurai and Ran; games of battles and warfare set in ancient Japan
- Risk; board game of geographic world conquest
- Road to the White House; simulates the race to become the U.S. president
- Ticket to Ride; card game featuring a cross-country train adventure

Connect games and books with units of study or celebrations of "this day in history." Look for help from *Libraries Got Game: Aligned Learning Through Modern Board Games* by Brian Mayer and Christopher Harris (2009). Encourage young people to share their favorite history-themed video games with you and talk about what they're learning and experiencing—leading them back to books wherever possible.

CONCLUSION

Historical fiction that is well written and engaging is just as compelling a story as any hip mystery or escapist fantasy. We just have to delve into the variety of current titles available to find a historical novel that will capture each young reader. Will it be humorous history? Medieval mystery? With an enthusiastic introduction by an adult, children can see that historical fiction has timeless relevance, lively writing, and interesting people. We can seek out those stories and help kids connect with people just like them. Interest often increases when we choose a historical novel to read aloud or booktalk, especially with interesting props. Many of these books can also be tied to film adaptations (e.g., *Sarah, Plain and Tall*) or audiobooks (e.g., *Dead End in Norvelt*, Macmillan Audio, 2011) and that often increases children's motivation to read the book version. Exposure to historical fiction will certainly better equip children to tackle their history homework, but even more significantly, we hope they can also find stories from the past that are relevant and meaningful to their lives today.

PROFESSIONAL RESOURCES FOR HISTORICAL FICTION

If you are interested in additional resources to help you explore this genre further, the following books can be helpful.

Altoff, Peggy, and Syd Golston. 2012. *Teaching Reading with the Social Studies Standards: Elementary Units That Integrate Great Books, Social Studies, and the Common Core Standards.* Silver Spring, MD: National Council for the Social Studies.

Barnhouse, Rebecca. 2004. *The Middle Ages in Literature for Youth.* Lanham, MD: Scarecrow Press.

Blumenthal, Bob. 2005. *A Parent/Teacher Guide to Children's Books on Peace and Tolerance.* Victoria, British Columbia: Trafford.

Chick, Kay A., and Deborah Ann Ellermeyer. 2003. *Multicultural American History Through Children's Literature.* Englewood, CO: Libraries Unlimited.

Coffey, Rosemary K., and Elizabeth F. Howard. 1997. *America as Story: Historical Fiction for Schools* (Second Edition). Chicago, IL: American Library Association.

Edinger, Monica. 2000. *Seeking History: Teaching with Primary Sources in Grades 4–6.* Portsmouth, NH: Heinemann.

Edinger, Monica, and Stephanie Fins. 1997. *Far Away and Long Ago: Young Historians in the Classroom.* Portland, ME: Stenhouse.

Hurst, Carol Otis, and Rebecca Otis. 1993. *In Times Past: An Encyclopedia for Integrating U.S. History with Literature in Grades 3–8.* New York: McGraw-Hill.

Kokkola, Lydia. 2002. *Representing the Holocaust in Children's Literature.* London: Routledge.

Krey, DeAn M. 1998. *Children's Literature in Social Studies: Teaching to the Standards.* Silver Spring, MD: National Council for the Social Studies.

Levstik, Linda S., and Keith C. Barton. 2010. *Doing History: Investigating with Children in Elementary and Middle Schools* (Fourth Edition). London: Routledge.

Miller, Wanda J. 1997. *U.S. History Through Children's Literature: From the Colonial Period to World War II.* Englewood, CO: Teacher Ideas Press.

Miller, Wanda J. 1998. *Teaching U.S. History Through Children's Literature: Post–World War II*. Englewood, CO: Libraries Unlimited.

Perry, Phyllis J. 1998. *Exploring Our Country's History: Linking Fiction to Nonfiction*. Englewood, CO: Libraries Unlimited.

Sandmann, Alexa A., and John F. Ahern. 2002. *Linking Literature with Life: The NCSS Standards and Children's Literature in the Middle Grades*. Silver Spring, MD: National Council for the Social Studies.

Schur, Joan Brodsky. 2007. *Eyewitness to the Past: Strategies for Teaching American History in Grades 5–12*. Portland, ME: Stenhouse.

Sullivan, Edward T. 1999. *The Holocaust in Literature for Youth*. Lanham, MD: Scarecrow.

Tunnell, Michael, and Richard Ammon. 1993. *The Story of Ourselves: Teaching History through Children's Literature*. Portsmouth, NH: Heinemann.

Veccia, Susan H. 2003. *Uncovering Our History: Teaching with Primary Sources*. Chicago, IL: American Library Association.

Walter, Virginia A. 2006. *War and Peace: A Guide to Literature and New Media, Grades 4–8*. Englewood, CO: Libraries Unlimited.

Zarnowski, Myra. 2006. *Making Sense of History: Using High-Quality Literature and Hands-On Experiences to Build Content Knowledge*. New York: Scholastic.

Standards in Action: National Curriculum Standards for Social Studies

As we work with children and their parents and teachers, questions come up about the school curriculum on a regular basis. We offer support in their reading as they tackle math and science and as they explore social studies (including history, geography, etc.). It can be helpful to familiarize ourselves with the curriculum standards in each relevant area. Each of these disciplines has its own professional association that advocates for learning and instruction and identifies appropriate standards. I would like to share just one example from the field of social studies. The National Council for the Social Studies published revised standards in 2010: *National Curriculum Standards for Social Studies: A Framework for Teaching, Learning, and Assessment* (http://www.socialstudies.org/standards). The revised standards, like the earlier social studies standards published in 1994, continue to be structured around the ten themes of social studies. These themes include specific "learning expectations," "class practices," "student products," and "skills and strategies, including literacy strategies" for each area. Here are the ten themes in a nutshell.

The Ten Themes of Social Studies
1. Culture
2. Time, Continuity, and Change
3. People, Places, and Environments
4. Individual Development and Identity
5. Individuals, Groups, and Institutions
6 Power, Authority, and Governance
7. Production, Distribution, and Consumption
8. Science, Technology, and Society

9. Global Connections
10. Civic Ideals and Practices

In our "One Book in Action" activities exploring *Hattie Ever After* we clearly tie in with theme #4, Individual Development and Identity: *"Social studies programs should include experiences that provide for the study of individual development and identity."* We look at how Hattie's experiences in San Francisco, in a new setting, with a new job, and with solving a family mystery shape the young woman she is becoming. You might also find this resource tied to the social studies standards helpful:

Sandmann, Alexa A., and John F. Ahern. 2002. *Linking Literature with Life: The NCSS Standards and Children's Literature in the Middle Grades.* Silver Spring, MD: National Council for the Social Studies.

Finally, I have written two articles about poetry and the social studies standards that might also be useful:

Vardell, S. M. 2003. "Poetry for Social Studies: Poems, Standards, and Strategies." *Social Education, 67* (4), 206–211.
Vardell, Sylvia M. 2011. "Everyday Poetry: Social Studies Poetry 'Notables.'" *Book Links* (September).

Assignments in Action: **Digging Deeper into Historical Fiction**

1. Historical Fiction Newbery Books
Study the historical fiction novels that have been Newbery medal winners or honor recipients. Analyze the settings to see whether they are based in or outside of the United States; which historical eras are depicted; how many protagonists are male, female, people of color, and so on. Do you see any patterns? Any shifts? Any holes? Examine circulation statistics to see which historical Newbery books are most popular. Analyze why that might be and consider strategies you might use to promote more reading of historical fiction.

2. Matching Books and Resources
Choose a favorite historical novel for young people and look for local resources that could provide enrichment experiences tied to the novel. What area museums have relevant exhibits? Are there local organizations with guest speakers available? Are there sources for maps, period clothing, primary source documents, and the like?

Check your local newspaper for stories and photographs and your area colleges and universities for history professors. How would you use these resources in the library? What kinds of displays or programs could you develop? For possible ideas, check out http://www.creativelibrarydisplays.com or http://schoollibrarydisplays .blogspot.com or these books: *Great Displays for Your Library Step by Step* by Susan P. Phillips (McFarland, 2008) or *Look, It's Books!: Marketing Your Library with Displays and Promotions* by Gayle Skaggs (McFarland, 2008).

3. Updating History

Some novels are contemporary fiction at the time they are written, but as time passes, they become historical. In some cases, roles, attitudes, and expectations may also change with the passing of time, so sharing older novels may become problematic. Their characters may now seem stereotypical, their attitudes dated. What to do? One suggestion is to match older works that are well-written, award-winning books with newer, more authentic historically based novels. For example, pair Laura Ingalls Wilder's much loved *Little House* books with Louise Erdrich's *The Birchbark House* series (Hyperion, 1999) for a more balanced depiction of Native American life in the nineteenth century. What other historical book pairs can you think of?

7

Fantasy

"It is our choices, Harry, that show what we truly are, far more than our abilities."
From *Harry Potter and the Chamber of Secrets* by J. K. Rowling (Scholastic, 1999)

In this chapter, we'll learn about the genre of fantasy literature for young people. We'll consider its unique nature and forms, including low fantasy, ghost stories, high fantasy, and science fiction. You'll investigate the big name authors known for writing fantasy as well as the awards that recognize excellence in this genre. We'll delve into fantasy series, graphic novels, audiobooks, the significance of Oz, and film adaptations of fantasy novels and peruse the criteria for evaluating fantasy.

INTRODUCTION

Some of the earliest books ever written for children have been fantasy novels including *Alice's Adventures in Wonderland*, published in England in 1865, and *The Wonderful Wizard of Oz*, published in the United States in 1900, among others. In fact, even before there was "children's literature," children read fantasy novels intended for adult audiences, such as *Gulliver's Travels* (1726). There is something especially timeless about fantasy. The magic of fantasy needs no particular historical setting, so the stories often transcend the time and place of their writing. They are grounded in the oral tales that are part of folklore and traditional literature; stories of heroes and magic, dragons and wishes. But even more, fantasy speaks to something deep within the human psyche—the wonder and worry about our place in the universe.

Some of our most beloved characters in children's literature come from fantasy novels, such as Winnie the Pooh, Peter Pan, Dorothy, and Pinocchio. These and others have also translated well into now-classic films, such as *Mary Poppins, Matilda,* and *Babe* (the pig). And consider some of the best-selling books for young people: *The Hunger Games,* which has sold 17.5 million copies and counting, and *Harry Potter,* the book that launched a reading resurgence and a panoply of new fantasy novels and series. What is it about the Harry Potter stories that so captivated hundreds of thousands of readers of all ages? Is it the "what if" posed by the books?

What if this is not my real family?
What if I have magical powers and I just don't know it?
What if there were a school where I could learn magic?

Or perhaps it is the underdog status of the lone misfit boy battling the forces of evil? Or maybe the author's vivid writing and action-packed scenes? All of these elements are often present in the best fantasy novels for young people.

History in Action: The Wizard of Oz

We don't have to look hard for a landmark work of fantasy literature for children. Frank L. Baum's *Wizard of Oz* is considered the great American fantasy book and has generated a veritable industry of Oz interpretations and spin-offs in the hundred years since its publication. Although it was widely dismissed as mediocre by librarians and critics at the time, it was immediately popular with the public. W. W. Denslow's inventive illustrations helped the book enormously. Baum and Denslow collaborated for the first Oz book, called *The Emerald City of Oz.* Since the publishing world had a superstitious belief that any title with a "gem" in it was doomed to fail, the title was changed to *The Wonderful Wizard of Oz.* It was originally published by the George M. Hill Company in Chicago in 1900 and has since been reprinted countless times, often under the title *The Wizard of Oz.*

The book has been in the public domain since 1956 and is available in full-text format online at Project Gutenberg (http://www.gutenberg.org/etext/55). Although Baum did not want to write another Oz book, he relented in 1904 and published thirteen more Oz books in all. Illustrator John Neill collaborated with Baum on the remaining Oz titles. After Baum's death in 1919, Ruth Plumly Thompson was selected by the publishers to continue writing books in the ongoing Oz series and did so annually until 1972.

The Wizard of Oz has been translated into more than forty different languages. Historians and literary scholars have generated countless interpretations of the significance of the Wizard of Oz phenomenon, and allusions and references to Oz characters and motifs proliferate throughout other works of literature. Oz-based phrases such as "there's no place like home," "ignore that man behind the curtain," "we're not in Kansas any more," and "follow the yellow brick road" are now part of our common parlance.

Theatrical and film adaptations of the Oz stories have also been a constant over the last 100 years, beginning with Baum's own collaboration with illustrator Denslow on a stage play in 1902, which offered a revised version of the story with Dorothy as an adult. Baum also produced the earliest Oz film series in 1908 and 1914 and twice featured the silent film actress Mildred Harris. Many more live action and animated film features followed, including the recent 3-D film, *Oz the Great and Powerful*, and the classic MGM 1939 movie starring Judy Garland, seen by more than a billion people worldwide and with a following all its own (http://thewizardofoz.warnerbros.com/). Children are often more familiar with this movie than with any of the Oz books and are often startled by the differences between the movie and the book(s) when they read the classic works.

Another enormously successful contemporary spin-off has been the musical adaptation of *Wicked* based on the book by Gregory Maguire. More unusual versions of Oz have appeared in comic book form in France and as several animated series in Japan. And fans of all ages maintain tribute websites to the books, movie, and iconology of Oz, such as Wendy's Wizard of Oz at http://www.wendyswizardofoz.com/.

For more in-depth study of the Oz literary legacy, consult these professional resources, among others:

Fricke, John. 1999. *100 Years of Oz: A Century of Classic Images*. New York: Stewart, Tabori and Chang.

Gardner, Martin, and Russell B. Nye. 2011. *The Wizard of Oz and Who He Was*. Whitefish, MT: Literary Licensing.

Green, David L., and Dick Martin. 1977. *The Oz Scrapbook*. New York: Random House.

Hearn, Michael Patrick. Ed. 2000. *The Annotated Wizard of Oz: The Centennial Edition*. New York: W. W. Norton.

Riley, Michael O. 1997. *Oz and Beyond: The Fantasy World of L. Frank Baum*. Lawrence, KS: University Press of Kansas.

Rogers, Katharine M. 2006. *L. Frank Baum: Creator of Oz*. New York: Da Capo.

Sunshine, Linda. 2003. *All Things Oz: The Wonder, Wit, and Wisdom of the Wizard of Oz*. New York: Crown.

Swartz, Mark Evan. 2002. *Oz Before the Rainbow: L. Frank Baum's "The Wonderful Wizard of Oz" on Stage and Screen to 1939*. Baltimore, MD: The Johns Hopkins University Press.

Woodhouse, Horace Martin. 2013. *The Essential Wizard of Oz: 101 Things You Didn't Know About the Most-Watched Movie in Film History*. Seattle, WA: CreateSpace.

The Library of Congress maintains a regular exhibit of Oz materials online at http://www.loc.gov/exhibits/oz/. Each new generation enjoys discovering the characters and themes of the land of Oz, a pivotal milestone of American literature for children.

DEFINITIONS

In a nutshell, the fantasy genre includes books in which something "make-believe" or impossible happens. Anderson (2013) observed that fantasy "contains some type of unreality or enchantment—what children call magic. The story elements break the natural physical laws of our world without explanation" (2013, p. 114). This may be as simple as having animal characters that talk, or as complex as creating whole imaginary worlds such as the Hogwarts school of magic in the Harry Potter books or the land of Middle-earth in Tolkien's *Lord of the Rings* series. Ghost stories, time travel tales, horror stories, and even tales of the supernatural are all fantasy stories. Even science fiction is considered a type of fantasy. Remember that we are talking about *novels* here, not picture books. In the realm of picture books there are also many talking animals and make-believe happenings, but here we are focusing on novel-length stories with elements of magic, time travel, the supernatural, and so on.

Fantasy is fantasy because it contains elements or events that cannot happen in the real world, as far as we know. These may be magic, but not necessarily. They may be technologically impossible, like time travel. This element of the "impossible," yet probable, is a big part of the appeal of modern fantasy literature. Reading fantasy books may help encourage those future inventors, scientists, and dreamers to envision a future of possibilities still unknown. On a practical level, fantasy literature is also helpful for guiding children in distinguishing fact from nonfact, as they sort through the details of a fantasy novel.

Fantasy novels attempt to tackle the unknown, even the subconscious. They celebrate the power of intuition, imagination, and intellect. Courage and risk are also important elements in fantasy novels. Failure is possible, and decision making and individual choice can be crucial. The reader who agrees to accept the fantasy world of the novel with "the willing suspension of disbelief" proposed long ago by Coleridge can gain self-knowledge while temporarily escaping reality. Tunnell, Jacobs, Young, and Bryan (2012) propose six basic ingredients or motifs that help establish the pattern or character of fantasy novels: magic, other worlds, good versus evil, heroism, character archetypes, and fantastic objects. Some books include many or all of these motifs. They are what we call "high" fantasy—a far departure from the reality of the present day. An example would be the *Lord of the Rings* trilogy or the *Harry Potter* books. Others may include just a few fantasy elements or only one motif. *Charlotte's Web* is an example of this type of fantasy, known as "low" fantasy. Nearly everything in *Charlotte's Web* could happen in the present day, *except* the talking animals.

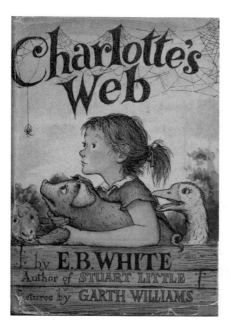

Who reads fantasy? Fantasy novels usually appeal to your brighter readers who are in the fourth grade and above for their recreational or independent reading. (Of course, there are always exceptions.) In fact, in their research, Jean Greenlaw and Margaret McIntosh (1986) found that children who are identified as "gifted and talented" are especially fond of fantasy. This makes sense, if you think about it. Fantasy novels are often longer and may contain challenging vocabulary—made-up words (like "Quidditch") and scientific concepts (like "tesseract"). This may be difficult to comprehend for a less able reader. In addition, fantasy novels often have a child protagonist who is a bit different—extremely bright, often misunderstood, possibly a loner. Gifted children often feel that way themselves, and thus identify with the character's struggles. But there are so many different kinds of fantasy that you can surely find some kind of fantasy that will appeal to all the different readers you know. You can find hilarious fantasy like the *Discworld* series by Terry Pratchett and scientific fantasy like the classic *Tripods Trilogy* by John Christopher, for example. We owe it to our children to present this genre to them in some form since it reflects many of our deepest wishes for the triumph of good in the world.

Librarians in Action: The Power of Audiobooks

Rose Brock, the librarian at Coppell Middle School West in Coppell, Texas, earned her master of library science (MLS) and PhD degrees at Texas Woman's University. In addition to writing supplementary teaching materials for several children's book publishers, Rose also partners with bestselling children's author Jon Scieszka on the national literacy project Guys Read/Guys Listen. Learn more about boys and listening from the Guys Listen Project at http://www.guyslisten.com.

Listen Up! The Power of Audiobook Collections in School Libraries by Rose Brock

My passion for connecting kids with audiobooks and understanding how audiobooks serve learners dates back to my time as a language arts classroom teacher. Even though I had a very liberal "Read *whatever* you want" policy for my students, interacting with any form of print was a heavy chore for some of them. After brainstorming ways to solve this issue, I realized that this problem became an opportunity for me to see if listening as a means of discovering a story would be welcomed. Armed with a very small budget, I bought a handful of high-interest young adult titles in audiobook format, some cheap CD players, and I offered my students a chance to experience books by "reading" them with their ears. While my classroom audiobook collection wasn't appealing to all students, it made all the difference for some of them, allowing me to witness firsthand the potential power of audiobooks.

After completing my MLS degree and becoming the campus librarian at the middle school where I taught, I began to dig into the research that supported what my experience had shown me and began sharing this research with administrators and discussing the rationale for building the school audiobook collection with the administration and faculty. The benefits of listening to audiobooks have been studied by many (largely focused on how audiobooks aid in reading comprehension or how they work well for targeted populations), and this data offered me a place to build my case for why my school library should have a robust, diverse audiobook collection.

After switching to a new school district and inheriting another middle school library collection devoid of an audiobook collection accessible to all students, I once again set out to educate my faculty on the benefits of providing students with access to audiobooks. In addition, I sought input from the entire student population via an online survey that questioned them about preferred genres, formats, and so on. Students were generous in sharing what they wanted, and with their input

I was able to select titles based on their recommendations. As my audiobook collection grew, listeners found their way to the collection, with guidance given by their language arts teachers and me. Helping students recognize that listening is a valid experience and delivery method helped audiobooks gain footing on an equal playing field in my school, and I've been able to get all my language arts teachers to expand their definition of "reading" to include audiobooks in their classrooms.

As I continued my graduate coursework and pursued a PhD in library science, I ultimately decided that I would complete a formal research study focused on audiobooks after years of sharing my experiences with teachers, administrators, and other librarians. In 2012, I conducted a study with school librarians throughout the state of Texas, surveying them about their attitudes regarding audiobooks. I tried to paint a picture of what typical library audiobook collections look like as well as what librarians perceive as their biggest challenges regarding collection development with audiobooks. While the findings of my study are far too numerous to detail here, the news worth celebrating is that almost 94 percent of librarians believed that audiobooks were good for all students, and 93 percent stated that their libraries already contained an audiobook collection. What those collections look like varied greatly, but learning that most librarians understand the value of audiobooks in regard to literacy was exciting. The biggest challenges reported to building large audiobook collections were cost, lack of funding and administrator support, and the evolution of formatting types.

As my study found, audiobooks are relatively expensive and the cost can be prohibitive for many libraries, especially those with small budgets. Finding funding for my school's audiobook collection has been an ongoing goal of mine; on numerous occasions, I have sought out and received funding from campus funds designated to benefit special populations of students. With that support, I've worked closely with special education teachers and the ESL/ELL/bilingual departments to provide materials ideal for these populations, all the while circulating audiobooks within the library to all students in compliance with providing the "least restrictive environment" and avoiding any stigma of differentiated materials. I've also found a number of local grants to obtain audiobooks and equipment, and a percentage of my "lost/damaged book money" accounts is also used to supplement the audiobook budget.

In Professor Teri Lesesne's (2006) presentation on the "Hows and Whys of Audiobooks" she recommended collaborating with the teachers in the reading department initially to purchase audio versions of required reading titles. She also suggested playing snippets of audiobooks for the kids when they enter the library and checking out books and audio together in one bag. She noted that audiobook checkout may need to extend beyond the usual book checkout period, since more hours may be needed for the listening experience.

The audiobook collection at my current school library currently includes approximately 700 physical titles housed centrally in the library, plus a growing collection of digital titles available to my students via an app, and they all circulate frequently. In my list of the best circulating titles of audiobooks, many of them are fantasy novels or fantasy series:

The Kane Chronicles
Percy Jackson and the Olympians series
The Heroes of Olympus series

The Inheritance series
The Hunger Games trilogy
Divergent trilogy
Matched trilogy
Harry Potter series
Artemis Fowl series
Inkheart series

Certainly fantasy novels are popular at my middle school and I think the audiobook format enables students at many different reading levels to enjoy this genre independently. I have found that all kinds of kids find the audiobook format satisfying—from kids who would rather not "read" print, to kids who are polishing their English, to kids who want to double their book time.

TYPES OF FANTASY

When it comes to modern fantasy novels, there is something for everyone. Short books, long novels, trilogies, series, and stories transformed into film. "Gentle" animal fantasies with very few magical elements, hilarious fantasies, and books about talking toys and tiny people can provide a good introduction to "low" fantasy for children. For children who enjoy more challenging reading and more challenging questions, the "high" fantasy of quest stories, supernatural mysteries, time travel tales, and science fiction may be just the thing. Let's consider the gamut of fantasy with some sample authors and titles for each type.

Low Fantasy

According to scholar and expert Charlotte Huck (2000), low fantasy features nonrational events that occur without explanation in the real world. The tone in low fantasy is usually lighthearted. The forms of low fantasy include stories about personified animals, personified toys, outlandish characters and humorous situations, magical powers, supernatural elements, tiny humans, and time slips. Even magical realism could be considered low fantasy where the miraculous seems perfectly natural and accepted, à la Louis Sachar's novel *Holes* (Frances Foster, 1998) or Rebecca Stead's Newbery medal book *When You Reach Me* (Random House, 2009). One example of an author whose work is considered "low" fantasy, is Roald Dahl, who gave us *Charlie and the Chocolate Factory* (Knopf, 1964), *James and the Giant Peach* (Knopf, 1961), and *Matilda* (Puffin, 1988), among others. His wild imagination, wicked sense of humor, and ruthless treatment of adult characters have won fans worldwide. All his stories occur in the world as we know it, more or less, with the addition of some unusual characters and magical powers that are out of the ordinary.

Of course, no discussion of fantasy can be complete without mention of the gentle, clever novels of E. B. White. If you have never read *Charlotte's*

Web (HarperCollins, 1952), promise yourself you will do so as soon as possible. It is one of those landmark works in children's literature: a deceptively simple story with a hint of a sophisticated, humorous layer for adults. The farm setting is largely realistic, with the addition of sentient, speaking animals that happen to have incredible spelling gifts, too. Other examples of this kind of low fantasy include the lyrical Newbery medal novel *The One and Only Ivan* by Katherine Applegate (HarperCollins, 2012); *The True Blue Scouts of Sugar Man Swamp* (Atheneum, 2013) and *The Underneath* (Atheneum, 2008), both by Kathi Appelt; the magical realism of *When You Reach Me* by Rebecca Stead (Random House, 2009); the sweet and sassy animal tales of Dick King-Smith; the hilarious *Time Warp Trio* series by Jon Scieszka; and even the popular Lemony Snicket, Eddie Dickens, and Spiderwick Chronicle stories. Many humorous fantasy series are examples of this type of reality-based "low" fantasy.

Ghost Stories and the Supernatural

Fantasy stories about ghosts, horror, and the supernatural are also very popular with many young readers, particularly as they move into their teen years. Psychologists tell us that this delight in horror stories leads to a natural catharsis that is quite healthy. Quite frankly, they genuinely scare me, I have to admit. But as a professional, I try to stay in step with what young people are reading, no matter what my personal preferences are, so I can make informed recommendations and converse knowledgeably with kids about their favorites. For example, R. L. Stine's *Goosebumps* series experienced huge popularity for quite some time, and it's now coming back in graphic novel form. Many of the classic ghost stories by John Bellairs still appeal to today's readers. Even Cornelia Funke has the humorous *Ghosthunters* series for the middle grades. Neil Gaiman is highly regarded for his treatment of dark forces and the supernatural, garnering him a Newbery medal for *The Graveyard Book* (HarperCollins, 2008). And Newbery honor distinctions went to Ingrid Law's story about average people with not so average powers, *Savvy* (Dial, 2008), and Grace Lin for her blending of Chinese legends into the family story of *Where the Mountain Meets the Moon* (Little, Brown, 2009). Rick Riordan's blending of mythology and reality created the very successful *Percy Jackson and the Olympians* series, as well as the *Heroes of Olympus* series and the *Kane Chronicles*. For a slightly older reader, look for Darren Shan's *Cirque Du Freak* series, which is extremely popular. Generally, these stories of ghosts, gods, fairies, vampires, and the supernatural are grounded in the real world (part of why they are frightening) and thus are generally considered low fantasy.

High Fantasy

High fantasy, on the other hand, takes place in a created secondary world far from the real everyday world in which we live. There are unusual creatures to befriend or vanquish, tasks to fulfill and quests to undertake, and magic to wield or escape. There are various categories of high fantasy including myth fantasy, gothic fantasy, epic/heroic fantasy, and sword and sorcery fantasy. These stories include settings far removed from present-day reality and often involve plotlines that are more grand in scale. For example, Jane Yolen is an established author of high fantasy and has written several series focused around the magical and powerful creature of the dragon, Merlin, and other hero motifs. T. A. Barron also has series that center around the Merlin myth, *Lost Years of Merlin* and the *Great Tree of Avalon*. The *Lord of the Rings* trilogy with its hobbits, orcs, goblins, and elves of Middle-earth is another gem of an example of high fantasy. Many authors walk in Tolkien's footsteps: Eoin Colfer's *Artemis Fowl* series, Jonathan Stroud's *Bartimaeus* series, Susan Cooper's *Dark Is Rising* series, Suzanne Collins's *Underland Chronicles*, Brian Jacques's *Redwall* series, and Philip Pullman's acclaimed *His Dark Materials* trilogy. The classic series *The Chronicles of Narnia* by C. S. Lewis continues to be a favorite, too. Probably the best known title in the series is *The Lion, the Witch and the Wardrobe* (HarperCollins, reprinted 1994) an allegorical story about four children, a magic kingdom, and a brave lion. And don't forget the best-selling and phenomenally popular fantasy character Harry Potter created by British author J. K. Rowling. Her novels tell the story of the modest but powerful Harry Potter as he gradually comes into his own, fighting evil every step of the way.

Science Fiction

High fantasy might also be seen to include science fiction or science fantasy, although these are usually viewed as a separate genre or subgenre entirely. Not too many children's books fall into the science fiction category because of the science and technology basis that can become fairly complex and complicated. Most sci-fi literature is written for adults or young adults because of the more demanding vocabulary and manifestations of technology generally incorporated into the story. However, there are several outstanding children's books that pivot around science and technology, including the groundbreaking book *A Wrinkle in Time* (Farrar, Straus & Giroux, 1962) and its sequels by Madeleine L'Engle. Margaret Peterson Haddix's series *Shadow Children* and *Double Identity* also place characters in a struggle against a technological and sociological evil. Science fiction asks questions about things we don't entirely understand yet, like how time works and how humankind and technology can coexist. Utopian and dystopian fantasies are also powerful reading in that they hypothesize a perfect world, or a perfect world gone awry. Lois Lowry's Newbery medal book *The Giver* (Houghton Mifflin, 1993) and its sequels could be considered science fiction with their utopian focus. Nancy Farmer proposes technologically challenging scenarios in her novels *The Eye, the Ear, and the Arm* (Orchard, reissued 2004) and *The House of the Scorpion* (Atheneum, 2002) and its sequel. The *Books of Ember* series by Jeanne DuPrau are also set in a world gone awry. For older readers, the *Enders* series by Orson Scott Card and the phenomenally successful *Hunger Games* trilogy by Suzanne Collins are hugely popular. These may seem like dark stories for children, but they place child characters in a technological world gone wrong and challenge them to cope and even triumph, and they do. As critic Zena Sutherland (2004) reminds us, ultimately fantasy also offers an affirmation of the "all rightness" of things.

Fantasy Series

Fantasy fiction attracts a serious readership, willing and eager to follow their favorite characters in book after book in trilogies and series. Some experts say people often become lifelong readers because of series books. With the appetite for Harry Potter adventures, for example, it has become clear that one book is not enough for the avid fantasy fan. In addition, many authors have even created multiple fantasy series, with new characters and new adventures to follow. The beauty of a series, of course, is that if a reader enjoys one book, there are many more to encourage ongoing reading. For children, this also provides invaluable reading practice and hours of escape and imagination building.

Fantasy Series

Here are some of the most popular series of fantasy books for young people, ranging from humorous escapades to complex quest narratives.

Humorous Fantasy Series

Time Warp Trio series by Jon Scieszka
Eddie Dickens and *Unlikely Exploits* trilogies by Philip Ardagh
A Series of Unfortunate Events by Lemony Snicket
Artemis Fowl series by Eoin Colfer
The Spiderwick Chronicles by Holly Black
Dragon Slayers' Academy series by Kate McMullan
Discworld series by Terry Pratchett
Bartimaeus series by Jonathan Stroud
Skulduggery Pleasant series by Derek Landy

Other Worlds, Creatures, and Quests Series

Chronicles of Prydain by Lloyd Alexander
The Lord of the Rings by J. R. R. Tolkien
The Lost Years of Merlin by T. A. Barron
The *Pit Dragons* series and *Young Merlin* series and more by Jane Yolen
The Dark Is Rising series by Susan Cooper
The Chronicles of Narnia by C. S. Lewis
The Underland Chronicles by Suzanne Collins
The *Wizard of Oz* series by L. Frank Baum
The Chrestomanci series by Diana Wynne Jones
Septimus Heap series by Angie Sage
Redwall series by Brian Jacques

Inheritance trilogy by Christopher Paolini
His Dark Materials trilogy by Philip Pullman
Guardians of Ga'hoole series by Kathryn Lasky
Earthsea series by Ursula Le Guin
Harry Potter series by J. K. Rowling
Pendragon series by D. J. MacHale
The Books of Bayern series by Shannon Hale

Magic in This World Series

Percy Jackson and the Olympians series, *Heroes of Olympus* series, *Kane Chronicles* series, all by Rick Riordan
The *Charlie Bone* series by Jenny Nimmo
Corydon trilogy by Tobias Druitt
The *Theodosia* series by R. L. Lafevers

Science Fiction Series

The (*Wrinkle in*) *Time Quartet* by Madeleine L'Engle
The *Enders* series by Orson Scott Card
The *Tripods Trilogy* by John Christopher
Shadow Children series by Margaret P. Haddix
The *Books of Ember* by Jeanne DuPrau
The Hunger Games trilogy by Suzanne Collins
The *Chaos Walking* trilogy by Patrick Ness

Ghost Story Series

The *Lewis Barnavelt* series by John Bellairs
Green Knowe series by L. M. Boston
Ghosthunters series by Cornelia Funke

CONTROVERSY

It is worth mentioning that modern fantasy has also been subject to challenge and censorship over the years. For a long time fantasy was accused of being "fluff," since it was full of "make-believe," and critics felt it was a waste of time for children to read. In more recent years, however, the criticism has been of a different sort. Some people have felt that fantasy's inclusion of magic and make-believe may be harmful reading for children. It may make them fearful or it may inappropriately glorify magic. Some feel it runs counter to their religious beliefs, too, in the presentation of magical creatures and powers. These are sensitive issues and deserve attention. But we have to be clear about what is the individual's right and what is the school's or library's responsibility. Having those collection development policies and book challenge protocols in place will be especially important. At the very least, we need to know about these books and read them ourselves to be fully informed.

MAJOR AUTHORS OF FANTASY

When you look for the best examples of modern fantasy, you may also be surprised to find some of the best children's literature being published in any genre. Many of the big award winners have been fantasy novels that create memorable characters and deal with powerful themes. Indeed, *The Giver* by Lois Lowry is considered one of the most important children's books *ever* written for young people. Each of these novels has used fantasy as the backdrop for putting young people (or mice who think like young people) in the position of saving the world (or at least their corner of the world). This vicarious reading experience can be very empowering for children who often feel powerless in the scary world of adults.

Fantasy Authors and Works in Audio Form

Each of the following individuals has an established reputation for creating quality fantasy novels for young people. For each name, an example of his or her work in the unabridged audiobook format is cited to get you started *listening* to fantasy. More new authors are emerging all the time, so be alert to the books kids are choosing and make a note of those new talents creating fantasy that kids enjoy. In addition, each of these big name authors has created many more enjoyable fantasy novels to look for. This is just a sampling.

Lloyd Alexander, *The Book of Three* (Listening Library, 2007)
Philip Ardagh, *A House Called Awful End* (Listening Library, 2003)
Natalie Babbitt, *Tuck Everlasting* (Audio Bookshelf, 2001)
T. A. Barron, *The Lost Years of Merlin* (Listening Library, 2000)
L. Frank Baum, *The Wizard of Oz* (Blackstone Audio, 2005)
Franny Billingsley, *The Folk Keeper* (Listening Library, 2000)
Holly Black, *The Spiderwick Chronicles* (Listening Library, 2007)
Eoin Colfer, *Artemis Fowl: The Last Guardian* (Listening Library, 2004)
Suzanne Collins, *The Hunger Games* (Scholastic, 2008)
Susan Cooper, *The Dark Is Rising* (Listening Library, 2000)
Roald Dahl, *Charlie and the Chocolate Factory* (HarperChildren's Audio, 2002)
Jeanne DuPrau, *The City of Ember* (Listening Library, 2006)
Nancy Farmer, *The House of the Scorpion* (Recorded Books, 2003)
Catherine Fisher, *Incarceron* (Listening Library, 2010)
Cornelia Funke, *Ghost Knight* (Listening Library, 2012)
Shannon Hale, *The Princess Academy* (Full Cast Audio, 2007)
Eva Ibbotson, *The Beasts of Clawstone Castle* (Recorded Books, 2006)
Brian Jacques, *Redwall* (Listening Library, 2005)
Diana Wynne Jones, *A Charmed Life* (Recorded Books, 2004)
Derek Landy, *Skulduggery Pleasant* (HarperChildren's Audio, 2007)
Madeleine L'Engle, *A Wrinkle in Time* (Listening Library, 2006)
C. S. Lewis, *The Chronicles of Narnia* (HarperChildren's Audio, 2004)

Lois Lowry, *The Giver* (Listening Library, 2001)
Christopher Paolini, *Eragon* (Listening Library, 2004)
Tamora Pierce, *Circle of Magic: Sandry's Book* (Full Cast Audio, 2003)
Terry Pratchett, *The Wee Free Men* (HarperChildren's Audio, 2005)
Philip Pullman, *The Golden Compass* (Listening Library, 2006)
Rick Riordan, *The Lightning Thief* (Listening Library, 2005)
J. K. Rowling, *Harry Potter and the Deathly Hallows* (Listening Library, 2007)
Lemony Snicket (Daniel Handler), *The Bad Beginning* (Listening Library, 2003)
J. R. R. Tolkien, *The Lord of the Rings* (Recorded Books, 2004)
Betty Ren Wright, *The Dollhouse Murders* (Live Oak Media, 1999)

For children new to fantasy, listening to a book in audio form can be a great way to introduce the genre. Since many fantasy novels are longer works, this format provides a storytelling experience that makes what can be a challenging work more accessible for some readers. And look how many fantasy novels have been recorded for listening in recent years.

Authors in Action: Grace Lin

Grace Lin is both an author and an illustrator with a variety of works and awards to her credit. She wrote and illustrated several popular picture books including her Lin Family books, *Dim Sum for Everyone!*, *Kite Flying*, *Fortune Cookie Fortunes*, and many others. She also has authored several novels, including the Pacy Lin series with *The Year of the Dog*, *The Year of the Rat*, and *Dumpling Days*; the easy reader series *Ling & Ting*; and the fantasy novels *Where the Mountain Meets the Moon*, a 2010 Newbery honor title and *New York Times* bestseller, and the companion book, *Starry River of the Sky*. Many of her books reflect her Taiwanese heritage and blend her childhood in upstate New York alongside the Chinese tales and legends of her culture. Here she addresses that unique combination and how it has shaped her as a writer and artist.

Why Couldn't Snow White Be Chinese? Finding Identity Through Children's Books
by Grace Lin

When I was in third grade, the class decided to put on a production of *The Wizard of Oz*. The news spread across the playground like an electrical current, energizing every girl to ask, "Who will play Dorothy?" The thought was thrilling and delicious, each of us imagining ourselves with ruby shoes. I whispered to my friend Jill, "Do you think I could be Dorothy?"

Jill stared at me in shock. "You couldn't be Dorothy. You're Chinese. Dorothy's not Chinese."

And then I remembered. I was different. I felt stupid for even thinking I could be the star of a play. That Dorothy, like everyone and everything else important, was not like me.

And what was I? Jill had bluntly termed me Chinese. But I didn't feel Chinese. I spoke English, I watched *Little House on the Prairie*, learned American history, and read books about girls named Betsy and boys named Billy. But I had black hair and slanted eyes, I ate white rice at home with chopsticks, and I got red envelopes for my birthday. Did I belong anywhere?

The books that I loved and read did not help me answer that question. Betsy and Billy were nice friends but they didn't understand. Neither did Madeline, Eloise, or Mike Mulligan. Cinderella, Snow White? I didn't even try to explain. *Rikki Tikki Tembo* and *Five Chinese Brothers* tried to be pals, but really, what did we have in common? Nothing. And so I remained different from my friends in real life, different from my fictional friends in stories . . . somehow always different.

I'm older now, and wiser, and I appreciate that difference. Instead of the curse I had felt it was during my childhood, I now treasure it. I realize the beauty of two cultures blending and giving birth to me (!), an Asian American.

When I decided to create children's books as my profession, I remembered my own childhood. I remembered the books I wished I had had when I was a child. Books that would have made me feel [that] I belonged, that there was someone else like me out there, and that who I was, was actually something great.

So with this in mind, I create my books. I try to make books that make readers appreciate Asian American culture. I try to make books that the contemporary child can relate to. I try to make books that encourage Asian American children to embrace their identities. For example, *The Ugly Vegetables* takes place in a suburban neighborhood and deals with one child's chagrin [at] having a Chinese vegetable garden while the rest of the neighbors grow flowers. *Dim Sum for Everyone!* takes place in Boston's Chinatown and shows a modern family enjoying this unusual cuisine. *Kite-Flying* shows the same family, driving a car, making and flying their own Chinese dragon kite. They are depictions of a present-day Asian American child's life.

Do these books make a difference? I think so. In my life, moments of insecurity and isolation could have been magically erased simply by having a book transform into a friend that shared what I saw and what I am. And, perhaps, if these books had been generously spread, exposing children of all races to the Asian part of the melting pot, perhaps then my childhood friend Jill would not have said, "Dorothy's not Chinese," but rather, "Sure, Dorothy could be Chinese." Why not? I'd click my heels three times to wish that.

This and other essays, interviews, and insights can be found at Grace Lin's website: GraceLin.com. This particular essay appears here with permission of the author.

One Book in Action: Where the Mountain Meets the Moon

Choosing a single title of fantasy for emphasis is one way of inviting children to sample the genre, particularly kids who might not have tried it before. Although many readers have become avid fantasy fans through the *Harry Potter* phenomenon, there are still children who may find the faraway settings strange and the length and vocabulary of fantasy novels challenging. Thus, it can be helpful to guide children's experiences with fantasy literature in purposeful and creative ways. For this chapter, we will center on Grace Lin's Newbery honor book, *Where the Mountain Meets the Moon* (Little, Brown, 2009), the story of a young girl in China who goes on a journey to find out how to change her fortune. This book was chosen by Al Roker as a selection for his *Today Show* Kids Book Club, and a fun video clip of Grace talking with Al and the kids appears on Grace's website. You'll also find reader and educator guides for many of Grace Lin's books, including extensive discussion questions and comprehension-building activities for *Where the Mountain Meets the Moon* at her publisher's website: http://www.gracelinbooks.com.

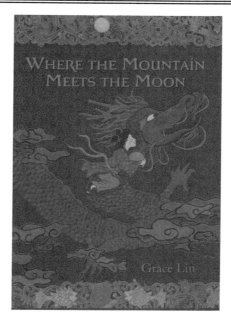

To Begin

Where the Mountain Meets the Moon is a lovely selection to read aloud, with its short chapters and mini-folktales and fairy tales and abundant dialogue. Invite volunteers to read aloud the Chinese "story" chapters (which are labeled "The Story of . . ." and appear in a different font). If time is short, just share Chapters Five and/or Six (each is three or four pages long) in which our heroine, Minli, sets off on her adventure. There is also an audio clip of the author reading an excerpt aloud on her website, plus the book is available as an unabridged audiobook from Listening Library. Then browse through the ten full-color illustrations Grace created for the book as well as the two-color pictures that open each chapter (and project them if you can) and invite the children to talk about what they think will happen in the book based on these illustrations. Many of these same images are woven throughout the book's digital trailer, which gives an evocative feeling for introducing the book (available at http://www.gracelin.com).

Making It Real

Take this fantasy novel and make it concrete for children by gathering objects referenced in the book or related in some way. In the story, Minli packs a variety of items as she sets off on her journey. See how many you can find to display along with the book: a needle, a pair of chopsticks, her white rabbit rice bowl, a small piece of dried bamboo, a hollow gourd full of water, a small knife, a fishnet, some uncooked rice, a large pot, and one copper coin. Talk about why she might have chosen to bring these items and predict how they might come in handy. She also uses some of these items to create a compass (rice bowl, water, and bamboo), which helps guide her on her way. Find, share, or make a compass together and talk about how to use a compass, an orienteering skill. And if you're really feeling adventurous, try bringing and keeping a pet goldfish, an auspicious and lucky creature in Chinese culture and a key figure in *Where the Mountain Meets the Moon*.

Poetry and Folktale Connections

Make connections to poetry with works by poets of Chinese heritage or poems on the topic of dragons and with Chinese folktale collections or picture book adaptations. Here are just a few examples. Bring books to browse and invite children to choose their favorite poem or tale to pair with Lin's novel.

Foster, John. 2004. *Dragon Poems*. New York: Oxford University Press.
Ho, Minfong. 1996. *Maples in the Mist: Poems for Children from the Tang Dynasty*. New York: Lothrop, Lee, & Shepard.
Mak, Kam. 2001. *My Chinatown: One Year in Poems*. New York: HarperCollins.
Prelutsky, Jack. 1993. *The Dragons Are Singing Tonight*. New York: Scholastic.
Tucker, Kathy. 2003. *The Seven Chinese Sisters*. Ill. by Grace Lin. Morton Grove, IL: Albert Whitman.
Whipple, Laura. Ed. 1996. *Eric Carle's Dragons, Dragons*. New York: Philomel.
Wong, Janet S. 2000. *Night Garden: Poems from the World of Dreams*. New York: McElderry.
Wong, Janet S. 2003. *Knock on Wood: Poems about Superstitions*. New York: McElderry.
Yep, Laurence. Ed. 1993. *American Dragons: Twenty-five Asian American Voices*. New York: HarperCollins.
Yolen, Jane. 1998. *Here There Be Dragons*. San Diego: Harcourt.
Young, Ed. 1989. *Lon Po Po*. New York: Philomel.
Young, Ed. 2004. *The Lost Horse: A Chinese Folktale*. New York: Houghton Mifflin Harcourt.
Young, Ed. 2005. *Beyond the Great Mountains*. San Francisco: Chronicle.

More Story Resources

Author Grace Lin offers an amazing variety of book-based resources for this and many of her works online at her website, http://www.gracelin.com. For example, for information about the creation of *Where the Mountain Meets the Moon*, you'll find a video clip of Grace talking about the book's "origins, themes, and character inspirations" as well as links to multiple interviews on her blog tour. You can also get ideas from her online book launch party complete with cupcakes and cookie recipes. Click on her "Activities" link, and you'll find an "Activity Book" with directions for making a compass, tips on drawing a dragon, information about Chinese symbolism and characters, and more recipes. Plus, there's a separate "Event Kit" that provides downloadable invitations, posters, and a puzzle game, perfect for Moon Festival celebrations or book club gatherings. In addition, there are even directions for making a simple board game created by an avid reader named Emme, age eleven!

Finally, for the latest on author/illustrator Grace Lin's life and work, look for her more informal blog, http://www.gracelinblog.com, where she posts pictures and vignettes, "Fortune Cookie Friday" thoughts, links to her travel blogs (to China, Hong Kong, and Price Edward Island), and where you can sign up for her *Gracenotes* newsletter and access the newsletter archives.

Other Books by Grace Lin

Children who enjoy the story of *Where the Mountain Meets the Moon* may want to continue reading additional books by author Grace Lin, particularly the companion novel, *Starry River of the Sky* (Little, Brown, 2012), with a boy protagonist who has his own adventure. At Grace Lin's website, you'll find an overview video, behind the story mini-documentary, awards and reviews, five activities including an event kit, interactive read aloud script, recipes, directions, and more for this companion novel.

Grace Lin is also the author of contemporary realistic fiction books including the Pacy Lin series: *The Year of the Dog* (Little, Brown, 2006), *The Year of the Rat* (Little, Brown, 2009), and *Dumpling Days* (2012), in which a young girl copes with everyday childhood concerns. But just as in her fantasy novels, Lin weaves two parallel stories together: Pacy's everyday experiences alongside her family's stories and memories. For younger readers, seek out her *Ling & Ting* series of easy readers or her engaging picture books that she has illustrated herself like her Lin Family books, *Dim Sum for Everyone!* (Knopf, 2001), *Kite Flying* (Dragonfly, 2004), *Fortune Cookie Fortunes* (Dragonfly, 2006), *Bringing in the New Year* (Knopf, 2008), *Thanking the Moon: Celebrating the Mid-Autumn Moon Festival* (Knopf, 2010), and others like *The Ugly Vegetables* (Charlesbridge, 2009). Sharing the works of Grace Lin helps children see the diverse interests an author can explore in her writing, as well as how she often weaves her own cultural heritage throughout her writing.

EVALUATION CRITERIA

According to critic Zena Sutherland (2004), fantasy must contain some imaginary or fantastic element as the most basic ingredient (ask yourself, "Can this really happen?"), but it is also important to look for "internal consistency." As the author creates rules for a fanciful world, those rules must be consistently maintained to sustain the alternative reality depicted in the book. In addition, we look for fantasy motifs in the writing, although some styles of fantasy are rich in symbols and motifs and others prefer to align closer with the ordinary. As we critically consider novels in this genre, we seek a balance of a plain, old-fashioned engaging story with the creation of a unique world or unusual perspective that is outside the ordinary—yet not so outside that we don't believe it. All of this must be artfully told so we keep reading, even when the names of places and people are odd or challenging. Thus, a good fantasy novel should also have the usual literary qualities we look for in any solid work of fiction: strong characterization, engaging plot, effective setting, worthwhile theme, and unique style.

Characters

The characters of fantasy are critical to the reader's engagement with the story. It should be possible to identify with the main character(s), even if they're not human. They may be strange or extraordinary, but we should still feel a kinship with the protagonist (or other characters), believing them worth the adventure. We should care about what happens to them. They should be credible and multidimensional individuals and grow a bit in the course of the story. For example, Harry Potter may be your basic good guy, but he has his foibles, too. Sometimes authors have one of the characters mirror the disbelief of the reader. The narrator or protagonist reassures readers that the fantastic events are normal or real. When a believable character who initially doubted the fantasy is convinced, readers are likewise convinced. The characters' attitudes toward their adventures color our own and their relationships set the stage for the conflicts that shape the plot.

Plot

The plot should be believable, logical, and internally consistent (within the story's fantasy framework), plus original and creative to keep the reader's interest. Many authors firmly ground a story in reality before gradually moving into fantasy. Plot in fantasy often involves quests or journeys with tasks to accomplish, obstacles to overcome, and villains to vanquish. This should proceed in a well-paced, clearly described fashion and it should grow out of the characters and how they behave in this fantasy world. For example, if the *Time Warp Trio* must have the magic book with them to travel through time, then they can't suddenly "poof" their way home at the end without it.

Setting

The setting can be especially important in fantasy, so the author must pay careful attention to setting and provide enough description to help the reader visualize the surroundings. Details of setting are an integral part of the story. Good authors make details so vivid that readers can see, hear, and feel the setting as they read the description. For example, in *The Lion, the Witch and the Wardrobe*, when the children go through the wardrobe, C. S. Lewis paints a clear picture of a winter climate that is in sudden contrast to their English home. Time and place can be critical here, so the reader needs a clear sense of setting to visualize the story events and characters.

Theme

Themes in modern fantasy are very important and generally reflect universal truths that transcend time and place. For example, common themes of fantasy include affirming that good is more powerful than evil, love is more important than power, and so on. This is where fantasy channels its roots in folklore, echoing ageless themes that are big in scope. This is part of why fantasy is so satisfying, too. After an arduous task, there is hope, victory—even when sacrifices are made. Fantasy novels help fulfill our need for something bigger than ourselves to believe in, no matter hold old we are. As Philip Pull-man, author of *The Golden Compass* (Knopf, 2006) and the *His Dark Materials* series, observed, "Thou shalt not is soon forgotten, but 'Once upon a time' lasts forever."

Style

The author should use language appropriate to the story (she or he may even coin new terms) and do enough but not too much explaining. There needs to be a clear and consistent point of view that encourages the reader to believe in this fantasy world and engage in the "willing suspension of disbelief" for the length of the novel. Authors should use consistent and distinct language for each character or group. The author's voice should create a distinctive frame-work for the story in the pacing, description, and dialogue, creating a place that comes vividly to mind in words and phrases that stay with us. One of my favorite examples is the opening line of Natalie Babbitt's classic fantasy novel, *Tuck Everlasting* (Farrar, Straus & Giroux, 1975), "The first week of August hangs at the very top of summer, the top of the live-long year, like the highest seat of a Ferris wheel when it pauses in the turning." What a vivid image this is and what great foreshadowing of what is to come in the story.

Sample Review

Let's put these evaluation criteria into action and consider one review and how it uses these criteria. Here's a sample review of a fantasy novel:

Funke, Cornelia. 2004. *Dragon Rider*. Trans. by Anthea Bell. New York: Scholastic.

Humans and their machines are developing land so close to the peaceful val-ley where a group of dragons live that fear of discovery spurs Firedrake and his brownie friend Sorrel to go in search of the legendary ancient dragon home known as the Rim of Heaven. Firedrake is a silver dragon energized by moonlight. Know-ing that they must fly half-way around the world, Firedrake and Sorrel enlist the help of a friendly young orphan named Ben who could be the dragon rider fore-told in prophetic lore. Along the way they encounter many fantastic creatures including mountain dwarfs, fairies, a thousand-eyed djinn, a basilisk, and a sea serpent. This arduous journey becomes extremely dangerous when Nettlebrand, a golden dragon created for the sole purpose of hunting and killing silver dragons, pursues Firedrake in the hope of finding the elusive Rim of Heaven and its silver inhabitants. The energy, action, adventure, and intrigue in this amazing story will capture the reader's interest. There are spies and counterspies, loyal friends and treacherous traitors. The strong plot and subplots are balanced perfectly with humor and clever dialogue. For example, Sorrel is an ill-tempered, sarcastic, pes-simistic creature, yet her witty banter and loyalty to Firedrake make her a lovable character. Lola Graytail, a skilled and intelligent rat, never addresses Twigleg, the homunculus, properly. She innocently refers to him as a "humpleklumpus," "hum-blecuss," "homuncupus," "hinclecompulsus," and so on. Funke's vivid imagination is clearly at work in this novel. Readers can escape into a world of fantastic creatures while remaining grounded in a classic story of good versus evil.

[By S. Zulema Silvia Bewley for *Librarians' Choices*. Used with permission.]

The reviewer immediately lets us know that this is a fantasy novel with the mention of dragons and a legend in the very first sentence. The fantasy setting of a "peaceful valley where a group of dragons live" is also identified in the beginning. Additional fantasy elements become apparent with the listing of characters: a dragon rider, "dwarfs, fairies, a thousand-eyed djinn, a basilisk, and a sea serpent"; "spies and counterspies, loyal friends and treacherous traitors"; and their unusual names, such as Firedrake, Sorrel, Nettlebrand, Lola Graytail, and Twigleg. Two specific characters are discussed to provide greater depth. "For example, Sorrel is an ill-tempered, sarcastic, pessimistic creature, yet her witty banter and loyalty to Firedrake make her a lovable character. Lola Graytail [is] a skilled and intelligent rat." These tidbits provide insight into the characterization as well as into the author's writing style.

The key elements of the story's plot are also articulated with the characters' "search of the legendary ancient dragon home known as the Rim of Heaven," their flight "half-way around the world," their enlistment of a friend, and their encounters with other fantastical creatures. A key plot conflict is also explicitly identified: "This arduous journey becomes extremely dangerous when Nettlebrand . . . pursues Firedrake." We get a sense of the overall nature of the plot with the description "energy, action, adventure, and intrigue in this amazing story" and the assessment that "the strong plot and subplots are balanced perfectly with humor and clever dialogue." Once again, the plot is addressed while also describing the author's style as humorous and clever.

The book's theme is summarized explicitly in the concluding sentence as "a classic story of good versus evil," but fantasy motifs that hint at the novel's theme are provided earlier in the review with the words "search," "prophetic lore," "arduous journey," and "loyal friends and treacherous traitors." A discussion of the author's style of writing is integrated into the analysis of characterization, plot, and even theme, along with a mention of "Funke's vivid imagination," but a specific example is also provided with Twigleg's many confused references to the "homunculus." Finally, the appeal to young readers is acknowledged with mention that "the energy, action, adventure and intrigue in this amazing story will capture the reader's interest" and "readers can escape into a world of fantastic creatures."

AWARDS FOR FANTASY

Over the years, many of the Newbery award–winning authors for the "most distinguished contribution to children's literature" for a given year have created works of modern fantasy. Books like *A Wrinkle in Time* by Madeleine L'Engle (Farrar, Straus & Giroux, 1962), *The High King* by Lloyd Alexander (Holt, 1968), *Mrs. Frisby and the Rats of NIMH* by Robert C. O'Brien (Atheneum, 1971), *The Grey King* by Susan Cooper (McElderry, 1975), *The Hero and the Crown* by Robin McKinley (Greenwillow, 1984), *The Giver* by Lois

Lowry (Houghton Mifflin, 1993), *Holes* by Louis Sachar (Frances Foster, 1998), *The Tale of Despereaux* by Kate DiCamillo (Candlewick Press, 2003), *The Graveyard Book* by Neil Gaiman (HarperCollins, 2008), *When You Reach Me* by Rebecca Stead (Random House, 2009), and *The One and Only Ivan* by Katherine Applegate (HarperCollins, 2012) have each been recognized with Newbery medals for outstanding writing. Keeping an eye on this prestigious award will help you discover some of the best fantasy written for children on a regular basis.

Although there are several distinctive awards for writers of fantasy and "speculative fiction" for adults, including the Hugo, Nebula, and World Fantasy awards, recognition of fantasy works for young people is also on the rise. Watching for these award announcements can help us keep up with the latest authors and trends in fantasy writing, too.

The Mythopoeic Fantasy Award for Children's Literature

Founded in 1967, The Mythopoeic Society is a nonprofit organization dedicated to the study of fantasy and mythic literature, especially the works of J. R. R. Tolkien, C. S. Lewis, and Charles Williams. Since 1992, the society has presented the Mythopoeic Fantasy Award for Children's Literature to honor books for younger readers (from picture books for beginning readers to young adult novels), written in the tradition of *The Hobbit* or *The Chronicles of Narnia*. Recent recipients include authors Jonathan Stroud, Terry Pratchett, Clare B. Dunkle, Catherine Fisher, Kristin Cashore, Grace Lin, and Megan Whalen Turner.

The Andre Norton Award

The Science Fiction and Fantasy Writers of America (SFWA) established an award to recognize outstanding science fiction and fantasy novels for young adults beginning in 2006. The award was named in honor of Andre Norton, author of more than 100 fantasy novels, many of them for young adult readers. Award recipients who write for young readers include Holly Black, J. K. Rowling, Catherynne M. Valente, and Terry Pratchett. The award targets the young adult population, but some works will be suitable for children, particularly those avid readers who are big fantasy fans.

Literature in Action: Expanding Reading with Audiobooks

As we strive to connect kids and books, we also need to keep in mind alternative formats that may help make that connection even more comfortable and likely for some young people. In particular, I have found that audiobooks are experiencing a resurgence of interest with many fantasy titles appearing in audio, as well as print. Personally, I am a huge fan of this format—particularly since I am a commuter. I can add at least a book a week to my routine by *listening* to a book. Plus, I enjoy the pleasure of listening to a professional narrator, hearing dialects pronounced properly, and so on. Kids enjoy these same features, as well as how relaxing audiobooks are—no struggling with decoding, just focusing on comprehension. And with the fantasy genre, many children enjoy listening to these longer, more challenging works. However, like anything, audiobooks have to be promoted. You have to let children know what they offer—listen to them yourself and talk about them, play tidbits to hook them, and so forth. Once children try them, word of mouth will sell them to other kids, especially 'tweens.

How Audiobooks Promote Literacy

Let's consider briefly why audiobooks are such an important medium. First, it taps into children's listening abilities. Researchers have consistently found that "Children who are better listeners are also better learners. . . . In particular, children who comprehend well through listening do the same when reading" (Lundsteen, 1979; Pinnell & Jagger, 1991). In fact, Kylene Beers (1998, p. 30) found that "Listening comprehension in the fifth grade was the best predictor of performance on a range of aptitude and achievement tests in high school." Clearly, listening promotes literacy. We know from reading aloud to children that they can follow along in a more advanced and difficult book than they might be capable of reading on their own, like fantasy novels, for example. That's because their listening vocabulary is always ahead of their knowledge of words in print. That is to say, there are words we know when we hear them, but we may not know how to spell or read them. Audiobooks can help bridge the gap. They can:

1. Foster an appreciation for literary language and expand vocabulary
2. Provide an example of fluent (even professional) models of oral reading
3. Model correct pronunciation of English, of various dialects, and of non-English words
4. Offer exposure to a variety of genres (including "harder" classics)
5. Help expand attention spans
6. Create a level playing field for a wide range of learners and abilities, including the need for material in multiple sensory modalities and for children with visual impairments
7. Inject a human factor, a personal connection, a sense of intimacy, a voice
8. Provide variety and a fun technological alternative

Recent surveys reveal that "fewer Americans are reading books than a decade ago, according to the National Endowment for the Arts, but almost a third more are listening to them on tapes, CDs, and iPods" (Harmon, 2005, p. 1). The growth in circulation of audiobooks is outpacing overall library circulation. Book clubs are increasingly made up of hybrid listener-readers, and the market for children's audiobooks is booming. Some librarians even lead "listening clubs" for which audio is the preferred medium. Clearly, we need to consider the audiobook format in our library collections.

Audiobook Publishers and Producers

As you look for audiobooks, you'll find that many print publishing houses produce their own audio versions alongside their print books, including Harcourt, Harper, Scholastic, and Simon & Schuster, for example. But there are also companies that specialize in producing only audiobooks, including my favorites Listening Library, Recorded Books, and Full Cast Audio. In fact, Listening Library, producer of the renowned audio versions of the Harry Potter series beautifully narrated by Jim Dale, often releases audio versions of titles simultaneously with their print publication. This enables readers *and* listeners to enjoy the best new books as soon as they're available. You'll also find free downloadable audio clips to use for booktalks and book discussions, as well as cover art, regular email newsletters and news alerts, and other educator resources at these publisher/producer websites. For a more complete listing of audiobook publishers, look for these names.

Bolinda Audio
Brilliance Audio
Cinco Puntos Productions
Crabtree Publishing
Findaway World (Playaways)
Full Cast Audio
Greathall Productions
Hachette Audio Books
Harcourt Children's Books
Harper Audio
Kidwick Books
Listen & Live Audio
Listening Library
Live Oak Media
Naxos of America
Recorded Books
Scholastic Audio
Simon and Schuster Audio
Smithsonian Books
Sourcebooks
Spoken Arts
Tantor Audiobooks
Warner Brothers
Weston Woods

If you're feeling especially enterprising, you can participate in creating your own recorded audiobooks. Books in the public domain can be read and recorded by anyone at Librivox.com and then made available worldwide. Tools like SoundCloud enable you to record your voice for any purpose. You could read a book excerpt for a digital booktalk or invite children to record their favorite paragraphs and add sound effects or background music—just be sure you're honoring copyright restrictions in choosing, recording, and disseminating your recordings.

Selecting Audiobooks

How do we know which audiobooks are best? A new award that is tremendously helpful was established to recognize excellence in audiobooks. The ALA Odyssey

Audiobook Award (sponsored by ALSC, *Booklist,* and YALSA) recognizes the best audiobook produced for children and/or young adults available in English in the United States. This award recognizes excellence by a producer for accomplishment and/or innovation in the production of an audio program. The winning title must exemplify the highest standards of direction, narration, engineering, and technical achievement. The stories of the wanderings of Ulysses are ascribed to the blind poet Homer and were originally told and retold in the oral tradition, hence the name for the Odyssey award, allowing us to return to the ancient roots of storytelling while living in our modern world.

For additional recommendations of outstanding audiobooks on an ongoing basis, check out these recommended lists:

- Grammy Awards for Spoken Word (www.grammy.com)
- Audio Publishers Association's Audie Awards (www.audiopub.org)
- ALSC Notable Children's Recordings
- YALSA Amazing Audiobooks for Young Adults

As we try to keep those children in the middle grades reading, at just the point when so many able readers stop, let's consider the value of audiobooks as an approach that may hook them on books for life, whether it's via tape cassette, compact disc (CD), or as downloadable audio files. Whether they are overscheduled overachievers or older children still struggling with reading mastery, audiobooks have great value in keeping books in their lives. Remember, "The idea is to put joy from listening into the lives of students who starve for beauty just as they starve for food" (Lundsteen, 1990, p. 224).

Audiobook Resources

As we seek out the best audiobooks for children, it helps to consult the experts on selecting, evaluating, and sharing audiobooks with young people. Mary Burkey, keeper of the acclaimed Audiobooker blog sponsored by *Booklist* and the author of *Audiobooks for Youth: A Practical Guide to Sound Literature,* suggests, "The best in recorded literature begins with the printed word and, through an ensemble of efforts, reflects and reshapes the text into an expressive new medium" (2012, p. 19). Consult these resources for more guidance on selecting and sharing audiobooks.

Audiobooker blog: http://audiobooker.booklistonline.com
Burkey, Mary. 2012. *Audiobooks for Youth: A Practical Guide to Sound Literature.* Chicago, IL: American Library Association.
Hannegan, Lizette, and Sharon Grover. 2011. *Listening to Learn: Audiobooks Supporting Literacy.* Chicago, IL: American Library Association.
Jon Scieszka's website on promoting listening to books: http://www.guyslisten.com
AudioFile Magazine, consumer magazine devoted to audiobooks: http://www.audiofilemagazine.com

SHARING FANTASY

Whether we're featuring fantasy audiobooks, reading a chapter aloud, or recommending new titles to eager readers, there are many possibilities for engaging kids in the reading of fantasy literature. We can seek out film adaptations of popular fantasy novels or look at the many new graphic novel formats for fantasy stories, for example. Kids themselves often have creative ideas for promoting the genre, too. In fact, readers of fantasy novels are often your brightest, most gifted kids—excellent allies in developing lists of recommended books, fantasy read-alike lists, posters and displays, author studies, digital trailers and glogs, and the like.

Novel-based Fantasy Films for Children

Many classic and beloved fantasy novels for young people have been adapted into live action and animated films, some multiple times by various filmmakers. Consider planning a "book and movie night" to promote reading and discussion of fantasy fiction. (Be sure to seek public performance rights.) Children in the middle grades particularly like to discuss the differences they see between book and movie versions. Often they have strong feelings about the difference between what their imaginations dream up and what they see on the screen. Create a book display featuring many of these fantasy film/ book titles (and DVDs) and have fantasy booklists ready. Of course, look for films based on comics such as Superman, Batman, Spiderman, Iron Man, and other superheroes. Here is just a sampling to consider.

Alice in Wonderland
Babe
The BFG
The Black Cauldron
The Borrowers
Charlie and the Chocolate Factory (or *Willie Wonka and the Chocolate Factory*)
Charlotte's Web
Chitty Chitty Bang Bang
The Chronicles of Narnia
City of Ember
The Dark Is Rising
Dr. Dolittle
Ella Enchanted
Ender's Game
Eragon
Five Children and It
Freaky Friday
Harry Potter films
The Hobbit
Holes
Howl's Moving Castle
Hugo
The Hunger Games
James and the Giant Peach
Lemony Snicket's A Series of Unfortunate Events
The Lord of the Rings trilogy
Mary Poppins

Matilda
Percy Jackson
Peter Pan
The Phantom Tollbooth
Pinocchio
Pippi Longstocking
The Secret of NIMH
Stuart Little
The Thief Lord
Tuck Everlasting
The Wind in the Willows
Winnie the Pooh
The Witches
The Wizard of Oz

The Mid-Continent Public Library maintains a handy database of movies based on books called "Based on the Book" (http://www.mcpl.lib.mo.us/readers/movies/). It is a compilation based on the Internet Movie Database (http://www.imdb.com) of over a thousand books, short stories, and plays that have been made into motion pictures released since 1980.

Graphic Novels for Children

A popular trend in publishing for children that builds upon the comics format is the graphic novel. In her book *Radical Change: Books for Youth in a Digital Age,* Eliza Dresang (H. W. Wilson, 1999) looks at the appeal of these new kinds of "handheld books" with graphic and nonlinear formats that today's young people find especially appealing. Many graphic novels are most appropriate for teen and adult readers, but there is a growing body of graphic novels and Japanese manga that is fun, appealing, and appropriate for children. In addition, comic books and cartoons are dominated by fantasy figures such as superheroes like Superman, Batman, and X-Men, and animated talking characters such as Road Runner, Bugs Bunny, and Mickey Mouse. Many comic strips, such as Garfield and Calvin and Hobbes, are also gathered in book format. And authors and illustrators are breaking the rules and creating new forms that blend text and visuals in innovative ways like Brian Selznick's Caldecott medal book, *The Invention of Hugo Cabret* (Scholastic, 2007) or his Schneider Award book, *Wonderstruck* (Scholastic, 2011). Thus, there is a fun connection here between fantasy fiction and graphic interpretation, and between the balance of text and visuals in book form. In an interview in *Children and Libraries,* Jennifer Holm, co-creator of *Babymouse,* commented, "I think certain genres, such as fantasy, especially lend themselves to graphic novels because of the opportunity for striking visuals. You can show an entirely new and fantastic world in a single panel" (Bird, 2007, p. 19).

Some libraries have had great success with comic, manga, and anime clubs devoted to this special niche. ALSC offers a recommended "Core Collection of Graphic Novels" list online at http://www.ala.org/alsc/compubs/booklists/

grphcnvls. The visual book format of the graphic novel has drawn many new readers to book clubs, particularly 'tweens and teens. Although there are graphic novels in nearly every genre, some of the most popular *fantasy* selections are presented here.

Baum, L. Frank. 2005. *The Wizard of Oz*. Adapted by Michael Cavallaro. New York: Puffin Books.

Dezago, Todd. 2001. *Tellos: Reluctant Heroes*. Illus. by Mike Wieringo. Berkeley, CA: Image Comics.

Eisner, Will. 2001. *The Last Knight*. New York: NBM Publishing.

Espinosa, Rod. 2003. *Courageous Princess*. San Antonio, TX: Antarctic.

Evanier, Mark. 2003. *Shrek*. Illus. by Ramon Bachs and Raul Fernandez. Milwaukie, OR: Dark Horse.

Grahame, Kenneth. 2003. *The Wind in the Willows: The Wild Wood*. Adapted and illus. by Michel Plessix. New York: NBM.

Harper, Charise Mericle. 2005. *Fashion Kitty*. New York: Hyperion.

Herge, Georges. 1994. *The Adventures of Tintin: Volume 1*. New York: Little, Brown.

Holm, Jennifer. 2005. *Babymouse: Queen of the World!* Illus. by Matthew Holm. New York: Random House.

Huddleston, Courtney. 2000. *Decoy*. Illus. by Don Jensen and others. Houston, TX: Penny-Farthing.

Krosoczka, Jarrett. 2009. *Lunch Lady and the Cyborg Substitute: Lunch Lady #1*. New York: Knopf.

Kunkel, Mike. 2003. *Herobear and the Kid: The Inheritance, v.1*. Toluca Lake, CA: Astonish Comics.

L'Engle, Madeleine. 2012. *A Wrinkle in Time*. Illus. by Hope Larson. New York: Farrar.

Morse, Scott. 2002. *Magic Pickle*. Portland, OR: Oni.

Nytra, David. 2012. *The Secret of the Stone Frog*. New York: TOON.

Pope, Paul. 2013. *Battling Boy*. New York: First Second.

Sfar, Joann. 2006. *Sardine in Outer Space*. New York: First Second/Roaring Brook.

Shelley, Mary. 2005. *Puffin Graphics: Frankenstein*. Adapted by Gary Reed. Illus. by Frazer Irving. New York: Puffin Books.

Smith, Jeff. 2003. *Bone: Out from Boneville, v.1*. New York: Scholastic/Cartoon Books.

Spiegelman, Art, and Françoise Mouly. Eds. 2003. *It Was a Dark and Silly Night*. New York: HarperCollins.

Stoker, Bram. 2006. *Puffin Graphics: Dracula*. Adapted by Gary Reed. Illus. by Becky Cloonan. New York: Puffin Books.

Tan, Shaun. 2007. *The Arrival*. New York: Scholastic.

Thompson, Jill. 2001. *Scary Godmother, v.1*. Sirius.

Torres, J. 2002. *Alison Dare: Little Miss Adventures*. Illus. by J. Bone. Portland, OR: Oni.

Trondheim, Lewis. 2006. *A.L.I.E.E.E.N. Archives of Lost Issues and Earthly Editions of Extraterrestrial Novelties*. New York: First Second/Roaring Brook.

Manga (comics translated from Japanese)

Kondo, Kazuhisa. 2002. *Mobile Suit Gundam 0079, v.1*. San Francisco, CA: Viz.

Miyazaki, Hayao. 1995. *Nausicaä of the Valley of the Wind Perfect Collection One*. San Francisco, CA: Viz.

Miyazaki, Hayao. 2002. *Miyazaki's Spirited Away, v.1*. San Francisco, CA: Viz.

Takeuchi, Naoko. 1998. *Sailor Moon, v.1*. Los Angeles, CA: Tokyopop.

Tanaka, Masashi. 2000. *Gon.* New York: DC Comics.
Tezuka, Osamu. 2002. *Astro Boy, v.1.* Milwaukie, OR: Dark Horse.

For more information on sharing graphic novels with kids, these resources may be helpful:

Goldsmith, Francisca. 2009. *The Readers' Advisory Guide to Graphic Novels.* Chicago, IL: American Library Association.
Gorman, Michelle. 2003. *Getting Graphic! Using Graphic Novels to Promote Literacy with Preteens and Teens.* Columbus, OH: Linworth.
Gorman, Michelle. 2007. Graphic Novels for Younger Readers. *Book Links.* May.
McCloud, Scott. 1994. *Understanding Comics: The Invisible Art.* New York: Morrow.
Pawuk, Michael. 2006. *Graphic Novels: A Genre Guide to Comic Books, Manga, and More.* Englewood, CO: Libraries Unlimited.

In their article, "Got Graphic Novels?" Baird and Jackson (2007) offer these helpful tips for librarians on collecting this graphic novel format:

- Include graphic novels in your library's collection development policy or statement
- Become knowledgeable about the genre through professional resources on this topic
- Read graphic novel reviews in library and education journals and preview books to help in the selection process
- Budget wisely and set aside funds to start up and maintain a viable collection, keeping in mind replacement costs
- Consider cataloging options, a separate place to house the collection with a graphic novel suffix
- Have a solid reconsideration and intellectual freedom policy
- Choose a well-placed display area with face-out shelving
- Be open to receiving suggestions from children (2007, p. 6)

You'll find additional "educator resources" at the Reading with Pictures website here: http://www.readingwithpictures.org/.

CONCLUSION

The genre of fantasy is rooted in ancient storytelling traditions of wonder and belief and stretches out toward an unknown future to speculate about what may lie ahead. For children, it offers something basic and something challenging at the same time. From complex high fantasy to deceptively simple low fantasy, from the milestone work *The Wizard of Oz* to the mega-bestsellers *Harry Potter* or *The Hunger Games*, from ghost stories to science fiction, fantasy literature provides an array of choices for readers of many ages, levels, and tastes. We have fantasy-based graphic novels, audiobooks, and films to choose from and a variety of connections to make. We can introduce avid fantasy fans to favorite series books or read aloud humorous fantasy to children less familiar with the genre. Either way, all children deserve exposure to this unique literature. As young Tiffany learns from the wise Mistress Weatherwax in Terry Pratchett's fantasy novel *A Hat Full of Sky* (HarperTeen, 2004, p. 202), "what I say is you have to tell people a story they can understand. Right now I reckon you'd have to change quite a lot of the world, and maybe bang Mr. Raddle's stupid fat head against the wall a few times, before he'd believe that you can be sickened by drinking tiny invisible beasts [that had been poisoning his well]. And while you're doing that, those kids of theirs will get sicker. But goblins, now, they makes sense today. *A story gets things done.*" We need facts and realism, of course, but make-believe stories can reveal important truths, too.

PROFESSIONAL RESOURCES IN FANTASY LITERATURE

If you are interested in additional resources to help you explore this genre further, the following books can be helpful.

Buker, Derek M. 2002. *Science Fiction and Fantasy Readers' Advisory: The Librarian's Guide to Cyborgs, Aliens, and Sorcerers.* Chicago, IL: American Library Association.

Garner, Joan. 2006. *Wings of Fancy: Using Readers Theatre to Study Fantasy Genre.* Englewood, CO: Libraries Unlimited.

Gates, Pamela S., Susan B. Steffel, and Francis J. Molson. 2003. *Fantasy Literature for Children and Young Adults.* Lanham, MD: Rowman & Littlefield.

Herald, Diana Tixier. 1999. *Fluent in Fantasy: A Guide to Reading Interests.* Englewood, CO: Libraries Unlimited.

James, Edward, and Farah Mendlesohn. 2012. *The Cambridge Companion to Fantasy Literature.* Cambridge, England: Cambridge University Press.

Johansen, K. V. 2005. *Quests and Kingdoms: A Grown-Up's Guide to Children's Fantasy Literature.* Sackville, New Brunswick: Sybertooth.

Manlove, Colin. 1999. *The Fantasy Literature of England.* New York: St. Martin's Press.

Marcus, Leonard. 2006. *The Wand in the Word: Conversations with Writers of Fantasy.* Cambridge, MA: Candlewick.

Nadelman, Lynn Ruth. 2005. *Fantasy Literature for Children and Young Adults: A Comprehensive Guide* (Fifth Edition). Englewood, CO: Libraries Unlimited.

Perry, Phyllis J. 2003. *Teaching Fantasy Novels: From* The Hobbit *to* Harry Potter and the Goblet of Fire. Englewood, CO: Libraries Unlimited.

Polette, Nancy. 2005. *Teaching Thinking Skills with Fairy Tales and Fantasy.* Englewood, CO: Libraries Unlimited.

Sandner, David. 1996. *The Fantastic Sublime: Romanticism and Transcendence in Nineteenth-Century Children's Fantasy Literature.* Westport, CT: Greenwood.

Sullivan, C. W. 1989. *Welsh Celtic Myth in Modern Fantasy.* Westport, CT: Greenwood.

Wadham, Rachel, and Tim Wadham. 1999. *Bringing Fantasy Alive for Children and Young Adults.* Columbus, OH: Linworth.

Yolen, Jane. 2005. *Touch Magic: Fantasy, Faerie and Folklore in the Literature of Childhood* (Expanded Edition). Atlanta, GA: August House.

Standards in Action: YALSA Competencies

The Young Adult Library Services Association (YALSA) is a division of the American Library Association (ALA) that supports library services to teens ages twelve to eighteen. When it comes to getting involved in ALA, we generally find a home in ALSC and/or YALSA, depending on whether we primarily serve children (ALSC focuses on ages birth to fourteen) or teens. You see there is overlap, so many people choose to belong to both organizations—as I do. Although we focus largely on children's literature in this book, the genres of longer fiction, particularly realistic novels and fantasy novels, become hugely popular as children mature in the teen years. Either way, I think it's important to familiarize ourselves with the professional competencies at both ends of the spectrum. We looked briefly at the ALSC competencies in Chapter One. YALSA developed these "Competencies for Librarians Serving Youth: Young Adults Deserve the Best" in 1981 and subsequently revised them in 1998, 2003, and 2010 (http://www.ala.org/yalsa/guidelines/yacompetencies2010). They include multiple objectives in each of the following categories.

Area I. Leadership and Professionalism
Area II. Knowledge of Client Group
Area III. Communication, Marketing, & Outreach
Area IV. Administration
Area V. Knowledge of Materials
Area VI. Access to Information
Area VII. Services

Reading this book and trying out many of the ideas and activities here will help prepare you to meet several of the YALSA competencies. In particular,

Area V. Knowledge of Materials

3. Demonstrate a knowledge and appreciation of literature for and by young adults in traditional and emerging formats.

Although the bulk of this book addresses literature for *children*, this chapter on fantasy, in particular, includes many authors and series that carry over to the field of young adult (YA) literature. Plus, we've considered alternative formats like the value of audiobooks. There is certainly a lot more to know when it comes to YA literature, so look for *Young Adult Literature in Action: A Librarian's Guide* by Rosemary Chance, the companion volume to this book, for more guidance.

Assignments in Action: Delving into Fantasy

1. Connecting with Traditional Tales

As presented earlier, many fantasy novels are rooted in the traditions of folk literature. Fantasy novels are original stories created from an author's imagination, rather than oral tales retold many times, yet they share many of the same attributes: archetypal characters such as the youngest child or gifted orphan or wise helper; settings in magical forests and faraway kingdoms; motifs such as transformations or the use of magical objects; patterns of three or four challenges or events. Choose a favorite fantasy novel and look for these elements from the oral tradition. Which ones are present? How do they affect the story? Why do you think the author included these and not others? Search the Internet for possible author interviews or the author's website to see if he or she addresses these allusions to folk literature.

2. Gifted Readers and Avatars and Second Life

Do you work with children who are identified as "gifted" or "talented?" For many gifted kids in the middle grades and up, fantasy is immensely popular, whether in the form of books, movies, graphic novels, or computer games. One outlet that is gaining increasing recognition is the creation of avatars, or unique online identities, for gaming, chatting, or online forums. Here, participants become authors of fantasy themselves. They do many of the things a fantasy author does: create and name a character, give it attributes and powers, and interact with other characters. Read more about this growing phenomenon, including concerns about child participation and child safety, here: http://www.gamestudies.org/0301/fromme/.

3. Manga Clubs and Comic Con

Graphic novels, anime, and manga are all very popular with 'tweens and teens, and many libraries have created clubs especially for fans of this medium. They gather to read, share, and compare their favorite titles, much like other book clubs. Look for a manga or anime club at a school or library in your community and attend a meeting. Which types and titles are favorites of the group? If possible, look for a comic con (or comic book-related convention) in your area to attend. These are also interesting sources of graphic novels, games, and other media for fans of fantasy.

8

Informational Books

"They had put man on the moon that day, true; but computers in 1969 barely had the computing power of today's hand-held calculators. So a lot of analysis was done the good old-fashioned way: paper, pencil, and brainpower."
From *Team Moon: How 400,000 People Landed* Apollo 11 *on the Moon* by Catherine Thimmesh (Houghton Mifflin, 2006)

In this chapter, we'll look at informational literature including biography. We will consider what is unique about this genre, what kinds of books are included, and how you evaluate them using unique criteria specific to this genre. You will also be introduced to major authors and awards in the genre, as well as resources and milestones worth noting. We'll review the variety of informational literature available nowadays from photo essay books to magazines and serials to series books. You'll read about ways to share nonfiction with children from reading aloud, to guiding research, to demonstrating the use of access features. We'll consider how this genre represents rich literature for recreational reading, as well as many excellent references for research and reporting.

INTRODUCTION

As informational literature for children enjoys more popularity than ever, it has also come under close scrutiny as we seek books that present factual information for children. Just how factual should a book for children be? Do children prefer a story over "straight" facts? Librarians, teachers, critics, and scholars are beginning to look closely at the writing of informational books and at children's responses to them. But just what do we mean when we talk about nonfiction for children? Critic Jo Carr divides nonfiction into two categories: "nonfiction that stuffs in facts, as if children were vases to be filled, and nonfiction that ignites the imagination, as if children were indeed fires to be lit" (1982, p. 710). For years and years, we had plenty of the former (facts) with woefully little of the latter (literature). However, as the genre has gained greater recognition, particularly through recent awards established to honor excellence in informational literature, more and more literary and engaging informational literature has been created for young people. In addition, the publishing industry continues to evolve with authors and illustrators experimenting with varying book format possibilities, approaching informational books in creative and sometimes unorthodox ways. Often the end result is a more appealing book for young people, if a more difficult book to pigeonhole.

Longtime nonfiction author Jean Fritz, perhaps the "grandmother" of honest biographies for children, wrote: "Thirty years ago when I started writing nonfiction for children, I was warned that I might find a hostile audience . . . children were apt to be suspicious of nonfiction as another ploy adults used to lure them to the academic world. I would have to invent dialogue, I was told, in order to disguise the factual nature of my books" (Fritz, 2001, p. 87). Of course, Fritz refused to do so and was one of the first authors for children to include source notes and bibliographies as well as dialogue that was documented in her informational works. Readers responded with enthusiasm. Child readers rose to the challenge and appreciated the frankness that Fritz brought to her biography writing. Telling a true *story* is fine, as long as the focus is on the truth.

Fortunately, there are many more choices in informational literature than ever before. A variety of topics, authors, and formats are abundant now. When I was growing up, most nonfiction consisted of dry, lengthy series books filled with small print and black and white pictures only. That has changed. The publishing world now provides a good variety of nonfiction for children on an amazing array of topics in formats that are colorful and appealing to the child reader. Many children are now also choosing informational books for their recreational reading—books about the *Titanic*, collections of gruesome facts, biographies of their favorite sports heroes, and so on. You may be surprised to learn that by grade five, many surveys of children's preferences show that boys, in particular, rate nonfiction books as their favorites. Nonfiction generally dominates the bestseller lists of adult books. In addition, many informational books for young people today are written with respect for the young reader, providing careful documentation of the research process. As author, editor, and teacher Marc Aronson has noted, "We are preparing students to catch ideas in flight, knowledge in formation." Whether we're looking for story-like nonfiction that contextualizes information, or a more journalistic approach, informational books for young people are not just for reference, research, and reports any more.

History in Action: Orbis Pictus

The *Orbis Pictus* or *Orbis Sensualium Pictus* (translated as "The Visible World" or "The World Around Us in Pictures"), published in 1657, is considered to be the first book planned and published for children. It also happens to be a work of nonfiction, an attempt to present the world in pictures for young people in a way that was intended to be visual and relevant. It was written by the Czech educator Jan Ámos Komenský (Johann Amos Comenius, 1592–1670) who had rather progressive notions about teaching children (both boys and girls) through illustrations that represented the real world. He was quite an important figure in the field of pedagogy and traveled the world lecturing on his ideas. His first book, *Orbis Pictus*, was something of an encyclopedia heavily illustrated with woodcuts of images of the natural world all labeled and described for young readers, the Renaissance counterpart to today's Eyewitness series.

The *Orbis Pictus* had 150 chapters and covered a wide range of subjects from botany to zoology to religion. Originally published in Latin and German in 1658 in Nuremberg, the book soon spread to schools in Germany and other countries. The first English edition was published in 1659, with quadrilingual editions to follow in Latin, German, Italian, and French in 1666. In the years 1670–1780, new editions were published in various languages with updated pictures and text. A version in English and Latin printed in 1777 is available in its entirety on Google Books via the University of Michigan. The University of Minnesota's Virtual Museum of Education Iconics offers a beautiful Orbis Sensualium Pictus Gallery with digitized images of several different versions of the *Orbis Pictus* (http://iconics.cehd.umn.edu/). Used as a picture book by young children and as a Latin textbook by older students, *Orbis Sensualium Pictus* was reprinted until well into the nineteenth century and remained a model for school books for 200 years. In fact, the very first book to be awarded the Newbery medal (in 1922), *The Story of Mankind* by Hendrik Willem van Loon, bears some similarities to *Orbis Pictus* in its wide sweep of subject matter, informational focus, and visual layout even though it appeared some 265 years later. *Orbis Pictus* is a worthy ancestor of our modern children's informational literature for several reasons:

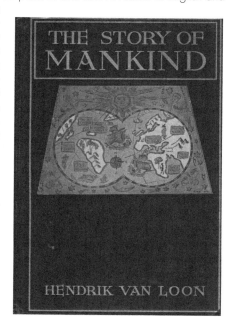

- It attempted to be relevant to children's curiosity about the real world.
- It provided abundant visuals to help children understand the concepts presented.
- It was well organized and sequenced with chapter headings, diagram labels, and an index.
- It was issued in bilingual and even quadrilingual editions to reach a wider readership.
- For its day, it reflected the author's passion for the subject matter in its content and design.

These are all worthy attributes of an outstanding book of informational literature even today. And that's why I'm pleased to boast that I suggested the name "Orbis Pictus" for the award for nonfiction established by the National Council of Teachers of English in 1990, when I served on that proposal committee. Yes, the NCTE Orbis Pictus Award for Outstanding Nonfiction for Children was named after the *Orbis Sensualim Pictus* because it was such a groundbreaking work for children. I'm lucky that my fellow committee members instantly loved it, and there was never any disagreement. Isn't it amazing that Comenius's vision still lives on in this way? Even the seal for the award reflects an image from the woodcut illustration in the original work. We're still looking for good nonfiction literature that shows kids the real world in a way that is appealing and informative—just as Comenius did in 1657.

DEFINITIONS

Many people in the field now use the label "informational books" to describe this genre. They prefer this phrase since they believe "nonfiction" to be a negative term. "Nonfiction" or "not fiction" suggests a negative association, a definition by non-example. On the other hand, the word "informational" is not entirely accurate either, since all books contain some information—even stories and poems. What is the answer? I tend to use the terms interchangeably because I'm interacting with different audiences including librarians, teachers, children, and families who may understand different labels. The key is understanding the genre and recognizing its purpose, seeing the wealth of information available on a wide range of subjects and the variety of approaches and formats that can engage readers of all ages.

The thing to keep in mind is this: usually the *purpose* of a nonfiction book is to inform. The typical purpose of fiction is to *entertain* or *provide escape*. Of course the lines between these two often get blurry. Many well-written informational books can be very entertaining. So don't worry about memorizing literary genre definitions as much as about making sure children have a steady diet of informational books available to them. Not only will you find that children enjoy them immensely, but this provides excellent preparation for the vast amount of information they'll be processing for the rest of their reading lives.

In *Edging the Boundaries of Children's Literature*, Carol Winters and Gary D. Schmidt (Allyn & Bacon, 2001) remind us that authors today look for a topic that engages them, researching it fully, documenting their sources, searching for the "telling detail," the "luminous anecdote," the perfect illustration. They focus on an event or a person and work at reproducing it in its complexity, not with "reductive simplicity." The best informational books for children have focus, directness, accessibility, and flair. They are not watered-down and simplistic.

Many people think of nonfiction as simply facts, but a close investigation of the genre reveals several different kinds of factual books within the general category of informational literature. Next, we'll consider a variety of subtypes of informational books currently available for young people.

Librarians in Action: Baby Steps in Researching with Children

Marnie Cushing received her bachelor of arts degree in English from the University of Texas of the Permian Basin in Odessa, Texas. She taught eighth grade English for several years in Andrews and Mesquite, Texas, as well as one year teaching U.S. history. She earned her master of library science degree from Texas Woman's University, was the librarian at Sue Ann Mackey Elementary School in Mesquite, Texas, for five years, and then moved to the high school level where she has found that researching with kids is the same whether they are kindergarteners or seniors—"baby" steps work with all levels! Here she writes about her efforts to promote research and inquiry with even the very youngest patrons.

Researching with First Graders
by Marnie Cushing

Don't be afraid of research. Children at any age can get excited about researching when it's made interesting and presented on a level they can understand. Research is a way to touch even the youngest students. Even kindergarteners ask questions, the foundation of the research and inquiry process.

At my school, Mackey Elementary, we try to break down the research process into chunks or components and introduce them incrementally at each grade level. For example, the first graders at my school love to come to the library to work on research. They are so excited to participate in something that at one time was only allotted to the "big" kids. Since we teach research at every level, K–5, the first grade students have already had some exposure to what they are about to do in the library. They can even tell me what they researched the previous year in kindergarten, and that is a great source of pride for the teachers *and* students.

One of the interesting units we work on during first grade is an animal unit. In our curriculum, the first grade students are expected to complete an informational chart on animals. We use this chart as our basis for introducing note taking. First graders are not adept at writing in the first semester, so we make the chart user-friendly with words to circle and simple, one-word answers to questions we propose. We also use a read aloud method that allows the students to hear the information and choose what they think needs to go into the chart. When the chart is completed over a three-day period (30 minutes each day in the library), we then discuss the similarities and differences between the animals. This may seem straightforward, but we take it one step further.

After we complete the reading and researching of facts about three different animals (bats, ants, and frogs), we then read informational picture books and picture storybooks that show these animals in humorous ways. One book we read is *I Saw a Bullfrog* by Ellen Stern (Random House, 2003), which features a drawing of a large frog's body with a bull's head attached to it on the cover of the book. The students get a big kick out of the funny fantastical animals. Then we ask the question, "How would the animals we studied be different if they were combined like the ones in the story?"

Each student then takes two out of the three pictures we provide them (a bat, an ant, or a frog), cuts them apart and mixes them together, making a "new" animal. They name their animals and then describe how the new animals would act differently with their new bodies. The names and pictures are so much fun and the students get a chance to create something unique and creative based on their knowledge of the facts.

Not only do the students enjoy the process, but the teachers do as well. This combination of reading, researching, and creative response activities is often something new for the teachers, too. It's important to me that the library is a place to make things fun and different, so there are new experiences for both kids and adults. Also, we're not interested in teaching the first graders how to fill out a proper note card or create a bibliography yet. We do explain why it is important to tell people where you found your information, and the children copy down the titles of the books we use in the library. That way, they have a foundation for what they will do in the coming years when they come back to the library for research. Then each year, we work on another piece of the research puzzle. Our hope is that when they get to middle school and high school they are completely comfortable with the research process and able to integrate the skills they have learned. Those baby steps occur in increments each year at Mackey Elementary School.

TYPES OF INFORMATIONAL BOOKS

For our purposes, we'll consider the following types of nonfiction or informational books based on the different purposes and formats of each: survey books, photo essays, concept books, social histories, informational storybooks, activity books, trivia books, series books, and other informational book formats. Each is defined by how it organizes or presents information for the child reader. Each has differing purposes for browsing, skimming, reading, or researching. Some lend themselves to reading aloud, like informational storybooks or social histories or concept books, while others are ideal for creating displays such as photo essays, activity books, and trivia books. This variety reminds us of the potential that this genre of literature offers for motivating young readers. Let's look at each type and consider a few example titles and authors.

Survey Books

Survey books acquaint readers with a topic by providing a general overview of that topic. This is probably the most abundant type of informational literature available for young people. As children's literature scholar Hepler reminds us, a survey work of nonfiction offers "an introduction to a topic and includes representative subtopics, but it may not necessarily cover all information" (1998, p. 9). For example, the prolific nonfiction author Gail Gibbons offers basic survey books in the picture book format with colorful cartoon-style illustrations, helpful captions, and exposition on nearly 200 different subjects. As children express interest in particular subjects, we can seek out more books for further reading. It is often here that we can discover the hidden, unexpressed reading interests of the reluctant reader, in particular. One example of an excellent survey-style book of informational literature is Steve Jenkins's amazing *The Animal Book: A Collection of the Fastest, Fiercest, Toughest, Cleverest, Shyest—and Most Surprising—Animals on Earth* (Houghton Mifflin Harcourt, 2013), a highly visual, comprehensive, and fascinating examination of 300 different animals. Or look for Karen Blumenthal's *Let Me Play: The Story of Title IX: The Law That Changed the Future of Girls in America* (Atheneum, 2005), about girls in sports and a mini-history of women's rights, too. Other authors who are known for creating outstanding survey books include Milton Meltzer, Franklyn Branley, Patricia Lauber, Dorothy Hinshaw Patent, Aliki, James Deem, and Caroline Arnold.

Photo Essays

Another very popular format for informational books for kids is the highly visual photo essay book. Much like a documentary film or an issue of *National Geographic Magazine*, photo essays document the text with photographs on nearly every page. The photo essay book "particularizes and personalizes information making it more emotionally involving for the reader or documents and validates the truth of the text with photographs" (Hepler, 1998, p. 8). These "junior" coffee table books are definitely designed for a wide audience of readers from the early grades through high school. Most of us use books such as these to gain an overview of a topic or to see visual representations to supplement our text-based knowledge. For this reason, photo essays transcend grade levels so long as the topic is appropriate to the reader's maturity level. One outstanding example is Sy Montgomery's ALA Sibert honor book, *The Tarantula Scientist* (Houghton Mifflin, 2004), with amazing photographs of the scientist in action by Nic Bishop. Authors who are known for creating outstanding photo essay books include George Ancona, Diane Hoyt-Goldsmith, Sandra Markle, Nic Bishop, and Seymour Simon.

Concept Books

Concept books present basic information about a single topic simply, distilled to its most basic terms with topics such as directionality (left/right), time, seasons, and so on. Concept books "explore the characteristics of a class of objects or of an abstract idea . . . typically size, color, shape, or spatial relationships . . . patterns in a class (for young children) . . . and cross-cultural concept books for older children" (Hepler, 1998, p. 7). This is probably the most popular form of informational literature for our very youngest readers. Thus, there is an essential and clear correlation between the topic and images, as well as between text and illustration. For instance, Tana Hoban used photographs illustrating groupings of objects for a variety of purposes in her photo-illustrated concept books for young readers. In contrast, Steve Jenkins uses collage illustrations in his works, including the concept book *What Do You Do with a Tail Like This?* (Houghton Mifflin, 2003). While these books are often thought of as books for young children, they can also be tremendously helpful for children learning new vocabulary in English, for example.

Authors who are known for creating outstanding concept books include Ann Morris and Ken Heyman, Mary Lankford, Bruce McMillan, Brian Floca, and Lois Ehlert.

Social Histories

A popular format for middle grade readers and above, social history books present information in the context of its impact on human history. For this type of informational book, primary source documents often help form the content of the book or provide organizational principles. This might include archival photographs, actual letters, eyewitness accounts, and so forth. Jim Murphy's dual Sibert and Orbis Pictus award-winning title *An American Plague* (Houghton Mifflin, 2003) or his fascinating *Invincible Microbe: Tuberculosis and the Never-Ending Search for a Cure* (Clarion, 2012) are both outstanding examples of this kind of top-notch social history for young readers. Susan Campbell Bartoletti's work, such as *They Called Themselves the K.K.K.: The Birth of an American Terrorist Group* (Houghton Mifflin Harcourt, 2010), offers vivid and disconcerting slices of history with a balanced perspective. These books are usually historical or sociological in nature, weaving together perspectives on how people have coped with challenges throughout history. Many of our most esteemed authors of nonfiction for children create award-winning social histories for kids, including Jim Murphy, Susan Campbell Bartoletti, Russell Freedman, Jerry Stanley, Rhoda Blumberg, Tonya Lee Stone, Kadir Nelson, Steve Sheinkin, Deborah Hopkinson, Phillip Hoose, Tonya Bolden, and James Cross Giblin.

Informational Storybooks

Informational storybooks are picture books that share information in a *story* context, such as in the Sibert and Orbis Pictus award-winning *Balloons over Broadway: The True Story of the Puppeteer of Macy's Parade* (Houghton Mifflin Harcourt, 2011) by Melissa Sweet, a fascinating and beautifully illustrated look at the story behind the famous Thanksgiving parade. This hybrid subgenre utilizes a story line to carry the information in a lively fashion, sometimes incorporating imaginative or fantastical happenings as in the *Magic School Bus* series—which provides an opportunity to help children see the difference between fact and "nonfact." For clues that a book is an informational book, look for a foreword, afterword, text notes, source notes, acknowledgments, and the like. However, scholar and expert Patricia Cianciolo cautions us that "Only if the story elements (characters, plot, etc.) are indeed skeletal, so that they do not distract from the author's primary and basic purpose (which should be to inform the reader) does it seem acceptable to couch information in a story (especially a fanciful one) or narrative verse" (2000, p. 23). Authors who are known for creating outstanding informational storybooks include Kathryn Lasky, Jim Arnosky, Robert Byrd, and Barbara Bash.

Activity Books

Activity books invite readers to engage in activities beyond reading by doing what they are reading about. The hands-on approach of how-to books, craft books, cookbooks, and experiment books directly involves children and is a very appealing format for the blossoming hobbyist. These books are designed to initiate activity and are full of diagrams, drawings, and examples. The text tends to be minimal in how-to books with an emphasis on directions, captions, sidebars, and so on, very much like a manual or guidebook or field guide. One fun and outstanding example is Jean Craighead George's *How to Talk to Your Dog*, illustrated with engaging and helpful cartoons by Sue Truesdell (HarperCollins, 2000), and another very popular example is Lee Ames's "drawing book" series including *Draw the Draw 50 Way: How to Draw Cats, Puppies, Horses, Buildings, Birds, Aliens, Boats, Trains, and Everything Else Under the Sun* (Watson-Guptill, 2012). Other authors who are known for creating outstanding how-to books include Herbert Zim and Vicki Cobb.

Trivia Books

Though literary critics would discount these as having any literary value at all, books of trivia, almanacs of facts, and accounts of strange and bizarre occurrences make up one of the most popular forms of informational books among children and young adults. Many are presented in short story narratives and usually make quick and pithy read alouds. They also often lure struggling readers into browsing through a book—or even reading a whole book—for the very first time. One example that is very popular is *The Top Ten of Everything* published annually by DK Publishing and full of fascinating lists based on statistical data on a diverse range of subjects, from blockbuster movies to crime data to popular drinks to tallest buildings. Similar books published on a regular basis include *The World Almanac and Book of Facts, The Scholastic Book of World Records, TIME for Kids Big Book of What*, and of course the *Guinness Book of World Records* (and its many spin-offs). National Geographic regularly produces highly visual books full of fun facts and trivia such as *Kids Quiz Whiz: 1,000 Super Fun, Mind-bending, Totally Awesome Trivia Questions* (2012), *5,000 Awesome Facts (About Everything!)* (2012), and *Weird but True! 5: 300 Outrageous Facts* (2013). These types of miscellany are often the most popular selections at book fairs and offer fun choices for quick browsing, reading aloud, and spontaneous sharing.

Series Books and Reference Tools

Nonfiction series books are generally defined by virtue of their *publisher*, rather than by author or even topic; they are usually initiated by a publishing house based on a perceived need, rather than by an author interested in a particular topic. Publishers count on the utility of the topic as a reference tool.

But many also experiment with organization and format to create a more reader-friendly book. For example, the Eyewitness series practically reinvented the survey format with its stark white backgrounds, close-up photographs, and catchy captions and reinvigorated the entire genre.

The advantage of the series is that they usually contain the most current information, are widely inclusive of topics (all 50 states in the United States, for example), cover topics that might not otherwise be written about, and enable us to meet the often idiosyncratic needs of the individual reader. Unfortunately, there are also some obvious disadvantages with series in that the books are not always models of lively writing, may lack depth and coherence, and may be a bit dry for the child reader. However, the variety of subject areas is impressive. There are series books for various age groups and reading levels (even in "I can read" formats). New topical series books pop up on unlikely subjects on a regular basis (e.g., food, diseases). What is the most unusual area you have noticed for a series of books to be written about? Publishers often welcome suggestions from librarians for new subject areas that may be needed.

Of course, dictionaries, thesauruses, atlases, encyclopedias, and other reference tools are also considered informational books and are an important part of a good nonfiction collection—whether in print or digital format. These do not usually circulate, but many children enjoy browsing through them and need some guidance in using these tools effectively.

Some authors create a kind of "series" of their own by virtue of the genre or type of books they regularly create (biographies by Russell Freedman), the book topic (science books by Seymour Simon, Sy Montgomery, Laurence Pringle, Gail Gibbons, or Dorothy Hinshaw Patent), or the consistent book format (picture book biographies by David Adler). The key difference here is that each of these books is the product of an author's personal interest in a topic based on careful research with sources cited and a lively, engaging writing style reflecting the individual voice and passion of the nonfiction author who chose the topic.

More Possible Formats for Informational Books

Nonfiction comes in all kinds of "packages"; there are picture books and reference works that also count as informational literature, yet we may not think of them in this genre. Many picture books shelved in the "easy" or "picture book" area are actually nonfiction, with a focus on sharing information, rather than telling a story. Or some nonfiction books are shelved in their Dewey categories but never sought for routine reports and research. But these nuggets of nonfiction all have potential for information and entertainment. In addition, when we recognize a book's purpose, we can approach it differently and maximize the book experience for children. Look for these additional formats for a great deal of informational literature:

- Counting books
- ABC books
- Journals
- Advice books

- Local history books
- Board books
- Predictable books
- Annuals/yearbooks
- Pop-up/moveable/engineered books
- Games, rules, and sports books

Magazines, Serials, and Periodicals

Magazines, serials, and periodicals are another format that is worth considering even though this format is in flux as more publications go strictly online. Magazines hold a great deal of appeal to kids since they seem very "grown-up," are highly visual and current, and are browsable and stigma-free for older struggling readers or new English learners. Generally informational in content, some magazines, like *Cricket*, include original fiction, too. Subscriptions are generally very affordable, and families often enjoy sponsoring subscriptions in honor of children's birthdays or other special occasions. We can even choose magazines with content specifically tailored to the interests of children at various age levels. Some magazines for children even accept submissions from their readers, which can encourage children's writing. Most magazines also maintain lively and interactive websites to supplement the print version, including puzzles, articles, apps, chat rooms, and other features. Some kids' favorites are the following:

Sports Illustrated for Kids
http://www.sikids.com

Cricket Magazine group
http://www.cricketmag.com

Time Magazine for Kids
http://www.timeforkids.com

Owl, Chirp, and Chickadee magazines
http://www.owlkids.com/

National Geographic Kids magazine
http://kids.nationalgeographic.com/

Cobblestone
http://www.cobblestonepub.com

Boy's Life
http://boyslife.org

Highlights for Children
http://www.highlightsforchildren.com

Kids Discover
http://www.kidsdiscover.com

Nickelodeon Magazine
http://www.nick.com

Skipping Stones
http://www.skippingstones.org

Stone Soup
http://www.stonesoup.com

Zoobooks
http://www.zoobooks.com

Mad Magazine
http://www.dccomics.com/mad/

Note: I know what you're thinking: magazines are a poor investment since they don't last long. True. However, for less than $20 for one year-long subscription, you can create a great deal of buzz in the library, have one issue travel across many, many readers, and build an ongoing enthusiasm for reading. For some kids, it may be the first time that they think of themselves as readers at all. That's a bargain, don't you agree?

Where Do Biographies Fit?

Biography is obviously a form of nonfiction. It is an informational book with a real person as its subject—a true story. However, in years gone by biography often resembled fiction more than nonfiction. In the past, biographers emphasized the *story*, often creating characters, dialogue, and events to "fill in the blanks" or add interest. Nowadays, we hold biography to the same standards we use for the writing of all nonfiction. Although there may be a story-like frame, the book should be accurate and factual, well organized, well designed, and well written.

Biographies are books that try "to breathe life and meaning into people and events," according to children's literature expert Charlotte Huck (2000, p. 634). Professor and scholar Donna Norton (2011) describes biography as the "story of a life" rather than as the "history of a life"; it should be "true to the reality of that person's life." When we read a biography of a person like Eleanor Roosevelt, for example, we want to know about her as a person, not just about the events and times in which she lived. It's kind of like literary people-watching. For children, the challenge is finding subjects that interest them (like athletes or celebrities), as well as providing scaffolding for their knowledge base about historical people so that they have some understanding about why this person is worth reading about. For example, not only was Eleanor Roosevelt a First Lady, but she was the first wife of a president to drive her own car, to travel by plane, and to earn her own money, as we learn in *Eleanor Roosevelt, a Life of Discovery* by Russell Freedman (Clarion, 1997).

Often we have to provide a "hook" or motivation to interest children in reading biographies of people in the past. But somehow, things change over the years because biography has become one of the most popular genres for *adult* reading. For example, check out the current as well as historical personalities and biographical profiles available online at http://www.biography.com. We are curious about how other people live and act, and biographies can help satisfy that curiosity. An effective librarian can also link this innate curiosity about people with books about the historical period or life events surrounding the biographical subject.

Biographies for children used to be limited to simplistic books mostly about presidents. In addition, these old biographies tended only to glorify the (dead white) man's achievements, without sharing any of his more human qualities. Thankfully, that has changed. Biographies for children today are much more varied. One of the major trends now is the availability of biographies on all kinds of people—women, people of color, ordinary citizens, even villains (such as Adolf Hitler). In addition, biographies now include a more well-rounded portrait of the subject that shares the flaws as well as the successes of the person. Some adults worry that children will lose their respect for our heroes of the past. But it seems as though we respect those heroes even more when we realize what personal flaws and obstacles they had to overcome to become successful. Hey, they're just like us, human beings—then maybe there is hope for all of us to do something meaningful with our lives.

Types of Biographies

There are several different types of biographies for young people worth considering, depending on the subject matter or the format. There are many traditional "cradle-to-grave" narratives about famous Americans, as well as biographies about a more diverse range of subjects, and even picture book formats for younger readers. In addition, many current biographies incorporate visuals such as photographs, facsimiles of primary source documents, and other illustrative material to add content and appeal to the biographical treatment.

Complete Biographies.   We generally begin sharing biographies with children with the intent to introduce them to famous people in history. And there are many strong examples of current biography that do a very good job of that. Jean Fritz ushered in a new era in honest biography writing for children when she penned her "collection" of brief, authentic, and humorous biographies of American Revolutionary figures for the U.S. bicentennial in 1976. Just consider *What's the Big Idea, Ben Franklin?* by Jean Fritz (Putnam, reissued 1996) in which one learns of Franklin's fierce competition with his brother, as well as about his penchant for invention. Several years later, Russell Freedman began writing biographies for children, and his *Lincoln, a Photobiography* (Clarion, 1987) even won the Newbery award for the best children's book of the year, a special distinction for nonfiction literature. It was from this book, for example, that I learned that this famous president hated to be called "Abe."

Indeed, Russell Freedman is generally considered the master of well-researched and well-documented biographies for young people, setting a high standard for others who choose to frame meaningful and interesting biographies for the middle grades and above. His subjects have included Ben Franklin, Martha Graham, Louis Braille, Franklin and Eleanor Roosevelt, Abraham Lincoln, the Wright brothers, Chief Crazy Horse, Babe Didrikson Zaharias, Confucius, and Marco Polo, running the gamut from the "usual suspects" in biography writing (presidents, first ladies) to surprising and significant choices of people whose lives provide interesting material for close study.

Since the late 1970s, authors have broadened their scope of biographical subjects to include a greater variety of people worth reading about. More books are being written about the lives of individuals who made significant contributions to society but were often overlooked in the history books. For example, Marian Anderson is the subject of Russell Freedman's *The Voice That Challenged a Nation: Marian Anderson and the Struggle for Equal Rights* (Clarion Books, 2004), which won both Orbis Pictus and Sibert honor distinctions for its excellent depiction of the life of this talented singer and civil rights icon. Tanya Lee Stone tells the compelling true story of the first African American paratroopers during World War II in *Courage Has No Color, the True Story of the Triple Nickles: America's First Black Paratroopers* (Candlewick, 2013).

Picture Book Biographies.   Enticing children to read biographies got a little bit easier with the arrival of picture book biographies. Here the presence of extensive illustrations adds visual interest along with pictorial details that enhance the authenticity of the time and place of the setting. In addition, the art helps personalize the subject. Therefore, the illustrations must be based on careful research and enhance the accuracy, as well as the appeal of the content. Of course, Diane Stanley's picture books are outstanding examples of this type of biography, with her treatment of *Leonardo da Vinci* (Morrow, 1996) winning the Orbis Pictus award and *Michelangelo* (HarperCollins, 2003) garnering Orbis Pictus honors. David Adler has also created many picture book biographies such as *A Picture Book of Harry Houdini* with Michael Adler, vividly illustrated by Matt Collins (Holiday House, 2009). More quality picture book biographies can be found by these authors as well as by Don Brown, Barbara Kerley, Tanya Lee Stone, Pam Muñoz Ryan, Jan Greenberg, Kathryn Lasky, Jen Bryant, Deborah Kogan Ray, Jonah Winter, and Jeanette Winter. Although these may be marketed as "first" books for young children, they provide a helpful, very visual introduction to important and interesting people for readers of any age.

Biography Series.   Many publishing companies have also created biographical series in which each book has a fairly standard appearance and content. Most of the time these are simply intended as curriculum resources for school or public libraries. They do, however, include biographical subjects who are often otherwise neglected, especially famous women and people of color. This includes the *DK Biography* series, *Time for Kids* biographies, *The Childhood of*

Famous Americans series, Graphic Library's *Graphic Biographies* series, and the popular Grosset & Dunlap *Who Was* series of "big head" biographies with a caricature cartoon image of the subject on the cover with an oversized head and small body.

Celebrity Biographies. Another trend in the publication of biography is the celebrity biography about the latest movie actor, rock star, or prize-winning athlete, often as part of a biography series. These may not be the most in-depth or well-balanced types of biography writing at its best, but they are often very popular with children and may lure them into reading and discussing the genre of biography when no other subject will. In fact, this is a good example of how biography reading can become pleasure reading, and not just reading about famous people for an assignment.

Collective Biographies. Collective biographies are also a helpful format in that several short biographies are presented together in one book, and they are usually linked in some way. Over the years, Kathleen Krull has built up quite a good reputation for writing excellent collective biographies, for example, seamlessly weaving together historical fact with hysterical details such as *Lives of the Presidents: Fame, Shame (and What the Neighbors Thought)* illustrated by Kathryn Hewitt (Houghton Mifflin Harcourt, 2011). Judith St. George and Cheryl Harness have each created interesting collective biographies as well, including St. George's Caldecott medal winner, *So You Want to Be President?* illustrated by David Small (Philomel, 2000).

Autobiographies. Autobiographies and memoirs are biographies written by the subjects themselves. Thus, these books can be biased or more subjective than those written by impartial authors, but they can also provide interesting personal insights into character and personality. Not many people write autobiographies intended for or suitable for children, but one series published by Richard Owen is a popular one. It's the "Meet the Author Collection," with individual authors and illustrators of children's books telling their own life stories in words and pictures. For other examples, look for *The Wall: Growing Up Behind the Iron Curtain* by Peter Sís (Farrar, 2007), depicting his youth in Communist Czechoslovakia, or *Bill Peet: An Autobiography* by Bill Peet (Houghton Mifflin, 1994) about the picture book author and artist who started out with Disney. For teen readers, there are even more choices, including popular celebrity autobiographies.

Evaluating Biography

In evaluating biographies, we hold them to the same rigorous criteria we apply to all nonfiction: accuracy, organization, design, and style. One of the "gold standards" is the presence of documentable dialogue. If a character speaks a line in a biography, there ought to be documentation of what journal or diary or record those words came from. Otherwise, the book is veering toward being considered historical fiction. Invented conversations are generally considered taboo and detract from the overall authenticity of a good biography. Of course, we also want to avoid glorifying the subject, while we still want subjects worthy of our attention. Maintaining objectivity and avoiding sentimentality are crucial; as much as we might want to preach to children, they are supremely resistant to moralizing lessons and deserve good stories, rather than good sermons, when it comes to good biographies.

MAJOR AUTHORS OF INFORMATIONAL BOOKS

Nonfiction books are written by many different kinds of people, from subject area experts to authors known more for their fiction writing. There are more and more writers who are writing only informational books and whose work has been recognized as both well researched and full of lively and interesting writing. They have established a reputation as thorough and careful researchers of content, as well as writers with a distinctive style and voice that captures readers of all ages. If you read several books by Seymour Simon, for example, you will find a consistent use of photographs gleaned from scientific sources. He is also known for his direct and focused style of writing that includes concrete comparisons that help readers visualize data and statistics, such as "the tongue of the blue whale weighs as much as a truck." Students who enjoy the area of science will find themselves drawn to the work of Seymour Simon.

Why not include nonfiction authors when we feature an author study or author center? Designate a set area, gather several books by one nonfiction author, post a booklist of her or his work, and display a few interesting biographical facts and perhaps a photo, now easier to find via author websites. Feature nonfiction authors/illustrators in booktalks, displays, and author visits. Children can be introduced to new authors whose work they may enjoy for their leisure reading, as well as gain exposure to high-quality expository writing, which can help inform their own attempts at composing reports.

Nonfiction Authors by the Numbers

Just for fun, some of the biggest names in nonfiction writing for young people today are listed below according to how one of their exemplary works is classified using the Dewey Decimal system. A quick glance reveals outstanding writers in every major category of nonfiction, with new titles and authors emerging all the time. Of course, each of the authors listed below has created many other informational books that may fall in many other Dewey categories. This is just a sampling.

100—Philosophy and Psychology
Kathleen Krull, *Sigmund Freud* (Penguin, 2006)

200—Religion
Diane Hoyt-Goldsmith, *Celebrating Ramadan* (Holiday House, 2005)

300—Social Sciences

David Adler, *Heroes of Civil Rights* (Holiday House, 2007)

Tonya Bolden, *M.L.K. Journey of a King* (Abrams, 2007)

Susan Kuklin, *Families* (Hyperion, 2006)

Kathryn Lasky, *John Muir: America's First Environmentalist* (Candlewick, 2006)

Ann Morris, *Grandma Hekmat Remembers: An Egyptian-American Family Story* (Lerner, 2003)

Jerry Stanley, *Children of the Dust Bowl: The True Story of the School at Weedpatch Camp* (Random House, 1993)

Tanya Lee Stone, *Almost Astronauts: 13 Women Who Dared to Dream* (Candlewick, 2009)

400—Language

Tana Hoban, *I Wonder* (Harcourt, 2003)

500—Science

Jim Arnosky, *Shimmer & Splash: The Sparkling World of Sea Life* (Sterling, 2013)

Franklyn Branley, *Volcanoes* (HarperCollins, 2008)

Joanna Cole, *The Magic School Bus and the Science Fair Expedition* (Scholastic, 2006)

Gail Gibbons, *Beavers* (Holiday House, 2013)

Steve Jenkins, *The Animal Book: A Collection of the Fastest, Fiercest, Toughest, Cleverest, Shyest—and Most Surprising—Animals on Earth* (Houghton Mifflin Harcourt, 2013)

Sandra Markle, *The Case of the Vanishing Honeybees: A Scientific Mystery* (Millbrook, 2013)

Sy Montgomery, *Kakapo Rescue: Saving the World's Strangest Parrot* (Houghton Mifflin, 2010)

Laurence Pringle, *Scorpions: Strange and Wonderful* (Boyds Mills Press, 2013)

Seymour Simon, *Killer Whales* (HarperCollins, 2007)

600—Technology

Patricia Lauber, *The True-or-False Book of Dogs* (HarperCollins, 2003)

Jim Murphy, *Invincible Microbe: Tuberculosis and the Never-Ending Search for a Cure* (Clarion, 2012)

Steve Sheinkin, *Bomb: The Race to Build—and Steal—the World's Most Dangerous Weapon* (Flashpoint/Roaring Brook, 2012)

Judith St. George, *So You Want to Be an Inventor?* (Penguin, 2002)

700—Arts and Recreation

Aliki, *Ah, Music!* (HarperCollins, 2003)

George Ancona, *Capoeira: Game! Dance! Martial Art!* (Lee & Low, 2007)

Jan Greenberg and Sandra Jordan, *Ballet for Martha: Making Appalachian Spring* (Roaring Brook, 2010)

Diane Stanley, *Michelangelo* (HarperCollins, 2003)

800—Literature

Don Brown, *American Boy: The Adventures of Mark Twain* (Houghton Mifflin, 2006)

Milton Meltzer, *Henry David Thoreau: A Biography* (Lerner, 2007)

900—History and Geography

Susan Campbell Bartoletti, *They Called Themselves the K.K.K.: The Birth of an American Terrorist Group* (Houghton Mifflin Harcourt, 2010)

Rhoda Blumberg, *York's Adventures with Lewis and Clark: An African-American's Part in the Great Expedition* (HarperCollins, 2004)

Lynn Curlee, *Parthenon* (Atheneum, 2011)

Russell Freedman, *Abraham Lincoln and Frederick Douglass: The Story Behind an American Friendship* (Houghton Mifflin, 2012)

Jean Fritz, *Who's Saying What in Jamestown, Thomas Savage?* (Penguin, 2007)

James Cross Giblin, *Good Brother, Bad Brother: The Story of Edwin Booth and John Wilkes Booth* (Houghton Mifflin, 2005)

Cheryl Harness, *Mary Walker Wears the Pants: The True Story of the Doctor, Reformer, and Civil War Hero* (Albert Whitman, 2013)

Favorite fiction authors typically get a fair amount of attention and admiration from children. Few nonfiction authors (or illustrators), however, get the same treatment. Yet many nonfiction authors are emerging as popular, engaging, knowledgeable, and productive. People like Gail Gibbons, Milton Meltzer, Russell Freedman, Kathleen Krull, Steve Jenkins, Sy Montgomery, and Seymour Simon (to name just a few) have each produced a dozen or more works of high quality and appeal. Encourage children to read a variety of works by an emerging favorite, to examine the element of style of writing in informational books, and to consider how an author's interests guide his or her choices of topics for their writing.

Authors in Action: Seymour Simon

Seymour Simon may well be one of the most prolific authors of nonfiction for children, with over 275 books published on a great variety of science topics, more than 75 of which have been named Outstanding Science Trade Books for Children by the National Science Teachers Association (NSTA). He has been recognized with an abundance of awards and recognitions, including the American Association for the Advancement of Science (AAAS)/Subaru Lifetime Achievement Award for his lasting contribution to children's science literature, and the Lifetime Achievement Award from the National Forum on Children's Science Books. He is also the founder of StarWalk Kids Media, a publisher of high-quality eBooks for children.

Born in New York and a former science and writing teacher in New York public schools for nearly 25 years, Simon has authored engaging nonfiction for children since the early 1970s, and his classic *The Paper Airplane Book* (Penguin Random House, 1971) is still in print. With topics ranging from space to animals, the natural world to the human body, weather disasters to optical illusions, you are sure to find an engaging nonfiction picture book by Seymour Simon for sharing with children. In fact, his name has become synonymous with the photo essay format, as he incorporates eye-popping photographs and graphics to grab the viewer and inform the reader. Here, he writes about his process for finding these amazing visuals, his ongoing quest to involve young readers in science on multiple fronts, and his foray into digital media.

Science in Action
by Seymour Simon

I've written more than 275 books on science subjects, so one might think that I've written books about every possible topic. Well, if one thought that, one would be wrong. I have so many new projects that I am interested in that it's difficult to even know where to start telling about them!

Let me begin by saying that I'm excited about the new books I'm writing for my ongoing HarperCollins photo essay series, which has grown to encompass 28 subjects, with four more in the works. I've just finished *Coral Reefs* (a companion to my other Earth Science/Environmental titles *Global Warming* and *Tropical Rainforests*), and I'm currently writing *Frogs* for that same series. Frogs are fascinating amphibians, and the photographs should be spectacular. I'm also very pleased to have a new series with Chronicle Books, publisher of my See More Readers a few years ago. These new books are very exciting to research and write because they are all about things that are "extreme." The first two books are *Extreme Earth Records* and *Extreme Oceans*. I love both the design and the fascinating information that we were able to convey with every spread. Kids are captivated by amazing details, to say nothing of imagining themselves in extreme environments like these!

All of these books are photo essay books, and finding and choosing the best photographs on each of these topics is part of creating the narrative. Text and images must work together to tell the story in a successful photo essay. These days, my photo research is largely done on the Internet, where I locate, view, and get permission to use pictures that I might want for one of my books. Of course, I also take many photographs in nature, so when I can I use one of my own shots for a particular book. The photographs that I use in my books must be scientifically accurate, informative, and highly dramatic, so they have to have a "gee-whiz" impact on the reader. A photo like that is often not easy to find, and that's why my photo research for an upcoming book may take weeks or even months.

The other exciting thing to report is that over the last two years I've written eight original eBooks for my children's digital publishing company, StarWalk Kids Media, including a major new space book that I am very proud of—*Earth: A Shipmate's Guide to Our Solar System*. I founded StarWalk Kids in 2011 with my wife and partner, Liz Nealon, who is the former creative director of Sesame Street. I could see that we were at the beginning of a profound digital shift in learning styles, and it was clear that there was going to be a need for high-quality literary nonfiction (and fiction) eBooks in schools and libraries. As I'm fond of saying, "I wanted my eBooks to be on the best possible platform, so I built it!"

I am extremely proud of our StarWalk Kids streaming collection. The eBooks are of the very highest quality, with gorgeous, professional narration. The books are not only mine but are also from other fine authors whose names you will recognize—Johanna Hurwitz, Emily Arnold McCully, Doreen Rappaport, Kathryn

Lasky, David Adler, Hudson Talbott, and Laura Vaccaro Seeger, to name a few. And because I'm a teacher myself, I knew we needed to address the challenges that educators face with technology in the classroom. So StarWalk Kids eBooks work on any device with Internet access (no special technology required). The program allows multiple children to use the same eBook at the same time, and the annual streaming subscription is made affordable for all schools and libraries with even the most modest materials budget. There are also curriculum specialists working on Common Core "Teaching Links" to go with every eBook, and 60 percent of the books in the StarWalk library are nonfiction, including exciting science books, books about history and social studies, biographies, and literary nonfiction on subjects ranging from dinosaur-hunting to World War II. It really is a great Common Core solution!

One of the things I love most about StarWalk Kids is that it has enabled the reclamation of good books that have gone out of print (mine as well as those by other writers) and [their] redesign/update . . . for digital editions. Like a phoenix rising from the ashes, a space book like *Saturn* is not only available again, but it has new photographs and up-to-date information. I've already revised *Planet Mars* to include the current mission by the Curiosity Rover. As new discoveries are made on the red planet, I'm sure I'll revise it again, record narration for the new pages, and the updated volume will simply appear in subscribers' existing collections.

I'm happy to report that I've also been hard at work on new books featuring a favorite fictional character of mine, Einstein Anderson! Yes, the science sleuth is back, but this time the series is called *Einstein Anderson: Science Geek*. These stories are about contemporary, tech-savvy kids who solve mysteries using their science knowledge and are very interactive. The books are a hybrid of fiction and nonfiction that not only present fun science mysteries but also include a real-life experiment or project to go with each story. The first four books are already available and there will eventually be 16 books in the series, illustrated by the talented and humorous Kevin O'Malley.

I can never get enough of exploring the world around me and the vast universe beyond. There is always something new to learn and share with my readers. For example, did you know that when astronauts are in space they can't cry? That's because in a low-gravity environment, the tears won't fall from their eyes. Hmmmm . . . that's an idea. Maybe my next book should be narrative nonfiction . . . the diary of an astronaut who can't cry! When I was a kid, I was always interested in the endless variety of the world around me. I still am. I hope my books are a kind of friendly guide and companion that help children become lifetime learners.

One Book in Action: Guts

We don't often think about featuring one book of nonfiction for literary study, but why not? If we can find a book that has kid-appeal, generates a lot of discussion, and encourages further reading, isn't that what a focus book should do? I have found that a well-chosen informational book can do all of the above, plus help validate the choice of young readers who prefer nonfiction and push other readers who might not choose nonfiction to give it a try. Older readers will find excellent discussion-worthy informational books by authors such as Russell Freedman, Jim Murphy, and Susan Campbell Bartoletti, but if you want to include younger readers, choosing an informational picture book is the way to go. And who creates some of the most amazing works of nonfiction in the picture book format? Seymour Simon, of course. Here's one example of how to develop a mini-study in informational literature focused on one book, *Guts: Our Digestive System* (HarperCollins, 2005).

Guts is an introduction to our gastrointestinal systems through 19 amazing, full-color photographs and clear and matter-of-fact prose. It presents this physiological system in the order that food would be processed, from teeth to esophagus to stomach to intestines and out, with a nod to the liver and the pancreas on the way. Simon doesn't shy away from the gross and presents all the parts and processes using the necessary factual labels (like "defecation"). He helps us understand a natural ongoing process that everyone experiences, describing it in a scientific approach that still manages to capture the wonder of the human body. It's this blending of writing that is never condescending with compelling scientific photographs and a topic of general interest that makes Seymour Simon's books effective across age ranges, too. Even as an adult, I learn something new and find myself poring over the photographs of pink heartburn or a green gallbladder. Clear labels help us know what we are seeing in the images and the large page format with alternating text and photograph (often on a black background) is striking and sophisticated. It's a book to read together with images you can project for further review, analysis, and discussion with children. When combined with Simon's other parallel books on human anatomy, you can have a comprehensive "health" study for World Health Day (April 7) or National Health Education Week (October 15–19), for example. Look for:

Bones: Our Skeletal System (HarperTrophy, 2000)
The Brain: Our Nervous System (Collins, 2006)
Eyes and Ears (HarperCollins, 2003)
The Heart: Our Circulatory System (Collins, 2006)
Muscles: Our Muscular System (HarperTrophy, 2000)

Read More

How do you follow up the reading and discussion of nonfiction? With more reading, research, guest speakers, and so on. For example, gather a selection of other books related to digestion, anatomy, health, and food. For younger readers this might include *What Happens to a Hamburger?* (in the *Let's-Read-and-Find-Out Science* series) by Paul Showers (HarperTrophy, 2001), or *Stomachaches* (from the *My Health* series) by Alvin Silverstein, Virginia B. Silverstein, and Laura Silverstein Nunn (Franklin Watts, 2003). Older readers may be interested in how scientists discovered how this digestive system works (in often startling ways) in *Guinea Pig Scientists: Bold Self-Experimenters in Science and Medicine* by Mel Boring (Holt, 2005) and *Invisible Allies: Microbes That Shape Our Lives* by Jeanette Farrell (Farrar, Straus & Giroux, 2005). Children of all ages may enjoy these more comical approaches:

- *101 Questions About Food and Digestion: That Have Been Eating at You . . . Until Now* by Faith Hickman Brynie (21st Century, 2002)
- *Head to Toe Science: Over 40 Eye-Popping, Spine-Tingling, Heart-Pounding Activities That Teach Kids About the Human Body* by Jim Wiese (Jossey-Bass, 2000)
- *The Body Owner's Handbook* (in the *Horrible Science* series) by Nick Arnold (Scholastic, 2002)

Follow-Up

Afterward, work together to create a "did you know?" display on a paper cutout of the human body (outline a volunteer lying down on craft paper) filled with fact-strips of odd or interesting tidbits the kids have gleaned from their reading. Follow up with the hilarious poetry of Allan Wolf in *The Blood-Hungry Spleen and Other Poems About Our Parts* (Candlewick, 2003), one of the few collections of anatomical poems for kids!

This may be an ideal opportunity to invite outside experts to come to talk to the children about their approaches to understanding and promoting healthy digestion, including physicians, nutritionists, or even restaurant owners. Children can prepare questions in advance based on their reading, "interview" the visitor, and summarize their findings afterward. Feeling brave? Children are often eager to share their own stories of upset stomachs, stomach viruses, food poisoning, appendectomies, and the like. (Set some ground rules for what is or is not acceptable or comfortable for group discussion.) For developing awareness and education, a bit of research will yield interesting information about food safety and healthy diet guidelines, including these websites:

United States Department of Agriculture (USDA)
Education and Outreach
Link to Youth Resources:
http://www.usda.gov

Government Food Safety Information
Link to Kids, Teens, and Educators:
http://www.foodsafety.gov/

MedlinePlus
U.S. National Library of Medicine and National Institutes of Health
For consumer health information:
http://medlineplus.gov/

Going Further

Another connection to explore with kids is the area of human waste and waste disposal. It's often an uncomfortable topic for adults, but children are usually very intrigued and curious. Luckily, there are several books that provide facts along with the squirms and giggles. Look for these:

- *Flush: The Scoop on Poop Throughout the Ages* by Charise Mericle Harper (Little, Brown, 2007)
- *Toilets, Toasters & Telephones: The How and Why of Everyday Objects* by Susan Goldman Rubin and Elsa Warnick (Harcourt, 1998)
- *The Truth About Poop* by Susan E. Goodman (Viking, 2004)

- *What You Never Knew About Tubs, Toilets, & Showers* by Patricia Lauber and John Manders (Simon & Schuster, 2001)

It might be more "tasteful" to explore the topic of food as a follow up to the study of human digestion. Consult a favorite kids' cookbook (e.g., *Everything Kids' Cookbook* by Sandra K. Nissenberg; Adams Media, 2002) and involve children in preparing a healthy snack; then close with some fun food poems from:

- Jorge Argueta's food-themed poetry collections including *Sopa de frijoles/Bean Soup* (Groundwood, 2009), *Arroz con leche: Rice Pudding* (Groundwood, 2010), and *Guacamole; Un poema para cocinar/A Cooking Poem* (Groundwood, 2012)
- Francisco Alarcón's *Laughing Tomatoes and Other Spring Poems/Jitomates Resueños y Otros Poemas de Primavera* (Children's Book Press, 1997)
- Lee Bennett Hopkins's *YUMMY!: Eating Through a Day* (Simon & Schuster, 2000)
- Pat Mora's haiku about foods indigenous to the Americas: *Yum! Mmmm! Que Rico!: America's Sproutings* (Lee & Low, 2007)
- Michael J. Rosen's anthology *Food Fight: Poets Join the Fight Against Hunger with Poems about Their Favorite Foods* (Harcourt, 1996)

Finally, readers who enjoy Seymour Simon's anatomy-based series may also want to read other books he has written in the areas of astronomy, animals, nature, and more. His "Einstein Anderson" fiction series follows a boy who solves mysteries through his science knowledge, and his "See More Readers" provide an entrée into informational literature for the youngest reader or the child still learning English using the same highly visual approach. For practical ideas on using Simon's astronomy books with kids, look for *Exploring Space: Using Seymour Simon's Astronomy Books in the Classroom* by Barbara Bourne and Wendy Saul (HarperCollins, 1994). Even more background information can be found on the author's website: http://www.seymoursimon.com/.

EVALUATION CRITERIA

When we select informational books for children and young adults, we want to make sure it meets the highest standards, if at all possible. But what are those standards? The usual literary elements of plot, character, setting, and theme do not apply to most informational books. We need different criteria based on the basic purpose of the genre. Remember, we go to nonfiction books for *information*. Therefore, the #1 criterion for quality in nonfiction writing is *accuracy* of information.

Accuracy

If the book contains inaccurate information, it doesn't matter how lovely the illustrations are or how positive the reviews, we are misinforming children if we share it with them. Accuracy is #1. But how do we know if a book on photosynthesis is accurate, if we are not well versed in the principles of photosynthesis ourselves? There are several ways. We look to reviewers who *are* knowledgeable. We seek input from experts in the field. We compare this book to others on the same subject. We also depend somewhat on the author's credentials and reputation in the field. Does he or she have sufficient background in this area? Are sources cited in notes or bibliographies that are included in the book? Is the author's point of view clear? Are stereotypes avoided? Are known facts clearly differentiated from theory? Is anthropomorphism avoided (talking animals, for example)? Are both illustrations and text correct? All these factors go into the mix. We should guide children in looking for accuracy in the books they read, as well. Encourage them to question, to look for notes and references, to compare and think critically. For example, Russell Freedman has said that he does not include a detail unless he can document it in three or more separate sources. Then he includes his sources, too. Look at his book *Abraham Lincoln and Frederick Douglass: The Story Behind an American Friendship* (Houghton Mifflin, 2012) and check for source notes, bibliographies, reading lists, and/or picture credits. Finding those tools noted in a book helps reinforce our appreciation of the accuracy and integrity of the work. As Marc Aronson has observed, "Notes, then, are not just proof that the author did his or her homework, nor assurance that basic facts are recorded correctly, or that quotations have been passed on accurately, rather they open up the version as given by the author to greater inquiry by the reader, the librarian, the teacher, the parent. Plus, they are a place for the author to put all the cool stuff he/she found that doesn't fit the main narrative."

Organization

The importance of organization in a nonfiction book is also crucial. How is the information presented? Remember, many informational books are not read from cover-to-cover. Therefore, it is important that the organization and layout of the book help the reader to pick and choose what she or he needs. Is the layout logical? Is there a clear sequence to the information? Are patterns provided (such as general-to-specific, simple-to-complex, etc.)? Are reference aids included (such as subheadings, a table of contents, index, etc.)? Then, of course, we also have to teach children how to use these tools. For a powerful example of excellent book organization, seek out the Sibert medal winner, *Black Potatoes: The Story of the Great Irish Famine, 1845–1850* (Houghton Mifflin, 2005) by Susan Campbell Bartoletti, a heartbreaking social history that blends a chronological telling with a political commentary, alongside effective use of many visuals from the time period.

Design

The artful appearance of the book is also an important factor in selecting and evaluating quality nonfiction. First, one considers whether the book is attractive, inviting, and readable. Will children even open it? But we're also concerned with whether the illustrations are appropriate and complement the text; whether pictures, tables, and other graphics are clear and placed appropriately. Even questions about type or font, size, and paper are relevant. Remember, we're asking if the design helps communicate the subject matter clearly and effectively. Look for the Sibert medal winner *Secrets of a Civil War Submarine: Solving the Mysteries of the H. L. Hunley* by Sally M. Walker (Carolrhoda Books, 2005) and imagine it as an old-fashioned book with lots of text and a few black and white photos. Things have changed, haven't they? Walker's book makes excellent use of photos and other images in full color, as well as creative use of color, font, and layout throughout this informational book. Plus, it's available as an audiobook, too.

Style

Finally, analysis of nonfiction books includes the element of style, too. Style is what makes an informational book a work of literature and not just a book of facts. Each nonfiction author has his or her unique style or voice, and you look for that distinctiveness in the presentation of the information. The writing should be clear, lively, and interesting. It should reveal the author's passion or enthusiasm for the subject; it should encourage curiosity and wonder on the part of the reader. The book should use appropriate vocabulary and not "talk down" to the reader. It should encourage critical thinking and more reading and not include too much information.

Sometimes people look "down" on nonfiction because they don't think of it as literature. But a close examination of the rigorous criteria that are applied to the very best informational books helps demonstrate that this genre is a valuable and even beautiful means of expression. Many authors such as Newbery medal winner (for *Lincoln*) Russell Freedman have devoted their entire lives to creating quality nonfiction that is just as worthwhile a literary experience as a good novel. I believe we owe it to children to introduce them to quality nonfiction as a literary experience that can be fun and pleasurable, as well as a tool for research and information-seeking.

Sample Review

Let's put these evaluation criteria into action and consider one review and how it uses these criteria. Here's a sample review of an informational picture book:

Kurlansky, Mark. 2006. *The Story of Salt*. Ill. by S. D. Schindler. New York: Putnam.

The Chinese used it for trade so successfully that it funded the Great Wall of China. The Egyptians used it so well to preserve their dead that centuries-old mummies exist today. George Washington's army used it to make gunpowder, and today it is used in ketchup and soft drinks. Who knew salt was so interesting? Kurlansky's thorough presentation of the history of salt is factual without boring the reader, and visually appealing with Schindler's colorful ink drawings featuring period clothing and scenery. Sidebars break up the pages with factual tidbits about salt, like the discovery of a 2000-year-old Celtic miner preserved in salt, and the story of a French prisoner who died, whose body was preserved in a barrel of salt for seven years to be brought to trial. *The Story of Salt* is an engaging choice that will provide readers with a thorough introduction to this common household ingredient. A "Salt Through the Centuries" timeline completes this informative picture book.

[By Tammy Korns for *Librarians' Choices*. Used with permission.]

Notice how this review opens with a listing of four facts that hint at the subject of the book rather than summarizing the subject explicitly. This subtly underscores the high interest factor of this informational book on the topic of *salt*. Next, the review makes this explicit with the comment, "Kurlansky's thorough presentation of the history of salt is factual without boring the reader." This statement also alludes to the accuracy of the work, one of the key elements for the analysis of informational literature. The element of organization is addressed with comments about the "sidebars [that] break up the pages with factual tidbits about salt" and the timeline of "Salt Through the Centuries." The story-like nature of the book is acknowledged and the importance of the illustrations is underscored with the mention of "Schindler's colorful ink drawings featuring period clothing and scenery," which are "visually appealing." These also contribute to the overall design of the book. The author's style is credited as being "interesting," "thorough," "factual without [being] boring," and "engaging." The inclusion of so many representative facts drawn from the book (about trade in China, mummification in Egypt, gunpowder ingredient, etc.) also suggests the thorough research of the author, the high interest of the content, and the appeal to the child reader—all important in evaluating nonfiction and a good strategy for reviewing books in this genre.

AWARDS FOR INFORMATIONAL BOOKS

Informational books are receiving more and more recognition from all the major awards in children's literature. Authors like Russell Freedman and Jim Murphy have received multiple Newbery honors, for example. Keeping up with the best informational books is a bit easier nowadays with the presence of two major awards specifically for this genre of nonfiction. Another award recognizes nonfiction writers for their total body of work. In addition, two major subject area organizations (science and social studies) regularly incorporate nonfiction into their annual "best" lists, as do more and more state lists and bibliographies. These distinctions provide an excellent barometer of quality and innovation in this informational genre.

The Orbis Pictus Award

The National Council of Teachers established the Orbis Pictus Award for Outstanding Nonfiction for Children in 1990 for promoting and recognizing excellence in the writing of nonfiction for children. Award and honor recipients are announced every spring and are listed on the NCTE website. Recent award recipients include *Monsieur Marceau: Actor without Words* by Leda Schubert (Roaring Brook, 2012), *Balloons over Broadway: The True Story of the Puppeteer of Macy's Parade* by Melissa Sweet (Houghton Mifflin, 2011), *Ballet for Martha: Making Appalachian Spring* by Jan Greenberg and Sandra Jordan (Roaring Brook, 2010), *The Secret World of Walter Anderson* by Hester Bass (Candlewick, 2009), *Amelia Earhart: The Legend of the Lost Aviator* by Shelley Tanaka (Abrams, 2008), and *M.L.K. Journey of a King* by Tonya Bolden (Abrams, 2007).

Robert F. Sibert Award

The Robert F. Sibert Informational Book Award established in 2001 is given annually by the Association of Library Service to Children to the author (and illustrator, if appropriate) whose informational book has made a significant contribution to the field of children's literature. Information books are defined as those written and illustrated to present, organize, and interpret documentable factual material for children. Award and honor recipients are announced every January and are listed on the ALA website. Recent medal books have included *Bomb: The Race to Build—and Steal—the World's Most Dangerous Weapon* by Steve Sheinkin (Roaring Brook, 2012), *Balloons over Broadway: The True Story of the Puppeteer of Macy's Parade* by Melissa Sweet (Houghton Mifflin Harcourt, 2011), *Kakapo Rescue: Saving the World's Strangest Parrot* by Sy Montgomery (Houghton Mifflin, 2010), *Almost Astronauts: 13 Women Who Dared to Dream* by Tanya Lee Stone (Candlewick, 2009), *We Are the Ship: The Story of Negro League Baseball* by Kadir Nelson (Disney–Jump at the Sun, 2008), *The Wall: Growing Up behind the Iron Curtain* by Peter Sís (Farrar/Frances Foster, 2007), and *Team Moon: How 400,000 People Landed Apollo 11 on the Moon* by Catherine Thimmesh (Houghton, 2006).

YALSA Award for Excellence in Nonfiction for Young Adults

The Young Adult Library Services Association established this award in 2010 to honor the best nonfiction book published for young adults (ages twelve to eighteen). A short list of up to five titles is named in the first week of December and the award-winning book is announced at the annual Midwinter conference of the American Library Association in January. Recent winners have included *Bomb: The Race to Build—and Steal—the World's Most Dangerous Weapon*, written by Steve Sheinkin (Roaring Brook, 2012), who had also won the previous year with *The Notorious Benedict Arnold: A True Story of Adventure, Heroism, & Treachery* (Roaring Brook, 2011), preceded by *Janis Joplin: Rise Up Singing* by Ann Angel (Amulet, 2010), and the first winner, *Charles and Emma: The Darwins' Leap of Faith* by Deborah Heiligman (Henry Holt, 2009).

Children's Book Guild and *Washington Post* Award for Nonfiction

In 1977, the Children's Book Guild inaugurated an annual award to honor "an author or author-illustrator whose total work has contributed significantly to the quality of nonfiction for children." The *Washington Post* joined the Guild in 1982 as the cosponsor of the award. Nonfiction is defined as written or illustrated work that arranges and interprets documentable facts intended to illuminate, without imaginative invention, the following fields of knowledge: science, technology, social science, history, biography, and the arts. Previous award winners have included Jan Greenberg and Sandra Jordan, Peter Sís, Kathleen Krull, Sy Montgomery, Susan Campbell Bartoletti, Doreen Rappaport, Sneed B. Collard, Caroline Arnold, Dorothy Hinshaw Patent, Steve Jenkins, Jim Murphy, Jim Arnosky, Brent Ashabranner, Isaac Asimov, Rhoda Blumberg, Joanna Cole, Russell Freedman, Jean Craighead George, Gail Gibbons, James Cross Giblin, Kathryn Lasky, Patricia Lauber, Albert Marrin, and Seymour Simon.

Outstanding Science Trade Books for Students K–12

The books that appear in this annually published annotated bibliography, "Outstanding Science Trade Books for Students K–12," are selected as outstanding children's science books published for young people in a given year, including many informational titles. They are selected by members by the National Science Teachers Association (NSTA) and the Children's Book Council (CBC). The list is published in the journal *Science and Children* every spring and is posted at http://www.cbcbooks.org as well as at the NSTA website.

Notable Social Studies Trade Books for Young People

This annual annotated book list is created by the National Council for the Social Studies (NCSS), also in cooperation with the Children's Book Council (CBC). It highlights children's literature that is appropriate for the social studies and includes many informational books. Their bibliographies of books for children in grades K–8 include both fiction and nonfiction. The list is published every spring in the journal *Social Education* and is posted at http://www.cbcbooks.org and at the NCSS website.

Literature in Action: **Introducing Access Features**

It's not always obvious to children that nonfiction books are arranged differently from fiction books and that readers can often approach them differently. Although some informational books are beautifully written literature and can be read from cover to cover, many nonfiction books serve more as reference sources that we "dip" into when seeking answers to questions or browse through just for fun. In addition, children will very likely be required to handle more and more nonfiction material throughout their adult lives. Thus, they need to be equipped with strategies for processing this "expository text" and for focusing their attention appropriately on the important information. We can help them with that in several ways, particularly by guiding them through the use of access features as these are used to organize informational books.

Access features provide a skeletal framework for the organization of informational text and come in both visual and verbal forms. They include the "reference aids" such as bibliographies and tables of contents, but go beyond. According to Rick Kerper in "Features for Accessing and Visualizing Information" (Kristo and Bamford, 2003), there are several major features for accessing and/or visualizing information in nonfiction texts. These include:

Visual Access Features
Illustrations (drawings and paintings)
Photographs (and captions)
Diagrams (cutaways, cross-sections, webs, timelines, flow diagrams, scale diagrams)
Maps
Tables (and rows and columns)
Graphs
Charts

Verbal Access Features
Table of contents (and chapter titles)
Index (to both verbal and visual material)
Glossary
Sidebars and inserts
Bibliography (primary and secondary sources)
Photo credits
Author/Illustrator notes (especially important for assessing accuracy and author credibility)
Subheadings
Page numbers

In her book *Texts and Forms and Features: A Resource for Intentional Teaching,* Margaret Mooney (2001) has dissected the typical nonfiction book to note nearly each and every form and feature of the genre. She provides an alphabetical listing of 39 access features and includes a definition of each along with a listing of the purpose and attributes of each feature. The list includes everything from abbreviations to blurbs to prefaces to timetables. For each of the elements, she provides a "why," "what," and "features" list that can be helpful for planning a mini-lesson.

If we do just a bit of planning, we can use informational books to explain what certain text elements are, providing children with the labels ("This is called a 'glossary'"), authentic examples ("Here is the glossary from Wilcox's book, *Mummies, Bones & Body Parts* [Carolrhoda, 2000]"), and explanations ("The glossary is a list of words and meanings, which helps us with this subject. Here is the word 'bog.' Let's read what a bog is"). In the give-and-take of an interactive read aloud session, we can help children clarify their understanding of all these "pieces" of text. Using high-quality informational books helps provide an interesting and meaningful context for identifying these elements. As children become more familiar with how these elements work in books they enjoy, they may be better equipped to experiment with recognizing them in their content area textbooks and with using these tools in their own writing.

These reference tools can also be presented quite naturally through nonfiction literature. Deciding which excerpt to read aloud can provide a need for referring to a table of contents. Reading aloud the table of contents can involve the children in choosing a starting chapter. Afterward, a discussion of how the author chooses titles for each chapter and why the chapters are organized the way they are is a rich opportunity for developing the thinking behind the writing and organizing of expository text.

The same kind of practice can be used for demonstrating the value of an index. This time, begin at the end by projecting an image of the index pages. Again, children can choose intriguing topics that interest them from the index. The adult or student leader then looks for the reference within the text. Show children how to read only the relevant material. So often, less able readers need "permission" *not* to read the entire page, not realizing that skimming and scanning are appropriate and necessary skills.

Expository text is full of all kinds of access features that can be systematically introduced through informational books. One at a time, in the context of a quality trade book, these tools can be demonstrated as the useful and informative devices they are. Jim Murphy's Orbis Pictus award–winning book, *The Great Fire* (Scholastic, 2006), is an excellent example of how helpful maps can be in telling a story. The scale and magnitude of the Great Fire of Chicago are vividly conveyed by the expanding gray area on the maps provided throughout the book. As the details of the fire unfold throughout the read aloud experience, projections of the maps can reveal the extent of the developing fire in a very concrete and visual way.

Other text features that can provide information and opportunity for quick instruction include the use of photographs and captions such as in *The Elephant Scientist* by Caitlin O'Connell and Donna Jackson with photographs by Caitlin O'Connell and Timothy Rodwell (Houghton Mifflin Harcourt, 2011), a timeline as in *Through My Eyes* by Ruby Bridges (Scholastic, 1999), and even pronunciation guides such as in *Leonardo da Vinci* by Diane Stanley (Morrow, 1996). Through a "show and tell" approach, we can actively engage children in understanding and interpreting these elements, their purpose and placement in the text, and their own responses to these information sources.

Access features can help us make better use of informational books. They can help us segment and comprehend material as we read a book or look back and look up material after we have read a book. They can enhance the organization of a book in terms of placement and sequence of text and visuals. They can also contribute to the overall design quality of the book. Imagine a book without *any* visual or access features. Text-only could be rather overwhelming or boring. Now, consider a book in terms of *only* the access features. Sketchy, but they can provide a skeleton for the contents of the book. However, children may not always pay attention to these valuable features. They may not understand the purpose they serve, or they may expend all their energies on focusing exclusively on the text. We need to help them discover these "gems" and guide them in how to use them before, during, and after their reading. Through sharing high-quality informational books, we can show children the care with which authors communicate their passion for their subject while also making the information accessible and comprehensible to the reader.

SHARING INFORMATIONAL BOOKS

We have been dubbed the information society—and with good reason: with improved technology for publication and communication, we have access to a greater volume of information than ever before. For example, more new information has been produced within the last three decades than in the last 5,000 years. In fact, over a million new books were published worldwide in 2013 alone. In one day, we are exposed to more information in a copy of *The New York Times* than the average person was likely to come across in an entire lifetime in seventeenth-century England (Wurman, 1989). In the future, it is projected that 90 percent of what children read in will be informational text. Thus, now more than ever, children need to be exposed, even immersed, in reading informational literature and learning how to use and understand this genre fully.

The first step in sharing nonfiction successfully is to recognize that there are many ways to share informational books. The traditional approach of choosing a book and reading the entire text out loud from cover to cover (in one session or across several sessions) is only one way. It can be an excellent way to introduce informational books. With this genre, however, this is probably not the most typical approach for presenting informational literature. Quite honestly, most informational books do not lend themselves to a cover-to-cover read aloud. The concept density is simply too intense for one sitting. That is, children may well be overwhelmed by the amount of new information and terminology presented in one book when presented with it all at once. Keep in mind, however, that many excellent works of fiction also do not lend themselves to being read aloud either, but are much more enjoyable when pored over individually in silent reading.

Reading aloud nonfiction at any age level can be as spontaneous and interactive as a baby's first board book experiences, pointing at pictures and labeling objects. There is no reason why such an approach cannot be just as pleasurable and meaningful in the library as it is at the bedtime reading for preschoolers (Vardell, 2003). For example, we might "preview" an informational book with a group, showing the incredible photographs, while inviting children to comment. "Wow, that looks interesting." "Listen again to how the author described this." "How is the author trying to make you feel?" "What words has the author used to persuade you to feel this way?"

Unfortunately, adults often fall into the trap of believing older children who are independent readers should be more systematic and thorough in their reading. They should proceed from beginning to end, reading every word. They should not look only at the pictures, and they should most certainly not read the ending first. But many informational books may best be enjoyed by browsing through the pictures first to develop a visual understanding of the phenomenon before tackling the vocabulary and explanations describing it within the text. Or older readers may want to use the index or table of contents to select the chapters that most interest them. Fortunately, the variety of nonfiction books being published today includes an incredible array of topics, formats, layouts, and styles to interest all kinds of readers.

Creative Follow-Up Activities for Nonfiction

When children encounter good books, they naturally want to share their reactions with each other. As we learn more about the new informational books available today on a vast array of topics, we can borrow from our files of ideas and activities usually earmarked to follow up fictional stories. When children need or want to follow their reading with a book project, why not let them choose a book of nonfiction and one of the following creative activities to go with it.

1. *Make a poster, book jacket, bookmark.* Children can apply their artistic and creative talents to creating something eye-catching and interesting, while exercising their comprehension and synthesizing abilities to highlight the most pertinent information about the nonfiction book or author they've selected.
2. *Make a model, mobile, mural, or collage.* For example, children might follow up their reading of Seymour Simon's *How to Build a Paper Airplane* with constructing examples of the various types of planes pictured in the book. These might then be suspended in a mobile or displayed against a mural of a sky scene or cityscape.
3. *Conduct a demonstration or experiment; gather a collection or display.* Many informational books encourage children's "hands-on" involvement as new concepts are introduced and explained. With supervision, have children try these activities. Other books encourage observation and examination of natural phenomena. Have children gather and display collections (or illustrations) of specimens sighted.
4. *Create illustrations, glog, scrapbook, or a map.* Some informational books come alive for children when they create their own illustrations or three-dimensional representations using pen and paper or digital tools à la Glogster. Creating their own scrapbook of pictures, drawings, facts, and the like may provide concrete personalization of new information. Locating a setting on a map and noting scale, context, and directions may also provide meaningful reinforcement of their learning.
5. *Read a portion orally; make an audio recording.* Many nonfiction books for children are so well written that they read well out loud. In addition, children may find certain portions of any text particularly fascinating because of their own individual interests. With that enthusiasm, they can make the book and the subject come alive for others by preparing and sharing an excerpt out loud, or by taping a portion or making a podcast (to accompany the book) for others to enjoy.
6. *Organize a "did you know?" bulletin board or display.* The collective curiosity of a group of children offers a lot of potential for large group activities that incorporate nonfiction. Children who enjoy *The Guinness Book of World Records* (and other similar books) may enjoy collaborating on creating a group display.
7. *Invite guest speakers from the community pertinent to the topic.* Many children choose informational books according to their special areas of

interests. Often children may be unaware there are individuals in the community with expertise in their interest area. Connecting nonfiction literature and book reading with personal interaction and interviewing can make the subject become real for everyone.

8. *Compare and contrast several informational works on the same subject.* For example, topics such as space travel, volcanoes, and dinosaurs have many book possibilities since these are topics that many authors have written about. Locate two or more books on the same topic or two biographies on the same individual and compare the coverage. Check for accuracy, currency, point of view; note what "facts" have changed over the years.

If you don't have a setting that enables ongoing planning and interaction for more in-depth activities, you can still:

- Choose high-quality nonfiction for read aloud time (and then model the use of some of the access strategies before, during, or after the read aloud)
- Recommend informational books during readers advisory for kids who have burning interests in special topic areas
- Recommend high-quality informational books when children need reference tools, and not just the usual reference works
- Include prize-winning nonfiction authors in your featured author area
- Include the Orbis Pictus award and Sibert award in your promotion of awards
- Create bibliographies and bookmarks for recommended nonfiction (on timely topics such as hurricanes, football, etc.)

As you can see, there are many possibilities for introducing and extending the nonfiction reading experience. Once you open the door to these ideas, children can suggest even more.

CONCLUSION

Children already think puddles and rainbows are magical—our job is to maintain and even enhance that sense of wonder with information that helps provide the how and why, but shows natural phenomena to be no less amazing. As children mature, they are increasingly called upon to process text from standardized tests, textbooks, news outlets, reference materials, and online sources. This lineup of required reading is daunting for kids, but reading informational books can help develop those skills and maintain interest. Using Internet resources and online databases yields masses of useful and accessible information, but it also takes an educated and critical user to assess and evaluate that information for accuracy and point of view. In addition, providing young readers with informational literature gives models of research and writing that can guide their own developing literacy skills. Choosing quality nonfiction books presents children with additional possibilities for their own independent reading as well as supporting the curriculum. The key is keeping current on what resources are available, then doing all we can to provide children with access to these books and tools. Once kids discover that answers to their questions about the world and how it works can be found in informational books, their interest in new nonfiction published each year will grow. As author Jean Fritz has said, "children will surely discover that books can be fun no matter which shelf they live on" (2001, p. 87).

PROFESSIONAL RESOURCES IN NONFICTION

If you are interested in additional resources to help you dig deeper in this genre, these selections are excellent.

Bamford, R., and J. Kristo. 2000. *Checking Out Nonfiction K–8: Good Choices for Best Learning.* Norwood, MA: Christopher-Gordon.

Baxter, Kathleen, and Michael Dahl. 2005. *Gotcha Covered!: More Nonfiction Booktalks to Get Kids Excited about Reading.* Englewood, CO: Libraries Unlimited.

Baxter, Kathleen, and Marcia Kochel. 1999. *Gotcha!: Nonfiction Booktalks to Get Kids Excited about Reading.* Englewood, CO: Libraries Unlimited.

Baxter, Kathleen, and Marcia Kochel. 2002. *Gotcha Again!: More Nonfiction Booktalks to Get Kids Excited about Reading.* Englewood, CO: Libraries Unlimited.

Baxter, Kathleen, and Marcia Kochel. 2006. *Gotcha for Guys!: Nonfiction Books to Get Boys Excited about Reading.* Englewood, CO: Libraries Unlimited.

Cianciolo, Patricia J. 2000. *Informational Picture Books for Children.* Chicago, IL: American Library Association.

Fredericks, Anthony D. 2007. *Nonfiction Readers Theatre for Beginning Readers.* Englewood, CO: Libraries Unlimited.

Freeman, Evelyn, and Diane Person. Eds. 1992. *Using Nonfiction Tradebooks in the Elementary Classroom.* Urbana, IL: National Council of Teachers of English.

Freeman, Evelyn, and Diane Person. 1998. *Connecting Informational Children's Books with Content Area Learning.* New York: Allyn & Bacon.

Harvey, S. 1998. *Nonfiction Matters: Reading, Writing, and Research in Grades 3–8.* Portland, ME: Stenhouse.

Kristo, J., and R. Bamford. Eds. 2003. *Making Facts Come Alive: Choosing Nonfiction Literature K–8* (Second Edition). Norwood MA: Christopher-Gordon.

Wyatt, Flora R., Margaret Coggins, and Jane Hunter Imber. 1998. *Popular Nonfiction Authors for Children: A Biographical and Thematic Guide.* Englewood, CO: Libraries Unlimited.

Zarnowski, Myra. 1990. *Learning About Biographies.* Urbana, IL: National Council of Teachers of English.

Zarnowski, Myra. 2003. *History Makers: A Questioning Approach to Reading and Writing Biographies.* Portsmouth, NH: Heinemann.

Zarnowski, Myra, Richard M. Kerper, and Julie M. Jensen. 2001. *The Best in Children's Nonfiction: Reading, Writing, and Teaching Orbis Pictus Award Books.* Urbana, IL: National Council of Teachers of English.

Standards in Action: Common Core and Nonfiction

We looked briefly at the Common Core State Standards (CCSS) for English Language Arts & Literacy in Chapter Two with a focus on reading literature (http://www.core standards.org/ELA-Literacy). But there are also specific Common Core State Standards that address learning to read *informational text* and *nonfiction*. This has some people concerned that we might neglect teaching and promoting fiction, but I hope we'll simply add a new emphasis on sharing nonfiction literature too—particularly since we have often neglected this genre in the past.

The standards charge us with developing children's skill to "perform the critical reading necessary to pick carefully through the staggering amount of information available today in print and digitally. They actively seek the wide, deep, and thoughtful engagement with high-quality literary and informational texts that builds knowledge, enlarges experience, and broadens worldviews." There are specific skills for reading and understanding "Informational Text" for grades K–12 in each of the four main areas below:

Reading: Informational Text

- Key Ideas and Details
- Craft and Structure
- Integration of Knowledge and Ideas
- Range of Reading and Level of Text Complexity

The activities and strategies described throughout the chapter address many of the standards in these areas. For example, in "Literature in Action: Introducing Access Features" we target skills in the "Craft and Structure" area including:

Grade 1: CCSS.ELS-Literacy.RI.1.5   *Know and use various text features (e.g., headings, tables of contents, glossaries, electronic menus, icons) to locate key facts or information in a text.*

Grade 2: CCSS.ELS-Literacy.RI.2.5   *Know and use various text features (e.g., captions, bold print, subheadings, glossaries, indexes, electronic menus, icons) to locate key facts or information in a text efficiently.*

Grade 3: CCSS.ELS-Literacy.RI.3.5   *Use text features and search tools (e.g., key words, sidebars, hyperlinks) to locate information relevant to a given topic efficiently.*

Grade 6: CCSS.ELS-Literacy.RI.6.5   *Analyze how a particular sentence, paragraph, chapter, or section fits into the overall structure of a text and contributes to the development of the ideas.*

Whether you work with teachers to find materials to support instruction in developing these Common Core standards or simply amp up your recommendation of engaging nonfiction books to the children you serve, it is wise to familiarize yourself with the latest relevant standards.

Assignments in Action: Investigating Informational Books

1. Information Power

The American Association of School Librarians has developed information literacy standards as part of their push for *Information Power: Building Partnerships for Learning* (available on the AASL website). Look these standards over, if you haven't already, and consider how the use of informational books might support these learning objectives. In addition, the Common Core standards also specify many objectives related to reading and understanding nonfiction text. Familiarize yourself with those standards, too.

2. How Nonfiction Has Changed

Look at how nonfiction for children has changed over the years. For example, see if you can find the book *My Puppy Is Born* by Joanna Cole first published in the 1970s. It was republished with new illustrations in 1991. Look at the difference that color photographs can make. Or compare other examples of informational books published before 1980 or 1990 with more current titles of informational books for children. How do the elements of accuracy, organization, design, and style translate then and now?

3. Series Books

Spend some time in the reference area of the children's section. Which resources seem most used? Which are consulted the least? Look at the series books in the nonfiction area, too. Where are they shelved? Do they seem to be circulating? Interview a librarian and find out how she or he decides on which reference tools and series books to order. Investigate how databases and eBooks are fitting into the budget, as well. Are users gravitating more toward use of databases and Internet sources and less toward print tools? How is the library handling that?

References

Ada, Alma Flor, Violet Harris, and Lee Bennett Hopkins. 1993. *A Chorus of Cultures: Developing Literacy through Multicultural Poetry*. Carmel, CA: Hampton-Brown Books.

Adams, Helen R. 2013. *Protecting Intellectual Freedom and Privacy in Your School Library*. Englewood, CO: Libraries Unlimited.

Akin, Lynn, and Donna MacKinney. 2004. "Autism, Children and Libraries: The 3 R's: Repetition, Routine, and Redundancy." *Children and Libraries, 1* (2), 57–63.

Akin, Lynn, and Erin O'Toole. 2000. "The Order of the Public Library and the Disorder of Attention Deficit." *Public Library Quarterly, 18* (3/4), 69–80.

Aldana, Patricia. 2004. *Under the Spell of the Moon: Art for Children from the World's Great Illustrators*. Toronto, Ontario, CA: Groundwood.

Altoff, Peggy, and Syd Golston. 2012. *Teaching Reading with the Social Studies Standards: Elementary Units That Integrate Great Books, Social Studies, and the Common Core Standards*. Silver Spring, MD: National Council for the Social Studies.

Amastae, Sharon. 2010. "Welcome to America, and to the Library." *Book Links Quick Tips*. August newsletter.

Ammon, Bette, and Gale W. Sherman. 1996. *Worth a Thousand Words: An Annotated Guide to Picture Books for Older Readers*. Englewood, CO: Libraries Unlimited.

Anderson, Nancy A. 2013. *Elementary Children's Literature: Infancy Through Age 13* (Fourth Edition). Boston: Pearson.

Asheim, Lester. "Not Censorship but Selection." http://www.ala.org/ala/oif/basics/notcensorship.htm. Accessed May 15, 2007.

Ashworth, Justin. 2006. "Letter to a First-Year School Librarian." *School Library Journal, 52* (9), 50.

Bader, Barbara. 1976. *American Picturebooks from Noah's Ark to the Beast Within*. New York: Macmillan.

Bagert, Brod. 1992. "Act It Out: Making Poetry Come Alive" in *Invitation to Read: More Children's Literature in the Reading Program*. Newark, DE: International Reading Association.

Baird, Zahra M., and Tracey Jackson. 2007. "Got Graphic Novels? More Than Just Superheroes in Tights!" *Children and Libraries, 5* (1), 5–7.

Bamford, R., and J. Kristo. 2000. *Checking Out Nonfiction K–8: Good Choices for Best Learning*. Norwood, MA: Christopher-Gordon.

Bang, Molly. 2000. *Picture This: How Pictures Work*. New York: SeaStar.

Banks, Carrie Scott, Sandra Feinberg, and Barbara Jordan. 2013. *Including Families of Children with Special Needs: A How-to-Do-It Manual for Librarians* (Revised Edition). Chicago: American Library Association.

Baring-Gould, William, and Cecil Baring-Gould. 1988. *The Annotated Mother Goose*. New York: Random House.

Barnhouse, Rebecca. 2004. *The Middle Ages in Literature for Youth*. Lanham, MD: Scarecrow Press.

Barr, Catherine, and John Gillespie. Eds. 2010. *Best Books for Children: Preschool Through Grade 6* (Ninth Edition). Englewood, CO: Libraries Unlimited.

Bartindale, Becky. 2007. "Librarian Leaves Mark at School." *The San Jose Mercury News*. January 29, 2007.

Barton, Bob, and David Booth. 2004. *Poetry Goes to School: From Mother Goose to Shel Silverstein*. Markham, Ontario, Canada: Pembroke.

Bauer, Caroline Feller. 1995. *Caroline Feller Bauer's New Handbook for Storytellers*. Chicago, IL: American Library Association.

Bauer, Caroline Feller. 1995. *The Poetry Break: An Annotated Anthology with Ideas for Introducing Children to Poetry*. New York: H. W. Wilson.

Bauman, Stephanie G. 2010. *Storytimes for Children*. Englewood, CO: Libraries Unlimited.

Baxter, Kathleen, and Michael Dahl. 2005. *Gotcha Covered!: More Nonfiction Booktalks to Get Kids Excited about Reading*. Englewood, CO: Libraries Unlimited.

Baxter, Kathleen, and Marcia Kochel. 1999. *Gotcha!: Nonfiction Booktalks to Get Kids Excited about Reading*. Englewood, CO: Libraries Unlimited.

Baxter, Kathleen, and Marcia Kochel. 2002. *Gotcha Again!: More Nonfiction Booktalks to Get Kids Excited about Reading*. Englewood, CO: Libraries Unlimited.

Baxter, Kathleen, and Marcia Kochel. 2006. *Gotcha for Guys!: Nonfiction Books to Get Boys Excited about Reading*. Englewood, CO: Libraries Unlimited.

Becker, Beverly C., and Susan M. Stan. 2002. *Hit List for Children 2: Frequently Challenged Books*. Chicago: American Library Association.

Beers, Kylene. 1998. "Listen While You Read." *School Library Journal, 44* (4), 30–35.

Bettelheim, Bruno. 2010. *The Uses of Enchantment: The Meaning and Importance of Fairy Tales*. New York: Vintage Books.

Bird, Elizabeth. 2007. "A Mouse in Their House: The Holm Siblings Banter about Babymouse." *Children and Libraries, 5* (1), 16–19.

Bishop, Kay. 2007. *The Collection Program in Schools: Concepts, Practices, and Information Sources* (Fourth Edition). Englewood, CO: Libraries Unlimited.

Bishop, Rudine Sims. 1992. "Making Informed Choices." In Violet Harris (Ed.), *Teaching Multicultural Literature in Grades K–8*. Norwood, MA: Christopher-Gordon.

Black, Alison, and Anna M. Stave. 2007. *A Comprehensive Guide to Readers Theatre: Enhancing Fluency and Comprehension in Middle School and Beyond*. Newark, DE: International Reading Association.

Blake, Quentin. 2003. *Magic Pencil: Children's Book Illustration Today*. London: British Library.

Blass, Rosanne J. 2002. *Booktalks, Bookwalks, and Read-Alouds: Promoting the Best New Children's Literature Across the Elementary Curriculum.* Englewood, CO: Libraries Unlimited.

Blass, Rosanne J. 2005. *Celebrate with Books: Booktalks for Holidays and Other Occasions.* Englewood, CO: Libraries Unlimited.

Blumenthal, Bob. 2005. *A Parent/Teacher Guide to Children's Books on Peace and Tolerance.* Victoria, British Columbia, Canada: Trafford.

Booth, David, and Bill Moore. 2003. *Poems Please! Sharing Poetry with Children* (Second Edition). Markham, Ontario, Canada: Pembroke.

Bosma, Bette. 1992. *Fairy Tales, Fables, Legends, and Myths: Using Folk Literature in Your Classroom.* New York: Teachers College Press.

Bourne, Barbara, and Wendy Saul. 1994. *Exploring Space: Using Seymour Simon's Astronomy Books in the Classroom.* New York: HarperCollins.

Bradbury, Judy. 2003. *Children's Book Corner: A Read-Aloud Resource with Tips, Techniques, and Plans for Teachers, Librarians and Parents,* Level Pre-K–K. Englewood, CO: Libraries Unlimited.

Bradbury, Judy. 2004. *Children's Book Corner: A Read-Aloud Resource with Tips, Techniques, and Plans for Teachers, Librarians and Parents for Grades 1 and 2.* Englewood, CO: Libraries Unlimited.

Brozo, William. 2002. *To Be a Boy, to Be a Reader: Engaging Teen and Preteen Boys in Active Literacy.* Newark, DE: International Reading Association.

Buker, Derek M. 2002. *Science Fiction and Fantasy Readers' Advisory: The Librarian's Guide to Cyborgs, Aliens, and Sorcerers.* Chicago, IL: American Library Association.

Burkey, Mary. 2012. *Audiobooks for Youth: A Practical Guide to Sound Literature.* Chicago, IL: American Library Association.

Buzzeo, Toni, and Jane Kurtz. 1999. *Terrific Connections with Authors, Illustrators, and Storytellers: Real Space and Virtual Links.* Englewood, CO: Libraries Unlimited.

Campbell, Melvin, and Joann V. Cleland. 2003. *Readers Theatre in the Classroom: A Manual for Teachers of Children and Adults.* Lincoln, NE: iUniverse.

Carr, Jo. 1982. *Beyond Fact: Nonfiction for Children and Young People.* Chicago, IL: American Library Association.

Cashdan, Sheldon. 2000. *The Witch Must Die: The Hidden Meaning of Fairy Tales.* New York: Basic Books.

Cavanaugh, Terence W. 2006. *Literature Circles through Technology.* Columbus, OH: Linworth.

Chance, Rosemary. 2008. *Young Adult Literature in Action: A Librarian's Guide.* Englewood, CO: Libraries Unlimited.

Chatton, Barbara. 1993. *Using Poetry Across the Curriculum.* Phoenix, AZ: Oryx Press.

Chatton, Barbara. 2010. *Using Poetry Across the Curriculum* (Second Edition). Santa Barbara, CA: ABC-CLIO.

Chick, Kay A., and Deborah Ann Ellermeyer. 2003. *Multicultural American History Through Children's Literature.* Englewood, CO: Libraries Unlimited.

Cianciolo, Patricia J. 2000. *Informational Picture Books for Children.* Chicago, IL: American Library Association.

Codell, Esme Raji. 2003. *How to Get Your Child to Love Reading: For Ravenous and Reluctant Readers Alike.* Chapel Hill, NC: Algonquin.

Codell, Esme Raji. 2007. http://www.planetesme.com/saharaspecial.html. Accessed June 16, 2007.

Coffey, Rosemary K., and Elizabeth F. Howard. 1997. *America as Story: Historical Fiction for Schools* (Second Edition). Chicago, IL: American Library Association.

Cullinan, Bernice, Marilyn Scala, and Virginia Schroder. 1995. *Three Voices: An Invitation to Poetry Across the Curriculum.* Portland, ME: Stenhouse.

Cummings, Pat. 1992. *Talking with Artists.* New York: Simon & Schuster.

Cummings, Pat. 1995. *Talking with Artists, Volume 2.* New York: Simon & Schuster.

Cummings, Pat. 1999. *Talking with Artists, Volume 3.* New York: Simon & Schuster.

Cummins, James. 2003. "Reading and the Bilingual Student: Fact and Friction." In G. Garcia (Ed.), *English Learners: Reaching the Highest Levels of English Literacy* (pp. 2–33). Newark, DE: International Reading Association.

Cummins, Julie. (Ed.) 1997. *Children's Book Illustration and Design II.* Los Angeles, CA: PBC International.

Cummins, Julie, and Barbara Kiefer. 1999. *Wings of an Artist: Children's Book Illustrators Talk About Their Art.* New York: Abrams.

Darling, Harold. 1999. *From Mother Goose to Dr. Seuss: Children's Book Covers 1860–1960.* San Francisco: Chronicle Books.

de Las Casas, Dianne. 2006. *Kamishibai Story Theater: The Art of Picture Telling.* Englewood, CO: Libraries Unlimited.

de Las Casas, Dianne. 2011. *Tell Along Tales!: Playing with Participation Stories.* Englewood, CO: Libraries Unlimited.

Diamant-Cohen, Betsy. 2006. *Mother Goose on the Loose.* New York: Neal-Schuman.

Diamant-Cohen, Betsy, and Selma K. Levi. 2008. *Booktalking Bonanza: Ten Ready-to-Use Multimedia Sessions for the Busy Librarian.* Chicago: American Library Association.

Donelson, Kenneth L. 1974. "What to Do When the Censor Comes." *Elementary English, 51* (3), 410–414.

Dresang, Eliza. 1999. *Radical Change: Books for Youth in a Digital Age.* New York: H. W. Wilson.

Durbin, Deborah. 1997. *Little Women, Louisa May Alcott: About the Author.* http://xroads.virginia.edu/~Hyper/ALCOTT/ABOUTLA.html. Accessed November 12, 2006.

East, Kathy, and Rebecca L. Thomas. 2007. *Across Cultures: A Guide to Multicultural Literature for Children.* Englewood, CO: Libraries Unlimited.

Edinger, Monica. 2000. *Seeking History: Teaching with Primary Sources in Grades 4–6.* Portsmouth, NH: Heinemann.

Edinger, Monica, and Stephanie Fins. 1997. *Far Away and Long Ago: Young Historians in the Classroom.* Portland, ME: Stenhouse.

Elleman, Barbara. 1999. *Tomie de Paola: His Art and His Stories.* New York: Putnam.

Elleman, Barbara. 2002. *Virginia Lee Burton: A Life in Art.* Boston: Houghton Mifflin.

Elleman, Barbara. 2009. *Drawings from the Heart: Tomie de Paola Turns 75.* Amherst, MA: Eric Carle Museum of Picture Book Art.

Elleman, Barbara. 2009. *Those Telling Lines: The Art of Virginia Lee Burton.* Amherst, MA: Eric Carle Museum of Picture Book Art.

Eric Carle Museum of Picture Book Art. 2007. *Artist to Artist: 23 Major Illustrators Talk to Children About Their Art.* New York: Philomel.

Ernst, Linda. 2007. *Baby Rhyming Time.* New York: Neal-Schuman.

Evans, Dilys. 2008. *Show and Tell: Exploring the Fine Art of Children's Book Illustration.* San Francisco: Chronicle Books.

Farmer, Lesley. 2013. *Library Services for Youth with Autism Spectrum Disorders.* Chicago: American Library Association.

Fitch, Sheree, and Larry Swartz. 2008. *The Poetry Experience: Choosing and Using Poetry in the Classroom.* Markham, Ontario, Canada: Pembroke.

Follis, Marianne. 2010. *Newbery and Notables 2000–2009: Investigating Trends.* Dissertation. Texas Woman's University.

Follos, Alison M. G. 2006. *Reviving Reading: School Library Programming, Author Visits and Books That Rock!* Englewood, CO: Libraries Unlimited.

Fox, Mem. 2008. *Reading Magic: Why Reading Aloud to Our Children Will Change Their Lives Forever* (Updated and Revised Edition). Boston: Mariner Books.

Franco, Betsy. 2005. *Conversations with a Poet: Inviting Poetry into K–12 Classrooms.* Somers, NY: Richard C. Owen.

Fredericks, Anthony D. 2007. *Nonfiction Readers Theatre for Beginning Readers.* Englewood, CO: Libraries Unlimited.

Freeman, Evelyn, and Diane Person. Eds. 1992. *Using Nonfiction Tradebooks in the Elementary Classroom.* Urbana, IL: National Council of Teachers of English.

Freeman, Evelyn, and Diane Person. 1998. *Connecting Informational Children's Books with Content Area Learning.* New York: Allyn and Bacon.

Fricke, John. 1999. *100 Years of Oz: A Century of Classic Images.* New York: Stewart, Tabori and Chang.

Fritz, Jean. 2001. "Nonfiction 1999." In Myra Zarnowski, Richard Kerper, and Julie Jensen (Eds.), *The Best in Children's Nonfiction: Reading, Writing, and Teaching Orbis Pictus Award Books.* Urbana, IL: National Council of Teachers of English.

Galda, Lee, Lawrence R. Sipe, L. A. Liang, and Bernice Cullinan. 2013. *Literature and the Child* (Eighth Edition). Independence, KY: Cengage Learning.

Gardner, Martin, and Russell B. Nye. 2011. *The Wizard of Oz and Who He Was.* Revised. Whitefish, MT: Literary Licensing.

Garner, Joan. 2006. *Wings of Fancy: Using Readers Theatre to Study Fantasy Genre.* Englewood, CO: Libraries Unlimited.

Garrity, Linda K. 1999. *The Tale Spinner: Folktales, Themes, and Activities.* Golden, CO: Fulcrum Resources.

Gates, Pamela S., Susan B. Steffel, and Francis J. Molson. 2003. *Fantasy Literature for Children and Young Adults.* Lanham, MD: Rowman & Littlefield.

Ghoting, Saroj, and Pamela Martin-Diaz. 2005. *Early Literacy Storytimes @ Your Library: Partnering with Caregivers for Success.* Chicago, IL: American Library Association.

Gillespie, John, and Corinne Naden. 2006. *The Newbery/Printz Companion: Booktalk and Related Materials for Award Winners and Honor Books* (Third Edition). Englewood, CO: Libraries Unlimited.

Glenn-Paul, Dierdre. 1997. "Toward Developing a Multicultural Perspective." In Violet Harris (Ed.), *Using Multiethnic Literature in the K–8 Classroom.* Norwood, MA: Christopher-Gordon.

Glover, M. K. 1999. *A Garden of Poets.* Urbana, IL: National Council of Teachers of English.

Goldsmith, Francisca. 2009. *The Readers' Advisory Guide to Graphic Novels.* Chicago, IL: American Library Association.

Goodwin, Katharine F. 2003. *In Search of Cinderella: A Curriculum for the 21st Century.* Arcadia, CA: Shen's Books.

Gorman, Michelle. 2003. *Getting Graphic! Using Graphic Novels to Promote Literacy with Preteens and Teens.* Columbus, OH: Linworth.

Gorman, Michelle. 2007. Graphic Novels for Younger Readers. *Book Links.* http://www.ala.org/ala/booklinksbucket/graphicnovelsforyounger.htm. Accessed May 21, 2007.

Green, David L., and Dick Martin. 1977. *The Oz Scrapbook*. New York: Random House.

Greene, Ellin, and Janice M. Del Negro. 2010. *Storytelling: Art and Technique* (Fourth Edition). Englewood, CO: Libraries Unlimited.

Greenlaw, M. Jean, and Margaret McIntosh. 1986. "Literature for Use with Gifted Children." *Childhood Education, 62* (4), 281–286.

Grenby, M. O., and A. Immel. Eds. 2010. *The Cambridge Companion to Children's Literature*. Cambridge, England: Cambridge University Press.

Gross, Ila Lane. 2001. *Cinderella Tales from Around the World* (LEAP's Global Understanding Book Series). New York: LEAP.

Gunning, Thomas. 2000. *Best Books for Building Literacy for Elementary School Children*. New York: Allyn & Bacon.

Hadaway, Nancy, and Marian McKenna. 2007. *Breaking Boundaries with Global Literature: Celebrating Diversity in K–12 Classrooms*. Newark, DE: International Reading Association.

Hadaway, Nancy, Sylvia M. Vardell, and Terrell Young. 2002. *Literature-based Instruction with English Language Learners*. New York: Allyn & Bacon.

Hall, Susan. 2007. *Using Picture Storybooks to Teach Literary Devices: Recommended Books for Children and Young Adults*, Volumes I, II, III, & IV. Englewood, CO: Libraries Unlimited.

Hannegan, Lizette, and Sharon Grover. 2011. *Listening to Learn: Audiobooks Supporting Literacy*. Chicago, IL: American Library Association.

Harmon, Amy. 2005. "Authors on Audio: Better a Listen Than a Pass." *The New York Times*, May 26, 2005.

Harris, Violet. Ed. 1997. *Using Multiethnic Literature in the K–8 Classroom*. Norwood, MA: Christopher-Gordon.

Harvey, S. 1998. *Nonfiction Matters: Reading, Writing, and Research in Grades 3–8*. Portland, ME: Stenhouse.

Haven, Kendall, and MaryGay Ducey. 2006. *Crash Course in Storytelling*. Englewood, CO: Libraries Unlimited.

Heard, Georgia. 1999. *Awakening the Heart: Exploring Poetry in Elementary and Middle School*. Portsmouth, NH: Heinemann.

Heard, Georgia. 2013. *Poetry Lessons to Meet the Common Core State Standards: Exemplar Poems with Engaging Lessons and Response Activities That Help Students Read, Understand, and Appreciate Poetry*. New York: Scholastic.

Hearn, Michael Patrick. 1996. *Myth, Magic, and Mystery: One Hundred Years of American Children's Book Illustration*. Lanham, MD: Roberts Rinehart.

Hearn, Michael Patrick. Ed. 2000. *The Annotated Wizard of Oz: The Centennial Edition*. New York: W. W. Norton.

Hearne, Betsy, with Deborah Stevenson. 1999. *Choosing Books for Children: A Commonsense Guide* (Third Edition). Urbana, IL: University of Illinois Press.

Heath, Shirley Brice. 1983. *Ways with Words: Language, Life, and Work in Communities and Classrooms*. Cambridge, England: Cambridge University Press.

Heiner, Heidi Anne. 2012. *Cinderella Tales from Around the World*. CreateSpace.

Heitman, Jane. 2004. *Teach Writing to Older Readers Using Picture Books: Every Picture Tells a Story*. Columbus, OH: Linworth.

Hepler, Susan. 1998. "Nonfiction Books for Children: New Directions, New Challenges." In Janice Kristo and Rosemary Bamford (Eds.), *Making Facts Come Alive: Choosing Nonfiction Literature K–8*. Norwood, MA: Christopher-Gordon.

Herald, Diana Tixier. 1999. *Fluent in Fantasy: A Guide to Reading Interests*. Englewood, CO: Libraries Unlimited.

Hielsberg, Amy. 1994. "Self-Censorship Starts Early: A Library School Student Learns an Unexpected Lesson When She Tackles a Touchy Topic." *American Libraries, 25*, 768–770.

Hilbun, Janet W., and Jane H. Claes. 2010. *Coast to Coast: Exploring State Book Awards.* Englewood, CO: Libraries Unlimited.

Hillman, Judith. 2002. *Discovering Children's Literature* (Third Edition). Upper Saddle River, NJ: Merrill Prentice Hall.

Holbrook, Sara. 2002. *Wham! It's a Poetry Jam: Discovering Performance Poetry.* Honesdale, PA: Wordsong/Boyds Mills Press.

Holbrook, Sara. 2005. *Practical Poetry: A Nonstandard Approach to Meeting Content-Area Standards.* Portsmouth, NH: Heinemann.

Holbrook, Sara, and Michael Salinger. 2006. *Outspoken: How to Improve Writing and Speaking Through Poetry Performance.* Portsmouth, NH: Heinemann.

Holdaway, Don. 1984. *The Foundations of Literacy.* New York: Scholastic.

Hollenbeck, Kathleen. 2003. *Teaching with Cinderella Stories from Around the World (Grades 1–3).* New York: Teaching Resources.

Hopkins, Lee Bennett. 1995. *Pauses: Autobiographical Reflections of 101 Creators of Children's Books.* New York: HarperCollins.

Horning, Kathleen. 2010. *From Cover to Cover: Evaluating and Reviewing Children's Books* (Revised Edition). New York: HarperCollins.

Huck, Charlotte. Ed. (2000). *Children's Literature in the Elementary School.* New York: McGraw-Hill.

Hunt, Peter. Ed. 2000. *Children's Literature: An Anthology, 1801–1902.* Oxford: Blackwell.

Hurst, Carol Otis, and Rebecca Otis. 1993. *In Times Past: An Encyclopedia for Integrating U.S. History with Literature in Grades 3–8.* New York: McGraw-Hill.

Inness, S. 1997. *Nancy Drew and Company: Culture, Gender, and Girls' Series.* Bowling Green, OH: Bowling Green State University Popular Press.

Isaacs, Kathleen T. 2012. *Picturing the World: Informational Picture Books for Children.* Chicago, IL: American Library Association.

James, Edward, and Farah Mendlesohn. 2012. *The Cambridge Companion to Fantasy Literature.* Cambridge, England: Cambridge University Press.

James, Helen Foster. 2002. *Author Day Adventures: Bringing Literacy to Life with an Author Visit.* Lanham, MD: Scarecrow.

Janeczko, Paul B. 2011. *Reading Poetry in the Middle Grades: 20 Poems and Activities That Meet the Common Core Standards and Cultivate a Passion for Poetry.* Portsmouth, NH: Heinemann.

Jarombek, Kathy, and Anne Leon. 2010. "Leadership at Its Best: Library Managers Spearhead Successful Special Needs Programming." *Children & Libraries 8,* 2, 54–57.

Jenkins, Carol Brennan. 1999. *The Allure of Authors: Author Studies in the Elementary Classroom.* Portsmouth, NH: Heinemann.

Jenkins, Carol Brennan, and Deborah White. 2007. *Nonfiction Author Studies in the Elementary Classroom.* Portsmouth, NH: Heinemann.

Jenkins, Diana R. 2004. *Just Deal with It!: Funny Readers Theatre for Life's Not-So-Funny Moments.* Englewood, CO: Libraries Unlimited.

Jenkins, Diana R. 2007. *All Year Long!: Funny Readers Theatre for Life's Special Times.* Englewood, CO: Libraries Unlimited.

Johansen, K. V. 2005. *Quests and Kingdoms: A Grown-Up's Guide to Children's Fantasy Literature.* Sackville, New Brunswick, Canada: Sybertooth.

Kennedy, X. J., and D. Kennedy. 1999. *Knock at a Star.* New York: Little, Brown.

Kerper, Rick. 2003. "Features for Accessing and Visualizing Information." In Janice Kristo and Rosemary Bamford (Eds.), *Making Facts Come Alive: Choosing Non-fiction Literature K–8* (Second Edition). Norwood, MA: Christopher-Gordon.

Kiefer, Barbara Z. 2010. *Charlotte Huck's Children's Literature* (Tenth Edition). Boston: McGraw-Hill.

Kiefer, B. Z., and C. Tyson. 2013. *Charlotte Huck's Children's Literature: A Brief Guide* (Second Edition). Boston, MA: McGraw-Hill.

Knowles, Elizabeth, and Martha Smith. 2007. *Understanding Diversity Through Novels and Picture Books*. Englewood, CO: Libraries Unlimited.

Kokkola, Lydia. 2002. *Representing the Holocaust in Children's Literature*. London: Routledge.

Kolencik, Patricia Liotta, and Carianne Bernadowski. 2007. *Teaching with Books That Heal: Authentic Literature and Literacy Strategies to Help Children Cope with Everyday Problems*. Columbus, OH: Linworth.

Krashen, Stephen. 2004. *The Power of Reading: Insights from the Research* (Second Edition). Portsmouth, NH: Heinemann.

Krey, DeAn M. 1998. *Children's Literature in Social Studies: Teaching to the Standards*. Silver Spring, MD: National Council for the Social Studies.

Kristo, J., and R. Bamford. Eds. 2003. *Making Facts Come Alive: Choosing Nonfiction Literature K–8* (Second Edition). Norwood, MA: Christopher-Gordon.

Kuharets, Olga R. 2001. *Venture into Cultures: A Resource Book of Multicultural Materials & Programs*. Chicago: American Library Association.

Langemack, Chapple. 2003. *The Booktalker's Bible: How to Talk About the Books You Love to Any Audience*. Englewood, CO: Libraries Unlimited.

Larson, Jeanette. 2004. *Bringing Mysteries Alive for Children and Young Adults*. Columbus, OH: Linworth.

LaRue, James. 2007. *The New Inquisition: Understanding and Managing Intellectual Freedom Challenges*. Englewood, CO: Libraries Unlimited.

Lesesne, Teri. 2006. "Why Listen: The Hows and Whys of Audiobooks." http://www.professornana.com/. Accessed May 22, 2007.

Levstik, Linda S., and Keith C. Barton. 2010. *Doing History: Investigating with Children in Elementary and Middle Schools* (Fourth Edition). London: Routledge.

Lewis, David. 2001. *Picturing Text: The Contemporary Children's Picturebook*. London: Routledge.

Lima, Carolyn, and Rebecca L. Thomas. 2010. *A to Zoo: Subject Access to Children's Picture Books* (Eighth Edition). Englewood, CO: Libraries Unlimited.

Lipson, Eden Ross. 2000. *The New York Times Parent's Guide to the Best Books for Children* (Third Edition). New York: Three Rivers Press.

Livingston, Myra Cohn. 1990. *Climb into the Bell Tower: Essays on Poetry*. New York: HarperCollins.

Livo, Norma J., and Sandra A. Rietz. 1991. *Storytelling Folklore Sourcebook*. Englewood, CO: Libraries Unlimited.

Lukens, Rebecca, Jacquelin Smith, and Cynthia M. Coffel. 2012. *A Critical Handbook of Children's Literature* (Ninth Edition). New York: Pearson.

Lundsteen, Sara W. 1979. *Listening: Its Impact at All Levels on Reading and Other Language Arts* (Revised Edition). Urbana, Illinois: National Council of Teachers of English.

Lundsteen, Sara. 1990. "Learning to Listen and Learning to Read in Perspectives on Talk and Learning." In Susan Hynds and Donald L. Rubin (Eds.), *NCTE Forum Series*. Urbana, IL: National Council of Teachers of English.

MacDonald, Margaret Read. 2006. *Storyteller's Start-Up Book*. Atlanta, GA: August House.

MacDonald, Margaret Read. 2006. *Ten Traditional Tellers*. Urbana, IL: University of Illinois Press.

MacDonald, Margaret Read, and Brian W. Sturm. 2001. *Storyteller's Sourcebook: A Subject, Title, and Motif Index to Folklore Collections for Children, 1983–1999*. Farmington Hills, MI: Thomson Gale.

Manlove, Colin. 1999. *The Fantasy Literature of England*. New York: St. Martin's Press.

Marantz, Sylvia. 1992. *Picture Books for Looking and Learning: Awakening Visual Perceptions Through the Art of Children's Books*. Phoenix, AZ: Oryx Press.

Marantz, Sylvia. 2013. *Artists of the Page: Interviews with Children's Book Illustrators*. Jefferson, NC: McFarland.

Marantz, Sylvia, and Kenneth A. Marantz. 2005. *Multicultural Picture Books: Art for Understanding Others* (Second Edition). Lanham, MD: Scarecrow.

Marantz, Sylvia, and Kenneth A. Marantz. 2006. *Creating Picturebooks: Interviews with Editors, Art Directors, Reviewers, Booksellers, Professors, Librarians and Showcasers*. Jefferson, NC: McFarland.

Marcus, Leonard S. 1994. *75 Years of Children's Book Week Posters: Celebrating Great Illustrators of American Children's Books*. New York: Knopf.

Marcus, Leonard. 1999. *A Caldecott Celebration: Six Artists Share Their Paths to the Caldecott Medal*. New York: Walker.

Marcus, Leonard. 1999. *Margaret Wise Brown: Awakened by the Moon*. New York: Harper.

Marcus, Leonard. 2002. *Ways of Telling: Conversations on the Art of the Picture Book*. New York: Dutton.

Marcus, Leonard. 2006. *Pass It Down: Five Picture Book Families Make Their Mark*. New York: Walker.

Marcus, Leonard. 2006. *Side by Side: Five Favorite Picture Book Teams Go to Work*. New York: Walker.

Marcus, Leonard. 2006. *The Wand in the Word: Conversations with Writers of Fantasy*. Cambridge, MA: Candlewick.

Marcus, Leonard. 2007. *Golden Legacy: How Golden Books Won Children's Hearts, Changed Publishing Forever, and Became an American Icon Along the Way*. New York: Random House.

Marcus, Leonard. 2012. *Show Me a Story! Why Picture Books Matter: Conversations with 21 of the World's Most Celebrated Illustrators*. Somerville, MA: Candlewick.

Mayer, Brian, and Christopher Harris. 2009. *Libraries Got Game: Aligned Learning Through Modern Board Games*. Chicago: American Library Association.

Mayes, Walter, and Valerie Lewis. 2004. *Valerie & Walter's Best Books for Children: A Lively, Opinionated Guide* (Second Edition). New York: Collins.

Maynard, Trisha. 2002. *Boys and Literacy: Exploring the Issues*. London: Routledge.

McCloud, Scott. 1994. *Understanding Comics: The Invisible Art*. New York: Morrow.

McClure, A. 1990. *Sunrises and Songs: Reading and Writing Poetry in the Classroom*. Portsmouth, NH: Heinemann.

McDaniel, Deanna J. 2007. *Gentle Reads: Great Books to Warm Hearts and Lift Spirits, Grades 5–9*. Englewood, CO: Libraries Unlimited.

McElmeel, Sharron L. 2000. *100 Most Popular Picture Book Authors and Illustrators: Biographical Sketches and Bibliographies*. Englewood, CO: Libraries Unlimited.

McElmeel, Sharron. L. 2001. *ABCs of an Author/Illustrator Visit* (Second Edition). Columbus, OH: Linworth.

McElmeel, Sharron, L., and Deborah L. McElmeel. 2005. *Authors in the Kitchen: Recipes, Stories, and More*. Englewood, CO: Libraries Unlimited.

McElmeel, Sharron, L., and Deborah L. McElmeel. 2006. *Authors in the Pantry: Recipes, Stories, and More.* Englewood, CO: Libraries Unlimited.

McKissack, Patricia. 2000. In Susan Lehr (Ed.), *Beauty, Brains, and Brawn: The Construction of Gender in Children's Literature.* Portsmouth, NH: Heinemann.

Mello, Robin. 2001. "Cinderella Meets Ulysses." *Language Arts, 78* (6), 548–555.

Miller, Donalyn. 2009. *The Book Whisperer: Awakening the Inner Reader in Every Child.* San Francisco: Jossey-Bass.

Miller, Wanda J. 1997. *U.S. History Through Children's Literature: From the Colonial Period to World War II.* Englewood, CO: Teacher Ideas Press.

Miller, Wanda J. 1998. *Teaching U.S. History Through Children's Literature: Post–World War II.* Englewood, CO: Libraries Unlimited.

Mitchell, Diana. 2003. *Children's Literature: An Invitation to the World.* Boston: Allyn & Bacon.

Mooney, Margaret E. 2001. *Texts and Forms and Features: A Resource for Intentional Teaching.* Katonah, NY: Richard C. Owen.

Mora, Pat. 2010. *Zing! Seven Creativity Practices for Educators and Students.* Thousand Oaks, CA: Corwin.

Morris, Betty J. 2004. *Administering the School Library Center* (Fourth Edition, Revised and Expanded). Englewood, CO: Libraries Unlimited.

Nadelman, Lynn Ruth. 2005. *Fantasy Literature for Children and Young Adults: A Comprehensive. Guide* (Fifth Edition). Englewood, CO: Libraries Unlimited.

Nespeca, Sue McCleaf, and Joan B. Reeve. 2003. *Picture Books Plus: 100 Extension Activities in Art, Drama, Music, Math, and Science.* Chicago, IL: American Library Association.

Nikolajeva, Mari, and Carole Scott. 2006. *How Picturebooks Work (Garland Reference Library of the Humanities).* London: Routledge.

Nodelman, Perry, and Mavis Reimer. 2003. *The Pleasures of Children's Literature* (Third Edition). Boston: Allyn & Bacon.

Norfolk, Sherry, Jane Stenson, and Diane Williams. 2006. *The Storytelling Classroom: Applications Across the Curriculum.* Englewood, CO: Libraries Unlimited.

Northrup, Mary. 2012. *Picture Books for Children: Fiction, Folktales and Poetry.* Chicago, IL: American Library Association.

Norton, Donna, and Saundra Norton. 2011. *Through the Eyes of a Child: An Introduction to Children's Literature* (Eighth Edition). New York: Pearson.

O'Connor, John S. 2004. *Wordplaygrounds: Reading, Writing & Performing Poetry in the English Classroom.* Urbana, IL: National Council of Teachers of English.

Odean, Kathleen. 2001. *Great Books About Things Kids Love: More Than 750 Recommended Books for Children 3 to 14.* New York: Ballantine Books.

Odean, Kathleen. 2003. *Great Books for Babies and Toddlers: More Than 500 Recommended Books for Your Child's First Three Years.* New York: Ballantine Books.

Ohler, Jason B. 2013. *Digital Storytelling in the Classroom: New Media Pathways to Literacy, Learning, and Creativity* (Second Edition). Thousand Oaks, CA: Corwin.

Opie, Iona, and Peter Opie. 1959. *The Lore and Language of Schoolchildren.* Oxford: Oxford University Press.

Opie, Peter, and Iona Opie. 1952. *The Oxford Dictionary of Nursery Rhymes.* Oxford: Oxford University Press.

Ordonez-Jasis, Rosario, and Robert W. Ortiz. 2006. "Reading Their Worlds: Working with Diverse Families to Enhance Children's Early Literacy Development." *Young Children, 61* (1), 42–48.

Pang, V. O., C. Colvin, M. Tran, and R. Barba. 1992. "Beyond Chopsticks and Dragons: Selecting Asian-American Literature for Children." *The Reading Teacher, 46* (3), 216–223.

Pawuk, Michael. 2006. *Graphic Novels: A Genre Guide to Comic Books, Manga, and More.* Englewood, CO: Libraries Unlimited.

Pearl, Nancy. 2007. *Book Crush.* Seattle, WA: Sasquatch Books.

Pearson, Molly Blake. 2005. *Big Ideas in Small Packages: Using Picture Books with Older Readers.* Columbus, OH: Linworth.

Pellowski, Anne. 1991. *The World of Storytelling.* New York: H. W. Wilson.

Pellowski, Anne. 2005. *Drawing Stories from around the World and a Sampling of European Handkerchief Stories.* Englewood, CO: Libraries Unlimited.

Pennac, Daniel. 1996. *Better Than Life.* Toronto, Ontario, Canada: Coach House Press.

Perry, Phyllis J. 1998. *Exploring Our Country's History: Linking Fiction to Nonfiction.* Englewood, CO: Libraries Unlimited.

Perry, Phyllis J. 1998. *Exploring the World of Sports: Linking Fiction to Nonfiction.* Englewood, CO: Libraries Unlimited.

Perry, Phyllis J. 2003. *Teaching Fantasy Novels: From the Hobbit to Harry Potter and the Goblet of Fire.* Englewood, CO: Libraries Unlimited.

Peterson, R., and M. Eeds. 1990. *Grand Conversations: Literature Groups in Action.* New York: Scholastic.

Phillips, Susan P. 2008. *Great Displays for Your Library Step by Step.* Jefferson, NC: McFarland.

Pilgreen, Janice. 2000. *The SSR Handbook: How to Organize and Manage a Sustained Silent Reading Program.* New York: Boynton/Cook.

Pinnell, Gay S., and Andrea M. Jagger. 1991. "Oral Language: Speaking and Listening in the Classroom." In J. Flood, Julie M. Jensen, D. Lapp, and J. R. Squire (Eds.), *Handbook of Research on Teaching the English Language Arts.* New York: Macmillan.

Polette, Nancy. 2000. *Gifted Books, Gifted Readers: Literature Activities to Excite Young Minds.* Englewood, CO: Libraries Unlimited.

Polette, Nancy. 2005. *Teaching Thinking Skills with Fairy Tales and Fantasy.* Englewood, CO: Libraries Unlimited.

Polette, Nancy. 2006. *Books Every Child Should Know: The Literature Quiz Book.* Englewood, CO: Libraries Unlimited.

Pollette, Nancy, and Joan Ebbesmeyer. 2002. *Literature Lures: Using Picture Books and Novels to Motivate Middle School Readers.* Englewood, CO: Teacher Ideas Press.

Postlethwaite, T. N., and K. N. Ross. 1992. *Effective Schools in Reading: Implications for Educational Planners.* The Hague: The International Association for the Evaluation of Educational Achievement.

Pratt, Anna Alcott. 1903. "A Letter from Miss Alcott's Sister about Little Women." *St. Nicholas,* May 1903, Vol. XXX: Part II, p. 631. Literature Resource Center Database. http://ezproxy.twu.edu. Accessed November 18, 2006.

Ray, Katie Wood. 1999. *Wondrous Words: Writers and Writing in the Elementary Classroom.* Urbana, IL: National Council of Teachers of English.

Reese, Debbie, and Naomi Caldwell-Wood. 1997. "Native Americans in Children's Literature." In Violet Harris (Ed.), *Using Multiethnic Literature in the K–8 Classroom.* Norwood, MA: Christopher-Gordon.

Reid, Rob. 1999. *Family Storytime.* Chicago, IL: American Library Association.

Reid, Rob. 2004. *Cool Story Programs for the School-Age Crowd.* Chicago, IL: American Library Association.

Reid, Rob. 2009. *More Family Storytimes.* Chicago, IL: American Library Association.

Reid, Rob. 2009. *Reid's Read-Alouds: Selections for Children and Teens.* Chicago, IL: American Library Association.

Reid, Rob. 2010. *Reid's Read-alouds 2.* Chicago, IL: American Library Association.

Riley, Michael O. 1997. *Oz and Beyond: The Fantasy World of L. Frank Baum.* Lawrence, KS: University Press of Kansas.

Roback, Diane, and Jason Britton. 2001. "All-Time Bestselling Children's Books." *Publishers Weekly.* December 17, 2001. http://www.publishersweekly.com/article/CA186995.html. Accessed February 21, 2007.

Rochman, Hazel. 1993. *Against Borders: Promoting Books for a Multicultural World.* Chicago, IL: American Library Association.

Rockman, Connie. Ed. 2008. *Tenth Book of Junior Authors and Illustrators.* New York: H. W. Wilson.

Rogers, Katharine M. 2006. *L. Frank Baum: Creator of Oz.* New York: Da Capo.

Rosenblatt, Louise. Reissued 1996. *Literature as Exploration.* New York: Modern Language Association.

Roser, Nancy L., and Miriam G. Martinez. 1995. *Book Talk and Beyond: Children and Teachers Respond to Literature.* Newark, DE: International Reading Association.

Ross, Virginia, and Lynn Akin. 2003. "Texas Public Libraries and Children with Learning Disabilities." *Public Library Quarterly,* 21 (4), 9–18.

Russell, David L. 2011. *Literature for Children: A Short Introduction* (Seventh Edition). New York: Pearson.

Salisbury, Martin. 2004. *Illustrating Children's Books: Creating Pictures for Publication.* Hauppauge, NY: Barron's Educational Books.

Salisbury, Martin, and Morag Styles. 2012. *Children's Picturebooks: The Art of Visual Storytelling.* London, England: Laurence King Publishers.

Saltman, Judith. Coll. 1985. *The Riverside Anthology of Children's Literature* (Sixth Edition). Boston: Houghton Mifflin.

Sandmann, Alexa A., and John F. Ahern. 2002. *Linking Literature with Life: The NCSS Standards and Children's Literature in the Middle Grades.* Silver Spring, MD: National Council for the Social Studies.

Sandner, David. 1996. *The Fantastic Sublime: Romanticism and Transcendence in Nineteenth-Century Children's Fantasy Literature.* Westport, CT: Greenwood.

Sawyer, Ruth. 1977. *The Way of the Storyteller.* New York: Penguin.

Scales, Pat R. 2001. *Teaching Banned Books: 12 Guides for Young Readers.* Chicago: American Library Association.

Scales, Pat R. 2009. *Protecting Intellectual Freedom in Your School Library: Scenarios from the Front Lines.* Chicago: American Library Association.

Schiller, Justin, Dennis David, Leonard Marcus, and Maurice Sendak. 2013. *Maurice Sendak: A Celebration of the Artist and His Work.* New York: Abrams.

Schneider, Dean, and Robin Smith. 2001. "Unlucky Arithmetic: Thirteen Ways to Raise a Nonreader." *The Horn Book,* 77 (2), 192–193.

Schur, Joan Brodsky. 2007. *Eyewitness to the Past: Strategies for Teaching American History in Grades 5–12.* Portland, ME: Stenhouse.

Shepard, Aaron. 2004. *Readers on Stage: Resources for Reader's Theater (or Readers Theatre), with Tips, Play Scripts, and Worksheets, or How to Do Simple Children's Plays That Build Reading Fluency and Love of Literature.* Olympia, WA: Shepard.

Short, Kathy, Carol Lynch-Brown, and Carl Tomlinson. 2014. *Essentials of Children's Literature* (Eighth Edition). Boston, MA: Pearson.

Shulevitz, Uri. 1997. *Writing with Pictures: How to Write and Illustrate Children's Books.* New York: Watson-Guptill.

Sierra, Judy. 1992. *Cinderella.* Phoenix, AZ: Oryx.

Sierra, Judy. 2002. *Can You Guess My Name?: Traditional Tales Around the World.* New York: Clarion.

Silvey, Anita. 2002. *The Essential Guide to Children's Books and Their Creators.* Boston: Mariner Books.

Silvey, Anita. 2005. *100 Best Books for Children: A Parent's Guide to Making the Right Choices for Your Young Reader, Toddler to Preteen.* Boston: Houghton Mifflin.

Silvey, Anita. 2012. *Children's Book-a-Day Almanac.* New York: Roaring Brook Press.

Sipe, Lawrence, and Sylvia Pantaleo. Eds. 2008. *Postmodern Picturebooks: Play, Parody, and Self-Referentiality.* London: Routledge.

Skaggs, Gayle. 2008. *Look, It's Books!: Marketing Your Library with Displays and Promotions.* Jefferson, NC: McFarland.

Slapin, B., and D. Seale. Eds. 1998. *Through Indian Eyes: The Native Experience in Books for Children* (Fourth Edition). Berkeley, CA: Oyate.

Sloan, Ann, and Sylvia M. Vardell. 2004. "Cinderella and Her Sisters: Variants and Versions." In T. A. Young (Ed.), *Happily Ever After: Sharing Folk Literature with Students.* Newark, DE: International Reading Association.

Smith, Michael, and Jeffrey D. Wilhelm. 2002. *"Reading Don't Fix No Chevys": Literacy in the Lives of Young Men.* Portsmouth, NH: Boynton/Cook.

Spitz, E. H., and R. Coles. 1999. *Inside Picture Books.* New Haven, CT: Yale University Press.

Stahl, J. D., Tina L. Hanlon, and Elizabeth Lennox Keyser. 2006. *Crosscurrents of Children's Literature: An Anthology of Texts and Criticism.* Oxford: Oxford University Press.

Stoodt-Hill, B. D., and L. B. Amspaugh-Corson. 2008. *Children's Literature: Discovery for a Lifetime* (Fourth Edition). New York: Pearson.

Sullivan, C. W. 1989. *Welsh Celtic Myth in Modern Fantasy.* Westport, CT: Greenwood.

Sullivan, Edward T. 1999. *The Holocaust in Literature for Youth.* Lanham, MD: Scarecrow.

Sullivan, Michael. 2003. *Connecting Boys with Books: What Libraries Can Do.* Chicago: American Library Association.

Sullivan, Michael. 2009. *Connecting Boys with Books 2: Closing the Reading Gap.* Chicago: American Library Association.

Sulzby, Elizabeth, and William Teale. 1996. "Emergent Literacy." In R. Barr, M. L. Kamil, P. B. Mosenthal, and P. D. Pearson (Eds.), *Handbook of Reading Research.* Mahway, NH: Lawrence Erlbaum.

Sunshine, Linda. 2003. *All Things Oz: The Wonder, Wit, and Wisdom of the Wizard of Oz.* New York: Crown.

Sutherland, Zena. Ed. 1983. *The Scott, Foresman Anthology of Children's Literature.* New York: Scott, Foresman.

Sutherland, Zena. 2004. *Children and Books* (Tenth Edition). New York: Longman.

Swartz, Mark Evan. 2002. *Oz Before the Rainbow: L. Frank Baum's "The Wonderful Wizard of Oz" on Stage and Screen to 1939.* Baltimore, MD: The Johns Hopkins University Press.

Tatar, Maria. 1992. *Off with Their Heads!: Fairy Tales and the Culture of Childhood.* Princeton, NJ: Princeton University Press.

Tatar, Maria. 1998. *The Classic Fairy Tales: Texts, Criticism (Norton Critical Editions)*. New York: W. W. Norton.

Tatar, Maria. 2003. *The Hard Facts of the Grimms' Fairy Tales* (Revised). Princeton, NJ: Princeton University Press.

Temple, Charles, Miriam Martinez, and Junko Yokota. 2011. *Children's Books in Children's Hands: An Introduction to Their Literature* (Fourth Edition). New York: Pearson.

Thomas, Cathlyn, and Carol Littlejohn. 2003. *Still Talking That Book!: Booktalks to Promote Reading Grades 3–12*. Columbus, OH: Linworth.

Thomas, Joseph T., Jr. 2007. *Poetry's Playground: The Culture of Contemporary American Children's Poetry*. Detroit, MI: Wayne State University Press.

Tiedt, Iris. 2000. *Teaching with Picture Books in the Middle School*. Newark, DE: International Reading Association.

Trelease, Jim. 2013. *The Read-Aloud Handbook* (Seventh Edition.) New York: Penguin.

Trites, Roberta S. 1997. *Waking Sleeping Beauty: Feminist Voices in Children's Novels*. Iowa City, IA: University of Iowa Press.

Tunnell, Michael, and Richard Ammon. 1993. *The Story of Ourselves: Teaching History Through Children's Literature*. Portsmouth, NH: Heinemann.

Tunnell, Michael, and James Jacobs, Terrell Young, and Gregory Bryan. 2012. *Children's Literature, Briefly* (Fifth Edition). Upper Saddle River, NJ: Prentice Hall.

Underdown, Harold. 2008. *The Complete Idiot's Guide to Publishing Children's Books* (Third Edition). New York: Alpha.

Vardell, S. M. 2000. "Looking at Literacy in Urban Families: Surveying the Scene." *English Leadership Quarterly*. National Council of Teachers of English. *22* (3), 6–9.

Vardell, S. M. 2003. "Poetry for Social Studies: Poems, Standards, and Strategies." *Social Education 67* (4), 206–211.

Vardell, S. M. 2003. "Using Read Aloud to Explore the Layers of Nonfiction." In Janice Kristo and Rosemary Bamford (Eds.), *Making Facts Come Alive: Choosing Nonfiction Literature K–8* (Second Edition). Norwood, MA: Christopher-Gordon.

Vardell, Sylvia M. 2006. "Don't Stop with Mother Goose." *School Library Journal* (April), 40–41.

Vardell, Sylvia M. 2006. "A Place for Poetry: Celebrating the Library in Poetry." *Children and Libraries 4* (2), 35–41.

Vardell, Sylvia M. 2007. "Linking Picture Books and Poetry: A Celebration of Black History Month." *Book Links*. http://www.ala.org/ala/booklinksbucket/linkingpoetry.htm. Accessed May 21, 2007.

Vardell, Sylvia M. 2007. *Poetry People: A Practical Guide to Children's Poets*. Englewood, CO: Libraries Unlimited.

Vardell, Sylvia M. 2011. "Everyday Poetry: Social Studies Poetry 'Notables.'" *Book Links* (September).

Vardell, Sylvia. 2012. *The Poetry Teacher's Book of Lists*. Princeton, NJ: Pomelo Books.

Vardell, Sylvia M. 2014. *Poetry Aloud Here 2: Sharing Poetry with Children* (Second Edition). Chicago, IL: American Library Association.

Vardell, Sylvia M. (2011). "From *Charlotte's Web* to the World Wide Web: The Impact of the Internet on the Field of Children's Literature." In April Bedford and Lettie Albright (Eds.), *A Master Class in Children's Literature: Trends and Issues in an Evolving Field*. Urbana, IL: National Council of Teachers of English.

Vardell, Sylvia M., and June M. Jacko. 2005. "Folklore for Kids: Exploring the Rhymes, Songs, and Games of Childhood." *Book Links 14* (4), 29–33.

Vardell, Sylvia M., and John E. Jacobson. 1997. "Teachers as Readers: A Status Report." *Journal of Children's Literature.* Children's Literature Assembly of the National Council of Teachers of English. *23* (1), 16–25.

Veccia, Susan H. 2003. *Uncovering Our History: Teaching with Primary Sources.* Chicago, IL: American Library Association.

Volz, Bridget Dealy, Cheryl Perkins Scheer, and Lynda Blackburn Welborn. 2000. *Junior Genreflecting: A Guide to Good Reads and Series Fiction for Children.* Englewood, CO: Libraries Unlimited.

Wadham, Rachel, and Tim Wadham. 1999. *Bringing Fantasy Alive for Children and Young Adults.* Columbus, OH: Linworth.

Walter, Virginia A. 2006. *War and Peace: A Guide to Literature and New Media, Grades 4–8.* Englewood, CO: Libraries Unlimited.

Webber, Desiree, and Sandy Shropshire. 2001. *The Kids' Book Club: Lively Reading and Activities for Grades 1–3.* Englewood, CO: Libraries Unlimited.

Wells, Gordon. 1986. *The Meaning Makers: Children Learning Language and Using Language to Learn.* Portsmouth, NH: Heinemann.

Wells, Kim. 1998. *Louisa May Alcott and the Roles of a Lifetime.* Master's Thesis. Southwest Texas State University. http://www.womenwriters.net/domestic goddess/thesis.htm. Accessed May 5, 2007.

Wilson, Patricia, and Karen Kutiper. 1994. "Beyond Silverstein and Prelutsky: Enhancing and Promoting the Elementary and Middle School Poetry Collection." *Youth Services in Libraries 7* (3), 273–281.

Winters, Carol, and Gary D. Schmidt. 2001. *Edging the Boundaries of Children's Literature.* New York: Allyn & Bacon.

Wolf, J. 1997. *The Beanstalk and Beyond: Developing Critical Thinking Through Fairy Tales.* New York: Teacher Ideas Press.

Woodhouse, Horace Martin. 2013. *The Essential Wizard of Oz: 101 Things You Didn't Know About the Most-Watched Movie in Film History.* Seattle, WA: CreateSpace.

Woolls, Blanche. 2004. *The School Library Media Manager* (Third Edition). Englewood, CO: Libraries Unlimited.

Worthy, Jo. 2005. *Readers Theater for Building Fluency: Strategies and Scripts for Making the Most of This Highly Effective, Motivating, and Research-Based Approach to Oral Reading.* New York: Scholastic.

Worthy, M. J., and J. W. Bloodgood. 1993. "Enhancing Reading Instruction Through Cinderella Tales." The *Reading Teacher, 46,* 290–300.

Wright, Cora M. 2002. *More Hot Links: Linking Literature with the Middle School Curriculum.* Englewood, CO: Libraries Unlimited.

Wurman, Richard Saul. 1989. *Information Anxiety.* New York: Doubleday.

Wyatt, Flora R., Margaret Coggins, and Jane Hunter Imber. 1998. *Popular Nonfiction Authors for Children: A Biographical and Thematic Guide.* Englewood, CO: Libraries Unlimited.

Yolen, Jane. 2005. *Touch Magic: Fantasy, Faerie and Folklore in the Literature of Childhood* (Expanded Edition). Atlanta, GA: August House.

York, Sherry. 2005. *Ethnic Book Awards: A Directory of Multicultural Literature for Young Readers.* Columbus, OH: Linworth.

Young, Terrell A. 2004. *Happily Ever After: Sharing Folk Literature with Elementary and Middle School Students.* Newark, DE: International Reading Association.

Zarnowski, Myra. 1990. *Learning About Biographies.* Urbana, IL: National Council of Teachers of English.

Zarnowski, Myra. 2003. *History Makers: A Questioning Approach to Reading & Writing Biographies.* Portsmouth, NH: Heinemann.

Zarnowski, Myra. 2006. *Making Sense of History: Using High-Quality Literature and Hands-On Experiences to Build Content Knowledge.* New York: Scholastic.

Zarnowski, Myra, Richard M. Kerper, and Julie M. Jensen. 2001. *The Best in Children's Nonfiction: Reading, Writing, and Teaching Orbis Pictus Award Books.* Urbana, IL: National Council of Teachers of English.

Zipes, Jack. 1994. *Fairy Tale as Myth, Myth as Fairy Tale.* Lexington, KY: University Press of Kentucky.

Zipes, Jack. 1997. *Happily Ever After: Fairy Tales, Children, and the Culture Industry.* London: Routledge.

Zipes, Jack. 2000. *The Great Fairy Tale Tradition: From Straparola and Basile to the Brothers Grimm (Norton Critical Editions).* New York: W. W. Norton.

Zipes, Jack. 2002. *Breaking the Magic Spell: Radical Theories of Folk and Fairy Tales.* Lexington, KY: University Press of Kentucky.

Zipes, Jack. 2003. *The Brothers Grimm: From Enchanted Forests to the Modern World* (Second Edition). New York: Palgrave Macmillan.

Zipes, Jack. 2006. *Why Fairy Tales Stick: The Evolution and Relevance of a Genre.* London: Routledge.

Zipes, Jack. 2011. *Fairy Tales and the Art of Subversion.* London: Routledge.

Zipes, Jack. 2012. *The Irresistible Fairy Tale: The Cultural and Social History of a Genre.* Princeton, NJ: Princeton University Press.

Zipes, Jack, Lissa Paul, Lynne Vallone, Peter Hunt, and Gillian Avery. Eds. 2005. *The Norton Anthology of Children's Literature.* New York: W. W. Norton.

Bibliography of Children's Books Cited

Aardema, Verna. 1975/2004. *Why Mosquitoes Buzz in People's Ears*. New York: Dial/Puffin.

Ada, Alma Flor. 1993. *The Rooster Who Went to His Uncle's Wedding: A Latin American Folktale*. New York: Penguin.

Ada, Alma Flor, and Isabel Campoy. Eds. 2003. *¡Pio Peep! Traditional Spanish Nursery Rhymes*. Translated by Alice Schertle. New York: HarperCollins.

Ada, Alma Flor, and Isabel Campoy. 2010. *Muu, Moo! Rimas de animales/Animal Nursery Rhymes*. New York: Rayo/HarperCollins.

Adler, David. 2007. *Heroes of Civil Rights*. New York: Holiday House.

Adler, David, and Michael Adler. 2009. *A Picture Book of Harry Houdini*. New York: Holiday House.

Alarcón, Francisco X. 1997. *Laughing Tomatoes and Other Spring Poems/Jitomates Resuenos y Otros Poemas de Primavera*. San Francisco, CA: Children's Book Press.

Alarcón, Francisco X. 1999. *Angels Ride Bikes and Other Fall Poems*. San Francisco, CA: Children's Book Press.

Aldana, Patricia. 1996. *Jade and Iron: Latin American Tales from Two Cultures*. Toronto: Groundwood.

Alexander, Lloyd. 1968. *The High King*. New York: Holt.

Alexander, Lloyd. 2007. *The Book of Three*. New York: Listening Library.

Aliki. 1988. *How a Book Is Made*. New York: HarperTrophy.

Aliki. 2003. *Ah, Music!* New York: HarperCollins.

Allard, Harry. 1984. *The Stupids Have a Ball*. Ill. by James Marshall. Boston: Houghton Mifflin.

Alvarez, Julia. 2009. *Return to Sender*. New York: Knopf.

Amateau, Gigi. 2005. *Claiming Georgia Tate*. Cambridge. MA: Candlewick.

Ames, Lee. 2012. *Draw the Draw 50 Way: How to Draw Cats, Puppies, Horses, Buildings, Birds, Aliens, Boats, Trains, and Everything Else Under the Sun*. New York: Watson-Guptill.

Ancona, George. 2007. *Capoeira: Game! Dance! Martial Art!* New York: Lee & Low.

Andersen, Hans Christian. 1999. *The Ugly Duckling.* Ill. by Jerry Pinkney. New York: HarperCollins.

Anderson, Laurie Halse. 2008. *Chains.* New York: Simon & Schuster.

Angel, Ann. 2010. *Janis Joplin: Rise Up Singing.* New York: Amulet.

Appelt, Kathi. 2008. *The Underneath.* New York: Atheneum.

Appelt, Kathi. 2013. *The True Blue Scouts of Sugar Man Swamp.* New York: Atheneum.

Applegate, Katherine. 2012. *The One and Only Ivan.* New York: HarperCollins.

Ardagh, Philip. 2003. *A House Called Awful End.* New York: Listening Library.

Argueta, Jorge. 2009. *Sopa de frijoles/Bean Soup.* Ill. by Rafael Yockteng. Toronto, ON, Canada: Groundwood.

Argueta, Jorge. 2010. *Arroz con leche: Rice Pudding.* Ill. by Fernando Vilela. Toronto, ON, Canada: Groundwood.

Argueta, Jorge. 2012. *Guacamole: Un poema para cocinar/A Cooking Poem.* Ill. by Margarita Sada. Toronto, ON, Canada: Groundwood.

Armstrong, Jennifer. 2006. *Once Upon a Banana.* Ill. by David Small. New York: Simon & Schuster.

Armstrong, William H. 1969. *Sounder.* New York: Harper.

Arnold, Nick. 2002. *The Body Owner's Handbook.* (The *Horrible Science* Series). New York: Scholastic.

Arnosky, Jim. 2013. *Shimmer & Splash: The Sparkling World of Sea Life.* New York: Sterling.

Avi. 2002. *Crispin: The Cross of Lead.* New York: Hyperion.

Aylesworth, Jim. 1992. *Old Black Fly.* New York: Holt.

Babbitt, Natalie. 1975. *Tuck Everlasting.* New York: Farrar, Straus & Giroux.

Babbitt, Natalie. 2001. *Tuck Everlasting.* Middletown, RI: Audio Bookshelf.

Bagert, Brod. 1999. *Rainbows, Head Lice and Pea-Green Tile: Poems in the Voice of the Classroom Teacher.* Gainesville, FL: Maupin House.

Balliett, Blue. 2013. *Hold Fast.* New York: Scholastic.

Bang, Molly. 2000. *Picture This: How Pictures Work.* New York: SeaStar.

Banyai, Istvan. 1995. *Zoom.* New York: Viking.

Barron, T. A. 2000. *The Fires of Merlin.* New York: Penguin.

Barron, T. A. 2000. *The Lost Years of Merlin.* New York: Listening Library.

Barron, T. A. 2000. *The Seven Songs of Merlin.* New York: Penguin.

Barron, T. A. 2001. *The Mirror of Merlin.* New York: Penguin.

Barron, T. A. 2002. *The Wings of Merlin.* New York: Penguin.

Barron, T. A. 2004. *The Merlin Conspiracy.* New York: HarperTrophy.

Barron, T. A. 2007. *The Lost Years of Merlin.* New York: Penguin.

Bartoletti, Susan Campbell. 2005. *Black Potatoes: The Story of the Great Irish Famine, 1845–1850.* Boston: Houghton Mifflin.

Bartoletti, Susan Campbell. 2010. *They Called Themselves the K.K.K.: The Birth of an American Terrorist Group.* Boston: Houghton Mifflin Harcourt.

Base, Graeme. 1987. *Animalia.* New York: Abrams.

Base, Graeme. 2013. *Little Elephants.* New York: Abrams.

Bass, Hester. 2009. *The Secret World of Walter Anderson.* Somerville, MA: Candlewick.

Baum, L. Frank. 2005. *The Wizard of Oz.* Ashland, OR: Blackstone Audio.

Baum, L. Frank. Reissued 2005. *The Wizard of Oz.* Adapted by Michael Cavallaro. New York: Puffin Books.

Beaumont, Karen. 2006. *Move Over, Rover.* Ill. by Jane Dyer. San Diego, CA: Harcourt.

Bertrand, Lynne. 2005. *Granite Baby*. Ill. by Kevin Hawkes. New York: Farrar, Straus & Giroux.

Bierhorst, John. 2001. *Latin American Folktales: Stories from Hispanic and Indian Traditions*. New York: Pantheon.

Billingsley, Franny. 2000. *The Folk Keeper*. New York: Listening Library.

Birdsall, Jeanne. 2005. *The Penderwicks*. New York: Knopf.

Black, Holly. 2007. *The Spiderwick Chronicles*. New York: Listening Library.

Blake, Quentin. 2003. *Magic Pencil: Children's Book Illustration Today*. London: British Library.

Bloom, Suzanne. 2001. *The Bus for Us*. Honesdale, PA: Boyds Mills Press.

Bloom, Suzanne. 2009. *A Mighty Fine Time Machine*. Honesdale, PA: Boyds Mills Press.

Bloom, Suzanne. 2011. *Feeding Friendsies*. Honesdale, PA: Boyds Mills Press.

Blumberg, Rhoda. 2004. *York's Adventures with Lewis and Clark: An African American's Part in the Great Expedition*. New York: HarperCollins.

Blume, Judy. 1970. *Are You There, God? It's Me, Margaret*. New York: Yearling.

Blumenthal, Karen. 2005. *Let Me Play: The Story of Title IX: The Law That Changed the Future of Girls in America*. New York: Atheneum.

Bolden, Tonya. 2007. *M.L.K. Journey of a King*. New York: Abrams.

Boring, Mel. 2005. *Guinea Pig Scientists: Bold Self-Experimenters in Science and Medicine*. New York: Holt.

Boynton, Sandra. 1982. *The Going to Bed Book*. New York: Simon & Schuster.

Boynton, Sandra. 2004. *Moo Baa La La La*. New York: Simon & Schuster.

Branley, Franklyn. 2008. *Volcanoes*. New York: HarperCollins.

Brett, Jan. 2011. *Beauty and the Beast*. New York: Putnam.

Brett, Jan. 2013. *Cinders: A Chicken Cinderella*. New York: Putnam.

Bridges, Ruby. 1999. *Through My Eyes*. New York: Scholastic.

Brown, Don. 2006. *American Boy: The Adventures of Mark Twain*. Boston: Houghton Mifflin.

Brown, Marcia. 1954. *Cinderella, or the Little Glass Slipper*. New York: Atheneum.

Brown, Marc. Reissued 2002. *Arthur*. New York: Little, Brown.

Brown, Margaret Wise. 1947. *Goodnight Moon*. Ill. by Clement Hurd. New York: Harper.

Brown, Peter. 2009. *The Curious Garden*. New York: Little, Brown.

Browne, Anthony. 2013. *One Gorilla: A Counting Book*. Somerville, MA: Candlewick.

Bruchac, Joseph, and James Bruchac. 2003. *Turtle's Race with Beaver*. New York: Dial.

Bruchac, Joseph. 2004. *Raccoon's Last Race: A Traditional Abenaki Story*. New York: Penguin.

Bryan, Ashley. 1998. *Ashley Bryan's African Tales, Uh-Huh*. New York: Atheneum.

Bryan, Ashley. 2003. *Beautiful Blackbird*. New York: Atheneum.

Bryan, Ashley. 2009. *Ashley Bryan: Words to My Life's Song*. New York: Atheneum.

Brynie, Faith Hickman. 2002. *101 Questions About Food and Digestion: That Have Been Eating at You . . . Until Now*. Fairfield, IA: 21st Century.

Buehner, Caralyn. 1996. *Fanny's Dream*. New York: Dial.

Burkert, Rand. Reteller. 2011. *Mouse & Lion*. Ill. by Nancy Ekholm Burkert. New York: Michael di Capua/Scholastic.

Burnett, Frances Hodgson. 1886. *Little Lord Fauntleroy*. New York: Scribner's.

Burns, Dal. 2007. *The Kookaburra and Other Stories*. Frederick, MD: PublishAmerica.

Calmenson, Stephanie, and Joanna Cole. Eds. 1990. *Miss Mary Mack*. New York: Morrow.

Canfield, Jack. 2001. *Chicken Soup for the Kid's Soul*. New York: Vermilion.

Carle, Eric. 1969. *The Very Hungry Caterpillar*. New York: Philomel.

Carle, Eric. 1993. *Today Is Monday*. New York: Philomel.

Carmi, Daniella. 2000. *Samir and Yonatan*. Translated by Yael Lotan. New York: Scholastic Press.

Cave, Kathryn. 2003. *One Child, One Seed: A South African Counting Book*. New York: Holt.

Cheng, Andrea. 2013. *Etched in Clay: The Life of Dave, Enslaved Potter and Poet*. New York: Lee & Low.

Chin, Jason. 2012. *Island: A Story of the Galápagos*. New York: Roaring Brook.

Choi, Yangsook. 2001. *The Name Jar*. New York: Knopf.

Choldenko, Gennifer. 2004. *Al Capone Does My Shirts*. New York: Putnam.

Choldenko, Gennifer. 2009. *Al Capone Shines My Shoes*. New York: Dial.

Choldenko, Gennifer. 2013. *Al Capone Does My Homework*. New York: Dial.

Christelow, Eileen. 1999. *What Do Illustrators Do?* New York: Clarion.

Cleary, Beverly. 1983. *Dear Mr. Henshaw*. New York: Morrow.

Clifton, Lucille. 1993. "Listen Children." In Wade Hudson (Comp.), *Pass It On, African American Poetry for Children*. New York: Scholastic.

Climo, Shirley. 1992. *The Egyptian Cinderella*. Minneapolis, MN: Econo-Clad.

Climo, Shirley. 1996. *The Korean Cinderella*. New York: HarperTrophy.

Climo, Shirley. 2001. *The Persian Cinderella*. New York: HarperTrophy.

Clinton, Catherine. Comp. 1993/1998. *I, Too, Sing America: Three Centuries of African American Poetry*. Boston: Houghton Mifflin.

Coburn, Jewell Reinhart, and Tzexa Cherta Lee. 1996. *Jouanah: A Hmong Cinderella*. Arcadia, CA: Shen's Books.

Coburn, Jewell Reinhart. 1998. *Angkat: The Cambodian Cinderella*. Arcadia, CA: Shen's Books.

Coburn, Jewell Reinhart. 2000. *Domitila: A Cinderella Tale from the Mexican Tradition*. Arcadia, CA: Shen's Books.

Codell, Esmé Raji. 2003. *Sahara Special*. New York: Hyperion.

Cole, Babette. 1999. *Prince Cinders*. Minneapolis, MN: Econo-Clad.

Cole, Joanna. 2006. *The Magic School Bus and the Science Fair Expedition*. New York: Scholastic.

Colfer, Eoin. 2004. *Artemis Fowl*. New York: Listening Library.

Collier, James, and Christopher Collier. 1974. *My Brother Sam Is Dead*. New York: Four Winds.

Collins, Suzanne. 2008. *The Hunger Games*. New York: Scholastic.

Cooper, Susan. 1975. *The Grey King*. New York: McElderry.

Cooper, Susan. 2000. *The Dark Is Rising*. New York: Listening Library.

Corcoran, Jill. Ed. 2012. *Dare to Dream . . . Change the World*. San Diego, CA: Kane Miller.

Craft, K. Y. 2001. *Cinderella*. New York: Seastar.

Creech, Sharon. 1994. *Walk Two Moons*. New York: HarperCollins.

Creech, Sharon. 2001. *Love That Dog*. New York: HarperCollins.

Creech, Sharon. 2005. *Replay*. New York: HarperCollins.

Creech, Sharon. 2008. *Hate That Cat*. New York: HarperCollins.

Crews, Nina. 2003. *The Neighborhood Mother Goose*. New York: Amistad.

Cronin, Doreen. 2000. *Click, Clack, Moo: Cows That Type*. Ill. by Betsy Lewin. New York: Simon & Schuster.

Cullinan, Bernice, and Deborah Wooten. Eds. 2009. *Another Jar of Tiny Stars: Poems by NCTE Award-winning Poets*. Honesdale, PA: Wordsong/Boyds Mills.

Cummings, Pat. 1992. *Talking with Artists*. New York: Simon & Schuster.

Cummings, Pat. 1995. *Talking with Artists, Volume 2*. New York: Simon & Schuster.

Cummings, Pat. 1999. *Talking with Artists, Volume 3*. New York: Simon & Schuster.

Cummins, Julie, and Barbara Kiefer. Eds. 1999. *Wings of an Artist: Children's Book Illustrators Talk About Their Art*. New York: Abrams.

Curlee, Lynn. 2011. *Parthenon*. New York: Atheneum.

Curtis, Christopher Paul. 1999. *Bud, Not Buddy*. New York: Delacorte.

Curtis, Christopher Paul. 2007. *Elijah of Buxton*. New York: Scholastic.

Cushman, Karen. 1994. *Catherine, Called Birdy*. New York: Clarion.

Cushman, Karen. 1995. *The Midwife's Apprentice*. New York: Clarion.

Cushman, Karen. 2000. *Matilda Bone*. New York: Clarion.

Cushman, Karen. 2012. *Will Sparrow's Road*. New York: Clarion.

Dahl, Roald. 1961. *James and the Giant Peach*. New York: Knopf.

Dahl, Roald. 1964. *Charlie and the Chocolate Factory*. New York: Knopf.

Dahl, Roald. 1988. *Matilda*. New York: Puffin.

Dahl, Roald. 2002. *Charlie and the Chocolate Factory*. New York: HarperChildren's Audio.

Dahl, Roald. 2002. "Cinderella." In Roald Dahl, *Revolting Rhymes*. New York: Knopf.

Dakos, Kalli. 2003. *Put Your Eyes Up Here: And Other School Poems*. New York: Simon & Schuster.

Daly, Jude. 2005. *Fair, Brown, and Trembling: An Irish Cinderella Story*. New York: Farrar, Straus & Giroux.

D'Aulaire, Ingri, and Edgar D'Aulaire. Reissued 1992. *Book of Greek Myths*. New York: Delacorte.

de Paola, Tomie. Reissued 1997. *Strega Nona*. New York: Simon & Schuster.

Dearden, Carmen Diana. 2003. *Little Book of Latin American Folktales*. Toronto, ON, Canada: Groundwood.

de Graaf, Anne. 2012. *Son of a Gun*. Grand Rapids, MI: Eerdmans.

Delacre, Lulu. 2004. *Arrorró Mi Niño: Latino Lullabies and Gentle Games*. New York: Scholastic.

Demi. 2003. *The Legend of St. Nicolas*. New York: McElderry.

Dezago, Todd. 2001. *Tellos: Reluctant Heroes*. Ill. by Mike Wieringo. Berkeley, CA: Image Comics.

Diakite, Baba Wague. 2001. *The Pot of Wisdom: Ananse Stories*. Toronto, ON, Canada: Groundwood.

diCamillo, Kate. 2000. *Because of Winn-Dixie*. Cambridge, MA: Candlewick.

diCamillo, Kate. 2003. *The Tale of Despereaux*. Cambridge, MA: Candlewick.

Dillon, Leo, and Diane Dillon. 2007. *Mother Goose: Numbers on the Loose*. San Diego, CA: Harcourt.

Dorris, Michael. 1992. *Morning Girl*. New York: Hyperion.

DuPrau, Jeanne. 2006. *The City of Ember*. New York: Listening Library.

Eastman, P. D. 1960. *Are You My Mother?* New York: Random House.

Eastman, P. D. 1961. *Go, Dog. Go!* New York: Random House.

Edwards, Pamela D. 1999. *Dinorella: A Prehistoric Fairy Tale*. New York: Hyperion.

Ehlert, Lois. 1993. *Eating the Alphabet: Fruits & Vegetables from A to Z*. New York: Voyager.

Ehlert, Lois. 2008. *Oodles of Animals*. San Diego, CA: Harcourt.

Eisner, Will. 2001. *The Last Knight*. New York: NBM Publishing.

Elliott, David. 2012. *In the Sea*. Somerville, MA: Candlewick.

Engle, Margarita. 2006. *The Poet Slave of Cuba: A Biography of Juan Francisco Manzano*. New York: Holt.

Engle, Margarita. 2008. *The Surrender Tree*. New York: Holt.

Engle, Margarita. 2009. *Tropical Secrets: Holocaust Refugees in Cuba*. New York: Holt.

Engle, Margarita. 2010. *The Firefly Letters: A Suffragette's Journey to Cuba*. New York: Henry Holt.

Engle, Margarita. 2011. *Hurricane Dancers: The First Caribbean Pirate Shipwreck*. New York: Henry Holt.

Engle, Margarita. 2013. *The Lightning Dreamer*. New York: Houghton Mifflin Harcourt.

Erdrich, Louise. 2012. *Chickadee*. New York: HarperCollins.

Espinosa, Rod. 2003. *Courageous Princess*. San Antonio, TX: Antarctic.

Evanier, Mark. 2003. *Shrek*. Ill. by Ramon Bachs and Raul Fernandez. Milwaukie, OR: Dark Horse,

Falconer, Ian. 2000. *Olivia*. New York: Atheneum.

Falwell, Cathryn. 1996. *Feast for 10*. New York: Clarion.

Farmer, Nancy. 2002. *The House of the Scorpion*. New York: Atheneum.

Farmer, Nancy. 2003. *The House of the Scorpion*. Prince Frederick, MD: Recorded Books.

Farmer, Nancy. Reissued 2004. *The Eye, the Ear, and the Arm*. New York: Orchard.

Farrell, Jeanette. 2005. *Invisible Allies: Microbes That Shape Our Lives*. Farrar, Straus & Giroux.

Fisher, Catherine. 2010. *Incarceron*. New York: Listening Library.

Fitzhugh, Louise. 1964. *Harriet the Spy*. New York: Harper & Row.

Fleischman, Paul. 1988. *Joyful Noise: Poems for Two Voices*. New York: Harper & Row.

Fleischman, Paul. 1990. *Saturnalia*. New York: HarperCollins.

Fleischman, Paul. 1993. *Bull Run*. New York: HarperCollins.

Fleischman, Paul. 2007. *Glass Slipper, Gold Sandal: A Worldwide Cinderella*. New York: Henry Holt.

Fleischman, Sid. 1986. *The Whipping Boy*. New York: Greenwillow.

Fleming, Candace. 2005. *Lowji Discovers America*. New York: Atheneum.

Fleming, Denise. 2012. *UnderGROUND*. New York: Beach Lane Books.

Florian, Douglas. 2005. *Zoo's Who*. San Diego, CA: Harcourt.

Florian, Douglas. 2012. *Unbeelievables: Honeybee Poems and Paintings*. New York: Beach Lane.

Forbes, Esther. 1943. *Johnny Tremain*. Boston: Houghton Mifflin.

Foster, John. 2004. *Dragon Poems*. New York: Oxford University Press.

Fox, Paula. 1973. *The Slave Dancer*. New York: Bradbury.

Freedman, Russell. 1987. *Lincoln, a Photobiography*. New York: Clarion.

Freedman, Russell. 1997. *Eleanor Roosevelt, a Life of Discovery*. New York: Clarion.

Freedman, Russell. 2004. *The Voice That Challenged a Nation: Marian Anderson and the Struggle for Equal Rights*. New York: Clarion.

Freedman, Russell. 2012. *Abraham Lincoln and Frederick Douglass: The Story Behind an American Friendship*. Boston: Houghton Mifflin.

Fritz, Jean. Reissued 1996. *What's the Big Idea, Ben Franklin?* New York: Putnam.

Fritz, Jean. 2007. *Who's Saying What in Jamestown, Thomas Savage?* New York: Penguin.

Frost, Helen. 2006. *The Braid*. New York: Farrar, Straus & Giroux.

Frost, Helen. 2008. *Diamond Willow*. New York: Farrar, Straus & Giroux.

Frost, Helen. 2009. *Crossing Stones*. New York: Farrar, Straus & Giroux.

Frost, Helen. 2013. *Salt*. New York: Farrar, Straus & Giroux.

Funke, Cornelia. 2004. *Dragon Rider*. Trans. by Anthea Bell. New York: Scholastic.

Funke, Cornelia. 2005. *Dragon Rider*. New York: Listening Library.

Funke, Cornelia. 2012. *Ghost Knight*. New York: Listening Library.

Gág, Wanda. Reissued 2006. *Millions of Cats*. New York: Puffin.

Gaiman, Neil. 2008. *The Graveyard Book.* New York: HarperCollins.

Gaiman, Neil, and Dave McKean. 2003. *The Wolves in the Walls.* New York: HarperCollins.

Gaiman, Neil, and Dave McKean. 2009. *Crazy Hair.* New York: HarperCollins.

Galdone, Paul. 2002. *Rumpelstiltskin.* Lexington, KY: Book Wholesalers.

Gantos, Jack. 1998. *Joey Pigza Swallowed the Key.* New York: Farrar, Straus & Giroux.

Gantos, Jack. 2011. *Dead End in Norvelt.* New York: Farrar, Straus & Giroux.

Garza, Carmen Lomas. 2005. *Family Pictures.* San Francisco, CA: Children's Book Press.

Geisert, Arthur. 2013. *Thunderstorm.* Brooklyn, NY: Enchanted Lion Books.

George, Jean Craighead. 2000. *How to Talk to Your Dog.* Ill. by Sue Truesdell. New York: HarperCollins.

George, Kristine O'Connell. 2002. *Swimming Upstream: Middle School Poems.* New York: Clarion.

George, Kristine O'Connell. 2009. *Emma Dilemma: Big Sister Poems.* Ill. by Nancy Carpenter. New York: Clarion.

Gerber, Carole. 2013. *Seeds, Bees, Butterflies, and More!: Poems for Two Voices.* New York: Holt.

Gerstein, Mordicai. 2003. *The Man Who Walked Between the Towers.* New York: Roaring Brook Press.

Gibbons, Gail. 2013. *Beavers.* New York: Holiday House.

Giblin, James Cross. 2005. *Good Brother, Bad Brother: The Story of Edwin Booth and John Wilkes Booth.* Boston: Houghton Mifflin.

Giff, Patricia Reilly. 1997. *Lily's Crossing.* New York: Delacorte.

Gipson, Fred. 1956. *Old Yeller.* New York: Harper.

Goble, Paul. 1978. *The Girl Who Loved Wild Horses.* New York: Bradbury.

Goodman, Susan E. 2004. *The Truth About Poop.* New York: Viking.

Grady, Cynthia. 2012. *I Lay My Stitches Down: Poems of American Slavery.* Ill. by Michele Wood. Grand Rapids, MI: Eerdmans.

Graham, Bob. Reissued 2001. *Queenie.* Cambridge, MA: Candlewick.

Grahame, Kenneth. 2003. *The Wind in the Willows: The Wild Wood.* Adapted and ill. by Michel Plessix. New York: NBM.

Gravett, Emily. 2006. *Wolves.* New York: Simon & Schuster.

Greenberg, Jan, and Sandra Jordan. 2010. *Ballet for Martha: Making Appalachian Spring.* New York: Roaring Brook.

Greenfield, Eloise. 1988. *Nathaniel Talking.* New York. Black Butterfly Children's Books.

Greenfield. Eloise. 2006. *The Friendly Four.* New York: HarperCollins.

Greenwald, Tommy. 2011. *Charlie Joe Jackson's Guide to Not Reading.* Ill. by J. P. Coovert. New York: Roaring Brook Press.

Grey, Mini. 2003. *The Very Smart Pea and the Princess-to-Be.* New York: Knopf.

Grimes, Nikki. 1998. *Jazmin's Notebook.* New York: Dial.

Grimes, Nikki. 2005. *It's Raining Laughter.* Honesdale, PA: Boyds Mills Press.

Grimes, Nikki. 2006. *The Road to Paris.* New York: Putnam.

Gunning, Monica. 2004. *America, My New Home.* Honesdale, PA: Wordsong/Boyds Mills Press.

Guy, Ginger. 2005. *Siesta.* New York: Greenwillow.

Haddix, Margaret P. 1999. *Just Ella.* New York: Pocket.

Hale, Shannon. 2007. *The Princess Academy.* Syracuse, NY: Full Cast Audio.

Hamilton, Virginia. 1974. *M. C. Higgins, the Great.* New York: Macmillan.

Hamilton, Virginia. 1988. *In the Beginning.* San Diego, CA: Harcourt.

Hamilton, Virginia. 1995. *Her Stories.* Ill. by Leo and Diane Dillon. New York: Blue Sky Press.

Hamilton, Virginia. 2007. *The People Could Fly.* New York: Random House.

Handler, Daniel (Lemony Snicket). 2003. *The Bad Beginning.* New York: Listening Library.

Harley, Avis. 2000. *Fly with Poetry: An ABC of Poetry.* Honesdale, PA: Wordsong/ Boyds Mills Press.

Harley, Avis. 2001. *Leap into Poetry: More ABCs of Poetry.* Honesdale, PA: Wordsong/Boyds Mills Press.

Harness, Cheryl. 2003. *Remember the Ladies: 100 Great American Women.* New York: HarperCollins.

Harness, Cheryl. 2013. *Mary Walker Wears the Pants: The True Story of the Doctor, Reformer, and Civil War Hero.* Morton Grove, IL: Albert Whitman.

Harper, Charise Mericle. 2005. *Fashion Kitty.* New York: Hyperion.

Harper, Charise Mericle. 2007. *Flush: The Scoop on Poop Throughout the Ages.* New York: Little, Brown.

Harrison, David. 2009. *Vacation, We're Going to the Ocean!* Honesdale, PA: Wordsong/Boyds Mills Press.

Havill, Juanita. 1980. *Jamaica Tag-along.* Ill. by Anne Sibley O'Brien. Boston: Houghton Mifflin.

Hazen, Lynn E. 2008. *Cinder Rabbit.* New York: Holt.

Heard, Georgia. Ed. 2012. *The Arrow Finds Its Mark: A Book of Found Poems.* New York: Macmillan.

Heiligman, Deborah. 2009. *Charles and Emma: The Darwins' Leap of Faith.* New York: Henry Holt.

Heller, Julek. 1998. *Eyewitness Classics: Robinson Crusoe by Daniel Defoe.* New York: Penguin.

Henkes, Kevin. 1996. *Lilly's Purple Plastic Purse.* New York: Greenwillow.

Henkes, Kevin. 2003. *Olive's Ocean.* New York: Greenwillow.

Henkes, Kevin. 2010. *My Garden.* New York: Greenwillow.

Heo, Yumi. 1996. *The Green Frogs: A Korean Folktale.* Boston: Houghton Mifflin.

Herge, Georges. 1994. *The Adventures of Tintin: Volume 1.* New York: Little, Brown.

Hesse, Karen. 1997. *Out of the Dust.* New York: Scholastic.

Hesse, Karen. 2001. *Witness.* New York: Scholastic.

Hesse, Karen. 2003. *Aleutian Sparrow.* New York: McElderry.

Hesse, Karen. 2004. *The Cats in Krasinski Square.* New York: Scholastic.

Hiaasen, Carl. 2002. *Hoot.* New York: Knopf.

Hiaasen, Carl. 2012. *Chomp.* New York: Knopf.

Hickox, R. 1999. *The Golden Sandal.* New York: Holiday House.

Ho, Minfong. 1996. *Maples in the Mist: Poems for Children from the Tang Dynasty.* New York: Lothrop, Lee, & Shepard.

Hoban, Russell. 1964. *Bread and Jam for Frances.* Ill. by Lillian Hoban. New York: HarperCollins.

Hoban, Tana. 1987. *26 Letters and 99 Cents.* New York: Greenwillow.

Hoban, Tana. 2003. *I Wonder.* San Diego, CA: Harcourt.

Hoban, Tana. 2007. *Black and White.* New York: HarperCollins.

Hoberman, Mary Ann. 2005. *You Read to Me, I'll Read to You: Very Short Mother Goose Tales to Read Together.* Ill. by Michael Emberley. Boston: Little, Brown.

Hoberman, Mary Ann. 2009. *All Kinds of Families.* New York: Little, Brown.

Hoberman, Mary Ann. Ed. 2012. *Forget-Me-Nots: Poems to Learn by Heart.* Ill. by Michael Emberley. New York: Little, Brown.

Hodges, Margaret. 1985. *Saint George and the Dragon*. Ill. by Trina Schart Hyman. New York: Little, Brown.

Hodges, Margaret. 2004. *The Legend of Saint Christopher*. Grand Rapids, MI: Eerdmans.

Holm, Jennifer L. 2005. *Babymouse: Queen of the World!* Ill. by Matthew Holm. New York: Random House.

Holm, Jennifer L. 2010. *Turtle in Paradise*. New York: Random House.

Hooks, William H. 1987. *Moss Gown*. New York: Clarion.

Hopkins, Lee Bennett. Comp. 2000. *Good Books, Good Times!* New York: HarperTrophy.

Hopkins, Lee Bennett. Comp. 1994. *Hand in Hand: An American History Through Poetry*. New York: Simon and Schuster.

Hopkins, Lee Bennett. Comp. 1999. *Lives: Poems About Famous Americans*. New York: HarperCollins.

Hopkins, Lee Bennett. Comp. 2000. *YUMMY!: Eating Through a Day*. New York: Simon & Schuster.

Hopkins, Lee Bennett. Comp. 2005. *Days to Celebrate: A Full Year of Poetry, People, Holidays, History, Fascinating Facts, and More*. New York: HarperCollins.

Hopkins, Lee Bennett. Ed. 2010. *Amazing Faces*. Ill. by Chris Soentpiet. Lee & Low.

Hopkins, Lee Bennett. 2011. *I Am the Book*. New York: Holiday House.

Howard, Elizabeth F. 2000. *Virgie Goes to School with Us Boys*. Ill. by E. B. Lewis. New York: Simon & Schuster.

Hoyt-Goldsmith, Diane. 2005. *Celebrating Ramadan*. New York: Holiday House.

Huddleston, Courtney. 2000. *Decoy*. Ill. by Don Jensen and others. Houston, TX: Penny-Farthing.

Hughes, Langston. 2007. *The Dream Keeper (and Seven Additional Poems)*. 75th anniversary edition. New York: Knopf.

Hughes, Langston. 2009. *My People*. Ill. by Charles R. Smith Jr. New York: Simon & Schuster.

Hurston, Zora Neale. Coll. 2005. *Lies and Other Tall Tales*. Ill. by Christopher Myers. New York: HarperCollins.

Hutchins, Hazel. 2007. *A Second Is a Hiccup*. New York: Scholastic.

Hyman, Trina Schart. 2001. *Rapunzel*. New York: Holiday House.

Ibbotson, Eva. 2006. *The Beasts of Clawstone Castle*. Prince Frederick, MD: Recorded Books.

Intrater, Roberta G. 2000. *Two Eyes, a Nose, and a Mouth*. New York: Scholastic.

Isaacs, Anne. 1994. *Swamp Angel*. Ill. by Paul Zelinsky. New York: Dutton.

Jackson, Ellen. 1998. *Cinder Edna*. New York: Mulberry.

Jacques, Brian. 2005. *Redwall*. New York: Listening Library.

Janeczko, Paul. Comp. 1994. *Poetry from A to Z: A Guide for Young Writers*. New York: Bradbury.

Janeczko, Paul. Comp. 2001. *A Poke in the I: A Collection of Concrete Poems*. Cambridge, MA: Candlewick.

Janeczko, Paul. Comp. 2002. *Seeing the Blue Between: Advice and Inspiration for Young Poets*. Cambridge, MA: Candlewick.

Janeczko, Paul. 2004. *Worlds Afire*. Cambridge, MA: Candlewick.

Janeczko, Paul. Comp. 2005. *A Kick in the Head: An Everyday Guide to Poetic Forms*. Cambridge, MA: Candlewick.

Janeczko, Paul. 2009. *A Foot in the Mouth: Poems to Speak, Sing, and Shout*. Ill. by Chris Raschka. Somerville, MA: Candlewick.

Janeczko, Paul B. 2011. *Requiem: Poems of the Terezín Ghetto*. Somerville, MA: Candlewick.

Jeffers, Susan. Reissued 2001. *Robert Frost's Stopping by Woods on a Snowy Evening*. New York: Dutton.

Jenkins, Steve. 2013. *The Animal Book: A Collection of the Fastest, Fiercest, Toughest, Cleverest, Shyest—and Most Surprising—Animals on Earth*. Boston: Houghton Mifflin Harcourt.

Jenkins, Steve, and Robin Page. 2003. *What Do You Do with a Tail Like This?* Boston: Houghton Mifflin.

Jenkins, Steve, and Robin Page. 2006. *Move!* New York: Houghton Mifflin.

Johnson, Stephen T. 1995. *Alphabet City*. New York: Viking.

Johnston, Tony. 2000. *Bigfoot Cinderrrrrella*. New York: Puffin.

Jones, Diana Wynne. 2004. *A Charmed Life*. Prince Frederick, MD: Recorded Books.

Judge, Lisa. 2011. *Red Sled*. New York: Atheneum.

Kadohata, Cynthia. 2004. *Kira-Kira*. New York: Atheneum.

Kadohata, Cynthia. 2006. *Weedflower*. New York: Simon & Schuster.

Katz, Alan. 2001. *Take Me Out of the Bathtub and Other Silly Dilly Songs*. New York: Scholastic.

Katz, Bobbi. Comp. 2000. *We, the People*. New York: Greenwillow.

Kellogg, Steven. 1995. *Pecos Bill*. New York: HarperCollins.

Kellogg, Steven. 2002. *A Rose for Pinkerton*. New York: Penguin.

Kennedy, Caroline. Ed. 2013. *Poems to Learn by Heart*. Ill. by John Muth. New York: Hyperion.

Ketteman, Helen. 2001. *Bubba, the Cowboy Prince*. New York: Scholastic.

Khan, Rukhsana. 2010. *Big Red Lollipop*. New York: Viking.

Kimmel, Eric. Reteller. 2008. *The McElderry Book of Greek Myths*. New York: Simon & Schuster.

Kimmel, Eric Kimmel. 2011. *The Golem's Latkes*. New York: Two Lions.

Klages, Ellen. 2006. *The Green Glass Sea*. New York: Viking.

Klages, Ellen. 2008. *White Sands, Red Menace*. New York: Viking.

Knudsen, Michelle. 2006. *Library Lion*. Cambridge, MA: Candlewick.

Kondo, Kazuhisa. 2002. *Mobile Suit Gundam 0079, v.1*. San Francisco, CA: Viz.

Konigsburg, E. L. 1967. *From the Mixed-Up Files of Mrs. Basil E. Frankweiler*. New York: Atheneum.

Konigsburg, E. L. 1996. *The View from Saturday*. New York: Atheneum.

Kontis, Alethea. 2006. *AlphaOops! The Day Z Went First*. Somerville, MA: Candlewick.

Kraske, Robert. 2005. *Marooned: The Strange but True Adventures of Alexander Selkirk, the Real Robinson Crusoe*. New York: Clarion.

Krosoczka, Jarrett. 2009. *Lunch Lady and the Cyborg Substitute: Lunch Lady #1*. New York: Knopf.

Krull, Kathleen. 2006. *Sigmund Freud*. New York: Penguin.

Krull, Kathleen. 2011. *Lives of the Presidents: Fame, Shame (and What the Neighbors Thought)*. Ill. by Kathryn Hewitt. Boston: Houghton Mifflin Harcourt.

Kuklin, Susan. 2006. *Families*. New York: Hyperion.

Kunkel, Mike. 2003. *Herobear and the Kid: The Inheritance, v.1*. Toluca Lake, CA: Astonish Comics.

Kurlansky, Mark. 2006. *The Story of Salt*. Ill. by S. D. Schindler. New York: Putnam.

Kuskin, Karla. 2003. *Moon, Have You Met My Mother? The Collected Poems of Karla Kuskin*. New York: HarperCollins.

Lai, Thanhha. 2011. *Inside Out and Back Again*. New York: HarperCollins.

Landy, Derek. 2007. *Skulduggery Pleasant*. New York: HarperChildren's Audio.

Larson, Kirby. 2006. *Hattie Big Sky*. New York: Delacorte/Random House.

Larson, Kirby. 2013. *Hattie Ever After.* New York: Delacorte/Random House.

Lasky, Kathryn. 1996. *True North.* New York: Scholastic.

Lasky, Kathryn. 2006. *John Muir: America's First Environmentalist.* Cambridge, MA: Candlewick.

Lattimore, Deborah Nourse. 2000. *Medusa.* New York: HarperCollins.

Lattimore, Deborah Nourse. 2002. *Cinderhazel: The Cinderella of Halloween.* New York: Scholastic.

Lauber, Patricia. 2003. *The True-or-False Book of Dogs.* New York: HarperCollins.

Lauber, Patricia, and John Manders. 2001. *What You Never Knew About Tubs, Toilets, & Showers.* New York: Simon & Schuster.

Law, Ingrid. 2008. *Savvy.* New York: Dial.

Lee, Jeanne. 1999. *I Once Was a Monkey.* New York: Farrar, Straus & Giroux.

Leedy, Loreen. 2001. *Monster Money Book.* New York: Scholastic.

Leedy, Loreen. 2004. *Look at My Book: How Kids Can Write and Illustrate Terrific Books.* New York: Holiday House.

L'Engle, Madeleine. 1962. *A Wrinkle in Time.* New York: Farrar, Straus & Giroux.

L'Engle, Madeleine. 2006. *A Wrinkle in Time.* New York: Listening Library.

L'Engle, Madeleine, and Hope Larson. 2012. *A Wrinkle in Time.* Ill. by Hope Larson. New York: Farrar.

Lester, Julius. 1994. *John Henry.* Ill. by Jerry Pinkney. New York: Penguin.

Lester, Julius. 2005. *Day of Tears: A Novel in Dialogue.* New York: Jump at the Sun.

Levine, Gail Carson. 1997. *Ella Enchanted.* New York: HarperCollins.

Lewis, C. S. Reissued 1994. *The Lion, the Witch and the Wardrobe.* New York: HarperCollins.

Lewis, C. S. 2004. *The Chronicles of Narnia.* New York: HarperChildren's Audio.

Lewis, J. Patrick. 1995. *Ridicholas Nicholas: More Animal Poems.* New York: Dial.

Lewis, J. Patrick. 1998. *The Little Buggers: Insect and Spider Poems.* New York: Dial.

Lewis, J. Patrick. 1999. *The Bookworm's Feast: A Potluck of Poems.* New York: Dial.

Lewis, J. Patrick. 2003. *Swan Song: Poems of Extinction.* Creative Editions.

Lewis, J. Patrick. 2004. *Scientrickery: Riddles in Science.* San Diego: Harcourt.

Lewis, J. Patrick. 2005. *Galileo's Universe.* Creative Editions.

Lewis, J. Patrick. 2005. *Monumental Verses.* Washington, DC: National Geographic.

Lewis, J. Patrick. 2005. *Please Bury Me in the Library.* San Diego: Harcourt.

Lewis, J. Patrick. 2005. *Vherses: A Celebration of Outstanding Women.* Mankato, MN: Creative Editions.

Lewis, J. Patrick. 2009. *Countdown to Summer: A Poem for Every Day of the School Year.* Ill. by Ethan Long. New York: Little, Brown.

Lewis, J. Patrick. 2009. *The Underwear Salesman: And Other Jobs for Better or Verse.* Ill. by Serge Bloch. New York: Simon & Schuster/Atheneum.

Lewis, J. Patrick. Ed. 2012. *The National Geographic Book of Animal Poetry.* Washington, DC: National Geographic.

Lewis, J. Patrick. 2013. *When Thunder Comes: Poems for Civil Rights Leaders.* San Francisco: Chronicle.

Lewis, J. Patrick, and Rebecca Kai Dotlich. 2006. *Castles, Old Stone Poems.* Honesdale, PA: Wordsong/Boyds Mills.

Lin, Grace. 2001. *Dim Sum for Everyone!* New York: Knopf.

Lin, Grace. 2004. *Kite Flying.* New York: Dragonfly.

Lin, Grace. 2006. *Fortune Cookie Fortunes.* New York: Dragonfly.

Lin, Grace. 2006. *The Year of the Dog.* New York: Little, Brown.

Lin, Grace. 2009. *The Ugly Vegetables.* Watertown, MA: Charlesbridge.

Lin, Grace. 2009. *Where the Mountain Meets the Moon.* New York: Little, Brown.

Lin, Grace. 2009. *The Year of the Rat.* New York: Little, Brown.

Lin, Grace. 2010. *Thanking the Moon: Celebrating the Mid-Autumn Moon Festival.* New York: Knopf.

Lin, Grace. 2012. *Dumpling Days.* New York: Little, Brown.

Lin, Grace. 2012. *Starry River of the Sky.* New York: Little, Brown.

Lionni, Leo. 1959. *Little Blue and Little Yellow.* New York: Astor-Honor.

Livingston, Myra Cohn. 1994. "Quiet." In Lee Bennett Hopkins (Comp.), *April Bubbles Chocolate: An ABC of Poetry.* New York: Simon & Schuster.

Long, Ethan. 2012. *Up, Tall and High!* New York: Putnam.

Lord, Cynthia. 2006. *Rules.* New York: Scholastic.

Louie, Ai-Ling. 1996. *Yeh-Shen: A Cinderella Story from China.* Ill. by Ed Young. New York: Puffin.

Lowell, Susan. 2001. *Cindy Ellen: A Wild Western Cinderella.* New York: Harper Trophy.

Lowrey, Janette Sebring. 1942. *The Pokmy Little Puppy.* New York: Simon & Schuster.

Lowry, Lois. 1989. *Number the Stars.* Boston: Houghton Mifflin.

Lowry, Lois. 1993. *The Giver.* Boston: Houghton Mifflin.

Lowry, Lois. 2001. *The Giver.* New York: Listening Library.

Lupica, Mike. 2012. *True Legend.* New York: Philomel.

Lyne, Sanford, Comp. 2004. *Soft Hay Will Catch You: Poems by Young People.* New York: Simon & Schuster.

Lyon, George Ella. 2011. *Which Side Are You On?* Ill. by Christopher Cardinale. El Paso, TX: Cinco Puntos Press.

Maccarone, Grace. 2013. *Princess Tales: Once Upon a Time in Rhyme with Seek-and-Find Pictures.* New York: Feiwel & Friends.

MacLachlan, Patricia. 1985. *Sarah, Plain and Tall.* New York: HarperCollins.

Maddern, Eric. 1993. *Rainbow Bird: An Aboriginal Folktale from Northern Australia.* New York: Little, Brown.

Maguire, Gregory. 1999. *Confessions of an Ugly Stepsister.* New York: Harper-Collins.

Mah, Adeline Yen. 2001. *Chinese Cinderella: The True Story of an Unwanted Daughter.* New York: Laurel Leaf.

Mak, Kam. 2001. *My Chinatown: One Year in Poems.* New York: HarperCollins.

Mandela, Nelson. Ed. 2004. *Favorite African Folktales.* New York: W. W. Norton.

Manna, Anthony, and Christodoula Mitakidou. 2011. *The Orphan: A Cinderella Story from Greece.* New York: Random House.

Marcus, Leonard. 2013. *Randolph Caldecott: The Man Who Could Not Stop Drawing.* New York: Farrar, Straus & Giroux.

Marino, Gianna. 2005. *Zoopa: An Animal Alphabet.* San Francisco: Chronicle.

Markle, Sandra. 2013. *The Case of the Vanishing Honeybees: A Scientific Mystery.* Brookfield, CT: Millbrook.

Martin, Bill Jr. 1967/2007. *Brown Bear, Brown Bear, What Do You See?* Ill. by Eric Carle. New York: Holt.

Martin, Bill Jr., and John Archambault. 1989. *Chicka Chicka Boom Boom.* Ill. by Lois Ehlert. New York: Simon & Schuster.

Martin, Bill Jr., and John Archambault. Reissued 2007. *Here Are My Hands.* New York: Henry Holt.

Martin, Rafe. 1998. *The Rough-face Girl.* Ill. by David Shannon. New York: Philomel.

Mavor, Salley. 2010. *A Pocketful of Posies.* Boston: Houghton Mifflin.

Mayer, Marianna. 1994. *Baba Yaga and Vasilisa the Brave.* New York: Morrow.

McBratney, Sam. 1995. *Guess How Much I Love You.* Ill. by Anita Jeram. Cambridge, MA: Candlewick.

McCloskey, Robert. 1941. *Make Way for Ducklings.* New York: Viking.

McDermott, Gerald. 1972. *Anansi the Spider*. New York: Holt.

McDermott, Gerald. 1974. *Arrow to the Sun*. New York: Viking.

McDonald, Meme. 1996. *The Way of the Birds*. St. Leonards, NSW, Australia: Allen & Unwin.

McDonnell, Patrick. 2011. *Me . . . Jane*. New York: Little, Brown.

McKinley, Robin. 1984. *The Hero and the Crown*. New York: Greenwillow.

McKissack, Patricia. 1989. *The Dark Thirty: Southern Tales of the Supernatural*. New York: Knopf.

McKissack, Patricia. 2001. *Goin' Someplace Special*. New York: Simon & Schuster.

McKissack, Patricia. 2006. *Porch Lies: Tales of Slicksters, Tricksters, and Other Wily Characters*. New York: Random House.

McLaughlin, Timothy P. Ed. 2012. *Walking on Earth & Touching the Sky: Poetry and Prose by Lakota Youth at Red Cloud Indian School*. Ill. by S. D. Nelson. New York: Abrams.

McLimans, David. 2006. *Gone Wild: An Endangered Animal Alphabet*. New York: Walker.

McMillan, Bruce. 1989. *Time To*. New York: Scholastic.

McMullan, Kate. 2002. *I Stink!* New York: HarperCollins.

McMullan, Kate, and Jim McMullan. 2006. *I Stink!* New York: HarperCollins.

Medina, Jane. 1999. *My Name Is Jorge on Both Sides of the River: Poems*. Honesdale, PA: Boyds Mills Press.

Meltzer, Milton. 2007. *Henry David Thoreau: A Biography*. Minneapolis, MN: Lerner.

Mercado, Nancy. Ed. 2004. *Tripping Over the Lunch Lady and Other School Stories*. New York: Dial.

Meyer, Marissa. 2012. *Cinder*. New York: Feiwel & Friends.

Millen, C. M. 2010. *The Ink Garden of Brother Theophane*. Ill. by Andrea Wisnewski. Watertown, MA: Charlesbridge.

Milne, A. A. 1924. *When We Were Very Young*. London: Methuen.

Milne, A. A. 1926. *Winnie-the-Pooh*. London: Methuen.

Milne, A. A. 1928. *The House at Pooh Corner*. London: Methuen.

Minters, Frances. 1999. *Cinder-Elly*. Minneapolis, MN: Econo-Clad.

Miyazaki, Hayao. 1995. *Nausicaä of the Valley of the Wind Perfect Collection One*. San Francisco, CA: Viz.

Miyazaki, Hayao. 2002. *Miyazaki's Spirited Away, v.1*. San Francisco, CA: Viz.

Montgomery, Sy. 2004. *The Tarantula Scientist*. Ill. by Nic Bishop. Boston: Houghton Mifflin.

Montgomery, Sy. 2010. *Kakapo Rescue: Saving the World's Strangest Parrot*. Boston: Houghton Mifflin.

Mora, Pat. 1996/1999. *Confetti: Poems for Children*. New York: Lee & Low.

Mora, Pat. 1997. *Tomás and the Library Lady*. New York: Knopf.

Mora, Pat. Comp. 2001. *Love to Mamá*. New York: Lee & Low.

Mora, Pat. 2005. *Doña Flor: A Tall Tale About a Giant Woman with a Great Big Heart*. Ill. by Raul Colón. New York: Knopf.

Mora, Pat. 2007. *Yum! Mmmm! Que Rico!: America's Sproutings*. New York: Lee & Low.

Mora, Pat. 2010. *Dizzy in Your Eyes: Poems About Love*. New York: Knopf.

Morales, Yuyi. 2003. *Just a Minute: A Trickster Tale and Counting Book*. San Francisco, CA: Chronicle.

Morris, Ann. 1995. *Shoes, Shoes, Shoes*. New York: HarperCollins.

Morris, Ann. 2003. *Grandma Hekmat Remembers: An Egyptian-American Family Story*. Minneapolis, MN: Lerner.

Morse, Scott. 2002. *Magic Pickle*. Portland, OR: Oni.

Murphy, Jim. 2003. *An American Plague: The True and Terrifying Story of the Yellow Fever Epidemic of 1793*. Boston: Houghton Mifflin.

Murphy, Jim. 2006. *The Great Fire*. New York: Scholastic.

Murphy, Jim. 2012. *Invincible Microbe: Tuberculosis and the Never-Ending Search for a Cure*. Boston: Clarion.

Murphy, Stuart. 2005. *It's About Time!* New York: HarperCollins.

Myers, Walter Dean. 2006. *Jazz*. Ill. by Christopher Myers. New York: Holiday House.

Myers, Walter Dean. 2011. *We Are America: A Tribute from the Heart*. Ill. by Christopher Myers. New York: HarperCollins.

Naidoo, Beverley. 2003. *Out of Bounds: Seven Stories of Conflict and Hope*. New York: HarperCollins.

Naylor, Phyllis Reynolds. 1991. *Shiloh*. New York: Atheneum.

Neitzel, Shirley. 1994. *The Jacket I Wear in the Snow*. New York: HarperTrophy.

Nelson, Kadir. 2008. *We Are the Ship: The Story of Negro League Baseball*. New York: Disney–Jump at the Sun.

Ness, Patrick. 2011. *A Monster Calls*. Ill. by Jim Kay. Somerville, MA: Candlewick.

Numeroff, Laura. 1985. *If You Give a Mouse a Cookie*. Ill. by Felicia Bond. New York: HarperCollins.

Nye, Naomi Shihab. Comp. 1992. *This Same Sky: A Collection of Poems from around the World*. New York: Four Winds Press.

Nye, Naomi Shihab. 2005. *A Maze Me: Poems for Girls*. New York: Greenwillow.

Nytra, David. 2012. *The Secret of the Stone Frog*. New York: TOON.

O'Brien, Robert C. 1971. *Mrs. Frisby and the Rats of NIMH*. New York: Atheneum.

O'Connell, Caitlin, and Donna Jackson. 2011. *The Elephant Scientist*. Boston: Houghton Mifflin Harcourt.

O'Dell, Scott. 1960. *Island of the Blue Dolphins*. Boston: Houghton Mifflin.

O'Neill, Mary. 1989. *Hailstones and Halibut Bones: Adventures in Color*. New York: Doubleday.

Onyefulu, Obi. 1994. *Chinye: A West African Folktale*. New York: Viking.

Opie, Iona. Comp. 1996. *My Very First Mother Goose*. Cambridge, MA: Candlewick.

Opie, Iona. 1999. *Here Comes Mother Goose*. Cambridge, MA: Candlewick.

Opie, Iona. 2007. *Mother Goose's Little Treasures*. Somerville, MA: Candlewick.

Opie, Iona, and Peter Opie. Eds. 1992/2012. *I Saw Esau: The Schoolchild's Pocket Book*. Cambridge, MA: Candlewick.

Orozco, José-Luis. 1997. *Diez Deditos: Ten Little Fingers and Other Play Rhymes and Action Songs from Latin America*. New York: Dutton.

Osborne, Mary Pope. 1989. *Favorite Greek Myths*. New York: Scholastic.

Palacio, R. J. 2012. *Wonder*. New York: Knopf.

Paolini, Christopher. 2004. *Eragon*. New York: Listening Library.

Park, Linda Sue. 2001. *A Single Shard*. New York: Clarion.

Paschen, Elise. Comp. 2005. *Poetry Speaks to Children*. Naperville, IL: Sourcebooks.

Paschen, Elise, and Dominique Raccah. Eds. 2010. *Poetry Speaks: Who I Am*. Naperville, IL: Sourcebooks.

Paterson, Katherine. 1977. *Bridge to Terabithia*. New York: Crowell.

Paterson, Katherine. 1978. *The Great Gilly Hopkins*. New York: Crowell.

Paterson, Katherine. 1980. *Jacob Have I Loved*. New York: Crowell.

Paterson, Katherine. 1997. *Jip*. New York: Scholastic.

Patron, Susan. 2006. *The Higher Power of Lucky*. Ill. by Matt Phelan. New York: Simon & Schuster.

Paul, Ann Whitford. 1999. *All by Herself: 14 Girls Who Made a Difference: Poems*. San Diego: Harcourt.

Paulsen, Gary. 1987. *Hatchet*. New York: Bradbury.

Paulsen, Gary. 1993. *Nightjohn*. New York: Delacorte.

Paulsen, Gary. 1998. *Soldier's Heart*. New York: Delacorte.

Pearson, Deborah. Comp. 2001. *When I Went to the Library*. Toronto, ON, Canada: Groundwood.

Peck, Richard. 2000. *A Year Down Yonder*. New York: Dial.

Peet, Bill. 1986. *Zella, Zack, and Zodiac*. Boston: Houghton Mifflin.

Peet, Bill. 1994. *Bill Peet: An Autobiography*. Boston: Houghton Mifflin.

Pelletier, David. 1996. *The Graphic Alphabet*. New York: Orchard Books.

Perkins, Lynne Rae. 2005. *Criss Cross*. New York: Greenwillow.

Phelan, Matt. 2009. *The Storm in the Barn*. Cambridge, MA: Candlewick.

Philip, Neil. Comp. 1994. *Singing America: Poems That Define a Nation*. New York: Viking.

Philip, Neil. 2000. *DK Read & Listen: Robin Hood*. New York: DK Children.

Pierce, Tamora. 2003. *Circle of Magic: Sandry's Book*. Syracuse, NY: Full Cast Audio.

Pinkney, Andrea Davis. 2010. *Sit-In: How Four Friends Stood Up by Sitting Down*. New York: Little, Brown.

Pinkney, Jerry. 1999. *The Ugly Duckling*. New York: HarperCollins.

Pinkney, Jerry. 2000. *Aesop's Fables*. San Francisco, CA: Chronicle.

Pinkney, Jerry. 2002. *Noah's Ark*. New York: SeaStar.

Pinkney, Jerry. 2006. *The Little Red Hen*. New York: Penguin.

Pinkney, Jerry. 2009. *The Lion & the Mouse*. New York: Little, Brown.

Pinkney, Jerry. 2013. *The Tortoise and the Hare*. New York: Little, Brown.

Polacco, Patricia. 1994. *Pink and Say*. New York: Philomel.

Polacco, Patricia. 2009. *January Sparrow*. New York: Philomel.

Polacco, Patricia. 2011. *Just in Time, Abraham Lincoln*. New York: Putnam.

Pollock, Penny. 1996. *The Turkey Girl: A Zuni Cinderella*. Ill. by Ed Young. New York: Little, Brown.

Pope, Paul. 2013. *Battling Boy*. New York: FirstSecond.

Potter, Beatrix. 1902. *The Tale of Peter Rabbit*. London: Frederick Warne.

Pratchett, Terry. 2004. *A Hat Full of Sky*. New York: HarperTeen.

Pratchett, Terry. 2005. *The Wee Free Men*. New York: HarperChildren's Audio.

Prelutsky, Jack. Comp. 1983. *The Random House Book of Poetry for Children*. New York: Random House.

Prelutsky, Jack. 1986. *Ride a Purple Pelican*. New York: Greenwillow,

Prelutsky, Jack. 1990. *Beneath a Blue Umbrella*. New York: Greenwillow.

Prelutsky, Jack. 1993. *The Dragons Are Singing Tonight*. New York: Scholastic.

Prelutsky, Jack. Comp. 1997. *The Beauty of the Beast*. New York: Knopf.

Prelutsky, Jack. Comp. 1999. *The 20th Century Children's Poetry Treasury*. New York: Knopf.

Prelutsky, Jack. 2006. *What a Day It Was at School!* New York: Greenwillow.

Pringle, Laurence. 2013. *Scorpions: Strange and Wonderful*. Honesdale, PA: Boyds Mills Press.

Pullman, Philip. 2006. *The Golden Compass*. New York: Listening Library.

Pullman, Philip. Reissued 2006. *The Golden Compass*. New York: Knopf.

Raschka, Chris. 2011. *A Ball for Daisy*. New York: Random House.

Raskin, Ellen. 1978. *The Westing Game*. New York: Dutton.

Raven, Margot Theis. 2002. *Mercedes and the Chocolate Pilot*. Farmington Hills, MI: Sleeping Bear Press.

Rawls, Wilson. 1961. *Where the Red Fern Grows*. New York: Doubleday.

Rey, H. A., and Margaret Rey. 1941. *Curious George*. Boston: Houghton Mifflin.

Rich, Mary Perrotta. Comp. 1998. *Book Poems: Poems from National Children's Book Week, 1959–1998.* New York: Children's Book Council.

Rinaldi, Ann. 2005. *The Color of Fire.* New York: Jump at the Sun.

Riordan, Rick. 2005. *The Lightning Thief.* New York: Hyperion.

Riordan, Rick. 2005. *The Lightning Thief.* New York: Listening Library.

Ritter, John H. 2012. *Fenway Fever.* New York: Philomel.

Rochelle, Belinda. Comp. 2000. *Words with Wings: A Treasury of African American Poetry and Art.* New York: HarperCollins.

Rosen, Michael J. 1996. *Food Fight: Poets Join the Fight Against Hunger with Poems About Their Favorite Foods.* San Diego, CA: Harcourt.

Ross, Gayle. 2003. *How Rabbit Tricked Otter and Other Cherokee Trickster Stories.* Minneapolis, MN: Tandem.

Rowling, J. K. 1997. *Harry Potter and the Sorcerer's Stone.* New York: Scholastic.

Rowling, J. K. 1999. *Harry Potter and the Chamber of Secrets.* New York: Scholastic.

Rowling, J. K. 2007. *Harry Potter and the Deathly Hallows.* New York: Listening Library.

Rubin, Susan Goldman, and Elsa Warnick. 1998. *Toilets, Toasters & Telephones: The How and Why of Everyday Objects.* San Diego, CA: Harcourt.

Ruurs, Margriet. 2005. *My Librarian Is a Camel.* Honesdale, PA: Boyds Mills Press.

Ryan, Pam Muñoz. 1996. *100 Is a Family.* New York: Hyperion.

Ryan, Pam Muñoz. 2004. *Becoming Naomi León.* New York: Scholastic, 2004.

Rylant, Cynthia. 1985. *Every Living Thing.* New York: Atheneum.

Rylant, Cynthia. 1992. *Missing May.* New York: Orchard.

Rylant, Cynthia. 2005. *Henry and Mudge and the Great Grandpas.* Ill. by Suçie Stevenson. New York: Simon & Schuster.

Sachar, Louis. 1998. *Holes.* New York: Frances Foster.

Sachar, Louis. 1998. *Sideway Stories from Wayside School.* New York: HarperCollins.

Salisbury, Graham. 1994. *Under the Blood-Red Sun.* New York: Delacorte.

San Souci, Daniel. 2002. *Cendrillon: A Caribbean Cinderella.* New York: Aladdin.

San Souci, Robert. 1998. *The Talking Eggs.* New York: Dutton.

San Souci, Robert. 2000. *Cinderella Skeleton.* San Diego, CA: Harcourt.

San Souci, Robert. 2000. *Little Gold Star: A Spanish American Cinderella.* New York: HarperCollins.

San Souci, Robert. 2006. *Sister Tricksters: Southern Tales of Clever Females.* Atlanta, GA: August House.

Sanderson, Ruth. 2002. *Cinderella.* New York: Little, Brown.

Sanderson, Ruth. 2008. *Mother Goose and Friends.* New York: Little, Brown.

Say, Allen. 2010. *The Boy in the Garden.* Boston: Houghton Mifflin.

Scanlon, Liz Garton. 2009. *All the World.* New York: Beach Lane.

Schertle, Alice. 2009. *Button Up.* New York: Houghton Mifflin.

Schlitz, Laura Amy. 2007. *Good Masters! Sweet Ladies!: Voices from a Medieval Village.* Somerville, MA: Candlewick.

Schmidt, Gary D. 2007. *The Wednesday Wars.* New York: Clarion.

Schneider, Josh. 2011. *Tales for Very Picky Eaters.* New York: Clarion.

Schroeder, Alan. 1996. *Minty: A Story of Young Harriet Tubman.* Ill. by Jerry Pinkney. New York: Dial.

Schroeder, Alan. 2000. *Smoky Mountain Rose: An Appalachian Cinderella.* New York: Puffin.

Schubert, Leda. 2012. *Monsieur Marceau: Actor without Words.* New York: Roaring Brook.

Schuett, Stacey. 1995. *Somewhere in the World Right Now.* New York: Knopf.

Schwartz, Alvin. 1992. *And the Green Grass Grew All Around*. New York: Harper-Collins.

Schwartz, David M., and Yael Schy. 2010. *What in the Wild? Mysteries of Nature Concealed . . . and Revealed*. Berkeley, CA: Tricycle.

Scieszka, Jon. 1989. *The True Story of the Three Little Pigs*. Ill. by Lane Smith. New York: Viking.

Scieszka, Jon. 1992. *The Stinky Cheese Man*. Ill. by Lane Smith. New York: Viking.

Scieszka, Jon. 1998. *Squids Will Be Squids*. Ill. by Lane Smith. New York: Viking.

Scieszka, Jon. 2001. *Baloney (Henry P.)*. Ill. by Lane Smith. New York: Penguin.

Scieszka, Jon. Ed. 2008. *Guys Write for Guys Read: Boys' Favorite Authors Write About Being Boys*. New York: Viking

Scieszka, Jon. Ed. 2010. *Guys Read: Funny Business*. New York: Walden Pond.

Scieszka, Jon. Ed. 2011. *Guys Read: Thriller*. New York: Walden Pond.

Scieszka, Jon. Ed. 2012. *Guys Read: The Sports Pages*. New York: Walden Pond.

Scieszka, Jon. Ed. 2013. *Guys Read: Other Worlds*. New York: Walden Pond.

Selznick, Brian. 2007. *The Invention of Hugo Cabret*. New York: Scholastic.

Selznick, Brian. 2011. *Wonderstruck*. New York: Scholastic.

Sendak, Maurice. 1964. *Where the Wild Things Are*. New York: HarperCollins.

Seuss, Dr. 1957. *The Cat in the Hat*. New York: Random House.

Seuss, Dr. 1960. *Green Eggs and Ham*. New York: Random House.

Seuss, Dr. 1960. *One Fish, Two Fish, Red Fish, Blue Fish*. New York: Random House.

Seuss, Dr. 1963. *Hop on Pop*. New York: Random House.

Seuss, Dr. 1990. *Oh, the Places You'll Go!* New York: Random House.

Sfar, Joann. 2006. *Sardine in Outer Space*. New York: First Second/Roaring Brook.

Sheinkin, Steve. 2011. *The Notorious Benedict Arnold: A True Story of Adventure, Heroism, & Treachery*. New York: Roaring Brook.

Sheinkin, Steve. 2012. *Bomb: The Race to Build—and Steal—the World's Most Dangerous Weapon*. New York: Flashpoint/Roaring Brook.

Shelley, Mary. 2005. *Puffin Graphics: Frankenstein*. Adapted by Gary Reed. Ill. by Frazer Irving. New York: Puffin Books.

Shields, Carol Diggory. 2002. *American History, Fresh Squeezed*. New York: Handprint.

Showers, Paul. 2001. *What Happens to a Hamburger?* (*Let's-Read-and-Find-Out Science* series). New York: HarperTrophy.

Sidman, Joyce. 2009. *Red Sings from Treetops: A Year in Colors*. Ill. by Pamela Zagarenski. Boston: Houghton Mifflin.

Sidman, Joyce. 2010. *Dark Emperor and Other Poems of the Night*. Boston: Houghton Mifflin Harcourt.

Siebert, Diane. Comp. 2006. *Tour America: A Journey Through Poems and Art*. San Francisco: Chronicle.

Sierra, Judy. 1997. *Counting Crocodiles*. San Diego, CA: Gulliver.

Sierra, Judy. 2000. *The Gift of the Crocodile*. New York: Simon & Schuster.

Sierra, Judy. 2005. *Schoolyard Rhymes: Kids' Own Rhymes for Rope Skipping, Hand Clapping, Ball Bouncing, and Just Plain Fun*. New York: Knopf.

Silverstein, Alvin, Virginia B. Silverstein, and Laura Silverstein Nunn. 2003. *Stomachaches* (*My Health* series). New York: Franklin Watts.

Silverstein, Shel. 1974. *Where the Sidewalk Ends*. New York: Harper & Row.

Silverstein, Shel. 1981. *A Light in the Attic*. New York: Harper & Row.

Silverstein, Shel. 1996. *Falling Up: Poems and Drawings*. New York: HarperCollins.

Simon, Seymour. 1976. *Paper Airplane Book*. New York: Puffin.

Simon, Seymour. 2000. *Bones: Our Skeletal System.* New York: HarperTrophy.

Simon, Seymour. 2000. *Muscles: Our Muscular System.* New York: HarperTrophy.

Simon, Seymour. 2003. *Eyes and Ears.* New York: HarperCollins.

Simon, Seymour. 2005. *Guts: Our Digestive System.* New York: HarperCollins.

Simon, Seymour. 2006. *The Brain: Our Nervous System.* New York: Collins.

Simon, Seymour. 2006. *The Heart: Our Circulatory System.* New York: Collins.

Simon, Seymour. 2006. *Weather.* New York: Collins

Simon, Seymour. 2007. *Killer Whales.* New York: HarperCollins.

Singer, Marilyn. 2000. *On the Same Day in March: A Tour of the World's Weather.* New York: HarperCollins.

Singer, Marilyn. 2012. *A Strange Place to Call Home: The World's Most Dangerous Habitats and the Animals That Call Them Home.* San Francisco: Chronicle.

Singer, Marilyn. 2013. *Rutherford B., Who Was He?: Poems About Our Presidents.* New York: Disney-Hyperion.

Sís, Peter. 2000. *Madlenka.* New York: Farrar, Straus & Giroux.

Sís, Peter. 2007. *The Wall: Growing Up Behind the Iron Curtain.* New York: Farrar/Frances Foster.

Smith, Cynthia Leitich. 2000. *Jingle Dancer.* New York: HarperCollins.

Smith, Cynthia Leitich. 2002. *Indian Shoes.* New York: HarperCollins.

Smith, Jeff. 2003. *Bone: Out from Boneville, v.1.* Scholastic: Cartoon Books.

Sneed, Brad. 2003. *Aesop's Fables.* New York: Dial.

Soto, Gary. 1990. *Baseball in April.* San Diego, CA: Harcourt.

Soto, Gary. 1992. *Neighborhood Odes.* San Diego: Harcourt.

Soto, Gary. 1995. *Chato's Kitchen.* Ill. by Susan Guevara. New York: Putnam.

Speare, Elizabeth George. 1958. *The Witch of Blackbird Pond.* Boston: Houghton Mifflin.

Spiegelman, Art, and Françoise Mouly. Eds. 2003. *It Was a Dark and Silly Night.* New York: HarperCollins.

Spier, Peter. 1977. *Noah's Ark.* New York: Doubleday.

Spinelli, Eileen. 2007. *Summerhouse Time.* New York: Knopf.

Spinelli, Jerry. 1990. *Maniac Magee.* New York: Little, Brown.

St. George, Judith. 2000. *So You Want to Be President?* Ill. by David Small. New York: Philomel.

St. George, Judith. 2002. *So You Want to Be an Inventor?* New York: Penguin.

Stanley, Diane. 1996. *Leonardo da Vinci.* New York: Morrow.

Stanley, Diane. 1997. *Rumpelstiltskin's Daughter.* New York: HarperCollins.

Stanley, Diane. 2000. *Michelangelo.* New York: HarperCollins.

Stanley, Diane. 2006. *Bella at Midnight.* New York: HarperCollins.

Stanley, Diane. 2007. *The Trouble with Wishes.* New York: HarperCollins.

Stanley, Jerry. 1993. *Children of the Dust Bowl: The True Story of the School at Weedpatch Camp.* New York: Random House.

Stead, Rebecca. 2009. *When You Reach Me.* New York: Random House.

Steig, William. 1969. *Sylvester and the Magic Pebble.* New York: Windmill Books.

Steig, William. 1982. *Doctor DeSoto.* New York: Farrar, Straus & Giroux.

Stein, David Ezra. 2010. *Interrupting Chicken.* Somerville, MA: Candlewick.

Steptoe, John. 1987. *Mufaro's Beautiful Daughters.* New York: HarperCollins.

Stern, Ellen. 2003. *I Saw a Bullfrog.* New York: Random House.

Sternberg, Julie. 2011. *Like Pickle Juice on a Cookie.* Ill. by Matthew Cordell. New York: Abrams.

Stevens, Janet. 1996. *From Pictures to Words: A Book About Making a Book.* New York: Holiday House.

Stoker, Bram. 2006. *Puffin Graphics: Dracula*. Adapted by Gary Reed. Ill. by Becky Cloonan. New York: Puffin Books.

Stone, Tanya Lee. 2009. *Almost Astronauts: 13 Women Who Dared to Dream*. Somerville, MA: Candlewick.

Stone, Tanya Lee. 2013. *Courage Has No Color, The True Story of the Triple Nickles: America's First Black Paratroopers*. Somerville, MA: Candlewick.

Stone, Tanya Lee. 2013. *Who Says Women Can't Be Doctors? The Story of Elizabeth Blackwell*. New York: Holt.

Sutcliff, Rosemary. Reissued 1987. *The Eagle of the Ninth*. Oxford: Oxford Press.

Sweet, Melissa. 2011. *Balloons over Broadway: The True Story of the Puppeteer of Macy's Parade*. Boston: Houghton Mifflin Harcourt.

Taback, Simms. 1997. *There Was an Old Lady Who Swallowed a Fly*. New York: Viking.

Taback, Simms. 1999. *Joseph Had a Little Overcoat*. New York: Viking.

Takeuchi, Naoko. 1998. *Sailor Moon, v.1*. Los Angeles, CA: Tokyopop.

Tan, Shaun. 2007. *The Arrival*. New York: Scholastic.

Tanaka, Masashi. 2000. *Gon*. New York: DC Comics.

Tanaka, Shelley. 2008. *Amelia Earhart: The Legend of the Lost Aviator*. New York: Abrams.

Tashjian, Janet. 2010. *My Life as a Book*. New York: Holt.

Tashjian, Virginia A. Ed. 1995. *Juba This and Juba That*. New York: Little, Brown.

Tate, Eleanora E. 1993. *Retold African Myths*. Logan, IA: Perfection Learning.

Taylor, Mildred. 1976. *Roll of Thunder, Hear My Cry*. New York: Dial.

Tezuka, Osamu. 2002. *Astro Boy, v.1*. Milwaukie, OR: Dark Horse.

Thayer, Ernest. 2000. *Casey at the Bat*. Ill. by Christopher Bing. New York: Handprint.

Thimmesh, Catherine. 2006. *Team Moon: How 400,000 People Landed* Apollo 11 *on the Moon*. Boston: Houghton Mifflin.

Thompson, Jill. 2001. *Scary Godmother, v.1*. Chicago: Sirius.

Thompson, Kay. 1955. *Kay Thompson's Eloise*. Ill. by Hilary Knight. New York: Simon & Schuster.

Tolkien, J. R. R. 2004. *The Lord of the Rings*. Prince Frederick, MD: Recorded Books.

Torres, J. 2002. *Alison Dare: Little Miss Adventures*. Illus. by J. Bone. Portland, OR: Oni.

Trelease, Jim. 1992. *Hey! Listen to This: Stories to Read Aloud*. New York: Penguin.

Trondheim, Lewis. 2006. *A.L.I.E.E.E.N. Archives of Lost Issues and Earthly Editions of Extraterrestrial Novelties*. New York: First Second/Roaring Brook.

Tucker, Kathy. 2003. *The Seven Chinese Sisters*. Ill. by Grace Lin. Morton Grove, IL: Albert Whitman.

Tullet, Hervé. 2011. *Press Here*. San Francisco: Chronicle.

Uchida, Yoshiko. 1981. *A Jar of Dreams*. New York: McElderry.

Van Allsburg, Chris. 1985. *The Polar Express*. Boston: Houghton Mifflin.

Vanderpool, Clare. 2010. *Moon Over Manifest*. New York: Random House.

Vardell, Sylvia, and Janet Wong. Eds. 2011. *Gift Tag*. PoetryTagTime.com.

Vardell, Sylvia, and Janet Wong. Eds. 2011. *PoetryTagTime*. PoetryTagTime.com.

Vardell, Sylvia, and Janet Wong. Eds. 2011. *P*TAG*. PoetryTagTime.com.

Vardell, Sylvia M., and Janet Wong. 2012. *The Poetry Friday Anthology (K–5)*. Princeton, NJ: Pomelo Books.

Vardell, Sylvia M., and Janet Wong. 2013. *The Poetry Friday Anthology for Middle School, Grades 6–8*. Princeton, NJ: Pomelo Books.

Vardell, Sylvia M., and Janet Wong. 2014. *The Poetry Friday Anthology for Science.* Princeton, NJ: Pomelo Books.

Viorst, Judith. 1972. *Alexander and the Terrible, Horrible, No Good, Very Bad Day.* New York: Atheneum.

Viorst, Judith. 1981. ". . . And Then the Prince Knelt Down and Tried to Put the Glass Slipper on Cinderella's Foot." In *If I Were in Charge of the World and Other Worries.* New York: Atheneum.

Volavkova, Hana. Comp. 1993. *I Never Saw Another Butterfly.* New York: Schocken Books.

Waber, Bernard. 1975. *Ira Sleeps Over.* Boston: Houghton Mifflin.

Walker, Sally M. 2005. *Secrets of a Civil War Submarine: Solving the Mysteries of the H. L. Hunley.* Minneapolis, MN: Carolrhoda Books.

Walters, Eric. Reteller. 2012. *The Matatu.* Ill. by Eva Campbell. Victoria, BC, Canada: Orca.

Ward, Cindy. 1992. *Cookie's Week.* New York: Putnam.

Wardlaw, Lee. 2011. *Won Ton: A Cat Tale Told in Haiku.* Ill. by Eugene Yelchin. New York: Henry Holt.

Weatherford, Carole Boston. 2002. *Remember the Bridge: Poems of a People.* New York: Philomel.

Weatherford, Carole Boston. 2005. *Freedom on the Menu: The Greensboro Sit-Ins.* New York: Dial.

Weatherford, Carole Boston. 2006. *Moses: When Harriet Tubman Led Her People to Freedom.* New York: Hyperion.

Weeks, Sarah. 2004. *So B It.* New York: HarperCollins.

Whipple, Laura. Ed. 1996. *Eric Carle's Dragons, Dragons.* New York: Philomel.

Whipple, Laura. 2002. *If the Shoe Fits: Voices from Cinderella.* New York: McElderry.

White, E. B. 1952. *Charlotte's Web.* New York: HarperCollins.

Wiese, Jim. 2000. *Head to Toe Science: Over 40 Eye-Popping, Spine-Tingling, Heart-Pounding Activities That Teach Kids About the Human Body.* Hoboken, NJ: Jossey-Bass.

Wiesner, David. 1991. *Tuesday.* New York: Clarion.

Wiesner, David. 1999. *Sector 7.* New York: Clarion.

Wiesner, David. 2001. *The Three Pigs.* New York: Clarion.

Wiesner, David. 2006. *Flotsam.* New York: Clarion.

Wilcox, Charlotte. 2000. *Mummies, Bones & Body Parts.* Minneapolis, MN: Carolrhoda.

Wilder, Laura Ingalls. 1953. *Little House in the Big Woods.* New York: HarperCollins.

Willard, Nancy. 1981. *A Visit to William Blake's Inn: Poems for Innocent and Experienced Travelers.* Ill. by Alice and Martin Provensen. Orlando, FL: Harcourt.

Willems, Mo. 2004. *Knuffle Bunny.* New York: Hyperion.

Willems, Mo. 2010. *We Are in a Book!* New York: Hyperion.

Williams, Vera. 2001. *Amber Was Brave, Essie Was Smart.* New York: Greenwillow.

Williams-Garcia, Rita. 2010. *One Crazy Summer.* New York: Amistad.

Winter, Jonah. 2011. *Born and Bred in the Great Depression.* New York: Random House.

Wisniewski, David. 1996. *Golem.* New York: Clarion.

Wolf, Allan. 2003. *The Blood-Hungry Spleen and Other Poems About Our Parts.* Cambridge, MA: Candlewick.

Wong, Janet S. 2000. *Night Garden: Poems from the World of Dreams.* New York: McElderry.

Wong, Janet. 2000. *The Trip Back Home.* San Diego, CA: Harcourt.

Wong, Janet. 2003. *Knock on Wood: Poems about Superstitions.* New York: McElderry.

Wong, Janet. 2008. *Minn and Jake's Almost Terrible Summer*. New York: Farrar, Straus & Giroux.

Wong, Janet. 2011. *Once Upon a Tiger: New Beginnings for Endangered Animals*. OnceUponaTiger.com.

Woodson, Jacqueline. 2003. *Locomotion*. New York: Putnam.

Woodson, Jacqueline. 2005. *Show Way*. New York: Putnam.

Woodson, Jacqueline. 2012. *Each Kindness*. Ill. by E. B. Lewis. New York: Putnam.

Worth, Valerie 1994. *All the Small Poems and Fourteen More*. New York: Farrar, Straus & Giroux.

Worth, Valerie. 2007. *Animal Poems*. New York: Farrar, Straus & Giroux.

Wright, Betty Ren. 1999. *The Dollhouse Murders*. Pine Plains, NY: Live Oak Media.

Wright, Blanche Fisher. Comp. 1916. *The Real Mother Goose*. New York: Rand McNally.

Yep, Laurence. Ed. 1993. *American Dragons: Twenty-five Asian American Voices*. New York: HarperCollins.

Yep, Laurence. 1993. *Dragon's Gate*. New York: HarperCollins.

Yep, Laurence. 1999. *The Dragon Prince: A Chinese Beauty and the Beast Tale*. New York: HarperCollins.

Yolen, Jane. Comp. 1994. *Sleep Rhymes Around the World*. Honesdale, PA: Boyds Mills/Wordsong.

Yolen, Jane. 1998. *Here There Be Dragons*. San Diego: Harcourt.

Yolen, Jane. 1999. *Bird Watch*. New York: Putnam.

Yolen, Jane. Comp. 2000. *Street Rhymes from Around the World*. Honesdale, PA: Boyds Mills/Wordsong.

Yolen, Jane. 2004. *Jason and the Gorgon's Blood*. New York: HarperCollins.

Yolen, Jane. 2004. *The Young Merlin Trilogy: Passager, Hobby, and Merlin*. San Diego, CA: Harcourt.

Yolen, Jane. Comp. 2006. *This Little Piggy: Lap Songs, Finger Plays, Clapping Games, and Pantomime Rhymes*. Cambridge, MA: Candlewick.

Young, Ed. 1989. *Lon Po Po*. New York: Philomel.

Young, Ed. 1992. *Seven Blind Mice*. New York: Philomel.

Young, Ed. 2004. *The Lost Horse: A Chinese Folktale*. New York: Houghton Mifflin Harcourt.

Young, Ed. 2004. *The Sons of the Dragon King*. New York: Atheneum.

Young, Ed. 2005. *Beyond the Great Mountains*. San Francisco: Chronicle.

Zelinsky, Paul. 1997. *Rapunzel*. New York: Dutton.

Zimmer, Tracie Vaughn. 2009. *Steady Hands: Poems About Work*. New York: Clarion.

Zimmer, Tracie Vaughn. 2011. *Cousins of Clouds: Elephant Poems*. New York: Houghton Mifflin.

Zolotow, Charlotte. 1972. *William's Doll*. New York: Harper.

Copyright Credits

CHAPTER OPENING IMAGES

The ALA photos are all available for free from the American Library Association Public Information Office. http://www.ala.org/ala/pio/campaign/prtools/downloadfree.htm

Chapter 1: Sister and baby brother reading together on the bed.

Chapter 2: Three African girls huddle around an open book in the lap of middle girl.

Chapter 3: Picture of father and son sitting on green couch in front of shelves. The Beyond Words: Celebrating America's Libraries Photo Contest courtesy of the American Library Association Public Information Office; First Place, Amateur. "Following in His Father's Footsteps" by Shirley Gray, Union Public Library, Union, NJ

Chapter 4: Close up of middle school girl and open book.

Chapter 5: Black and white close up photo of girl's face looking up. The Beyond Words: Celebrating America's Libraries Photo Contest courtesy of the American Library Association Public Information Office; ALA President's Prize; "A Reach for Knowledge" by Susan Matsubara, Lexington Public Library, Lexington, KY

Chapter 6: Color photo of girl reading with pile of textbooks in front of her. The Beyond Words: Celebrating America's Libraries Photo Contest courtesy of the American Library Association Public Information Office; Third Place, Youth; "Exploring" by Veronica Marzonie, Flint Public Library, Flint, MI

Chapter 7: Black and white photo of boy sitting between all the shelves. The Beyond Words: Celebrating America's Libraries Photo Contest courtesy of the American Library Association Public Information Office; Honorable

Mention, Amateur; "Zachary" by Marlene Hodge, Timberland Regional Library, Centralia, WA

Chapter 8: Black and white photo of boys grouped around books and a computer. The Beyond Words: Celebrating America's Libraries Photo Contest courtesy of the American Library Association Public Information Office; First Place, Youth; "Eyes on the Print" by Tracy Conti, Coral Reef Senior High School Library, Miami, FL

TEXT PERMISSIONS

Zapped by "Dia" by Pat Mora. Copyright © 2008 by Pat Mora. Reprinted by permissions of Curtis Brown, Ltd.

Denise Fleming interview reprinted with permission from TeachingBooks.net.

Kirby Larson interview used courtesy of KidsRead.com.

Standards for the English Language Arts, by the International Reading Association and the National Council of Teachers of English, Copyright 1996 by the International Reading Association and the National Council of Teachers of English. Reprinted with permission. Available at http://www.ncte.org/standards.

COVER IMAGE PERMISSIONS

Reprinted with the permission of Atheneum Books for Young Readers, an imprint of Simon & Schuster Children's Publishing Division from BEAUTIFUL BLACKBIRD by Ashley Bryan. Copyright © 2003 Ashley Bryan.

Reprinted with the permission of Beach Lane Books, an imprint of Simon & Schuster Children's Publishing Division from UNDERGROUND by Denise Fleming. Copyright © 2012 Denise Fleming.

Cover from A SINGLE SHARD by Linda Sue Park. Jacket and case cover copyright © 2001 by Jean and Mousien Tseng. Used by permission of Clarion Books, an imprint of Houghton Mifflin Harcourt Publishing Company. All rights reserved.

Cover from THE MIDWIFE'S APPRENTICE by Karen Cushman. Jacket illustration copyright © 1995 by Trina Schart Hyman. Used by permission of Clarion Books, an imprint of Houghton Mifflin Harcourt Publishing Company. All rights reserved.

Cover from JUMANJI by Chris Van Allsburg. Copyright © 1981 by Chris Van Allsburg. Used by permission of Houghton Mifflin Harcourt Publishing Company. All rights reserved.

Cover from THE GIVER by Lois Lowry. Copyright © 1993 by Lois Lowry. Used by permission of Houghton Mifflin Harcourt Publishing Company. All rights reserved.

Cover from LINCOLN: A PHOTOBIOGRAPHY by Russell Freedman. Jacket copyright © 1987 by Houghton Mifflin Company. Used by permission of Clarion Books, an imprint of Houghton Mifflin Publishing Company. All rights reserved.

Index

Academy of American Poets, 123, 143
Aesop, 83–84
Aesop's Fables, 82, 89
Aesop Prize, 103
Al Capone Does My Homework, 197
Al Capone Does My Shirts, 197
Al Capone Shines My Shoes, 197
ALA Graphics, 7, 64
Alcott, Louisa May, 153–154
Alexander and the Terrible, Horrible, No Good, Very Bad Day, 70, 144
Alice series, 164
Alice's Adventures in Wonderland, 39, 221
Alif Laila, 4
All the King's Men, 116
All the World, 54
The Allure of Authors: Author Studies in the Elementary Classroom, 27
Alvin Ho, 163
Amanda Pig, 50
Amastae, Sharon, 6
Amber Was Brave, 124
Amelia Bedelia, 50
American Association for the Advancement of Science (AAAS), 270
American Association of School Librarians, 10, 33, 74, 288; standards for the 21st-century leaner, 112

American Girl series, 154, 198
American History, Fresh Squeezed, 201
American Library Association, 19–20, 22, 29–30, 36, 66, 94, 143, 177; Library Bill of Rights, 36; Odyssey Audiobook Award, 243–244; 100 Frequently Most Banned/Challenged Books of 2000–2009, 164
An American Plague, 260
American Rhetoric, 214
Ames, Lee, 261
Ananiz, Cynthia, 216
Andersen, Hans Christian, 45, 91
Anderson, Laurie Halse, 211
The Andre Norton Award, 241
The Animal Book: A Collection of the Fastest, Fiercest, Toughest Cleverest, Shyest—and Most Surprising—Animals on Earth, 259, 314
The Annotated Mother Goose, 116
Appelt, Kathi, 228
Applegate, Katherine, 144, 228, 241
Are You My Mother?, 24
Are You There, God? It's Me, Margaret, 164, 175, 189
The Arrow Finds its Mark, 132
Association for Library Services to Children, 8, 20, 29, 33, 178; ALSC Competencies, 36

Association of American Publishers, 36
Audiobooks, 225–227, 232–233, 242–244; promoting literacy with, 242; publishers and producers, 243; resources, 244; selecting, 243–244
Author Day Adventures: Bringing Literacy to Life with an Author Visit, 27, 295
Avi, 181, 209

Babbitt, Natalie, 239
Baby Rhyming Time, 118
Babymouse, 246
Bader, Barbara, 42
Bagert, Brad, 138
Balloons Over Broadway: The True Story of the Puppeteer of Macy's Parade, 260
Bank Street College, 137
Baring–Gould, William and Ceil, 116
Barr, Catherine, 14
Barron, T.A., 229
Bartoletti, Susan Campbell, 260
Barton, Bob, 146
Baseball in April, 161
Batchelder Award, 178
Bats! Furry Fliers of the Night, 74
Bauer, Caroline Feller, 139, 146
Baum, L. Frank, 222, 230, 247
Beatrix Potter Society, 42
Beaumont, Karen, 47, 124
Beautiful Blackbird, 96–97
The Beauty of the Beast, 121
Because of Winn-Dixie, 161
Becoming a Nation of Readers, 11–12
Becoming Naomi León, 158
Beers, Kylene, 242
Bell, Anthea, 239–240
Bell, Babs, 13
Best Books for Children: Preschool Through Grade 6, 14
Best lists, 22–23
Bewley, S. Zulema Silvia, 239–240
Bibliomania, 193
Bing, Christopher, 50
Biographies, 264–268; autobiographies, 267; celebrity, 267; collective, 267; complete, 265; evaluating, 267–268; picture book, 266; series, 266–267; types of, 265–267
Bird, Betsy, 18
Bishop, Rudine Sims, 3–4, 62, 174
Black and White, 48
Blass, Rosanne J., 185

The Blood-Hungry Spleen and Other Poems About Our Parts, 274
Bloom, Suzanne, 43–44
Blubber, 164
Blue Rose Girls, 17
Blume, Judy, 156–157, 164, 189
Blumenthal, Karen, 259
Bond, Felicia, 47
Book blogs, 17–18
Book! Book! Book!, 13
Book It pizza certificates, 7, 185
Booklist, 16
Books Kids Will Sit Still For series, 12
Books of Ember series, 229, 231
Booktalking, 185–186, 190
Booth, David, 146
Born and Bred in the Great Depression, 198
Boston Globe/Horn Book awards, 15
Bound to Stay Bound Books, 20
Boys and books, 183–184
Boy's Life, 263
Brack, Rose, 225–227
The Bridge Is Up, 13
Bridge to Tarabithia, 164
Bringing in the New Year, 237
Bronzo, William, 184
Brown, Margaret Wise, 60, 124
Brown, Peter, 54
Brown bag book reports, 179–180
Brown Bear, Brown Bear, 49, 124
Browne, Anthony, 48
Bruchac, Joseph and James, 90
Bryan, Ashley, 66, 94–98
Buckalo, Mary D., 101–102
Bud, Not Buddy, 209
Buker, Derek M., 249
Bulletin of the Center for Children's Books (BCCB), 16
The Bus for Us, 44
Buss, Deborah, 13
Button Up, 137
Byars, Betsy, 156

Caldecott, Randolph, 19, 25, 39–40
California Department of Education, 11
The Cambridge Companion to Fantasy Literature, 249
Card, Orson Scott, 229
Carle, Eric, 48–49, 73
Carmi, Daniella, 178
Carol Otis Hurst's Children's Literature Site, 24

Carroll, Lewis, 39
Casey at the Bat, 50
Castaway, 193
The Cat in the Hat, 24, 49–50
The Cats in Krasinski Square, 198
Cave, Kathryn, 48
Censorship, 165–166, 231
Center for Children's Books at the University of Illinois, 24
Chains, 211
Chance, Rosemary, 250
Charlotte Zolotow Award, 67
Charlotte's Web, 25, 227–228
Charlie and the Chocolate Factory, 227
Charlie Joe Jackson's Guide to Not Reading, 175–176
Charlotte's Web, 224
Chasse, Emily, 85–86
Chatton, Barbara, 143, 21
Cheng, Andrea, 200
Chickadee, 211
Chicken Spaghetti, 17
Chika Chicka Boom Boom, 47, 124
Child at Heart Gallery, 64
Children and Books, 59
Children and Libraries, 246
Children's Book Council (CBC), 24, 26, 212
Children's Book Guild, 280
Children's Choices, 22
Children's Literature Assembly of the National Council of Teachers of English (CLA/NCTE), 33
Children's Literature Association, 33
Choldenko, Gennifer, 197
A Chorus of Cultures: Developing Literacy through Multicultural Poetry, 146
Christopher, John, 225
Christopher, Matt, 161
Cianciolo, Patricia, 260
Ciardi, John, 122
Cinderella, 84–85, 88, 104–105; novels, 107; parodies, 107–108; poems, 107; studying, 106; variants, 104–105; websites, 108
Claes, Jane, 22
Claudia Lewis Award, 137
Cleary, Beverly, 12, 156–158
Clementine, 163
Click, Clack, Moo: Cows That Type, 45
Clinton, Catherine, 200
Coast to Coast: Exploring State Book Awards, 22

Cobblestone, 263
Codell, Esmé Raji, 9, 159, 189
Cole, Joanna,
Collier, Bryan, 66
Collins, Suzanne, 229, 231
Commission on Reading, 12
Common Core State Standards, 118–119, 146–147, 189, 287–288
The Complete Idiot's Guide to Publishing Children's Books, 45
Conin, Doreen, 13
Contemporary realistic fiction, 151–190; adventure, 160; animals, 160–161; awards for, 176–178; characters, 171–172; controversy and, 164–166; culture, 173–175; definition of, 154–155; evaluating, 171–176; gender, 173–175; history, 151–152; major authors of, 166–168; mystery, 160; plot, 172; professional resources in, 186–187; sample review, 175–176; series, 163–164; setting, 172; sharing, 183–186; short stories, 161–162; sports, 161; style, 173; subgenres, 159–161; subtopics, 157–159; theme, 172–173; transitional novels, 162–163; types of, 156–164
The Cooperative Children's Book Center (CCBC), 16–17, 38
Coppell Middle School West, 225
Corcoran, Jill, 200
Coretta Scott King award, 19–20, 66, 94
Creature from My Closet, 163
Creech, Sharon, 172, 176, 181
Cricket Magazine group, 263
Crispin, 209
Criss Cross, 173, 176
A Critical Handbook of Children's Literature, 61
Cronin, Doreen, 45
Cullinan, Bernice, 8
Cummings, James, 72
The Curious Garden, 54
Curtis, Christopher Paul, 212
Curtis, Paul, 209
Cushin, Marnie, 257–258
Cushman, Karen, 197, 209
Cynsations, 17

Dahl, Roald, 227
Dalat International School, 155
Danielson, Julie, 17

Dark Emperor and Other Poems of the Night, 65

The Dark Thirty: Southern Tales of the Supernatural, 91

Dashdondog, Jambyn, 4

Days to Celebrate: A Full Year of Poetry, People, Holidays, History, Fascinating Facts, and More, 121, 200, 313

Dead End in Norvelt, 197, 211, 217

Dear America series, 154, 198

Dear Mr. Henshaw, 158

Decade for Childhood, 7

Defoe, Daniel, 192–193

Denslow, W.W., 222–223

Diamond Willow, 137

Diamant-Cohen, Betsy, 118, 185

Diary of a Wimpy Kid, 6, 163

DiCamillo, Kate, 241

Dickinson, Emily, 134

Dictionary of Literary Biography, 26

Dim Sum for Everyone!, 233–234, 237

Discworld series, 225, 230

The Diverting History of John Gilpin, 40

Dork Diaries, 163

Double Identity, 229

Down on the Farm, 13

Dragon Rider, 239–240

Draw the Draw 50 Way, 261

Dresang, Eliza, 11, 246

Drop Everything and Read day, 12

Duke, 207

Dumpling Days, 158, 233, 237

DuPrau, Jeanne, 229, 231

Earnst, Linda, 118

Earth: A Shipmate's Guide to Our Solar System, 271

Eastman, P.D., 24

Edging the Boundaries of Children's Literature, 256

Ehlert, Lois, 48–49, 260

El día de los niños/El día de los libros, 11, 28, 31

Elijah of Buxton, 212

Emerson Elementary School, 73

Enders series, 229

English-language learners, 6–7, 119–120, 263

Erdrich, Louis, 211

ESPN Deportes, 6

Evans, Shane, 66

The Eye, the Ear, and the Arm, 229

Ezra Jack Keats Award, 67

Fair Weather, 197

Fantasy, 3, 164, 221–251; awards for, 240–244; characters, 237–238; controversy in, 231; definitions of, 223–225; evaluating, 237–240; films, novel-based, 245–246; ghost stories and the supernatural, 228; high, 228–229; history, 221–222; low, 227–228; major authors of, 232–237; plot, 238; professional resources in, 249–251; sample review, 239–240; science fiction, 229–230; series, 230–231; setting, 238; sharing, 244–248; style, 239; theme, 238–239; traditional tales and, 251; types of, 227–231

Fantasy Literature for Children and Young Adults, 249

Farmer, Nancy, 229

Favorite Poem Project, 123

Feeding Friendsies, 43

The Fences Between Us, 207

Fenway Fever, 161

The First Day of Winter, 13

Fisher, Aileen, 136

Fitzhugh, Louise, 151

Fleischman, Paul, 136

Fleischman, Sid, 197–198

Fleming, Candace, 13, 158

Fleming, Denise, 13, 52–55

Floca, Brian, 260

Fluent in Fantasy: A Guide to Reading Interests, 249

Fly With Poetry: An ABC of Poetry, 132

Follett's Titlewave, 15

Follis, Marianne, 12–13, 180, 185

Follos, Alison M. G., 27

Fortune Cookie Fortunes, 233, 237

The Foundations of Literacy, 8

Fox, Mem, 9

Freedman, Russell, 265–266, 276–277

Freedom on the Menu: The Greensboro Sit-Ins, 199

Freeman, Nancy, 12

Fricke, John, 223

The Friendship Doll, 207

Fritz, Jean, 254, 286

From Cover to Cover: Evaluating and Reviewing Children's Books, 15, 61

Frost, Helen, 137
Frost, Robert, 123
Full Cast Audio, 243
Funke, Cornelia, 239
Fuse #8, 18

Gaiman, Neil, 241
Galileo's Universe, 132
Gaming the Past, 216
Gantos, Jack, 159, 197, 211
Gardner, Martin, 223
Garland, Judy, 223
Garner, Joan, 249
Gates, Pamela S., 249
Geisel Award, 49, 66
George, Kristine O'Connell, 149
Gerstein, Mordicai, 70
Gibbons, Gail, 258
Giggle Poetry, 123
Giggle Giggle Quack, 13
Gillespie, John, 19
Gipson, Fred, 161
The Giver, 229, 232, 241
Glenn–Paul, Dierdre, 3
Go, Dog, Go!, 24
Goin' Someplace Special, 144
Golden Books, 24
The Golden Compass, 239
González, Xelena, 43–44
Good Masters! Sweet Ladies, 136
Goodnight Moon, 49, 60, 124
GoodReads, 35
Google Lit Trips, 215–216
Gooney Bird, 163
Goose & Bear series, 43
Gore, Al, 74–75
Grady, Cynthia, 200
Graphic novels, 246–248; manga, 247–248, 251
Gravett, Emily, 62
The Graveyard Book, 241
Great Books About Things Kids Love: More Than 750 Recommended Books for Children 3 to 14, 14
The Great Fire, 282
The Great Gilly Hopkins, 157–158, 164
GreatKidBooks, 73
Green Eggs and Ham, 24
The Green Glass Sea, 210–211
Greenfield, Eloise, 144
Greenlaw, Jean, 224

Greenwald, Tommy, 175–176
Grey, Mini, 92
Grimes, Nikki, 144, 149
Grimm, Jakob and Wilhelm, 82, 89
Grissom, Susi, 175
The Gryphon Award, 66
Guess How Much I Love You, 46
Gulliver's Travels, 221
Gutman, Dan, 161
Guts: Our Digestive System, 272–275
Guy, Ginger, 48
Guys Read, 225

Haddix, Margaret Peterson, 229
Halvorsen, Gail S., 194
Hank Zipzer, 163
Hans Christian Andersen Award, 19, 67, 178
Hardy Boys series, 25
Harley, Avis, 132
Harness, Cheryl, 206
HarperCollins, 22
Harriet the Spy, 151
Harris, Christopher, 216
Harris, Mildred, 223
Harris, Violet, 146
Harry Potter, 24–25, 82, 221, 229, 248
A Hat Full of Sky, 249
Hatchet, 175, 193
Hattie Big Sky, 203, 205
Hattie Ever After, 191, 203–207
Haygood, Hilary, 119–120
Heard, Georgia, 132, 148
Hearne, Betsy, 2
Heath, Shirley Brice, 5
Heelis, William, 41
Heller, Julek, 193
Help Me Mr. Mutt, 14
Henkes, Kevin, 54, 164
Herald, Diana Ticier, 249
Herald, Kelly, 141
The Hero and the Crown, 241
Hesse, Karen, 198
Heyman, Ken, 260
The Higher Power of Lucky, 176, 180
Highlights for Children, 263
Hilbun, Janet, 22
A Hippopotamusn't, 129
His Dark Materials, 239
Historical fiction, 164, 191–220; awards for, 211–214; blending genres,

Historical fiction (*continued*)
199–200; characters, 208; definitions of, 193–194; drama, 215; evaluating, 207–211; historical simulation games and, 216; introduction to, 191–192; major authors of, 201–207; notable social studies trade books, 212; picture books, 198–199; plot, 208; poetry and, 200–201; professional resources for, 217–218; sample review of, 210–211; series, 198; setting, 208–209; sharing, 214–216; stereotyping in, 210; style, 209; theme, 209; types of, 195–200; U.S. history, 195–197; virtual travel, 215–216; world history, 197–198
Hoban, Tana, 48, 73
Hodges, Margaret, 91
Holbrook, Sara, 201
Holdaway, Don, 8
Holes, 144, 227, 241
Holm, Jennifer, 246
Holocaust Museum Houston, 213
Hop on Pop, 24
Hopkins, Lee Bennett, 121, 136, 148, 200
Horn Book Magazine, 15, 182–183, 211
Horning, Kathleen T., 15, 17, 38, 61
Horsey, Marleen Gould, 194–195
The House at Pooh Corner, 115
The House of the Scorpion, 229
How to Get Your Child to Love Reading: For Ravenous and Reluctant Readers Alike, 9, 169
Huck, Charlotte, 42, 90, 227, 264
Hughes, Langston, 122, 144
The Hunger Games trilogy, 227, 229, 231, 248
Hurst, Carol Otis, 215
Hurston, Zora Neale, 90
Hyman, Trina Schart, 91

I Never Saw Another Butterfly, 201
I Saw a Bullfrog, 257
If You Give a Mouse a Cookie, 47
In the Small, Small Pond, 52–54
In the Tall, Tall Grass, 53–54
Informational books, 253–288; activity books, 261; accuracy, 275–276; awards for, 278–282; biographies, 264–268; concept books, 259–260; definitions of, 256; design, 276–277; evaluating, 275–278; follow–up activities for, 284–285; informational storybooks, 260; introduction to, 253–256; magazines, serials, and periodicals, 263–264; major authors of, 268–275; organization, 276; photo essays, 259; reference tools, 261–262; sample review of, 277–278; series books, 261–262; sharing, 283–285; social histories, 260; style, 277; survey books, 258–259; trivia books, 261; types of, 258–268
Ingram's iPage, 15
The Inheritance series, 227
The Ink Garden of Brother Theophane, 137
International Board on Books for Young People, 19, 32
International Children's Book Day, 31
International Children's Digital Library, 24
International Children's Literature Digital Library, 63
International Reading Association, 22–23; Promising Poet Award, 136
Internet Movie Database, 246
The Invention of Hugo Cabret, 246
Island of the Blue Dolphins, 193
It's Raining Laughter, 144
Ivy and Bean, 163

James, Edward, 249
James, Helen Foster, 27
James and the Giant Peach, 227
Jane Addams Book Award, 212
Jane Addams Peace Association, 212
Janeczko, Paul, 140, 148
Jazz, 135
Jeffers, Susan, 123
Jenkins, Carol Brennan, 27
Jenkins, Steve, 258–259
Jeram, Anita, 46
John Henry, 90
Joey Pigza, 159
Jones, Leigh Ann, 34
Jones, James Earl, 71
Joseph Had a Little Overcoat, 49
Joyful Noise, 136
Judge, Lisa, 47
Judy Moody, 163
Junie B. Jones, 163
Just One More Book, 26
Justin Case, 163

Kadohata, Cynthia, 212
The Kane Chronicles, 226
Katz, Alan, 138
Katz, Bobbi, 200
Kay Thompson's Eloise, 46
Kazim, Syeda Basarat, 4
Kennedy, X.J., 122
Kerper, Rick, 281
A Kick in the Head: An Everyday Guide to Poetic Forms, 140
Kids Discover, 264
KIDSWWWRITE, 3
King, Coretta Scott, 20
King, Martin Luther, Jr., 20
King, Stephen, 189
Kinney, Jeff, 6
Kirkus Reviews, 16, 54, 74
Kisses from Rosa, 63
Kite Flying, 233–234, 237
Klages, Ellen, 210
Knight, Hilary, 46
Knuffle Bunny, 45
Knudsen, Michelle, 1
Komenský, Jane Ámos, 255
Konigsburg, E.L., 151, 176
Korns, Tammy, 62, 210, 278
Krashen, Stephen, 10, 12
Kraske, Robert, 193
Krull, Kathleen, 120
Kruse, Ginny Moore, 38
Kurlansky, Mark, 277–278
Kuskin, Karla, 136, 144
Kutner, Merrily, 13

Lakewood Elementary School, 11
Lankford, Mary, 260
Larson, Kirby, 203–207
L'Engle, Madeline, 229
Leap Into Poetry, 132
Lear, Edward, 123
Lee Bennett Hopkins Award, 136–137
Lesesne, Teri, 226
Lewis, C.S., 238
Lewis, J. Patrick, 122, 129–132, 138, 149, 200
Lewis, Valerie, 14
Libraries Got Game: Aligned Learning Through Modern Board Games, 216
Library Lion, 1
The Library of Congress, 214; Poetry and Literature Center, 123
Libravox.com, 243

Lies and Other Tall Tales, 90
A Light in the Attic, 122
Lima, Carolyn, 14
Lin, Grace, 158, 233–237
The Lion & the Mouse, 45, 90
The Lion and the Unicorn, 137
Lipson, Eden Ross, 9
Listservs of children's literature, 33–34
Literacy; becoming literate, 2–5; celebrations, 31–32; cloze procedure, 69–70; development, 5–9, 285–286; echo reading, 69; emergent, 8–9; -related activities, 6; resources for supporting family, 7; visual, 69
Literature-based Instruction with English Language Learners, 72
Little House novels, 210, 234
Little Read Wagon, 43
The Little Red Hen, 101–102
Little Women, 151, 153–154
Litwin, Eric, 13
Livingston, Myra Cohn, 136, 138
Lobel, Arnold, 120–121
A Long Way from Chicago, 197
Lord, Cynthia, 159, 178
Lord of the Rings, 223–224, 230
Lotan, Yael, 178
Lottridge, Celia Barker, 138
Lowji Discovers America, 158
Lowrey, Janet Sebring, 24
Lowry, Lois, 208, 229, 232, 241
Lupica, Mike, 161

McBratney, Sam, 46
Mackin, 15
MacKinney, Donna, 30–31
Mad Magazine, 264
Magic School Bus series, 260
Make Way for Ducklings, 46
Making Books with Children, 63
Maniac Magee, 177
Marcus, Leonard S., 64, 66
Marooned: The Strange but True Adventures of Alexander Selkirk, the Real Robinson Crusoe, 193, 314
Mathers, Petra, 63
Mayer, Brian, 216
Mayes, Walter, 14
Martin Jr., Bill, 47, 73, 124
Marvin Redpost, 163
Matilda, 227
Maynard, Trisha, 184

McCall, Jeremiah, 216
McCloskey, Robert, 46
McCord, David, 136
McElmeel, Sharron L., 27, 51–52
McGuire, Gregory, 223
McIntosh, Margaret, 224
McKinley, Robin, 241
McKissack, Patricia, 144, 210
McLoughland, Beverly, 138
McMillan, Bruce, 260
Medina, Jane, 138
Melcher, Frederick, 19
Mendlesohn, Farah, 249
Mercado, Nancy, 162
Mercedes and the Chocolate Plot, 194
Merriam, Eve, 136, 138
Mid-Continent Public Library, 246
The Midwife's Apprentice, 197, 209
A Mighty Fine Time Machine, 44
Millen, C.M., 137
Miller, Donalyn, 9, 18
Milne, A.A., 115
Minnich, Cindy, 18
Minty: A Story of Young Harriet Tubman, 199
Missing May, 173, 177
Mobile libraries, 3–4
Molson, Francis J., 249
Montgomery, Sy, 259
Mooney, Margaret, 281
Mora, Pat, 28–30, 121–122, 179
Morris, Ann, 260
Mother Goose on the Loose, 118
Mother Goose Society, 118
Move Over, Rover, 47, 124
Museum resources, 213
Muncha! Muncha! Muncha!, 13
Murphy, Jim, 260, 282
My Friend Rabbit, 14
My Garden, 54
My Librarian is a Camel, 3
My Life, 163
My Life as a Book, 168–170
My Name is America series, 198
My Puppy is Born, 288
Myers, Christopher, 90, 135
Myers, Walter Dean, 135, 137, 181, 200
The Mythopoeic Fantasy Award for Children's Literature, 241

Naden, Corinne, 19
Naidoo, Beverly, 162

Nancy Drew series, 1, 25
The National Archives, 214
National Association to Promote Library Services ...(REFORMA), 20
National Children's Book Week, 11, 32, 64
National Council for the Social Studies (NCSS), 212, 280
National Council of Teachers of English (NCTE), 23, 256; Award for Excellent in Poetry for Children, 20, 129, 136; Orbis Pictus Award for Outstanding Nonfiction for Children, 20, 256, 260, 279; Standards for the English Language Arts, 187–189
National Curriculum Standards for Social Studies, 218–219
National Geographic; Book of Animal Poetry, 130–132; *Kids*, 263
National Poetry Month, 32, 143
National Science Teachers Association (NSTA), 270, 280
Naylor, Phyllis Reynolds, 164, 177, 179–180
Neil, John, 222
Nelson, Kadir, 66
Nerdy Book Club, 18
The New York Times Parent's Guide to the Best Books for Children, 9, 296
Newbery, John, 25, 157
Newbery Medal, 1, 12, 15, 18, 21, 65, 136, 144, 172–173, 176–177, 180, 197, 208–209, 211, 227–228, 229, 235, 255, 277
Nickelodeon Magazine, 264
Noah's Ark, 91
Nodelman, Perry, 145
Norton, Donna, 264
Notable Books for a Global Society, 22
Notable Books in the Language Arts, 23
Number the Stars, 208
Numeroff, Laura, 47
Nye, Naomi Shihab, 138, 200
Nye, Russell B., 223

O'Dell, Scott, 21, 193, 211
Odean, Kathleen, 8
Old Yeller, 161
Olive's Ocean, 164
O'Malley, Kevin, 272
The One and Only Ivan, 144, 228, 241
One Child, One Seed: A South African Counting Book, 48

One Crazy Summer, 211
One Fish, Two Fish, Red Fish, Blue Fish, 24
One Gorilla: A Counting Book, 48
100 Most Popular Picture Book Authors and Illustrators: Biographical Sketches and Bibliographies, 51–52
Opie, Peter and Iona, 117
Orbis Pictus, 20, 39, 255–256
Otterbein College, 129
Our Choice: A Plan to Solve the Climate Crisis, 74–75
Our Choice: How We Can Solve the Climate Crisis, 74–75
Out of Bounds: Seven Stories of Conflict and Hope, 162
The Oxford Dictionary of Nursery Rhymes, 117
Oz, the Great and Powerful, 223

Palacio, R.J., 158–159
The Paper Airplane Book, 270, 284
Parish Peggy, 50
Park, Linda Sue, 208
Parrot, Kiera, 64
Paterson, Katharine, 157–158, 164
Patron, Susan, 176, 180
Paul, Ann Whitford, 200
Paulsen, Gary, 160, 180, 193
Peaceable Kingdom Press, 64
Pearson, Deborah, 162
Peck, Richard, 197, 208
Pennypacker, Sara, 163
Percy Jackson and the Olympians series, 226, 231
Perkins, Lynne Rae, 173, 176
Pete the Cat and His Four Groovy Buttons, 13
Pew Report, 7
Phelan, Matt, 176, 211
Philip, Neil, 200
Picture books, 39–80; alphabet books, 47, 124; awards for, 65–68; board books, 49; book–based apps, 73–75; characters, 59; concept books, 48; counting books, 47–48, 72–43, 124; cultural markers, 62, 72–73; definition of, 42–43; digital books, evaluating, 64–65; easy readers, 49–50; English–language learners and, 72; ebooks, 57, 64–65; engineered books, 48–49; evaluation criteria, 59–65;

illustration, 55–58, 61; individual poet compilations, 122; introduction to, 39–41; involving families, 71; media awards, 68; older readers and, 75–76; plot, 59–60; poem, 123–124; predictable, 46–47; resources on making, 58, 77–78; sample review, 62–63; setting, 60; sharing, 68–76; storybooks, 45–46; style, 60–61; survival language and, 72–73; theme, 60; types of, 44–50; wordless, 46
Pilgreen, Janice, 12
Pinkney, Brian, 55, 61
Pinkney, Jerry, 45, 66, 90–91, 101–102
Playground lore, 109
Please Bury Me in the Library, 138
Poet(s); birthdays, calendar of, 125–129; major, 125–129; poet-in-resident programs, 128; visiting, 128
Poetry, 115–130; across the curriculum, 143; awards for, 136–140; definitions, 118–120; discussing, 142; displays, 128; emotion, 133; evaluating, 132–136; folktale connections, 236; form, 140; Fridays, 141–142; general anthologies, 120–121; imagery, 133; introduction to, 115–116; language, 124–125, 133; pairing, 143–144; picture books, 123–124; practice checklist, 145; predictable, 124; professional resources in, 146; promoting, 144; rhyme, 133; sample review, 134–135; sharing, 140–145; sharing, steps for, 141–142; sound, 133; topical or thematic collections, 121–122; types of, 120–125; verse novels, 124
Poetry Aloud Here: Sharing Poetry with Children, 139
The Poetry Break, 146
The Poetry Friday Anthology K-5, 142, 148
Poetry from A to Z: A Guide for Young Writers, 140
Poetry Goes to School: From Mother Goose to Shel Silverstein, 146
Poetry Lessons to Meet the Common Core State Standards: Exemplar Poems with Engaging Lessons and Response Activities That Help Students Read, Understand, and Appreciate Poetry, 148
Poetry People: a Practical Guide to Children's Poets, 128

The Poetry Teacher's Book of Lists, 131, 201

The Poky Little Puppy, 24

Potato Hill Poetry, 123, 143

Potter, Beatrix, 24, 40–41

Pratchett, Terry, 225, 230, 249

Prelutsky, Jack, 115–116, 120–121, 138, 149

Press Here, 50

Project Gutenberg, 193, 222

Professor Kay Vandergrift's Children's Literature Site, 24

Public Library Association, 8

Publishers Weekly, 16, 24, 53

Pullman, Philip, 239

Pura Belpré award, 19–20, 66, 158

Ralph Caldecott Medal, 15, 19, 45, 49, 52, 65–66, 70, 90–91, 102–103, 136, 246

Ralph Caldecott: The Man Who Could Not Stop Drawing, 66

The Random House Book of Poetry, 120–121

Raschka, Chris, 140

Raven, Margot Theis, 194

Rawls, Wilson, 161

Read Across America, 31

The Read-Aloud Handbook, 12

Readers' advisory, 14

Readers' Theater, 155–156, 181–182; Authors, 181

Reader's Bill of Rights, 15

Reading; aloud, 11–12; DEAR time, 12; free voluntary, 12; incentive programs, 184–185; sustained silent (SSR), 12

Reading is Fundamental, 185

Reading Magic, 9

Reading Poetry in the Middle Grades: 20 Poems and Activities That Meet the Common Core Standards and Cultivate a Passion for Poetry, 148

Reading with Pictures, 248

ReadRoger, 18

Recorded Books, 243

Red Sings from Treetops:, 136

Red Sled, 47

Reimer, Mavis, 145

Reviving Reading: School Library Programming, Author Visits and Books That Rock!, 27

Riordan, Rick, 89, 231

Robert F. Sibert Award, 279

Robinson Crusoe, 191–193

Rockman, Connie, 27

Rohmann, Eric, 14

Roll of Thunder, 191

Rowling, J.K., 24–25, 82, 221, 229

The Royal Diaries series, 198

Ruby Lu, 163

Rules, 159, 178

Rumpelstiltskin's Daughter, 92

Russell, David, 42, 90

Rutherford B., Who Was He? Poems About Our Presidents, 201

Ruurs, Margriet, 3–4

Ryan, Pam Muñoz, 158

Ryder, Winona, 154

Rylant, Cynthia, 161, 173, 177

Sabuda, Robert, 48

Sachar, Louis, 144, 162, 227, 241

The Saggy Baggy Elephant, 24

Sahara Special, 159, 189

Saint George and the Dragon, 91

Sam, 163

Samir and Yonatan, 178

San Andres Elementary School, 119

San Antonio Public Library, 43

San Francisco Chronicle, 206

Sarah, Plain and Tall, 217

Savage, Stephen, 47

Scanlon, Liz Garton, 54

Scarry, Richard, 24

Schneider, Dean, 182–183

Scholastic, 198

Schroeder, Alan, 199

Scieszka, Jon, 92

Society of Children's Book Writers and Illustrators Golden Kite Award, 67

Schertle, Alice, 137

Scheuer, Mary, 73

Schindler, S.D., 277–278

School Library Journal, 15–16, 18, 74

Science Fiction and Fantasy Readers' Advisory; The Librarian's Guide to Cyborgs, Aliens, and Sorcerers, 249

Scieszka, Jon, 184

Schlitz, Laura Amy, 136

School Zone Dallas, 195

Schmidt, Gary D., 256

Scott O'Dell Award for Historical Fiction, 21, 211

A Second is a Hiccup, 48

Secret of a Civil War Submarine: Solving the Mysteries of the H. L. Hunley, 277

Seeing the Blue Between: Advice and Inspiration for Young Poets, 140

Selznick, Brian, 246

7-Imp, 17

Seuss, Dr., 24, 40, 49–50, 66, 123, 125

Seven Blind Mice, 81

Shadow Children, 229

Sharp, Colby, 18

Shields, Carol Diggory, 201

Shiloh, 161, 175, 177, 179–180

Sibert, Robert F., 19–20

The Sibert Award, 19–20

Sideway Stories from Wayside School, 162

Sidman, Joyce, 65, 136

Siebert, Diane, 201

Siesta, 48

Silverstein, Shel, 24, 115–116, 122, 138

Silvey, Anita, 9, 27

Simon, Seymour, 270–273, 284

Simon & Schuster, 22

Singer, Marilyn, 201

A Single Shard, 208

Sis, Peter, 61, 198

Skipping Stones, 264

Smith, Charles R., Jr., 66

Smith, Cynthia Leitich, 17, 26

Smith, Lane, 56

Smith, Robin, 182–183

Smithsonian Institution Traveling Exhibition Service, 213

So, Meilo, 121

So B It, 159

Social Education, 212

Society of Children's Book Writers and Illustrators, 26

Son of a Gun, 178

Soto, Gary, 138, 161

Sparknotes.com, 202

Spier, Peter, 91

Spinelli, Jerry, 177

Sports Illustrated for Kids, 263

Squids Will Be Squids, 92

The SSR Handbook, 12

Stanley, Diane, 92

Starry River of the Sky, 236

StarWalk Kids, 271–272

Stead, Rebecca, 227–228, 241

Steffel, Susan B., 249

Steig, William, 70–71

Steinkamp, Mia, 155–156

Stern, Ellen, 257

Stevens, Janet, 13

Stink, 163

The Stinky Cheese Man, 92

Stone, Tanya Lee, 206

Stone Soup, 162, 264

A Storm in the Barn, 211

The Story of Mankind, 255

The Story of Salt, 277

Storytelling, 109–110

Storytime favorites, 12–14

Sue Ann Mackey Elementary School, 257–258

Summer Reading Club, 7

Sutherland, Zena, 59, 61, 151, 192, 211, 230, 237

Swan Song: Poems of Extinction, 132

Sweet, Melissa, 260

The Swiss Family Robinson, 193

Sylvester and the Magic Pebble, 70–71

Taback, Simms, 49

The Tale of Despereaux, 241

The Tale of Peter Rabbit, 24, 40–41, 44–45

Tales of a Fourth Grade Nothing, 157

Tales of Mother Goose, 82, 116–118

TheTarantula Scientist, 259

Tashjian, Jake, 170–171

Tashjian, Janet, 168–170

Taylor, Mildred, 191, 208

Teacher's Choices, 22

Teen Read Week, 143

Texas Essential Knowledge and Skills (Teks), 146–148

Texts and Forms and Features: A Resource for Intentional Teaching, 281

Thayer, Ernest, 50

There Is a Bird on Your Head, 14

Thimmesh, Catherine, 253

Thomas, Rebecca, 14

Thompson, Kay, 46

Thompson, Ruth Plumly, 222

Thomsen, Susan, 17

Time Magazine for Kids, 263

Time Warp Trio, 238

Tolstoy, Leo, 158
Tom Sawyer, 194
Tomás and the Library Lady, 30–31, 179
Tootle, 24
The Tortoise and the Hare, 90
Tour America: A Journey Through Poems and Art, 201, 321
Traditional Tales, 81–113; anthologies, evaluating, 101; awards for, 102–103; beast, 88; characters, 98–99; culture, 100–101; cumulative, 88; definition of, 84–85; evaluation criteria, 98–12; fables, 90; fairy, 88; fairy, fractured, 91–92; fantasy and, 251; folktales, 87–88, 103–105; from Africa, 93; from Asia, 92–93; from Australia, 94; from Europe, 94; from North America, 93; from South America, 93–94; illustrations, 100; introduction to, 81–84; legends, 89; literary, 91; myths, 89; noodlehead, 88; plot, 99; pour quoi, 88; realistic, 88; religious, 90–91; resources for, 111–112; retellers of, 92–98; sample review, 101–102; setting, 99; sharing, 108–110; style, 99–100; tall, 90; theme, 99; trickster, 88 types of, 87–92
Trelease, Jim, 9, 12, 184
Tripods Trilogy, 225
The Trouble with Wishes, 92
The True Blue Scouts of Sugar Man Swamp, 228
True Legend, 161
The True Story of the Three Little Pigs, 92
Truesdale, Sue, 261
Tuck Everlasting, 239
Tullet, Hervé, 50
Turtle's Race with Beaver, 90
Twain, Mark, 194
The 20ᵗʰ Century Children's Poetry Treasury, 121

Ugly Duckling, 45, 91
The Ugly Vegetables, 234
UnderGROUND, 53–55
The Underneath, 228
Undertown, Harold, 45
United States Board on Books for Youth, 33
U.S. National Library of Medicine, 213
University of Minnesota, 255
University of Virginia, 154

Up, Tall and High!, 66
Using Poetry Across the Curriculum, 143, 201

Valerie & Walter's Best Books for Children: A Lively, Opinionated Guide, 14
Van Leeuwen, Jean, 50
Van Loon, Hendrik Willem, 255
Vardell, Sylvia M., 27, 128–130, 148, 201
The Very Hungry Caterpillar, 49
The Very Smart Pea and the Princess-to-Be, 92
The View from Saturday, 151, 176
Viorst, Judith, 70, 143–144
Visiting/guest authors, 119–120, 212–213, 284–285
Volavkova, Hana, 201
VOYA (Voice of Youth Advocates), 16

W. K. Kellogg Foundation, 28–29
Walk Two Moons, 172, 176
Walker, Sally M., 277
TheWall, 198
Wardlaw, Lee, 137
Warren, Robert Penn, 116
Washington Post, 280
Wayland, April Halprin, 149
Weatherford, Carole Boston, 199, 201
Weedflower, 212
Weeks, Sarah, 159, 181
Weisner, David, 56
Wells, Gordon, 5
When I Went to the Library, 138 162
When You Reach Me, 227–228, 241
Where the Mountain Meets the Moon, 234–237
Where the Red Fern Grows, 161
Where the Sidewalk Ends, 115–116
Where's Walrus, 47
The Whipping Boy, 197–198
White, Deborah, 27
White, E.B., 25, 227–228
Wilder, Laura Ingalls, 210
Willems, Mo, 14, 45, 50, 61
Williams–Garcia, Rita, 211
Wings of Fancy: Using Readers Theatre to Study Fantasy Genre, 249
Winter, Jonah, 198
Winters, Carol, 256
Wolf, Allan, 274
Wolves, 62
Women Children's Book Illustrators, 42

Women's International League for Peace and Freedom (WILPF), 212
Wonder, 158–159
The Wonderful Wizard of Oz, 221, 222–223, 233, 248
Wonderstruck, 246
Wong, Janet, 148–149
World Wide School Library, 154
Worth, Valerie, 138
A Wrinkle in Time, 229
Wyeth, N.C., 193

A Year Down Yonder, 197
The Year of the Dog, 158, 233, 237

The Year of the Rat, 158, 233, 237
Young, Ed, 81
Young Adults' Choices, 22
Young Adult Library Services Association (YALSA), 33, 250; Award for Nonfiction for Young Adults, 279–280
Young Adult Literature in Action: A Librarian's Guide, 250
YouTube, 13, 26

Zagarenski, Pamela, 136
Zimmer, Tracie Vaughn, 138
Zoobooks, 264

About the Author

SYLVIA M. VARDELL is professor in the School of Library and Information Studies at Texas Woman's University, where she teaches graduate courses in children's literature. Her research has focused particularly on sharing poetry with young people. Her published work includes Libraries Unlimited's *Poetry People: A Practical Guide to Children's Poets* as well as *Poetry Aloud Here: Sharing Poetry with Children in the Library*; The Poetry Friday Anthology series (with Janet Wong); *The Poetry Teacher's Book of Lists*; as well as her blog on sharing poetry with kids, PoetryForChildren at Blogspot. Vardell writes a regular "Everyday Poetry" column for *Book Links* magazine and has served on several award committees, including the Laura Ingalls Wilder Award, the Sibert Medal, the Odyssey Award, the Orbis Pictus Award, and the National Council of Teachers of English Poetry Award.